The Politics of Immortality in Rosenzweig, Barth and Goldberg

Also available from Bloomsbury

Another Finitude, by Agata Bielik-Robson
Immanent Transcendence, by Patrice Haynes
Locke on Knowledge, Politics and Religion, edited by Kiyoshi Shimokawa and Peter R. Anstey
The Ethics of Generating Posthumans, edited by Calum MacKellar and Trevor Stammers
Why God Must Do What is Best, by Justin J. Daeley

The Politics of Immortality in Rosenzweig, Barth and Goldberg

Theology and Resistance Between 1914–1945

Mårten Björk

BLOOMSBURY ACADEMIC
LONDON · NEW YORK · OXFORD · NEW DELHI · SYDNEY

BLOOMSBURY ACADEMIC
Bloomsbury Publishing Plc
50 Bedford Square, London, WC1B 3DP, UK
1385 Broadway, New York, NY 10018, USA
29 Earlsfort Terrace, Dublin 2, Ireland

BLOOMSBURY, BLOOMSBURY ACADEMIC and the Diana logo are trademarks
of Bloomsbury Publishing Plc

First published in Great Britain 2022
This paperback edition published 2023

Copyright © Mårten Björk, 2022

Mårten Björk has asserted his right under the Copyright, Designs and Patents Act,
1988, to be identified as Author of this work.

For legal purposes the Acknowledgements on p. vi constitute an extension of
this copyright page.

Cover design by Charlotte Daniels
Cover image: Plane in Rotation, called Black Circle (1915), Kazimir Severinovich Malevich.
Private Collection. (© Fine Art Images / Heritage Images / Getty Images)

All rights reserved. No part of this publication may be reproduced or transmitted in any
form or by any means, electronic or mechanical, including photocopying, recording, or
any information storage or retrieval system, without prior permission in writing from the
publishers.

Bloomsbury Publishing Plc does not have any control over, or responsibility for, any third-
party websites referred to or in this book. All internet addresses given in this book were
correct at the time of going to press. The author and publisher regret any inconvenience
caused if addresses have changed or sites have ceased to exist, but can accept no
responsibility for any such changes.

A catalogue record for this book is available from the British Library.

A catalog record for this book is available from the Library of Congress.

ISBN: HB: 978-1-3502-2822-1
PB: 978-1-3502-2826-9
ePDF: 978-1-3502-2823-8
eBook: 978-1-3502-2824-5

Typeset by Deanta Global Publishing Services, Chennai, India

To find out more about our authors and books visit www.bloomsbury.com and
sign up for our newsletters.

Contents

Acknowledgements		vi
Introduction		1
1	Yearning for a system: Franz Rosenzweig and the great paganism of life	15
2	Abundance and scarcity: Karl Barth and the struggle for existence	71
3	The animal of the infinite: Oskar Goldberg and the science of evil	119
4	Life outside life: Theology and resistance	183
Notes		201
Bibliography		239
Index		258

Acknowledgements

This book is based on my dissertation, *Life Outside Life: The Politics of Immortality, 1914-1945*, that I defended at Gothenburg University in September 2018. The dissertation also included a chapter on the German theologian Erik Peterson which I plan to expand to a book on its own. The chapters on Rosenzweig, Barth and Goldberg together with the introduction and conclusion have been rewritten and developed for this book. I should also mention that all translations from works in German, Spanish and Swedish are my own.

    I dedicate this book to my true hope and true love Natacha L. Balbontin, and I want to especially mention my mother, Eva Björk, and my father, Bengt Björk (RIP), my supervisors in Gothenburg, Arne Rasmusson and Ola Sigurdson, my opponent at my defence, Rinse Reeling Brouwer, and Jade Grogan at Bloomsbury. This book would not have existed without the support and friendship of many people, including Jacob Andersson, Johan Andersson, Sigurd Baark, Linnea Carlsson, Peter Carlsson, Petra Carlsson, Bo I. Cavefors (RIP), John Clegg, Dritëro Demjaha, Karolina Enquist Källgren, Lottie Eriksson, Erik Erlanson, Hjalmar Falk, Cooper Francis, Rev'd James Hanway SJ, Michael J. Hollerich, Anton Jansson, Werner Jeanrond, Carsten Juhl, Jakob Kaae, Simone Kotva, Joel Kuhlin, Jaroslaw Kurek OSB, Travis LaCouter, Grégoire Langouët, Göran Larsson, Olle Larsson, Jeff Love, Rob Lucas, Neil Maclean, Mattias Martinson, Alberto Moreiras, Gerardo Muñoz, Håkan Möller, Andreas Nordlander, Tormod Otter Johansen, James Payne, Adam Persson, Christine Quarfood, Idris Robinson, Cecilia Rosengren, Ida Simonsson, Anna and Gustav Sjöberg, Richard Steenvorde OP, Zöe Sutherland, Anton Svanqvist, Marcello Tarì, Davide Tarizzo, Andrzej Tichý, Marius Timmann Mjaaland and Manfred Voigts (RIP).

Introduction

The question of eternal life is inherently political. The long tradition in the West that has articulated the hope of a victory over death, be it in the form of an immortality of the soul, a resurrection of the flesh or a recapitulation of the dead in a new cosmos, cannot be separated from the question about the good life and how society should be organized.[1] This was not only true during antiquity or in the medieval period when the theology of eternal life informed politics and was a crucial part of many cosmologies. The dialectic between politics and immortality is alive in contemporary discussions on transhumanism and singularity.[2] It also haunted our recent past, such as the catastrophic years from 1914 to 1945, which are at the centre of this study.

Perhaps most famous for drafting the constitution of Austria in 1920, Hans Kelsen published three years after the *Machtübernahme* in Germany an article on the political character of immortality aptly titled 'The Soul and the Law'.[3] His simple, but at the same time congenial, thesis was that the ideas of immortality should be understood as ethical and political ideologies promoting distinct ways of being in the world. The significant concepts of the modern theory of the state are, as Carl Schmitt had argued in 1922, secularized theological notions.[4] But theological ideas are also necessarily ethical and political. The development of the 'Platonic doctrine of the soul and its immortality' is part of a conservative ideology according to Kelsen, whereas 'the belief in the resurrection of the body, and in a final judgment which should assure eternal life to the just in the Kingdom of God' has a 'revolutionary character'.[5]

In this study I examine how the German Jewish philosopher of religion Franz Rosenzweig, the Swiss Reformed theologian Karl Barth and the Jewish philosopher of myth Oskar Goldberg, long forgotten but at the centre of the intellectual debates in Berlin in the 1920s, defended a politics of immortality. This implied a resistance against the transformation of the idea of immortality that Hans Blumenberg has traced in *The Legitimacy of the Modern Age*.[6] Blumenberg argued that at the same time as 'immortality is pushed forward by Lessing, Kant, and Herder to the point of the idea of reincarnation' in the modern era, it is also 'moralized'.[7]

The change is radical, if at the same time easy to overlook, since immortality has always involved an ethical and a political dimension. But, Blumenberg continued, with the modern discussion on immortality, it is no 'longer God who is the primary "object" of one's attention in the "beyond". On the contrary, that attention continues the theoretical interests and moral obligations of this world, that is, it loses its quasi-worshipful character so as to satisfy, instead, what one's finite individual life denies'.[8] The legitimacy of a modern theory of immortality is now found in the intersection between a moralization and a detheologization of the world that is parallel with a view on life as primarily a biological and material phenomenon.

Biologists, economists and philosophers began during the eighteenth and nineteenth centuries to view life as 'the root of all existence'.[9] Life was conceptualized as a struggle for survival both in an economical and a biological sense. Humanity was seen to labour under 'the threat of death: any population that cannot find new resources is doomed to extinction; and, inversely, to the degree that men multiply, so they undertake more numerous, more distant, more difficult, and less immediately fruitful labors'.[10] It was from this strife that culture and human society arose.

Charles Darwin himself ended *The Origin of Species* by stating that the 'Struggle of Life' shows that 'from the war of nature, from famine and death, the most exalted objects which we are capable of conceiving, namely, the production of the higher animals, directly follows'.[11] This does neither entail that a Darwinian perspective is simply based on the violent economy of life, nor that it excludes the possibility or even necessity of inter- and extra-species cooperation. But the idea of natural selection as a struggle became a political and even metaphysical postulate in the period between 1914 and 1945, to the point that these years have been described as a biocentric era.[12] As Richard Weikart has showed, Darwinist notions were also instrumentalized for political reasons in Nazi Germany.[13]

In this 'age of life' the understanding of living organisms as ruled by adaptation and fitness even became a philosophical postulate, a metaphysics of the modern period.[14] Darwin's real insight was turned to a universal principle explaining inorganic systems as well as organic ones and became applicable outside biology, such as in economics and cosmology. 'Biology departments are actually the place where the *true* metaphysics of modernity continues to be produced.'[15]

The theologies of immortality that Rosenzweig, Barth and Goldberg developed confronted this new conception of life and reflected the distress during the period from 1914 to 1945, with its conflicts and wars. Germany's experience of the crisis of capitalism, represented by the hyperinflation of the 1920s and the Great Depression of the 1930s, has rightly been described as a profound 'theologico-political cultural crisis precipitated by the collapse of the Protestant synthesis of the Wilhelmine period'.[16] The hope for immortality became in this era, as we will see, a way to resist the reduction of life to biology, culture and history and a refusal to identify human existence with political concepts such as race, state and nation.

In Germany, before 1914, 'racial hygiene had been decisively rejected by the Imperial administration as a violation of prevailing ethical codes and of personal liberty'.[17] It was, however, institutionalized and accepted in academic and other public institutions during the Weimar Republic. Prominent scientists and visionaries like the zoologist Ernst Haeckel, the physician Wilhelm Schallmayer and the biologist Alfred Ploetz (founder of the Society for Race Hygiene, the first eugenics society) had, before the Weimar period, argued for the need for a politics that secured the health of the nation.[18]

Schallmayer professed already in 1905 his belief in a biological politics, *biologische Politik*, in order to assure the hygiene and health of the people of the German Empire.[19] His proposition was that in a modern, technological state, both 'the products of culture' and 'the generative human worths of inheritance' must be 'the subject of politics'.[20] He identified a conflict between supposed interest of race, *Rasseinteresse*, and social interest, *Sozialinteresse*.[21] The racial interest accentuated the need to cultivate a politics that secured the biological survival and health of the people as such. At the same time, Schallmayer, who was a socialist, openly rejected Aryan ideologies as pseudo-scientific.[22] It was not only fascists or right-wing militants who spurred the eugenics movements; some argued that eugenics could even be used for liberal or progressive aims, thus assuring the health of the population.[23] Other more utopian scientists, such as the biologist Paul Kammerer, attacked racism and developed a program of organic technology with the purpose of harnessing the evolution of the human species.[24]

This politicization of life also transformed the conception of immortality. Kammerer compared, for example, his form of eugenics with the Christian idea of the resurrection.[25] Immortality implied more and more a longing for survival rather than a belief in a future judgement of the inequities of the world. It was no longer primarily about the beyond. Immortality was about this life. Present life. But can life rest in the present? Is it possible to reduce life to its embodied, biological state? Is life, first of all, a struggle for survival?

My aim with this book is to discuss how Rosenzweig, Barth and Goldberg confronted the biologization of politics in the years between 1914 and 1945. By focusing on the intersection between a transformation of the notion of life and the discussion on immortality in this period of planetary wars, I examine how these three theologians addressed the biocentrism of their era.[26] They challenged several of the historicist and naturalist positions that had become hegemonic as guidelines for academic research and even seen as ontological truths explaining the structure of reality and the meaning of human existence.[27] Their theologies of eternal life implied a critique of the basis of the 'age of life', and they resisted openly the detheologization of life and immortality that Blumenberg, rightly, viewed as defining the modern era.

My study tells this story through three main analytical chapters, where I examine the politics of immortality defended by Rosenzweig, Barth and Goldberg in this order. This takes us to a conclusion where I summarize the research and return to the question of how their discussion of immortality challenges the 'age of life' and complicates Blumenberg's theory of the transformation of the understanding of immortality during the modern era. We will see that the politics of immortality defended by Rosenzweig, Barth and Goldberg questions the Darwinian logic behind 'the human self-assertion' that according to Blumenberg characterizes modernity.

A generation against history

In his discussion on the transformation of the concept of immortality, Blumenberg was clearly influenced by Ludwig Feuerbach, and referring to this lapsed theologian he wrote: 'The idea of immortality is curiosity that does not yet understand itself in its rational economy; it is the negation of history, insofar as history withholds things from every present time. Man only wants to know what *man* can know.'[28] The domains of this species-knowledge are history and nature. Any idea of immortality that transcends the confines of the natural and historical world is seen as an illusion that must be transformed into a knowledge of what man *can* know. Human knowledge does not go beyond the human.

According to Blumenberg, Feuerbach showed that it was possible to naturalize and historicize immortality as the reproduction of the human species.[29] The individual dies but can have its afterlife in the posterior life of coming generations. This interpretation of the emergence of specifically modern ideas of immortality is strengthened by Claude Lefort in his examination of the memorialization of immortality and life during the era of the American and French revolutions.[30]

Influenced by Hannah Arendt's discussion on immortality in the ancient Greek *polis* as the remembrance of the free and virtuous citizens' political deeds, Lefort argued that immortality was viewed as a memory of grand men and their actions in the modern era. In the years of the French and American revolutions, the revolutionaries sought to 'break with the Christian ethic – sometimes without realising it, they were able to rehabilitate life on earth, they passionately set themselves the task of building an eternal city and identified their own immortality with that of their political achievement'.[31] Lefort makes it quite easy for himself since he fails to acknowledge the profound role of Christians in the American Revolution, and thereby he also fails to understand how what he describes as a specifically Christian idea of the afterlife shaped the revolution.[32] However, his idea of a transformation of the sense of immortality is essentially correct. Immortality survives in modernity as a new sense of posterity. It is no longer primarily spurred by a faith that the dead are inscribed in an eternal domain or waiting for the resurrection.[33] Christianity is increasingly adapted to what Blumenberg called the legitimacy of the modern age. The hope for an afterlife does not disappear, but it is given a new form in what has been called a post-Christian world.[34]

It is important to stress that the modern age entailed more than the emergence of a new notion of immortality. It also transformed the understanding of what immortality meant in the past, namely, what functional or political role it had for engendering specific forms of life. According to Kelsen, the 'metaphysical dogma of the immortality of the soul' depended primarily on 'the justificatory or ethical-political function of religion, not on its explanatory or scientific function'.[35] Although 'religion has more than an ethical and political aspect and aims not only to give a basis for duty, but still more to reveal the ground of being', the jurist argued that the rationality of the belief in immortality was to be found in its ethical and political dimension.[36] Yet, axiology, the philosophical study of value – or what Kelsen called the justificatory dimension of the theology of immortality – and ontology, the explanatory dimension of ideas on eternal life, are hard to differentiate. Moral and political ideologies necessarily involve explanations that justify them and theology, metaphysics and cosmology are in themselves often profoundly political.

The understanding of life as a biological and historical process ruled by adaptation and heredity transformed theology and politics, and the subjects of my study were without doubt formed by this new awareness of the embodied and historical character of human existence. Rosenzweig based the beginning of his whole philosophy on the mortality of creaturely existence. Goldberg embraced in a similar manner the psychophysical constitution of human life and developed a biological interpretation of religion and myth. Famous for his critique of historicism, Karl Barth praised the materialism of Feuerbach, and pointed to Haeckel and other well-known nineteenth-century scientists and philosophers such as Karl Vogt, Ludwig Büchner and Jacob Moleschott as reminders to theology of the embodied nature of our species.[37] Yet, Barth argued that the condition of possibility for this type of materialism was 'not to be found in the researches and results of biology and physiology, but in the rise of . . . [a] form of humanity': the modern proletariat.[38]

The appearance of this mode of human life, entrapped in an industrialized civilization and formed by the modern nation state, implied according to the Swedish conservative state theorist Rudolf Kjellén a biopolitical problem. In *Staten som Lifsform*, widely read in Germany after its translation in 1917, Kjellén underlined that life itself had become the problem of politics.[39] But what kind of life? This was the question raised by the theologies of eternal life and immortality that Rosenzweig, Barth and Goldberg defended. Their theories of immortality were political discourses criticizing the biopolitical perspective that Kjellén was one of the most famous defenders of, and even if Rosenzweig, Barth and Goldberg's theologies were in many senses radically different their distinct notions of immortality revealed a common attempt to rethink the sense and meaning of life.

There is no research that has put Barth, Goldberg and Rosenzweig into a common constellation, nor read their ideas of eternal life as a confrontation of the biopolitics of modern era. Commentators in their own time recognized, however, similarities between them.

In 1930, the Berlin-based Junker und Dünnhaupt Verlag published an introduction to philosophy of religion by Hans Leisegang.[40] Leisegang turned to Barth, Rosenzweig, Goldberg and the latter's friend, the philosopher Erich Unger, as examples of the contemporary philosophical and theological discussion on religion.

Leisegang was not alone in noticing commonalities between Barth, Goldberg and Rosenzweig. Nine years later, in 1939, the scholar of religion Schalom Ben-Chorin described these three theologians as heralds of a theology transcending liberalism and orthodoxy.[41] In a similar manner, the influential German Jewish philosopher Margarete Susman underlined the interconnection between Goldberg, Barth, and Rosenzweig in a lecture that Manfred Voigts has saved from oblivion.[42] The parallels between Barth, Goldberg and Rosenzweig do not in any sense negate the important differences between them. But there is a clear unanimity in their revival of traditions such as angelology and demonology, and in their discussion on myth and polytheism as political problems.

Another, and perhaps much more important, unanimity is that the subjects of this study belonged to those intellectuals in the Weimar period who 'resisted history' by reacting against the historicism and naturalism of the modern era.[43] It is important to emphasize that Barth, Rosenzweig and Goldberg never denied the importance of the methods of critical philology and academic historiography. On the contrary, they mastered them. Their understanding of human existence implied, however, a rejection of history and nature as ultimate categories. There existed something beyond the confines of human, and therefore spatio-temporal, existence.

The resistance against historicism and naturalism has been viewed as a dangerous form of irrationality, and even as laying the ground for fascism and Nazism. Mark Lilla has famously interpreted Barth and Rosenzweig as figures belonging to a generation who paved the way for totalitarianism and Nazism by 'turning to the Bible for political inspiration. To compound the puzzle, these thinkers were universally hostile to the thinking that had given rise to modern liberal democracy, and more than a few defended the most repugnant ideologies of the twentieth century, Nazism and Communism.'[44] Thomas Mann, who initially read and admired Goldberg, came to see him as a herald of anti-democratic thought. The German author based the portrait of the fascist Jew Dr Chaim Breisacher on Goldberg in his novel *Doctor Faustus*. The narrator of *Doctor Faustus*, Serenus Zeitblom, describes Breisacher as a herald of 'the new world of anti-humanity, of which my easy-going soul till then had known nothing at all'.[45] As Manfred Voigts has pointed out, Goldberg saw his attack on Western civilization as a critique of the world that produced fascism, and Mann's obsession with the Jewish mythologist has been interpreted as a sign of his own residual antisemitism.[46]

There were anti-historicists who rejected modernity in a reactionary manner just as Lilla argues. Barth, however, was a staunch social democrat and anti-militarist who opposed the First World War. He openly supported democracy and the Weimar Republic, and later became one of the leading theologians who attacked Nazism to the point that he was expelled from Germany in 1935.[47] Rosenzweig, on the other hand, was a more conservative thinker who only reluctantly accepted the Weimar Republic. But his hope for a multicultural transnational empire comes into sharp conflict with the rise of Nazism in Germany.[48]

It is also important to keep in mind that the parliamentary victory of NSDAP in 1933 did not in any sense entail a rejection of the economic and political development that laid the basis for the biologization of politics that Rosenzweig, Barth and Goldberg openly challenged by seeking to rethink human existence.

Race and culture, spirit and nature, biology and theology were intermixed in a biopolitical discourse that was parallel to the transformation of the idea of immortality in the biocentric era. This was the world that Rosenzweig, Barth and Goldberg questioned.

Franz Rosenzweig

Franz Rosenzweig (1886–1929) is rightly recognized as one of the most important European intellectuals during the twentieth century, to whom dozens of articles and monographs have been devoted.[49] A classic reading of Rosenzweig is to view him as an existentialist philosopher who rejected the systematic task of German idealism.[50] This interpretation has been contested by Benjamin Pollock, who describes Rosenzweig's philosophy as a systematic attempt to understand 'the All' – being itself or the totality of all that is – that transcends, but also deeply relies on, the tradition of German idealism which he mastered.[51]

Pollock's reading of Rosenzweig's philosophy as what I call a yearning for a system is interrelated with the complex interpretation of the political and religious trajectory of humanity in *The Star of Redemption* from 1921.[52] In this work, which Rosenzweig began to write when he served in the infantry at the *Balkanfront* during the First World War, he developed a historical genealogy of philosophical and religious ideas of immortality culminating in a description of the diasporic life of the Jews as a participation in the eternal life of God.

The First World War gave Rosenzweig the hope that Germany could become the centre of what the theologian and liberal politician Friedrich Naumann called a *Mitteleuropa* – a new European imperial order where Germany had aligned itself with the Austro-Hungarian Empire.[53] But while Naumann focused almost exclusively on Central Europe, the Germanist Jörg Kreienbrock has recently argued that 'Rosenzweig's phantasmatic geopolitical vision goes beyond European borders, including Turkey and Egypt'.[54] His hope was essentially a hope for a New Levant with Germany as its pounding heart. The inclusion of new peoples and cultures in the empire would change Europe both culturally and politically into a true multicultural order.[55]

Consequently, Rosenzweig had enlisted in the army in 1915 as someone who struggled for a new world. At the front, in 1917, he wrote a series of texts where he argued for a geopolitical re-orientation of Germany as a new imperial order.[56] When Rosenzweig understood that Germany would lose the war he began the work on what became *The Star of the Redemption*. Now he laid out a theological strategy for a transnational community. His hope for a world interconnected to a global sphere was still living but became intertwined with his theology of immortality and eternal life. This, what he called 'new thinking', was a serious engagement with the finitude of life that he could not ignore as a soldier.[57] But it was also an attempt to think that which transcends death.

Rosenzweig was born in Kassel in a secular Jewish middle-class family; he died of amyotrophic lateral sclerosis when he was only forty-five years old. As a young man he began to study medicine but switched over to philosophy and history. As an academic, Rosenzweig mastered the art of philology and historical criticism. His dissertation on G. W. F. Hegel and the state was well received.[58] Soon Rosenzweig became disaffected with the academic life and abandoned his promising university career. Instead, he founded the *Freie jüdische Lehrhaus* in Frankfurt in 1920, a centre for the education of Jewish adults, which attracted many German Jewish intellectuals who would later gain fame.

In the chapter devoted to Rosenzweig I examine primarily his discussion of eternal life and immortality in his major work – *The Star of Redemption* – his introduction to this book – *Understanding the Sick and the Healthy* – which was published after his death, some of his letters written during the war and in the 1920s and several of the essays gathered in *Zweistromland*.[59] I shall show that eternal life for Rosenzweig involved an explanation of human history as a process that unfolded towards a life beyond life where the All, the totality of everything that is, is explained and reflected in the struggle for a world common to all humans that defied the nationalism of his time.

Karl Barth

The Swiss Reformed pastor Karl Barth (1886–1968) has been devoted a whole industry of articles, essays and monographs, and his legacy is a highly contested territory where rival factions struggle over the interpretation of the master.[60] Barth's understanding of immortality, resurrection and eternal life has recently been discussed by Nathan Hitchcock and R. Dale Dawson, and Yo Fukushima has written a useful book on the concept of life in Barth's writings.[61]

Barth was born in Basel, Switzerland, and spent his childhood in Bern.[62] His father was a theologian and pastor with interests in philosophy. Barth studied theology in Bern, Berlin, Tübingen and Marburg, and was as a young theologian impressed by liberal theologians and philosophers such as Adolf von Harnack, Hermann Cohen and especially the Marburg theologian, Wilhelm Herrmann, whose *Ethik: Grundriss der theologischen Wissenschaften* had a profound impact on his thinking.[63]

I shall to a large extent follow Bruce McCormack's suggestion of four variations of a common theme in the period from 1914 to 1936, where the continuity is 'the (seemingly impossible) attempt to think from a standpoint lying in God Himself'.[64] The first development of this understanding of God's majesty can, according to McCormack, be found in the years between 1915 and 1920.[65] Barth had in July 1911 moved to Safenwil in Aargau, a northern canton in Switzerland plagued by poverty and class conflicts, to serve as a preacher there. Soon Barth was known as the red pastor, since he preached a political gospel for the poor and, in 1915, joined the Swiss Social Democratic Party and became a militant anti-militarist.[66]

Nevertheless, the First World War radicalized Barth's theological and political positions. On the one hand he became disillusioned with Harnack, Herrmann and his other teachers' support of German militarism and consequently saw their theology as bankrupt. On the other hand he was utterly disappointed by the fact that the German Social Democratic Party voted in favour of the war credits that enabled Germany to go to war in 1914.

These two catastrophes prompted Barth to emphasize that the relation between God and the world had to be understood as a *diastasis*, 'a relation in which the two members stand over against each other with no possibility of a synthesis into a higher form of being'.[67] It is this diastasis that is invariable in Barth's intellectual development, and it has a tremendous impact on his view on eternal life as a divine life, a life that is incarnated in a human being, namely Jesus of Nazareth, yet transcending the limited and mortal life of creaturely existence.

Barth came to underline this diastasis even more in the second phase of his theological development, between 1920 and 1924. The deepening of the diastasis to a crisis for human subjectivity forced him to rewrite *The Epistle to the Romans*, whose first edition had been published in 1919.[68] In the second edition the relationship between God and creation was conceptualized as a crisis that the human has to go through when he comes to believe that there is an exteriority to creation in God.

In 1921, Barth moved to Göttingen and was given the newly founded chair of Reformed Theology. Three years later, in 1924, he wrote his criticism of Friedrich Schleiermacher, *The Theology of Schleiermacher*, and began his so-called *Göttingen Dogmatics*, which according to McCormack was the beginning of the third phase that lasted until around 1936. This period was a concentration 'on the actualization of the revelation by the Holy Spirit in the present', and it prompted Barth to begin the work with his *Church Dogmatics* in 1932.[69] The turn to dogmatics was not an abandonment of his belief in the diastasis between God and creation.[70] It enabled Barth to interpret the tradition of classical Christian doctrine from the perspective of the diastasis between God and creation, eternity and time, creaturely existence and eternal life.

McCormack plays down the importance of Barth's book on Anselm, *Fides quaerens intellectum* from 1931, although, according to Hans Urs von Balthasar, it signified a shift in Barth's theological development.[71] Even if I think that McCormack's description of Barth's development as a theologian is essentially correct, I agree with Sigurd Baark and Manfred Josuttis that Barth's book on Anselm is of crucial importance in order to understand his method of *Nachdenken*.[72]

Theology was for Barth biblical theology and had three essential dimensions: observation (*Beobachtung*, *explicatio*: the explication of the tradition); reflection (*Nachdenken*, *meditatio*: the study of the logic of theological texts) and appropriation (*Aneignung*, *application*, *usus*: the application of theology in practice).[73] And, as I shall argue, Barth's understanding of *Nachdenken* is directly related to the idea of resurrection and eternal life as he developed it in the *Church Dogmatics* during the 1940s. It even affected his understanding of prelapsarian existence as a life that is not ruled by the Darwinian struggle for existence.

The final phase of Barth's theological development commences according to McCormack in 1936, after Barth had listened to a lecture in Geneva on the election of creation through Christ by the pastor Pierre Maury.[74] This period consolidated what has been called Barth's Christocentrism.[75] He now emphasized the concept of election and affirmed that theology must interpret human reality, and even creation as such, from the life, death and resurrection of Jesus Christ.

In my analysis of Barth's theology of eternal life and resurrection I discuss texts from all four periods that McCormack traces: sermons from the First and Second World Wars; his lecture on Feuerbach from 1922; the second edition of the *Epistle of the Romans*; the *Göttingen Dogmatics*; his book on political theology, *Church and State*, from 1938; his lectures on ethics in 1928 and 1929; and the volumes of *Church Dogmatics* published between 1932 and 1945.[76] What I emphasize in these often dense studies is the dialectic between time and eternity revealed in Christ that according to Barth traverses the human and differentiates our species into a lapsed being and a redeemed creature. I shall argue that this disjunction gives the human creature the possibility to counter the struggle for survival that seems to be the destiny of creaturely existence and thereby the human can become a reflection of God's eternal life.

Oskar Goldberg

Oskar Goldberg (1885–1953) was a Jewish philosopher of myth, a trained physician and initiator of several important philosophical societies in the Weimar period, for example the *Philosophische Gruppe*, which was frequented by authors and philosophers such as Günther Anders, Berthold Brecht, Walter Benjamin, Karl Korsch, Alfred Döblin, Gershom Scholem and Robert Musil.[77] The polyglot Goldberg was the son of an orientalist and studied at Dr Joseph Wohlgemuth's orthodox seminary, and later at the Jewish theological school Beit Hamidrash under the rabbi Abraham Biberfeld.[78]

Goldberg became famous for his reading of the Torah, *Die fünf Bücher Mosis-ein Zahlengebäude*, published in 1908 when he was only twenty-three years old.[79] In this numerological hermeneutics of the Torah, in the tradition of what is called *gematria*, he discerned a mathematical pattern reflecting the divine mind.[80] Perhaps surprisingly this profoundly mystical book did not only find readers among fellow believers and those interested in Jewish mysticism. It was recognized by the noted historians of religion Robert Eisler and Franz Dornseiff, 'although they disputed his claim that it was beyond the power of human intelligence to fabricate' the pattern that Goldberg disclosed.[81]

In his study *Die Wirklichekit der Hebräer* from 1925, a biological, and to some readers even magical, examination of myth in the Torah based on research done between 1903 and 1908, Goldberg would relate his numerological reading of the Torah to on the one hand a complex theology of eternal life, and on the other an anthropological explanation of the rites that constitute the Hebrews as a people living in relation to God. *Die Wirklichekit der Hebräer* would raise even more heated discussions than *Die fünf Bücher Mosis* and found prominent readers in Martin Buber, Franz Rosenzweig, Thomas Mann, Hans Leisegang, Edgar Dacqué and Erwin Reisner.

The research conducted for *Die fünf Bücher Mosis* and *Die Wirklichkeit der Hebräer* was presented for the so-called Goldberg circle, *Goldberg-Kreis*, whose inner core, besides the philosopher Erich Unger and the legal and economic historian Adolf Caspary, was constituted by Edgar Zacharias and Erwin Loewenson.[82] The fate of Goldberg was tragic. He died forgotten and unknown in Nice. If it had not been for Manfred Voigts's almost archaeological excavation of Goldberg's work he would probably still be unknown.

Scholem described Goldberg and his circle as one of the three most remarkable sects that modern German Jewry produced, namely: the groups around the Aby Warburg library; Max Horkheimer's *Institut for Sozialforschung*; and Oskar Goldberg and his so-called collective of 'metaphysical magicians'.[83] Scholem reacted very negatively, perhaps jealously, to Goldberg, and said that he was 'inclined to regard him as a representative of the devil in our generation'.[84] He was not alone in viewing Goldberg as a problematic figure. As I have stated, Thomas Mann came to view him as a dangerous reactionary.

Still, Mann asked Goldberg to collaborate as a writer for the anti-fascist journal *Mass und Wert* and helped him to migrate to the United States when Goldberg had to flee Europe after he had been interned in France for some months in 1941. Mann had read *Die Wirklichkeit der Hebräer* carefully and used it for his four-part novel *Joseph and His Brothers*, which portrays the cultic and mythical roots of what Goldberg called *Urjudentum*.[85] Yet, in the end, Mann chose to portray Goldberg as a herald of the irrationality of Nazism rather than as a philosopher who tried to explain the existence of suffering and evil in the world. From his own perspective, Goldberg sought to revive the messianic task of Judaism as a hope for the redemption of the creation as such. As I will argue, his critique of civilization was not a nostalgic longing for the past. It should be understood in relation to Adolf Caspary's complex reading of Karl Marx's theory of machinery. Only thereby can one truly grasp the core of Goldberg's philosophy.

I shall primarily use *Die Wirklichkeit der Hebräer*, his study on numerology and his book on Maimonides – *Maimonides: Kritik der Jüdischen Glaubenslehre* – in order to discern his theology of immortality.[86] We will see that Goldberg's interpretation of the Torah can be described as a ponerology, a science of evil, culminating in a political theory of the spectral life of the dead.

1

Yearning for a system

Franz Rosenzweig and the great paganism of life

When Franz Rosenzweig's *Hegel und der Staat* was published in 1920 it may have seemed as if his hope for a German *Mitteleuropa* had been buried under the debris of war. The soldier-philosopher added a postscript beginning with the laconic phrase '[w]e are at the end', signalling that the political trajectory he traced in the book was now over.[1] One year later, *The Star of Redemption* (from now on called *The Star*) was published, his definite farewell to the hopes he once held for idealistic philosophy and German politics. In 1920, Rosenzweig concluded *Hegel und der Staat* with a stanza from Friedrich Hölderlin's poem 'An die Deutschen', indicating that he, against all odds, still believed in the geopolitical task that he had theorized during the First World War.

> Our life time is narrowly defined,
> The number of our years we see and count,
> But the years of the people,
> Did a mortal eye ever see them?[2]

The years of our individual lives may be counted and limited, but the poet indicates that the years of the people might be immortal since a mortal eye cannot grasp them. For Rosenzweig, the life of a people without doubt exceeds the short existence of the individual. Yet, the life of the species surpasses the life of a people, tied as it is to the autochthonic spatiality of the nation state. Eternal life, a life that overcomes the boundaries of finite life, is a life that does not only transcend the life of the individual. It transcends the life of the people, the life of humanity and moves beyond life itself. For Rosenzweig, such a life beyond life, transcending the limits of finite existence, was not only a theological question. It was a geopolitical problem.

It was from a similar perspective that Rosenzweig argued in 1917, when he served in the infantry, that the meaning of the world war should ultimately be found in the overcoming of the nation state and the formation of a European community.³ In his essay 'Vox Dei?', he hoped that a Unified States of Europe, a *Vereinigte Staaten Europas*, would emerge as an outcome of the First World War.⁴ Perhaps even more importantly, in 'Die neue Levante' he explicitly stated that the goal of this Europe was the expansion to a New Levant, an international community that included Turkey and parts of Africa.⁵

In contrast to Hegel, and even more so to his teacher Friedrich Meinecke, Rosenzweig did not believe that the course of history was bound to the nation or the state.⁶ He reproached, as Duncan Celly rightly comments, Meinecke for not thinking 'in terms of associations or federations of states (*Staatenverbände*)'.⁷ The task of German imperialism must be the creation of a new international order.

Rosenzweig's critique of Meinecke was a contribution to the debate in which Friedrich Naumann, Ernst Troeltsch and several other prominent German sociologists, theologians and philosophers discussed how modern politics could direct 'the German working classes towards the goal of a strong, industrializing nation-state'.⁸ Rosenzweig's philosophical and religious work, including *The Star*, was part of this *Geisterkampf*.⁹ The essays written during the First World War, such as 'Globus: Studien zur weltgeschichtlichen Raumlehre', that were supposed to compose a war opus, *Kriegsopera*, laid the basis for his geopolitical ponderings.¹⁰ In these texts he explained the rationality for what he, in a letter to his parents, saw as the true goal of the war.

> Meinecke's fundamental mistake [*Grundfehler*] is that *malgré tout* he still thinks of states [*Staaten*], and not unions of states [*federations, Staatenverbände*]. He says: unions of states make wars useless, they introduce nothing politically creative, by this Meinecke means that wars creatively influence only the single state. However, states are no longer the carriers of history, rather it is unions of states, and it is precisely on them that war, this war in fact, has a creative influence. The real-politically true principal point [*realpolitisch berechtigte Kern*] of the idea of pacifism is: to overcome the national within the federal state [*die Überwindung des Nationalen im Verbandsstaat*].¹¹

Rosenzweig had hoped for a multicultural empire beyond the existing nations. With *The Star* he took a new step. Now he anticipated a global home for our species grounded in Judaism and Christianity or, as we will see, in something '*überjudisch*' and '*überchristlich*'. *The Star* was therefore also an intervention in the geopolitical discussion of his days. The term 'geopolitics' had been coined by Rudolf Kjellén – whom Rosenzweig read – in 1899, and the translations of the Swedish political scientist's work was widely discussed in Germany.¹²

Rosenzweig's teacher, Meinecke, lauded Kjellén's theories, and edited a translation of his writings, and Kjellén's geopolitical and biopolitical treatise *Staten som Lifsform* was translated and published in Germany in 1917.[13] The discussion in which Kjellén's geopolitical and biopolitical theories had a role provides a good example of the political context that shaped *The Star*.

After Germany's defeat in 1918, Rosenzweig did not abandon his hope for a new empire. If he had fought for a multicultural empire, with Germany as its heart, he now claimed that a transformed Christianity and Judaism could lay the basis for an international community beyond the nation, even if this meant a conflict with Islam, a religion he portrayed in a simplistic and Eurocentric manner.[14]

Rosenzweig, who had pondered converting to Christianity, argued in *The Star* that Christianity and Judaism were produced by the same revelation. They promised a unanimity of our species and gave Rosenzweig the means to develop a profoundly geopolitical theology after he had accepted that Germany would no longer be able to build a *Vereinigte Staaten Europas*.

Rosenzweig began to write *The Star* when he served as an artillery observer, and increasingly came to understand, as Jörg Kreienbrock has aptly written, 'the impossibility of having a complete overview of the battlefield from the perspective of the individual soldier. There is no absolute point of view in which a complete overview would be possible'.[15] This emphasis on our finitude, so radical that Rosenzweig in a text on the famous debate between Ernst Cassirer and Martin Heidegger defended the latter as the true heir to Hermann Cohen, had a profound impact on his political and philosophical imagination.[16] There is a limit to life and what we can know. Nevertheless, the quotation from Hölderlin that Rosenzweig concluded *Hegel und der Staat* with indicates that even if there is no objective orientation for the mortal eye, there may be a perspective on life that is eternal.

Tellingly, *The Star* concludes with an eschatological perspective beyond life. The finite and mortal life, even death itself, is part of an eternal life that has knowledge of what is and what could be. Philosophy must become theology and get a glimpse of the world from the point of redemption, where the world has been completed. This new perspective is what Judaism promises with its messianic faith, and which Christianity seeks by embedding all nations in the eschatological end of life that Rosenzweig called God.

However, *The Star* is a critique of current existing Christianity and Judaism by depicting them more as what they could be rather than what they are. He had hoped for a new multicultural Germany or even a New Levant. Now he articulated the need for a transformed Judaism and Christianity and even came to allude to the need of an order beyond these religions. In this sense Rosenzweig was true to Hermann Cohen's interpretation of Judaism as a religion that arises from the difference between is and ought.[17] Philosophy should not only describe reality but seek to transform it and, for Rosenzweig, only a transformed world can make us grasp the All.

The cognition of the All

The Star commences famously with death and concludes with a description of the eternal life that death is said to bestow upon the human creature. Read carefully, the first pages give a hint of the reversal of the relation between death and life that Rosenzweig defended: 'From Death, it is from the fear of death that all cognition of the All begins. Philosophy has the audacity to cast off the fear of the earthly, to remove from death its poisonous sting, from Hades his pestilential breath.'[18] The whole work that Rosenzweig devoted his life to – philosophy – emerges out of death and leads to life: 'a life beyond life'.[19]

What Rosenzweig called 'the cognition of the All' was the hope of an ordered and systematic description of the world as a totality.[20] It is the revelation of the intelligibility of a life constantly threatened and limited by death and, therefore, an orientation beyond the finite perspective of the individual. This systematic task of philosophy, the orientation of human cognition into a system of knowledge ultimately grasping the All, was, for Rosenzweig, a discovery of German idealism. But the system needed an existential basis in the mortal life of the individual. This was something that Immanuel Kant, with his insistence on the transcendental limits of thought, and F. W. J. Schelling, with his philosophy of revelation, rather than J. G. Fichte and G. W. F. Hegel had come close to understand. It was, however, Arthur Schopenhauer and Friedrich Nietzsche who took the last step.[21] They liberated German philosophy from its false universalism but Schopenhauer and Nietzsche failed to grasp the possibility to anchor the systematic task of philosophy in human life and such a project necessitated a new critique of Western philosophy.

Modern philosophy was part of what Rosenzweig mockingly described as 'the whole venerable brotherhood of philosophers from Ionia to Jena' – that is from the inception of Greek philosophy with Thales in Ionia (modern Turkey) to G. W. F. Hegel in Jena, Germany – since in Thales's thesis, '[a]ll is water', the systematic and unitary structure of the world is postulated.[22]

The All is contested by death. The mortal individual does not see unity but a reality that looks fragmented and contingent. Every death is something that rips a creature out of the order of existence and exposes the unsystematic character of the world and the contingency of life.

Historically the task of philosophy was not only to explain the rationality of the world but to teach us how to die. It was only by overcoming the fear of death, the destroyer of every system, that the world could be said to be rational and have a systematic meaning.[23] Philosophy in the ancient period was, as Pierre Hadot has argued, never a purely academic exercise. It was a 'philosophical way of life ... which consists in *living* logic, physics, and ethics'.[24] To become a philosopher one must join one of the different schools moulding human life in relation to a diverse set of cosmological theories or religious practices which fostered the ability to understand reality and to live a good life. In pagan antiquity, Rosenzweig emphasized, there was 'not simply a – polytheism, but a "polycosmism," a "polyanthropism"' – a manifold of perspectives.[25]

The Platonists, for instance, affirmed the widespread belief of the pagan world that the soul is, Rosenzweig wrote, 'the natural something that already by its nature is incapable of dying ... The soul, it is asserted, cannot die; but since it is interwoven into nature, the inability to die becomes an inexhaustible capacity for transformation; the soul does not die, but it migrates through bodies'.[26] Epicurus, on the other hand, meant that we should acquaint ourselves with death, the most awful of evils, and learn that death is nothing: 'It is nothing, then, either to the living or to the dead, for with the living it is not and the dead exist no longer'.[27] This instruction to see death as nothing, whether it is based on Epicurean or Platonist ideals, is the 'compassionate lie of philosophy'.[28] Compassionate by trying to ease the pain of mortality. Yet still a lie.

The ancient definition of philosophy as an instrument to differentiate oneself from the material world was alive during Rosenzweig's time. His teacher in Freiburg, Heinrich Rickert, argued in a platonic manner that '[o]nly when a human has *separated* himself from his atheoretical interests of "life" and "existence", and only tries to think theoretically about himself and his environment, does he reach the *independence* which he needs to get to see everything which there is in the world, that is the world-totality'.[29]

Rickert's insistence on philosophy as a theoretical life liberated from ordinary, concrete existence was perhaps most evident in *Die Philosophie des Lebens* from 1920.[30] In this critique of *Lebensphilosophie* Rickert claimed that 'since every man who is concerned with philosophy is not only a living being, but also a thinking being' the philosopher must distance himself from life in order to grasp what Rosenzweig called the All.[31]

Rickert asked rhetorically, 'if . . . living beings only could live and experience . . . According to the modern philosophy of life, it sometimes looks like that. The bare life seems to it a blessedness of life.'[32] *Lebensphilosophie* reduced human life to the non-contemplative existence that Plato depicted with scorn, and which Rickert urged his students to leave behind in order to be capable to comprehend the world as a totality.

At the *Balkanfront*, with dying comrades and enemies around him, Rosenzweig attacked this kind of philosophy and wrote that it 'abandons the body to the power of the abyss, but above it the free soul floats off in the wind'.[33] He continued, 'the fear of death knows nothing of such a separation in body and soul.'[34] The soldier dying in war who 'yells I, I, I and wants to hear nothing about a deflection of the fear onto a mere "body" – matters little to philosophy'.[35] Socrates's death proved, Rosenzweig wrote, that 'the ultimate conclusion' for philosophy is that 'death would be – nothing. But actually, this is not an ultimate conclusion, but a first beginning, and death is truly not what it seems, not nothing, but a pitiless something that cannot be excluded.'[36] Death is always the death of what Rickert called a bare or mere life – *bloßes Leben* – and therefore a death of a specific individual.[37]

Against the philosophers, Rosenzweig decried that one should neither cast aside the fear of death, nor exorcize what he called the fear of the earthly. The earthly is our carnal and embodied existence. One should 'stay' in the fear of death for the 'fear of the earthly should be removed from him only with the earthly itself'.[38] The soldier waiting for the next battle in the trenches, with the image of war and death on his retina, and the ageing or sick with the hope to live on with her loved ones know that death is not nothing. For them, just as for all other mortals who grasp death, death is always the death of someone. It is the death of a creature; the death of a living being; the death of a naked life, which is more than a soul or a mind. This is why Gérard Bensussan has described Rosenzweig's critique of philosophy as a refusal of idealism.[39]

This is true to an extent since, for Rosenzweig, the essential problem with the whole tradition of philosophy from Ionia to Jena was that it did not understand why '[t]he All, which would be both everything and whole, can neither be known honestly nor experienced clearly; only the dishonest cognition of idealism, only the obscure experience of the mystic can make itself believe it has grasped it.'[40] The All cannot be experienced since thought and being never are identical from a finite perspective. Death proves this by revealing the limits that differentiate the unity of being to a manifold of beings: the world is always a world of worlds.

There is a 'non-identity of being and thinking'.[41] Reality exceeds thinking. It is always greater than human thought. Yet, the cognition of the All, that is the systematic attempt to formulate a philosophy of being, is the goal of philosophy. *The Star*, Rosenzweig emphasized, was 'a system of philosophy', commencing in the angst of death.[42]

Commencing but not culminating. *The Star* ends in what Rosenzweig described as a perspective beyond cognition which seems to be that obscure non-knowledge of the mystic that he initially rejected: 'The All must be grasped beyond cognition and experience, if it is to be immediately grasped.'[43] The weakness of philosophy, namely, its belief in a cognition of the All, is also its strength.

The philosophical desire to understand the world may be flawed, but it reflects a real longing that could be satisfied through a critique of traditional philosophy. The birth of a new thinking is made possible by the experience of the fact that death is inevitable for everyone. The unanimity of death is the path to a perspective 'beyond cognition and experience'.[44]

A true system of philosophy needs to transgress the boundaries of finite life and at the same time it has to be anchored in the concrete and embodied existence of human life. Rosenzweig strives to answer why 'man comes upon the thought to put himself above life' and even more show why this striving beyond life must begin in the life of the individual who knows that her life and cognition are finite.[45] It was this movement that he described in the three books that constitute *The Star* which moves from the shattering of the unity of being through death to a system of the All revealed in what is described as eternal life. I will give a dense overview of the strange blending of theological philosophy, geopolitics and cultural history that constitutes the three books of *The Star* that will be fleshed out in this chapter.

In the first book – 'The Elements or the Everlasting Primordial World' – Rosenzweig examined the rise of subjectivity, a soul or a self that fears death and discovers the manifold of existence. Life, in this everlasting primordiality, is a multitude of perspectives, organisms, and individuals just as the primordial world itself is a world of divergent worlds, cultures and histories. This world belongs to an individual who lacks a complete overview of existence; a creature curved into himself because of the fear that death gives it. The primordial individual, both identified with the pagan of antiquity and the modern human who died in the trenches during the First World War, can through its fear begin to understand that the world transcends thought and that philosophy is a vain endeavour to identify being with thinking. Being, and even more life, exceeds thinking. The philosophical systems from Ionia to Jena belong to the primordial world since they are attempts to understand the world as world, namely, as something that lacks what Rosenzweig describes in the second book: redemption and renewal – the discovery of that which is outside us.

In the second part of *The Star* – 'The Path or the Ever Renewed World' – the primordial individual's discovery of an exteriority is examined; this is the story of how a you ensouls the I as a person whom the I is responsible for. This care for the other has been part of all ages and cultures. However, the discovery of the you as a you signals for Rosenzweig the birth of Judaism and Christianity as religions calling the individual who is curved into the primordial world to love and to be open for that which is outside him. The discovery of the other as a you is a discovery of something new: an alteriority and exteriority to the self-identity of the primordial world.

The third, concluding book – 'The Configuration or the Eternal Supra-World' – describes the rise of a nameless we out of the I's discovery of the other as a you. It is in this new collective life form – the we beyond the I and the you – where a cognition of the All may be possible. This we belongs to a new world, the Eternal Supra-World – *Die Ewige Überwelt* – which is the world revealed from the point of view of redemption. There is no transhuman configuration of the species or any *Übermensch* only a supra-world, *Überwelt*, and the unfolding of the knowledge of the All is related to the revelation of this world beyond the world. The All implies an eschatological relation, the we, between the I and you that – as we will see – commences with and returns to what is common to all creaturely existence: the primordial and ultimately pagan subjectivity discovered in the fear of death.

Creaturely existence

In a letter from 1926 to Ernst Simon, Rosenzweig wrote apropos Oskar Goldberg: 'Yesterday I noticed by your manner how dangerous it is to say something about Goldberg; after five minutes you already treated me as if I thought he was right.'[46] But even if Rosenzweig distanced himself from Goldberg, he recognized the significance of the Jewish philosopher's magnum opus, *Die Wirklichkeit der Hebräer*, from 1925. Goldberg's description of the relation between myth and ritual in the Pentateuch had struck a chord in Rosenzweig who in *The Star* insisted upon the liturgical and ritual character of Judaism. He even described the Jewish liturgical life as possessing a 'mythic unity' that, as I shall show in the last section of this chapter, binds Jewish life to the eternal life of God.[47]

Like Goldberg, Rosenzweig traced what he called the 'Jew's myth' to the pagan universe of the ancient period.[48] He even developed a philosophy of paganism in the first book of *The Star*, since, for him, 'paganism is definitely no mere religio-philosophical bogeyman for adults, which is the way it is used by the orthodoxy of earlier centuries and, curiously enough, in Max Brod's recent well-known book. Rather it is – no more and no less than the truth.'[49] Brod had attacked racist and fascist movements in Europe for signifying a regress to paganism.[50] Instead he should have, Rosenzweig emphasized, understood that paganism is the truth. But the truth of what?

Rosenzweig agreed with Brod that 'today's pagans call themselves Christians . . . they like to walk about in the wraps of pagan animal hides' since the Christians are unable to completely wrest themselves out of the pagan world that both Rosenzweig and Brod ultimately saw as the state and the nation.[51] However, for Rosenzweig this was not merely, as Brod wrote in 1921, a warning against paganism as a power 'dedicated to the idea of the continuation of this world' which materialized itself in all the 'Aryans, Germanics, swastika people . . . [who] eagerly revert to the unbaptized state of their respective nations'.[52]

Brod, in this sense more prophetic than Rosenzweig, wrote a warning against fascism among what he called the Caucasian peoples. This use of paganism was, for Rosenzweig, ideological since it refused to see paganism as a truth: the truth that the creature belongs to the world. The rich history of non-Jewish and non-Christian religious traditions revealed the truth of human life as a creaturely existence – even the Platonist flight from the material world was a way to tackle the fear of death – and expressed thereby a truth of our earthly condition. Truth, Rosenzweig wrote, 'to be sure in an elemental, invisible, nonrevealed form', but still a truth.[53]

In what sense can paganism be the unrevealed truth of earthly existence, and why does the Christian world reproduce the truth of paganism? One can find answers to these questions in a letter from November 1917 to Rudolf Ehrenberg where Rosenzweig described Hegel and Johann Wolfgang von Goethe, in a rather simplistic manner, as two modern and Christian pagans who on the one hand grasped the structure of the world, and on the other described the lived reality of life.[54] Goethe's love for nature, and Hegel's identification of God with the human spirit, made them pagan in the sense that both of them came close to identifying the divine with the world and the human. Their work reflected the monistic trend in philosophy and implied a reduction of life to its historical and biological substrate and of the divine to the world of nature. Their work belonged therefore, paradoxically, more to the primordial world of paganism than to the renewed world of Judaism and Christianity.

Rosenzweig wrote to Ehrenberg, 'what else is paganism' than 'the idea of immanence' and hence the idea of a world as a world without an exteriority, something transcendent?'[55] Tellingly, in 'Paralipomena' – Rosenzweig's wartime notes from 1916 to 1917 – the soldier-philosopher argued explicitly that paganism does not know any form of transcendence. Even Plato was a monist who identified the good and thereby the divine with nature (if only the nature of the eternal forms): 'For revelation, however, nature is completely nature (the creator *creates* nature and *reveals* goodness). Platonic idealism is only the counterpart to pagan materialism, and not at all "transcendental". Moses, not Plato, is transcendental.'[56] Ignoring the essential fact that Plato posits the good outside being, Rosenzweig argued that Moses points to a *creatio ex nihilo*, the revelation of a God that creates nature as nature from nothingness, whereas Plato represents a world that emanates out of the divine.

Rosenzweig came thereby close to reproducing Brod's view on paganism as an identification of being, or the reality of the All, with creation or nature. But he refused to see this as a proto-totalitarian idea. The identification of being with nature was the unrevealed truth of paganism.[57] Unrevealed, but still the truth for 'the essence of myth . . . [is] a life that knows nothing above or beneath itself; a life that knows neither of things ruled over nor of ruling gods, a life purely in itself, whether the bearers of this life are gods, people or things'.[58] Thereby paganism is also a life profoundly afraid of death that philosophy seeks to console by arguing that death is nothingness since such a life knows nothing beyond nature.

Plato, Rosenzweig wrote, only knows the nothingness of death and cannot depict a world that has transcended death in the Christian or Judaic sense: 'Paganism never really reaches beyond death because it never realizes that "death is swallowed by victory", because it knows no life that *affirms* death and *therefore* is beyond it.'[59] I have to define what a death-affirming life entails later; what is important at this point in my argument is that the primordial world of paganism is enclosed by death to something of a circle that knows nothing outside itself.

The pagan notion of immortality is not something that disrupts the circularity and closedness of nature since it entails reincarnation, or some kind of afterlife in another plane of this world, and not the birth of a new creation where 'death', as Paul wrote to the Corinthians, is 'swallowed up in victory'.

The brilliance of Hegel, according to Rosenzweig, is that he disclosed the structure of the primordial world as the mythical Ouroboros, the serpent eating its own tail: 'the earth rests on the great serpent and the great serpent supports itself by biting its own tail, that is what Hegel teaches and for sure this does give an exhaustive explanation of the system of the earth-serpent.'[60] The closure of the Hegelian system seals the world from the exteriority which, according to Rosenzweig, upholds it and this is a truthful description of the world as a primordial world. For even if Hegel 'does not explain why this system does not now fall as a whole I say: It does not fall and it does not hover, for there is no space "wherein" it could fall. The serpent fills all possible space; it is just as *massive as the earth* that rests on it'.[61] This is the truth of the primordial world that seals itself from every exteriority and transcendence: matter is matter, nature is nature, bare life is bare life, and God is, in the end, the world totality and identical with what is.

Still, Rosenzweig insisted, even if the truth of the world is the primordial world, this primordiality is a vestige pointing outside itself for the limit of life, and therefore of the cosmos it belongs to, opens paganism itself to the path of revelation.

No system of thought can explain away the pain of death and fixate life onto itself since mortality posits a threshold that may give rise to the speculation that there is something else than this life and, even more, something other than the cycles of worlds and reincarnations that constitute the multiverse of the primordial world. Thus, even if the essence of pagan myth, also in its modern Hegelian form, is 'a life that knows nothing above or beneath itself', Rosenzweig comes close to Goldberg's insistence, that myths, be they pagan or not, are more than discoveries of the immanence of the world.[62] Myths can be viewed as revelations of a radical transcendence. They indicate, Rosenzweig writes apropos Goldberg, that nothing, not even myths or stories, is merely subjective.

> There is nothing that is only subjective. Neither mistakes nor dreams. Just think of Freud! Everything subjective has a relation to something objective. There can be no believed gods without the will of God. Goldberg is right in his struggle against the subjectification of the content of pagan belief; that is really a thoughtless and deeply unbelievable opinion . . . The decisive difference does not go between subjective-objective, but between the creator and the created. The false gods are created.[63]

When even the deities of the world are revealed as being objective, they are not revealed to be divine but, for instance, psychological, sociological or natural phenomena belonging to the world of human life and therefore, Rosenzweig underlines, created by the divine. They point beyond themselves by constantly raising the question if it is really true, like the philosophers say, that the world snake can uphold itself. Is there, really, no need of a God and what would the existence of a God entail philosophically?

In 'Paralipomena', Rosenzweig answered that question by making a clarifying comment on the relation between paganism – the primordial world – and the supra-world that revelation reveals *in* paganism as a renewal of the latter and wrote: 'With Christen*dom* emerges heathen*dom*'.[64] Christianity discloses heathendom; a unifying quality of the pagan world that does not exist as one world, but as a manifold of religions, philosophies and worlds or – once again – as not only a polytheism but also a polycosmism and polyanthropism, by revealing that the unity of these worlds is their lack of the exteriority that the Abrahamic religion calls God.[65]

According to Rosenzweig, the different religious and philosophical currents that Christianity reveals as a heathendom – that is a common world – are in a sense sublated to a renewed world that discloses something outside its own immanence. For, Rosenzweig writes, 'God plainly did not create religion, but rather the world. And when he reveals himself, the world not only continues to exist everywhere, indeed it is hereafter for the first time really created. Revelation does not in the least destroy genuine paganism, the paganism of creation.'[66] What revelation reveals is that nature, just because it is nature and not something divine, is created. This is why paganism is the unrevealed truth of nature, and revelation essentially revealed paganism; 'the paganism of creation' rather than the divinity of nature or, for that matter, the pure immanence of the cosmos.

Consequently, in his essay 'The New Thinking', Rosenzweig stated that the pagan 'did not live in the cosmos, but in the created world, whose sun, our sun, also shone for Homer; and he was not a hero of the Attic tragedy, but a poor human being like us'.[67] Likewise, when the Greek pagan 'prayed, [he] was, to be sure, not heard by Zeus or Apollo, but of course by God'.[68] The circular movement of paganism, the cosmological identification of nature with the divine world, is shattered by death and by the longing that the pagans expressed in their prayers to Zeus and Apollo that were heard by God. This argument certainly assumes its result by simply claiming that the world does not only point beyond itself but opens itself to the divine through its limits. But the crucial thing for Rosenzweig was the undeniable fact that our sun was also Homer's sun, and the problems of human life were also the problems of the hero in the Attic tragedy. The moderns, dying on the battlefields of the Great War, share the same created universe as the pagans – the primordial world – and all creatures live in relation to what Rosenzweig viewed as the common God to all existence, and described as the 'God of Gods'.[69]

Thus, even if the myriad pagan gods were only figments of the imagination these deities are born from real psychophysical needs and therefore, as Goldberg would say, objective. And, Rosenzweig insisted, these needs must be acknowledged theologically and sociologically as forces that bind us modern humans to the men and women of antiquity since we share the same world and often the same troubles as Homer.[70]

We can mirror ourselves in the pagan world by learning great insights from the stories of the Greek gods. The mythological constructions of paganism are, as everything else in the world, part of a common existence that unites all organic and inorganic creatures in a shared and unified reality – the creation. This is the truth of paganism. It discloses an invariable urge in the human, a profound and deep feeling that we belong to the earth and should stay in the earthly or, at least, need to learn how to tackle the question of death by learning how to die. But if the pagan traditions reveal the truth of what Rosenzweig calls creation they can also reproduce, which will be evident in the next section, a dangerous fetishization of life.

The struggle for survival

The danger with philosophy in its classical form as a teaching of how to die is that it disconnects the human from the reality of death. Even worse, philosophy may become so abstract that it separates itself from the concrete life of the human who does not only die but also lives and nourishes himself as a psychophysical creature with biological, cultural and economic needs. By denying death as the annihilation of an individual who, Rosenzweig writes, 'wants to live', philosophy falsifies what life can teach us about existence and the All.[71]

The emphasis on life reveals that Rosenzweig was a biocentric thinker. As a soldier he understood life as a struggle for existence, a work against death: 'Animals and plants, and every "organism" in the wider secondary sense, are not mere products and mere results of forces, but once there, a something that seeks to affirm itself in its own form against all forces.'[72] To be alive is to affirm one's own existence. This definition of life as an almost Darwinian struggle for survival prompted Rosenzweig to argue that *everything* 'that seek[s] to affirm itself in its own form against all forces' can be said to live: 'Not only living essences exist, but also institutions, societies, feelings, things, works – everything, really everything can be alive. But what does this being-alive mean, then, as opposed to mere existence? . . . Life offers resistance; it resists, that is to say, death.'[73] Life is a struggle against death.

What is death? The biologist Rudolf Ehrenberg, whose *Theoretische Biologie* from 1923 according to Rosenzweig was part of the reconfiguration of philosophy towards the new thinking that the soldier-philosopher endorsed, wrote that '[d]eath is the catastrophic ending of a process, be it great or small and it does not matter if it is at the same time a new beginning or not, it is the discontinuity, the leap in the sequence of events'.[74] Death is what makes life possible. It constitutes the possibility of all life since life is finite life: 'Not: no life without death. But: without death no life.'[75] Life is something that necessarily ends, and ends catastrophically, just as the stream of the water running down the mountain eventually ends in the sea.[76]

The great merit of Ehrenberg's *Theoretische Biologie* was, according to Rosenzweig, that it 'subsumes the doctrine of organic nature for the first time under the law of real, irreversible time'.[77] In *The Star*, Rosenzweig expressed this temporalization of organic nature as a critique of the reduction of death in philosophy to a nothing. This discovery of death as the death of something, or even the death of thousands of somethings, is the truth of paganism since even if the 'temples of the gods have rightly fallen . . . the invocation that called out to them from a tormented breast, and the tears shed by the Carthaginian father, who offered up his son as a sacrifice to Moloch, cannot have remained unheard or unseen'.[78]

The father from Carthage who sacrifices his child to Moloch (the biblical name of a deity often associated with child sacrifices) is a human being in time who, by being finite, is heard by God. For, Rosenzweig writes, the pagan must have been heard by the divine: 'Or should God have waited for Mount Sinai, or even Golgotha?'[79]

Behind the paganism of the Carthaginian father who painfully sacrificed his child is the same fear of death that fills us modern men and women, and which expresses a basic truth that philosophy and theology must conceptualize: 'the paganism of creation'. By arguing that God did not wait for Israel but wanted to redeem the pagan father who sacrifices his son to Moloch, Rosenzweig stressed how the primordial world of paganism becomes a renewed world through its inner logic; the primordial world opens itself to something outside it simply because it is threatened by suffering and death.

Thus, contrary to Hans Blumenberg who saw the disclosure of the immanence of the world as a detheologization of existence, Rosenzweig described our finitude and worldliness as a sign that God created a world full of life that struggles for its survival, and that longs for a liberation from this endless strife. The truth of paganism is the truth of the primordial reality of life, namely, that it struggles for existence. The primordial world can therefore be defined as the urge to live.

In 1915, Rosenzweig examined the rise of nationalism as a regress to a paganism in a manner that came close to Brod's view on heathendom: 'The "national being" had forgotten that nationalism is nothing more ... according to its deepest meaning than that of which it is – ethnicism! – the literal translation: paganism.'[80] Some years later Rosenzweig identified in a similar manner the 'eternal gods of paganism in whom paganism will survive until the eternal end, the State and the arts, the former the idol of material gods, the latter the idol of personal ones'.[81] The order of the state, and the domains of art and culture, infest the world with a certain (pseudo)eternity – the seemingly endlessness of the primordial world – by fighting for their life and hence being alive.

If the state and the arts are living forces they are also forces that will perish if only at what Rosenzweig terms the eternal end. It was in this vein he wrote in *The Star*, shortly after the defeat of Germany in 1918, that 'if the State might dam up the river of time in the eras of world history, and art try to drain it off into the endless canal system of experiences – so let them!'[82] By being *living* institutions these institutions will die since life is cast into the irreversible flood of time that annihilates everything.

Rosenzweig continued his critique of the paganism of the state and the arts – and therefore certainly of Christian civilization itself – by writing: 'He who sits in heaven mocks them; he contrasts to their already conflicting interaction the silent work of created nature in whose truth the deified world is limited and fashioned for eternal life, the deified man is humbled and sent onto the eternal way, and thus both, world and man together are subject to God's rule.'[83] This enigmatic passage indicates that it is the order of created nature – the natural life of every being – and not the world of politics or culture that shall be turned to a supra-world, *Überwelt*, where creation is redeemed and death overcome.

It is in what Rosenzweig called 'the silent work of created nature' one can find a truly providential order of eternal life. Providence – the divine care for creation – cannot exactly be found in the order of the states which Rosenzweig had hoped when he wrote his *Kriegsopera* and neither in the life of nations as Meinecke was close to believe. It was because of the unity of the world as a world of nature that providence could act through politics and more specifically through the destruction of nations by potentially unifying humanity in a new global order. Although Rosenzweig criticized all attempts to deify history in

The Star, his theological interpretation of existence made him insist that God's providence is a geopolitical task given to the world as a world. God's providence is the process that reveals the primordial world as a renewed world. The Jew and the Christian should not only interpret the world as potentially becoming a planetary human community: the kingdom of God. The political order must actively be transformed to reflect the coming unity of the world that Rosenzweig thought was unfolding in 'the silent work of creation' and that the cry of 'the Carthaginian father' revealed as the secret longing of pagan life.

In a lecture from 1920, Rosenzweig said that '[t]he world demands a myth of eternal life', and world here is nothing but created nature, and he continued by stating: 'The eternal people *is* such a myth.'[84] The Jews, that is the eternal people, are such a myth because they could live *outside* the struggle for existence that rule the nations and states. Even if this myth of eternal life is *in* the Jews, and in no other nation of the world, since they lack a nation – Rosenzweig wrote before the constitution of Israel as a state – it is still something that goes forth *from* them. It is revealed to the world as the promise that every people may be embedded in the eternal life of God if they partake in the movement beyond the struggle for life and therefore beyond the primordial world of tribes and nations that, in a sense, is the world itself: the pagan world beyond the paganism of state and nation.

This almost organic growth of humanity into a new form of life that begins with but goes beyond the eternal people is the trajectory that Christianity commences by being the religion 'that tolerates no borders'.[85] The birth of Christianity through the belief that Jesus is the Son of God is the turn of world history – *die Wende der Weltgeschichte* – and the emergence of 'the new geographical principle: the expansion over the world begins . . . In this quantitative sense, there is progress. The world becomes more and more circular'.[86] Rosenzweig underlines now against his earlier hope of a federation of states that even the multinational empire, such as Naumann's *Mitteleuropa* or the Roman Empire of antiquity, has borders. In contrast, Christianity knows no limits and, Rosenzweig argues, seeks to create an international community and thereby liberate the world. If it does not want to regress to its inherent paganism it has to conjure a new human figure: an individual no longer only living for his own survival but ready to love the stranger and move beyond the limits of nation, state and empire.

> The Church no longer sets any outer limits for itself as the empire did; it is on principle not satisfied with any border, it has no knowledge of renunciation. As it outwardly throws its protective cloak around the destiny of the whole world,

so, too, within its bosom, no one may remain only for himself. It demands of everyone the immediate sacrifice of his Self, but it fully returns this to everyone in its motherly love; each is a precious and irreplaceable child, always unique in spite of all others. Hence, through it, the individual's life depends immediately on the life of the whole world. The bond that ties him, like the Mother Church itself, to the destiny of the world is love.[87]

It is the insistence that 'the destiny of the world' is a love that rejects all limits which explains why Rosenzweig's planetary and deeply eschatological geopolitics comes into conflict with Meinecke and Kjellén's appraisal of the nation. The goal of world politics, or what Rosenzweig continues to call 'messianic politics', is the creation of a human community that has no other limit than the earth itself.[88]

At the end of *Staten som Lifsform*, Kjellén rhetorically asked if the 'pursuit of geographical individuality, nationality, autarky and interest groups – is all of this not only different forms of the *return to nature*, that is a connection to the life of instincts, which Rousseau preached to the individual!'[89] This rhetoric is close to Rosenzweig's insistence that the human should stay in the earthly, and it is a similar perspective that can make him maintain that the state is a profoundly autochthonic phenomenon differentiating humanity in a world of nations. But, for Rosenzweig, the destruction of these entities in, for example, wars becomes the seed for a new life outside these regional structures.

Kjellén insisted that 'subhuman' symbols, such as trees, forests and land, are necessary metaphors in order to reveal the truth of the state as a biological organism.[90] The state should be viewed through the lenses of 'the modern anthropogeographics' as 'a highly developed piece of land' since the state is 'of earth', in other words 'a developed surface of soil' where human beings root themselves.[91] By using the term 'anthropogeography', Kjellén emphasized the geopolitical work of the renowned German geographer Friedrich Ratzel, a student of Ernst Haeckel famous for coining the term *Lebensraum* in his *Politische Geographie*.[92] Ratzel had in his two-volume book *Anthropogeographie* depicted the relation between anthropology and geography, and claimed that a people is something of a living organism forced to migrate and expand its territories due to population growth.[93]

Dams, motorways, bridges and tunnels were the equivalent to the metabolic system of an animal body struggling for its existence. Interestingly, Ratzel was hostile to all racial theories and his use of the term *Lebensraum* did not justify racist politics. Ratzel emphasized that almost all peoples of the world were racially diversified since life itself forced humans to migrate.[94] His studies of the

United States made him argue that ethnic and cultural diversity improved the vigour of a society.⁹⁵ Nonetheless, his view of the state as an organism fighting for its survival made Ratzel's work easy to appropriate by racial theorists.

Rosenzweig was influenced by the conservative, if not reactionary, tradition of Kjellén and Ratzel – later his and Buber's translation of the Hebrew Bible would be criticized by Siegfried Kracauer for being *völkisch* – and he found the morphological philosophy of Oswald Spengler especially interesting.⁹⁶ Rosenzweig even described *The Decline of the West* as the greatest vision of our world since Hegel's work on history.⁹⁷

Spengler had an organic view of history and saw the rise and decline of civilizations as akin to the growth, blooming and death of flowers and plants that never crossbreed. For Rosenzweig, however, the collapse of cultures and nations forces humanity out of the cycle of civilizations and helps to renew the world as an intermixed globe rather than a conglomerate of separate cultures and nations: 'Therefore *decline* must indeed occur, so that new things can take place. And decline *occurs*. Great external events are necessary: World War and World Revolution.'⁹⁸ The fall of empires and the chaos of war are providential.

The decline of the West promised a new planetary community by renewing the world and pushing European humanity out of its primordial existence. Our species does not belong to any special piece of soil and can only find a permanent dwelling place in its wandering on the crust of the earth.

Just as for Ratzel, migration was, according to Rosenzweig, a necessity for life. But this wandering between the nations must be unfettered from the limits of the state and make the globe as such a common home for homo sapiens: an empire of creatures. In this he differed radically from the nationalist or imperialist perspective of Meinecke, Kjellén and Spengler. Kjellén tied the life of a people to the soil of a specific nation and underlined that the eternal life of the state depended on the individuals who constituted the people.

> The life of the state lies in the end in the hand of the individuals. It is in their power both to strengthen and weaken it, extend or shorten it. We do not know if eternal life will be bestowed on any state or even any nation; but we see that it to a decisive extent depends on the individuals themselves if their state will *live long on earth*!⁹⁹

From Rosenzweig's perspective, this hope for a form of institutional eternal life reflects the basic logic of all organizational life as the vain attempt to postpone their death: 'All mere organization lives as if we could not die at every moment.'¹⁰⁰ Rosenzweig even wrote that 'organizations live as if it were certain that the moment bridges to future moments' and this is certainly not true: death is also immanent to the life of institutions.[101] It is only a life that knows that it is finite and affirms death, and consequently the fall of nation, state and empire that it belongs to, that can wrest itself out of the cycles of history and embed itself in the eternal.

The common sense of death

In the preceding section, I showed that life for Rosenzweig is a resistance against the catastrophe of death. Dying is the temporal process of the world which moves every finite being, be it organic or not, towards a coming end. The world common to the pagan and the modern human is the primordial world of the creature: the creaturely and finite life that seeks to avoid death. Thus, when philosophy urges us to flee the sting of death and view death as nothing, this is not only a retreat from what Rosenzweig regards as the point of departure for his new thinking: the bare life that seeks survival. It is also a flight from the common sense, *von dem gesunden Menschenverstand*, that the reality of death implies.[102]

Rosenzweig argued that the 'new thinking knows, just like the age-old [thinking] of common sense, that it cannot know independently of time – which was the highest claim to glory that philosophy up to now assumed for itself'.[103] Rickert is one of many who claimed that a philosophy unable to move beyond a temporal perspective will never be able to develop a *Weltanschauung*, a conception of the world in its totality. It will only be a *Zeitanschauung*, a mere understanding of time which all true philosophy must transcend.[104] Rosenzweig affirmed instead that, from a philosophical perspective, one could wager that the time of the world reveals a coming or at least possible unity and a corresponding systematic knowledge of the All.

The temporality of the world was a providential sign that 'the world is becoming. The world is not yet complete. Laughter and tears are still in it. And the tears are not yet wiped away on all faces'.[105] The temporal process that can renew the primordial world to a supra-world implies the decline of cultures, nations, and states that a conservative like Spengler bemoaned but which Rosenzweig meant was the necessary consequence of the passage of time. Consequently, a true knowledge of the All must include the 'state of becoming, of incompletion' as a necessary feature of every part of the world, and, Rosenzweig insisted, '[w]e ourselves along with our world concepts belong to the world.'[106] When we grasp our temporal finitude as a constitutive part of the world, we become aware of the disjointed state of the world itself. Time reveals that the world is non-identical since it exists in becoming.

The sense of our own mortality is ontologized by Rosenzweig as a sense of the time of the world. Common sense as the common sense of death shatters every endeavour to grasp the All: death reveals the world as a manifold and a multiverse. In fact, the All can only be completed through the unfolding of time. This is what the common sense of time implies for Rosenzweig: death completes the system by moving life towards its end.

Rosenzweig's turn to common sense is, as Cass Fisher has argued, 'so preposterous that scholars have largely ignored this interpretive clue to the work'.[107] *The Star* is anything but clear and commonsensical in its persistence on the need to move thought to a point beyond life and experience. The book is, Rosenzweig writes with ironic understatement, 'really not intended for the everyday use of every member of the family'.[108] Yet, he identifies his philosophy with common sense, and implicitly makes the case that it is a book for everyone since everyone can understand the commonality of death.

His posthumous volume *Das Büchlein vom gesunden und kranken Menschenverstand* – translated as *Understanding the Sick and the Healthy* – clearly reveals that Rosenzweig defended a healthy common sense – *gesunder Menschenverstand*. He even claimed that his philosophy was nothing else than a transformation of common sense into a method of scientific and speculative thinking.[109] It does this by positing the finitude of temporality as a limit to philosophical speculation itself, and the healthy common sense accepts this limit by knowing that everything will end and, in this end, achieve a certain unity.

It is from the perspective of a radical finitude that Rosenzweig can declare that death is 'the law of unity' in life and write:

> one day the law of unity is suspended over . . . life . . . Knowledge is knowledge of one's own unity. Precisely: the will toward – one's own death. For only death makes life a unity. As long as the human is still living the multiplicity of idols remains in him. Indeed, he would not be living if these idols lost their power. He would hasten toward death.[110]

In order to make this argument legible, I have to remind the reader of Rosenzweig's thesis of the non-identity between thinking and being. I can now deduce that this non-identity is given by the temporality of the world. Only a being that no longer is in the present has unity and can be understood as being completed and identical with itself.

Death brings the multiplicity of life, what Rosenzweig calls 'the paganism of creation', to an end. The paganism of creation is the manifold of worldviews which the human existence expresses to the point that Rosenzweig writes: 'Culture in itself is polytheistic.'[111] Not even a monotheistic civilization can end this polytheism of worldviews – it constantly produces new perspectives and heresies (from the Greek *haíresis* originally meaning choice or thing chosen) – for the goal of revelation is not to dissolve paganism but to reveal its truth. Even if *The Star* was written *against* those who Rosenzweig called 'the fanatics', those who seek to hasten the end of the polytheism of life, Rosenzweig stipulated a coming unity in death and saw this as a messianic event.[112]

Rosenzweig stressed that *The Star* is driven 'by the task of overcoming the danger of understanding the new thinking, perhaps, in a sense, or rather the nonsense, of irrational tendencies such as the "philosophy of life".'[113] For, 'everyone clever enough to have steered clear of the jaws of the idealistic Charybdis seems nowadays to be drawn into the dark whirlpool of this Scylla.'[114] The Scylla is to view life as the ultimate horizon for thought when thinking, according to Rosenzweig, seeks to transcend the philosophy that absolutizes creaturely or biological existence. Thus, even if the new thinking commences with the yearning for survival common to all life, it aims to transcend finite life. It seeks to go from the primordial world to the supra-world, from life to what in *The Star* is enigmatically called 'a life beyond life'.[115]

Peter Gordon is right to emphasize that Rosenzweig's philosophy remains within the bounds of creatureliness.[116] For him, Rosenzweig's hermeneutics of life confirms that 'we are creatures (*Geschöpfe*), precisely insofar as we do not possess the truth as a whole. Being creatures we remain "within the boundaries of mortality".'[117] If God were to grant us more than our portion of the truth, this would require that we surpassed the boundaries of human life, Gordon argues. Still, according to Rosenzweig, this is what death implies for the creature. Death casts the human out of the boundaries of human finitude into the domain of eternity by forever making life to what it was: a specific life with a specific history.

According to Gordon, *The Star* 'should not be read as a progressive argument, but rather as a hermeneutic investigation'.[118] Even if I accept Gordon's suggestion that Rosenzweig writes from the perspective of creaturely life, it is still the case that this life progresses towards death because every creature is a mortal being. There is an evolution in *The Star* towards a perspective on the life of the creature from the vantage point of eternity or the supra-world given by death. The aim with the book is to describe how the revelation prompts us to believe in 'a life beyond life' and this revelation is a renewal of the primordial world of the creature struggling against death and thereby a redemption of the life caught in history.[119]

This 'life beyond life', it is true, is for Rosenzweig 'nothing different than what I was permitted to perceive already in the centre of life; the difference is only that I see it, no longer merely hear'.[120] In life we can hear the rumour of a revealed God, by for instance, listening to stories and myths of Abraham and Moses, and when we are given the opportunity to *see* revelation we can understand what we before have only *heard*; and what one sees is life from the vantage point of redemption that certainly moves us beyond our creaturely confines.

Now we are no longer in the middle of life. We are given a perspective beyond life even if we only see that the meaning of eternal life is – Rosenzweig writes, referring to Mic. 6.8 – 'to do justice and to be good with all your heart and to walk humbly with your God'.[121] Only a life of justice is a life that has begun to move out of the primordial urge to survive – which in its cultural, and sublated form, can certainly seem to be something other than mere creaturely survival but that still is ruled by what Rosenzweig called the pagan gods of the state and the arts – and can take part of the redemption of life that God, essentially, is.

This is why, the 'last' – 'the life beyond life' – for Rosenzweig is the 'nearest', something already given to us in the commandment to love our neighbour.[122] To *see* this goodness, to *see* the world redeemed and loved, and not only to *hear* the commandment that we should love the neighbour in a world full of death, is a sight that liberates us from our creaturely life which so evidently is filled with suffering. For Rosenzweig, life was a life of war, of sickness with malaria at the *Balkanfront*, and then a painful death in 1929 from the muscular degenerative disease amyotrophic lateral sclerosis. He wrote, as I have already stated, that '[p]aganism never really reaches beyond death because it never realizes that "death is swallowed by victory", because it knows no life that *affirms* death and *therefore* is beyond it'.[123]

First, it is important to note that the affirmation of death is an affirmation of bodily life and only in this sense a critique of paganism. Rosenzweig writes that '[t]he separation of "Body" and "Soul" is specifically pagan. The absolute *unity* of the human is revealed.'[124] To affirm this unity is to affirm its essentially mortal character and to define the victory over death as the hope for a world that can redeem itself from death by affirming it.

Second, the triadic development of *The Star* from a primordial world, where the human encounters death, to a renewed world, is a transformation of the world defined by death to a cosmos where death has been defeated.

To an extent Gordon may be right that there is no progression in *The Star*, but rather a circular movement that begins with life – the life that fears death and struggles against death – and that ends with a life that emerges from death. However, this is a life that partakes in the eschatological process to redeem the world that time itself implies. It is even a life that can be affirmed as being outside the confines of mortality since it can now see and not only hear that death has been overcome.

Elliot Wolfson has noticed this mystical tendency in Rosenzweig's thinking by stating that the leitmotif of *The Star* is 'the victory of eternity over time', and that '[d]eath is only the beginning, the way that leads unto life'.[125] Death, Wolfson writes, comparing Rosenzweig to Heidegger, is not in any sense an appropriation of one's own *Sein-zum-Tode* but 'the recognition of one's essential relatedness to the eternal life that is other than oneself'.[126] Wolfson's emphasis that eternal life is *other than oneself* is of crucial importance. To experience the otherness of eternity produces the belief that life, just as the whole order of creation, has not its origin in itself. But to experience this otherness is not simply to experience the revelation that constitutes the belief in the Judaic God, the 'God of Gods'; it is to understand life as a kind of task or mission that can help us affirm death as a passage into new life. Rosenzweig did not mean that only Jews, and later Christians, viewed death as a possibility for new life. He argued that these two religions could make us understand that the life of the other was the meaning of eternal life and he thought that these religions were, or at least should be, based on the chastening of the primordial will of life that according to him expressed itself historically as different forms of paganism.

This does not imply that we should view Rosenzweig as a mystic against his will. But the knowledge of the All that he sought is only possible for someone who '*affirms* death and *therefore* is beyond it'. Rosenzweig explicitly wrote that a 'healthy man has the strength towards the grave. The sick man invokes death and lets himself be carried away in mortal fear. . . . Health is in good terms with Death.'[127] This nearness to death is, as Zachary Braiterman has shown, something that is often overlooked in the discussion on Rosenzweig.

The soldier-philosopher was strangely unburdened by the horror of war. He wrote essays, parts of whole books, when he was at the front, and did not complain over the loss of comrades or the killing of enemies, in his letters from the front. He even consoled his mother for her husband's, and hence his father's, death in 1918 by writing in a manner that reminds of the pagan traditions he criticized: 'The less I fear death, indeed *the more I love it*, the more freely can I live. Happiness and life are two different things and it's no wonder that men finally came to ascribe bliss to the dead alone. In any event, it is not the portion of the living.'[128]

In *Understanding the Sick and Healthy* Rosenzweig could state that a healthy human – a human with a common sense – 'must direct his life to no other goal but death. Only then does life become simple, inasmuch as it no longer seeks to elude death, being willing to chant the dirge at any moment, while advancing in the face of death.'[129] These are bewildering and confusing words from a thinker who accuses philosophy of having cast off the fear of death, and they have been interpreted by Nahum Glatzer as standing in striking contrast to the words which conclude *The Star*: 'INTO LIFE.'[130]

At first glance, it appears that Glatzer is right. There seems to be a contradiction between Rosenzweig's exhortation to fear death in *The Star*, and his acceptance of death in *Understanding the Sick and Healthy*. Pollock has implicitly given an answer to this contradiction by arguing that 'there is an important difference between the morbidity of one who views death as the task of the hour, and that of one who sees death as the positive ending of a fully lived life.'[131] This seems to be true, because as Rosenzweig wrote, 'we are not supposed to "flee" "from the narrow, stifling life into the realms of the ideals." We are supposed to live.'[132] To live is to be mortal and to be mortal is to face death as a necessary part of life, even as a gate – which is the name of the last section of his book on eternal life – to 'the life beyond life'.

It is what I call the common sense of death, in other words Rosenzweig's argument that death is not a nothing but rather the cessation of concrete and temporal life, that forces his thinking out of the domain of life, into the completion which death implies for *all* life. Rosenzweig understood that death is not only the positive ending of what Pollock calls a fully lived life. Death is also the completion of a life that never had the possibility to live fully. The truth of such an unfulfilled life is that it can be lamented by the living who can hope for its resurrection in God's eternal life or simply mourn its end. It is in this way that death can be said to reveal the truth of a life. All death, even the most horrid death, is, if not a completion, at least an end, allowing the living the possibility to understand the meaning of a life once lived, if only as something that must be lamented as seemingly meaningless.

I must now ask: On what grounds can Rosenzweig argue that death is the revelation or what he also calls a verification of a truth? And what existence is ready to affirm death? One answer to these two questions can be found in the second book of *The Star*, where Rosenzweig claims that the martyr, the witness ready to die for a truth, exposes the experiential character of truth.

Truth, Rosenzweig writes, is 'not, as Scholastics think, recognized in the error; truth attests itself; it is one with all the real; it does not separate in it'.[133] Truth is for Rosenzweig reality: what is true is real or can become real. Truth is not first and foremost a coherent and logical truth, such as the mathematical truth, whose content is revealed for everyone under the right circumstances. Truth is a truth that one believes may be attested, and thus judged, to be real: 'Truth does not prove reality, but reality upholds truth. The essence of the world is this upholding... of truth.'[134] The concept of verification, *Bewährung*, is a key concept in *The Star* where it is used to prove the temporality of truth itself: 'Truth in this way ceases to be what "is" true, and becomes that which, as true – wants to be verified [*bewährt*]. The concept of the verification of the truth becomes the basic concept of this new theory of knowledge.'[135] Truth is something that becomes true in the order of time. Truth becomes real by being attested as having reality as what is common to all and therefore able to be known.

Martin Kavka has pointed out that Rosenzweig was not alone in professing a form of verificationism among 'the major Jewish philosophers of the Weimar period'.[136] Kavka emphasizes that *Bewährung*, which can also be translated as testing or affording, has a forensic and juridical meaning, and should be understood as a judgement of something being or coming to be true.[137]

Rosenzweig describes his theory of verification as a 'messianic theory of knowledge, which evaluates truths according to the price for its verification and to the bond that they establish among human beings'.[138] This verificationism has not much in common with the logical positivists' insistence that only empirically verifiable statements are cognitively meaningful, and his idea of truth can be attacked from a Popperian perspective for not being falsifiable.[139]

The positivists' verification thesis was a harsh rejection of ethics, metaphysics and theology, whereas for Rosenzweig these modes of thought can be verified empirically since truth is not necessarily 'those least important truths, of the type "two times two is four," on which people easily can agree... the path leads over the truths that have cost man something, on towards those that he cannot verify except with the sacrifice of his life'.[140] It is martyrdom that binds truth to death through the concept of verification. Truth is something which one is prepared to witness for even at the price of death.

David Baumgardt, who for a while belonged to Oskar Goldberg's circle, has criticized Rosenzweig for confusing truth with the feeling of truth.[141] The martyr's feeling or belief may be untrue even if she is ready to die for her belief in what is true. But Rosenzweig does not only view truth as a reality that is verified in time because of his understanding of death as something that completes and even reveals the truth of a life. He is also prompted to view truth as something that verifies itself because he believed in the existence of a messianic truth: a truth of redemption that can reveal the meaning of life through death and even retroactively save the past through the redemption of the dead.

Rosenzweig's messianic theory of knowledge is directly related to his understanding of the importance of lamentation. His perspective on death as a verification of the truth of life implies that the martyrs may be just those who never lived their lives fully, like those men and women who died during the First World War and revealed the murderous truth of Western civilization. Life was nothing harmonious or idyllic. It was a life of war, pain and suffering, a struggle for survival, and it was this that made Rosenzweig yearn for redemption. No life – not even the life blessed by peace or the life of the academic in his ivory tower – can avoid the verification that death entails.

> It is so difficult to realize that all verification lies ahead, that death is the ultimate verification of life, that to live means to die. He who withdraws from life may think that he has avoided death; however, he has merely foregone life, and death, instead of being avoided, closes in from all sides and creeps into one's very heart, a petrified heart. If he is to be restored to life he must recognize the sovereignty of death.[142]

Death is what verifies life, for every death is potentially a martyrdom, in other words a witness to the fact that life ultimately may only reveal the banality, injustice or tragedy of existence. What Baumgardt does not discuss is that it is not the feeling of truth as such that makes Rosenzweig identify truth with verification. It is a specific feeling, or rather longing, that makes him defend his theory of verification.

Rosenzweig's postulation that verification lies ahead was based on his belief that philosophy requires theology to grasp what can be believed, but not necessarily known, namely, that death verifies life. 'Philosophy today requires, in order to be freed of its aphorisms, and hence precisely for its scientific character' that 'theologians do philosophy. But theologians in a different sense, of course ... For ... the theologian who[m] philosophy requires for the sake of its scientific character is himself a theologian who desires philosophy – out of concern for integrity.'[143]

The problem with theology is that it lacks authority and legitimacy in a modern world where the human is no longer seen as a created being but a contingency of the process of evolution. Rosenzweig comments on this predicament by noticing that modern theology has not been able to find 'a positive *auctoritas* for it, which founds its truth through cognition'.[144] It is philosophy, Rosenzweig argued, which can give theology the positive authority to ground revelation in the idea of death as the common sense of life, and thus to begin in what is common to all mortal creatures: death. Theology can, in a sense, find its immanent and natural legitimacy in death.

The perspective beyond life that Rosenzweig sought in *The Star* was, obviously, not possible to verify among the living. But the common limit to all living organisms makes theology legitimate as a suggestion that the sense of life is the otherness to existence that Rosenzweig called eternal life. The life that feels that the rumour of redemption is worth living and dying for is the life that lives for something other than sheer survival and such a life verifies the truth that some are ready to live for the eternal by affirming death.

Rosenzweig's turn to common sense is an intrinsic part of his theology of death, since his aim is to ground philosophy in the singular perspective of the finite individual only to push it to a theological perspective beyond life. Philosophy could give theology legitimacy in a period where immortality was increasingly viewed as a perpetuation of our existence and present interests. However, Rosenzweig wanted to go further. He defended a theological metaphysics which posited that there is something more than life and death.

It is not by coincidence that Nathan Rotenstreich already in 1967 criticized Rosenzweig for not being able to free 'himself from the traditional and rational basis of philosophy' since *The Star* is 'a highly speculative system erected for the purpose of impugning speculation itself'.[145] Rotenstreich fails to mention that Rosenzweig's turn to common sense is an appropriation of key insights from F. W. J. von Schelling's philosophy of revelation and not in itself an attempt to flee philosophy.[146] It is true that Rotenstreich recognizes that 'the *terminus a quo*' for Rosenzweig is 'speculation and not healthy understanding, but this speculation penetrated so deeply into what Rosenzweig calls the real man that it seemed to him, as it were, common sense'.[147] But the purpose of Rosenzweig's turn to common sense is not to banish speculation from philosophy, and absolutely not to differentiate German idealism and philosophy in general from common sense.

Rosenzweig tried to make speculative philosophy, or what he also called science, a necessary part of mortal life and in doing so he once again comes quite close to ancient philosophy. He insisted that 'science can renounce life if need be' and

> the principal works of our Jewish science have consistently sought and found their public much less in the breadth of the world it lives than in the length of

the next century. . . . Life, however, cannot do without science. It needs it, true, not like bread; but already Scripture says that man does not live by bread alone: life needs science as its soul.[148]

Science is not only the natural or social sciences. It is the science of faith and the love for wisdom: theology in its scientific and systematic sense and philosophy in the tradition of German idealism as a systematization of the All.

It is not a coincidence, even if Rosenzweig wrote that it is something that surprised him, that his union of philosophy and theology in a 'coitus' had theosophy as offspring and not philology: 'Thus theosophy – I myself am still astonished and resistant to this thought – is joined to theology and philosophy concluding the triangle of the sciences. The rest is philo-logy, that is silence.'[149] This is not surprising since *The Star* is not a neutral description of history. It commences with philosophy, in the first book on the primordial world, continues with theology in the second book on the renewed world, and culminates in the theosophy of the third book that promises a vision beyond life. Here we are given a wisdom of God – theosophy – beyond the love of wisdom, philosophy, and the Word of God, theology. Theosophy is the capacity to see what we can only hear in the midst of life: the redemption of the world.

Rosenzweig is resistant to this begetting of theosophy since he is afraid to fall back into the metaphysics that he eschewed. However, the wisdom of God that the coitus between philosophy and theology generated is a wisdom of the concrete and everyday life of the human who lives and wants nothing but to live. Life craves science, even the systematic science of theology, which for Rosenzweig was a science of redemption that postulated the legitimacy to believe in a future vision of the world 'in its redemptive unity which is God'.[150] Only through the concept of revelation can philosophy find a perspective that is beyond life and thereby reach the point of view of a redemption that even redeems God from the violence of his creation.

The redemption of God

In *Philosophie der Offenbarung*, Schelling's famous lectures on the concept of revelation held in Berlin in 1841 and 1842, the German philosopher distanced his own positive philosophy from what he called negative philosophy.[151] The latter was constructed upon an illegitimate identity between thought and being if it transgressed its limits. This identification of reality and thought is legitimate for logic which grasps the content of thought as if it were real. It asks, in other words, for essences. Still, ontology, and especially philosophy of nature, is a positive philosophy beginning from the acknowledgement that being, or what Schelling described as the mere positivity of existence, precedes thought: *'The beginning of positive philosophy is the being which comes before all thinking. It goes from being, which no concept precedes, to the concept, to "transcendence"'*.[152]

Being, here identified with the vast domain of reality as such, is before thought since no human concept precedes it. So even if we cannot grasp being without language or thinking since there is no immediate access to reality without the mediation of language or thought, we still cannot identify being with thinking or language. There is, Kant would say, a noumenal world that reveals itself conceptually through the fact that we humans belong to a world that we cannot fully understand in and for itself. Or, as Rosenzweig would say, there is a non-identity between being and thinking since we cannot be sure that what we think or experience is true, just as we cannot avoid trusting the common sense of reality as a world that exists independently from us.

The content of negative philosophy, Schelling wrote, is 'the a priori intelligible being' whereas '*the positive* [philosophy seeks to understand] *the a priori unintelligible being, so that it becomes intelligible a posteriori*'.[153] This, Schelling continues, is why positive philosophy is a rational science based on revelation.

Reality reveals itself for thinking as a non-identity to thought in the form of an intelligible concept that can be shared and understood as signifying a *common* reality and therefore indicating something that we may rationally believe is true through a *common* revelation.

The process of knowledge for Schelling does therefore not begin in thought.[154] It begins in what Schelling terms the *prius*, the 'first', before thinking, the sensing and willing which comes before knowing.[155] Yet, Rosenzweig argued, if willing and experiencing come before knowledge and knowing, this is only because the world comes before the will. The everyday confrontation with the interconnection of things reveals the commonsensical fact that the 'world is already made'.[156] It is the positivity of being – the fact that it is created – that is the *prius* of both knowledge and willing. Every experience is an experience of a cause that gives rise to experience, such as an injury that implies pain, a lover who creates suffering, a flower that arouses scent, or a book that produces knowledge.

The fact that the world is already made, and a common reality for all that is, is for Rosenzweig what constitutes the common ground of the multitude of almost monadic worldviews that experience one and the same world but in a myriad of different and often contradicting ways.

Modern philosophy, especially the perspectivism of Schopenhauer and Nietzsche, has conceptualized this inherent difference of the world, Rosenzweig claims, so radically that it postulates that '[p]hilosophy does not have as object the objective, thinkable All and the thinking of this objectivity; rather, it is a "view of the world," the idea with which an individual mind reacts to the impression the world makes on it'.[157] This is clearly not the task of the new thinking which still seeks to understand the unity of reality. Still, Rosenzweig was a modern thinker who understood the legitimacy of the new perspectivism which sought to understand the 'multidimensional form' of reality.[158]

For Rosenzweig, a philosophy capable of expressing the multitude of viewpoints of the world as a common reality must show that the difference in perspectives is inherent in being itself. The world *is* a manifold of perspectives. Borrowing the idea of a non-verbality of being, in other words the postulation that being is 'non-verbal', outside thought and language, from Ludwig Feuerbach, who listened to Schelling's lectures on revelation, Rosenzweig claimed that the 'non-identity of being and thinking must appear in being and thinking themselves'.[159]

The reason why the non-identity of thought and reality reflects a non-identity in being itself is because being is inherently temporal. Being is becoming. Since the world, which Rosenzweig calls the 'Space-Time-World', is a radically unfinished totality moving towards its end, Rosenzweig can postulate that everything which is is not identifiable with itself.[160] That which is only becomes itself when it is in rest and therefore is dead. In life, and consequently in time, that which is is a primordial world that constantly renews itself through its temporality, and by renewing itself it moves towards its state as a supra-world by dying and becoming complete. This is the eschatological process from death into life that *The Star* sketches by affirming the finite life of the creature as the beginning of the knowledge of the All.

However, the non-identity inherent in being is not only expressed eschatologically in the movement of present time towards a future which creates the past as a land of the dead that the living can hope will one day be redeemed. The non-identity between thought and being is already apparent in the distinction between concept and nature, essence and existence, and therefore revealed in the present. Schelling underlined that the primordial structure of reality discloses that the philosopher of nature does not choose the objects he tries to understand: '*The philosophy of nature will not deduce any real plants; every real existing plant is a now and here.*'[161] The now and here of a real plant, and by extension of reality itself, is not immanent to thinking. It is something that reveals itself as an exteriority to thought. Reality is, Rosenzweig wrote, borrowing an important concept from Hans Ehrenberg's *Die Parteiung der Philosophie*, metalogical.[162] The real transcends the structure of thought.

Common sense, in other words the sense of a common reality, which can be said to be shared by all sentient beings, even if they experience it in radically divergent ways, grasps the positivity of existence. This is not a relapse into pre-critical and pre-Kantian metaphysics, which stubbornly accepts what is given and builds an ontology of being as something disclosing itself through the positivity of non-immanent reality. What should be doubted, and what is a legitimate doubt, is, Rosenzweig writes in a Kantian manner, not the question if the world exists, but '[w]hether it really is as it appears to us?'[163]

Even if Rosenzweig writes sneeringly against the academic philosophers that only a professional scholar would argue that friendship is solely subjective since only *I* can experience it; it is still necessary to doubt our experiences of the world. Friendship may be false. Reality is, as I have insisted, constituted as a manifold of perspectives that we must understand as perspectives and not as truths: 'Regarding the world there are worldviews. That is, (objectively applied) there are worlds. Worlds that telescope into each other, that have their own laws, set their own task. The world of art, of law, of work, of faith, of nature, of the spirit *e tutti quanti*.'[164] Philosophy neither should nor can identify experience with the reality or truth of the world.

Philosophy must, as we have seen, critically verify the experience of positivity as something real, and by doing so it can move beyond finite experience to a cognition of the All. Yet it is the fact that the world is a world of worlds that explains why Rosenzweig insisted that philosophy should learn from the daily, mundane experience of a world common to all sentient beings. He therefore accepts that what Schelling called negative philosophy never can become a thinking of the positivity of the real. A philosophy of revelation is needed.

Negative philosophy cannot grasp the sheer positivity and thatness of reality, which for Rosenzweig shows its singularity in the experience of the death of a living organism or the end of an occurrence. This is why all deaths, I can now deduce, are more than nothings. They are the end of somethings, since being is a manifold of worlds, and life a multitude of creatures. Death and the destruction of living and inanimate beings, be they animals, plants or minerals, just as the end of occurrences, are the *somethings* which bind together the totality of worlds to a common, temporal reality. There is unity in the world because there is death.

Death completes being since, we remember, 'only death makes life a unity' for life always evolves beyond the unified.[165] But death gives not only unity. It also gives eternity for, Rosenzweig writes, when 'a form of the world dies it is ... made eternal'.[166] What has been is forever what it was. It now exists once for all. The dead rest in the order of the preceding as something eternal waiting for its renewal. '[E]ach individual event', Rosenzweig wrote, 'is a rigidifying, a non plus ultra. In this sense one can say that nature at every moment rigidifies to "eternal being" ("being is eternal"), that it is full of death. (Law of entropy!).'[167]

The second law of thermodynamics gives time an irreversible direction evolving from the past into the future, and was in Rosenzweig's time interpreted as an accumulation of the entropy of the universe to the point of the destruction of the cosmos in its totality. This process was seen as a threat to the idea of immortality and resurrection since it posits the end of everything, but it is death that gives the being eternity, according to Rosenzweig. By being past life, life enters the domain of eternity and can be said to be the accumulated ground of both present and future life. Life is always a life after itself.

Every death is part of the past that is the condition of possibility of the present and coming existence for, Rosenzweig writes, the 'being of the world is its being-already-there [*Schon-da-sein*] ... [W]e now see the characteristic of Creation in general when we understand existence [*Dasein*] as being-there [*Da-sein*], already-being-there [*Schon-da-sein*], no longer as a simple universal being, but as being which gathers all the singular in itself.'[168]

If the being of the world is its being-already-there then everything that is *exists after itself* and since the past is eternal being the land of the dead is the world of eternity. It is the past that makes being into being-already-there. Yet the past is not only the condition of possibility for existence by being eternal but for knowledge itself. The past, as the ground of being, precedes thought and knowledge. Rosenzweig writes explicitly that 'all concepts that attempt to embrace reality universally try to adopt the form of the past [*die Form der Vergangenheit*] ... the concept of "cause," of "origin," of "presupposition," of "a priori": each time, the world is projected into the past in order to be knowable'.[169] The temporality of the world embeds all created things – be they animate or inanimate, organic or inorganic, historical or natural – in the form of the preceding that makes knowledge possible. Knowledge is always a form of history: it searches for a cause, an origin or a presupposition of what is real. Truth, as I have claimed, presupposes according to Rosenzweig reality and knowledge is a knowledge of the causes, origins and presuppositions of reality and therefore of the eternal being of the past.

At the same time, the past is not possible without a future, and even if Rosenzweig to an extent privileges the past as the eternal being that makes present and future existence possible, it is still the future that explains the past in his system. The past is a beginning. It is in this sense that his epistemology is profoundly messianic. The future is only future by producing a past, namely, the end of a beginning. The future completes everything by making it part of the eternity of the past since only when something is completed in the future can it be judged and, hopefully, redeemed. The past is thereby not finished as long as there is a future. It is part of the becoming of the world that links that which was to that which will be through the redemption that even can change the past. The redemption arises from the fact that if everything exists after itself, the past is the beginning of the future that gives meaning to that which was.

This is why Rosenzweig's system is not only a philosophy of time but a theology of redemption. His theory of the past as eternal being is part of an eschatological clarification of how the dead can be said to partake in the eternal life of God and thereby be redeemed. The arrow of time that entropy signifies is the eternalization of the world in the past through the completion that the future gives life since, he writes, above everything temporal 'stands a promise of the end, a thought of completion. . . . The eternal cycle of the world-law is ruptured by the promise of the *happiness* of peace (Nirvana, death).'[170] Death is what liberates humanity from the struggle of life.

By describing death as the promise of happiness that is bestowed on the living when it reaches completion, Rosenzweig identifies an antagonism between the eternal being of the past, which he comes close to identifying with the unity of God, and the polytheism of the living in the course of history; 'against the unity of God there is the multiplicity of the – idols. *Fight* is here between unity and multiplicity. Of this the philo*sophy* of unity knows nothing. . . . For only death makes life a unity.'[171] A philosophy of unity knows nothing of this struggle since philosophy cannot reach the point beyond life that theology seeks. Only theology can wager that the eternal being of the past is embedded in the life of God.

If life is polytheistic by being a manifold, then death is monotheistic by promising unity and even more redemption. This evolution towards redemption is expressed in a yearning that permeates every living, and perhaps even every dead, part of the cosmos, in a Paulinian manner: 'The longing of the world is called happiness. The longing of the human is called completion.'[172] Life desires rest from its struggle for survival and this rest is what happiness ultimately is for Rosenzweig: a carefree existence; a life unbothered by surviving to the point that it even goes beyond the finite joy of life which is always a life of laughter and tears. Rosenzweig does not urge us to seek death. We should stay in the earthly. But he argued that there is a greater and eternal happiness that surpasses the laughter and sorrow of earthly life.

To love death, which Braiterman accuses Rosenzweig of coming close to doing, is, for the author of *The Star*, only legitimate as a love of eternity. The existence that can affirm death is an existence that seeks to love the eternal life that promises completion. Love must be a love for the God that is the God of the future. But God is only the God of the future by being the God that made creation a temporal world that gradually moves towards its end, just as every being in the world is given temporal completion in its cessation. 'You don't have the *end* until you have the complete conquest of time and with it the restoration of eternity. The end therefore solves the why-question of temporality by setting an end to temporality. When an artist has *completed* his work – not before – it is subject to the judgment of eternity.'[173] The reason why there is death in the world is because the world is a temporal process that one day will become eternal by being completed.

It is this coming completion of existence that makes it possible for every human to partake in the finishing of the world as a work of redemption rather than as something that, vainly, seeks to restrain the decline of the world. This is why Rosenzweig emphasizes the temporality of the world as something that moves that which is into the eternity of the past by dying and giving room for new life. There is, for him, no point in defending the world as it is since the world is becoming. Thus, logically, an act of love, and love is for Rosenzweig the force that seeks to bring humanity nearer the All, is greater than every action primarily belonging to the (pseudo)eternity of the state and the arts, since it is an act of eternal life that can redeem the past. It is an act that seeks to complete that which is and was and make past and present life part of the All. Love is not something that upholds existence, it changes and renews creation to the point that the past itself is redeemed, it reveals that the world is in a process of completion. It is what can transform the philosophy of revelation to a theology of redemption.

In contrast, the acts that seek to uphold a world that primarily fights for its survival are part of a vain work that, from the perspective of eternity, shall be judged exactly as it always was: a meaningless power struggle that even may postpone our redemption from the laughter and suffering in the world. For Rosenzweig, the promise of redemption that humanity can take part in by doing the good that he identifies with eternal life is not only a redemption of the world. It is a redemption of God himself from the decline, death and suffering that the process of completion means for a finite life that necessarily is a temporal, and therefore mortal, life.

> In the Redemption, that of the world through man and that of man through the world, God gives himself his own Redemption. Man and the world fade out in Redemption, God completes himself. It is only in Redemption that God becomes that which the human spirit, in its temerity, constantly sought everywhere and affirmed everywhere, yet without ever having found it, for this was not yet: the One and the All. The All of philosophers that we had reduced to dust with full knowledge of the facts, here in the dazzling light of the midnight where Redemption is fulfilled, has finally, truly finally, come together to become the One.[174]

The completion of the world is the point when man and world fade out in the redemption and, interestingly, 'God completes himself' through humankind's salvation of the world. In the German original, Rosenzweig explicitly writes '*Mensch und Welt verschwinden in der Erlösung*.'[175] Man and world disappear, *verschwinden*, but only because they no longer are simple parts of the primordial world, the world that struggles for survival, and which only knows present life: a life with a beginning and an end, whereas God's life is eternal and necessarily transcending the normal order of time. God can even redeem the past and thereby transform everything that was, but he needs help. It is only through '[r]edemption, that of the world through man and that of man through the world . . . that God becomes that which the human spirit . . . constantly sought everywhere . . . yet without ever having found it'. For, and this is crucial, there is no 'All', and in a specific sense no God, before the completion and redemption of everything that is, was and will be.

God seeks to become redeemed from the violence of his own creation through humanity's redemption of the world and the world's redemption of humanity: 'It is only when and where the members of this living organism are covered by the breath of love for the neighbour, a breath that breathes soul into them, it is only when they add to their life what life itself could not give them: a soul, eternity.'[176] Life could not give the living organism an eternal soul since life is, as we have seen, a struggle for survival. It is a struggle to uphold the manifold, even polytheism, of existence that does not know 'the One and the All' that is God's own redemption. For Rosenzweig, 'the One and All' reveals itself before the completion of time as the task of the human to ensoul his world by living for something else than the struggle for survival.

The unfinished character of the world explains, for Rosenzweig, why philosophy fails. The classical philosopher wants to understand the world in its totality before it is completed and such a completion is identical with its redemption. The world is not in any sense an 'All' here and now since it, and therefore God himself, is not redeemed. Yet, the world is given a unitary character by being made one through the redemption that for the human entails the birth of the soul and the task to love the other. To be ensouled is to anticipate the unity of the world by ordering life towards the God that seeks the point when everything, finally, has become one and this oneness includes the dead for in redemption mankind and the world fade away in God's own completion.

If *The Star* begins in death, and moves to life, this is because the process of redemption that Rosenzweig tries to follow reverses the normal course of existence and seeks to bring life out of the completion of death. The fading out of life promises a resurrection of life out of the suffering process of time into the oneness of the divine. This does not entail that everything becomes God. On the contrary, it reveals that everything is made eternal in the unity that God gives himself through his redemption from the violence of the world that can only mean a transformation of the past. For, we remember, revelation is the revelation of 'the paganism of creation'. It is the revelation of the unity for the world that has lacked such commonality by being fragmented in tribes, nations and empires. But in what sense is this unity related to the liberation of that which was?

'To live', Rosenzweig emphasized when he describes the liturgical life of the Jews at the end of *The Star*,

> means to live between beginning and end. He who would want to live outside of time – and he who wants to live not that which is temporary, but an eternal life, must want this – he who therefore wants this must deny that 'between'. Such a denial . . . would result not merely [in] a not-living-in-time, but a positive living-eternally.[177]

The denial of the between of life, what Rosenzweig calls a *living-eternally*, is a reversal of the ordinary and causal structure of life as a process between a beginning and an end. It is even a reversal of the historical process that rules the life of the state and the people. And to 'reverse a between means to make its after into the before and its before into the after, the end into the beginning, the beginning into end'.[178] Those who desire this living-eternally must, before the end of time, live as if the end and beginning of life have faded out from the world and thereby act as if they could alter past. They must view life and the whole domain of time as something that is more complex than an evolution from a beginning to an end by hoping for the possibility of the redemption of that which already is there, namely, the world. The world is the accumulation of the past that is open for the future by being in becoming. The redemption of the world must therefore also be the redemption of the past. This is how the path into death can lead to life.

Yet even those who seek a positive living-eternally belong to those who have not disappeared into the eternity of God. They are living in a world that is still not an 'All', still not one. In difference to other creatures of life, they endeavour to bind themselves to a loving community that includes the dead and not only the dead of one's own tribe, state or people but the whole world of the past.

Such a community would be a new kind of people transcending the struggle for existence that characterizes the course of life and history. It would be an eternal people: a people called out from the course of history by living in relation to the promise of rest that Rosenzweig finds in the eternity of the past. This is what the matrilineal bloodline of the Jewish people represents. The diasporic life of the Jews transcends all geographic borders and signals to humanity that it can live outside state and empire and not only live for the living but for the dead who strangely enough, according to Rosenzweig, can be liberated by the acts of those who come after them.

The eternal being of the past is what urges the living to hope for the redemption of the dead. The dead are not only or even primarily dead. They are made eternal and they are interpellating humanity to live for something greater than the beginning and end of present life. They urge us to live for God's own completion which we now can identify with the redemption of time.

This task of completing God by redeeming time itself is what it entails to live eternally, and this eternal life is directly related to the geopolitics that Rosenzweig defended in 1917 when he wrote his theory of world historical space, 'Globus', and sketched the providential unfolding of the world to a supra-world. Just as death completes life, warfare is something of the motor of history, even 'the unavoidable effect – quasi-necessary and immemorial – of the limiting force that produces borders'.[179] 'For God, who, as it is written, is a warrior, created only One heaven and One earth', and directs us towards eternal life.[180]

Subtraction and expansion of history

'Globus' commences in a mythical past when a human draws a border and says this is mine: 'The first human, who enclosed a part of the soil of the earth to his and his family's own property, unlocked the world history. For when he said

Mine he did not only make what was His to His, but also all the rest to the Theirs of everybody else: with Mine he created Yours and His.'[181] Rosenzweig's almost Rousseauian myth of the rise of history through property and borders is the beginning of world history. The rise of new borders and limitations of land does not only imply the transgression of old limits but the connection of the world to a globe.

The world of limits progresses towards a whole without borders where 'the first limited I' – *das begrenzte erste Ich* – which exhorts this is mine, is transformed to 'the unlimited last we' – *das unbegrenzte letzte Wir* – which does not know the difference between mine and yours.[182] This unlimited last we is in *The Star* termed the supra-world, *Überwelt*, and defined as an absolutely inclusive we: 'The We is always "We all"' and this we is the we of every human in history or perhaps even every creature in the long story of the world.[183] The states try to limit this collectivization of life to a we by tying it to a specific time and place, Rosenzweig implied, for in 'uncurbed change and alteration history seems to die away. Then comes the State and hangs its law over alteration. Now something is suddenly there that persists.'[184] However, even the states are thrown into the past by the movement of time and thereby become part of the we of eternal life. For, according to Rosenzweig, '[l]ife can be either only rest or only movement. And, since time cannot be denied, movement triumphs'.[185] With movement comes death since only a being in rest can live eternally.

In the first part of 'Globus', called the oecumene, *Ökumene*, Rosenzweig sought to define this movement beyond the nations as something potentially arising from the conflicts of the First World War.

> Only the attempt at an international organization of the world will emerge from the current world fire, and because it is only an attempt, therefore, just in a multitude of forms. . . . In this struggle the spatial confinement of the whole earth will be grounded in the oecumenical thoughts. One has spoken of eternally separate cultures. I do not believe that. For the God, who, as it is written, is a warrior, created only One heaven and One earth.[186]

War commences the transformation of the earth to a globe by forcing together populations in new empires and nations. There is, according to Rosenzweig, a providential meaning in the wars of the world. They indicate the need for a new international community.

This was not only a critique of Meinecke, but also of his teacher and friend, the earlier mentioned social democrat and German nationalist Hermann Cohen who in his war tractate *Deutschtum und Judentum* from 1915 argued for the necessity of the German Jew to be a proud member of the nation state.[187] This Rosenzweig could not accept, for even if he also was a German patriot he claimed in his critique of Cohen's essay that if 'Adam was born of the earth, the Jew has wandered into' the nation which he always can leave.[188] Thus, according to Rosenzweig, 'from Abraham onwards the myth of the people is a succession of such immigrations into the Land, which is not the "Land of Birth", but rather "that which I'll show you"'.[189] The Jews are therefore no longer pagans centred in a nation. They are members of a coming community and represent, for Rosenzweig, the future liberation of humanity as such.

Interestingly, this argument is a reminiscent of Ratzel's argument of the necessity of migration for the development of the nation. But if migration for Ratzel implied a theory of a people's *Lebensraum*, that so easily could become an imperialist and racist concept, Rosenzweig argued that the world itself must be organized so that humanity is given the possibility to freely wander on the earth's crust. Our whole planet must become a room for a life beyond the state. Yet, such a world could only be born from the conflicts and wars that pervade human history and in this sense Rosenzweig's work was an apology of imperialism. In 'Globus' he even described the colonization and globalization that Vasco de Gama and Christopher Columbus initiated as the birth of the globalization that can push us beyond the state.

> Vasco and Columbus's work has entered into history, but the connecting work of de Magalhães is still something that awaits completion today. Already, the waters are roaring around Africa's three coasts to form one sea. But the dry earth has not yet closed itself to a globe. Humanity is not yet in one home. Europe is not yet the soul of the world.[190]

Vasco de Gama and Christopher Columbus had begun a new chapter in history by their expeditions to India and America, respectively. The geopolitical task of making the world a globe, *einen Rund*, heralded by these two historical figures, was the formation of a planetary community, symbolized by the Portuguese explorer Fernão de Magalhães, Magellan, whose expedition to the East Indies from 1519 to 1522 resulted in the first circumnavigation of the globe.

It is important to note the words *awaits completion* in the quotation above. Rosenzweig saw himself as something of a Jewish activist, fighting for a planetary community with religion as an instrument for change. His work was always a public and political affair for him, related to world history and to the course of actions that he thought was needed to be taken. Even if he struggled for a German victory in the war, he hoped that his nation could become a multicultural empire and force history to enter its eschatological completion.

This did not happen. Germany lost the war. Yet, as I have claimed, Rosenzweig did not abandon his eschatological interpretation of the course of history. On the contrary, in 'The New Thinking' Rosenzweig emphasized that '[m]essianic politics, that is a theory of war' is the subject matter of the third book of *The Star*.[191] In this concluding book he examines Christianity and Judaism as the two forces that follow Abraham's exodus out of the autochthonic relation to the earth and, as we have seen, even beyond empire.

Judaism *subtracts* itself from the history of nations and wars by dwelling inside the pagan nations as a diaspora signalling the possibility of a life outside the states. Christianity, in contrast, is a religion of *expansion* transgressing the borders and limits of the world. The discovery of *The Star* is the idea of the Jewish diaspora as a subtraction from history (and therefore implicitly from rectilinear time as an unbending process from a beginning to an end) and Christianity as a movement of expansion that seeks to move history to an end (and therefore the transformation of the past through its completion in the future). But the goal of this double path out of history is clearly anticipated in 'Globus' where the goal of history, the unity of the world, reflects the prehistorical past that knew no borders and states. Rosenzweig underlined in this essay that even if the world is a world of borders, there exists a natural phenomenon which points beyond the inhabited world, the closed *oecumene*, and this is the sea that Fernão de Magalhães has united with his voyage around the world.

> The earth is determined from the creation to be crossed by boundaries at all times. Limitability is its nature, limitlessness is only the ultimate goal, but since the ultimate goals of history always have their firm and visible foundation in the things of nature, we have the same case here. The boundlessness that remains the ultimate goal of the earth is inherent in the sea from the beginning.[192]

Creation, by being something which comes before human history, indicates the possibility of unity and it does so 'from the beginning'. It is, as we have seen, 'the silent work of created nature' and not the pagan deities of state and culture which fashions the world 'for eternal life'.[193]

Decades before Carl Schmitt's *Land and Sea*, Rosenzweig depicted the sea in a mythical manner as an image of the infinite, unlimited world and described the conquest of America as the birth of a new global order.[194] However, according to the conservative Rosenzweig, this was an order that still needed Europe at its centre since only this continent could enliven what he saw as the senility of Asia and the juvenility of America.[195]

Rosenzweig was still loyal to what Max Brod called the culture of the Caucasian peoples whose amalgamation of Christianity and paganism Brod traced to the ominous year 1492.[196] The fact that Columbus, when he 'had discovered the first American island' wrote 'in his diary: "These kind-hearted people must make good slaves"' implied for Brod that the 'Christian and pagan instincts had concluded peace. Here is the decisive factor, the tragic guilt of Christianity – it was not strong enough to resist an intensified paganism.'[197]

Not unlike Rosenzweig, Brod pointed to the discovery of America as a world historical event that implied the 'appearance of the *Homo capitalisticus* . . . . In 1494 it was a monk who started bookkeeping by double entry. Where Christianity and paganism came closest, in Italy, early capitalism blossomed first.'[198] Rosenzweig heralded this development of colonialism and war. Yet, he wrote in *The Star* that the Christians 'cannot at all know how far God's will is realized in the warlike destinies of their States', and the decline of their civilization may be providential since it may turn it 'to a stone in the edifice of the Kingdom'.[199]

Rosenzweig accentuated that 'the consciousness of the individual decides nothing concerning this; the war alone decides, which rages on above the consciousness of the individual'.[200] The world of war and colonialism against which Brod warns is for Rosenzweig a part of the providential order of making the world an interconnected globe. Even in 1920, some years after he had abandoned his book on war, he could argue: 'The world is round. The sun of Europe descends only to rise again over the world.'[201] This roundness and circularity was, for Rosenzweig, how the world could redeem humankind and how humankind could redeem the world: its spherical shape could make the world a global order for all. Nature made globalization possible.

However, something has happened, Rosenzweig continued this clandestine conversation with Spengler's theory of the decline of the Occident, by defining the Jews or what he called the oldest people, as the force which can renew the world and make it a globe:

> The eternal youth of the world triumphs over the senility of the Occident. (China and India prove nothing. For they are young only because they have remnants of the youth of primordial humanity), but we [i.e. the Jews] prove, for we were quite entangled in this declining Occident. And we rise from it. The most senile proves itself to be the youngest of the peoples.[202]

The dying Occident can be revitalized by the Jews who, by lacking not only nation but also empire and state, reveal the need of a world beyond not only the existing states but, in a sense, politics as such. The spherical shape of the world now reflected the power of the future to alter the past that those who refuse to live between the beginning and end enact in the world. The future redemption desired by Rosenzweig will change the course of the past since by being embedded in a life outside time, the life beyond life of God, even the irreversibility of time can be transformed.

Now, after the defeat of Germany in 1918, the struggle against the polytheism of culture and nations was more explicitly connected to the life of the Jews which, Rosenzweig hoped, could renew the Occident and even open the world for the last, unlimited we that shall reunite humanity in a world community without borders and nations. Nevertheless, it is in the West that one can find 'the guides of our breed on the road of clarity'.[203] These guides of our breed on the road of clarity, or as the original German reads in a troubling manner revealing the *völkisch* tendencies in *The Star*, '*die Führer unseres Geschlechts auf den Weg der Klarheit*', are primarily the Greek pagans, and the breed – *Geschlecht* – that should follow them is not only the German Jews.[204] It is the world of the Western peoples.

In spite of all the criticism of the Occidental metaphysical tradition for which Rosenzweig is famous, the soldier-philosopher explicitly writes that it 'is no coincidence that the Revelation, when it went out into the world, did not take the path of the East but that of the West'.[205] Even if Rosenzweig hoped for another side of the West, a West beyond the nations, even a West beyond Christendom, this new world could only emerge through a conflict between the West and the East.[206] Rosenzweig was, *avant la lettre*, a theorist of the clash of civilizations but one that hoped for a unified world beyond the existing states and cultures.

The inability of Western philosophy to accept death comes, according to Rosenzweig, from its Eastern heritage. Philosophy is motivated by a feeling that life is only a mirage, a veil, a dream, an existence in a cave that he traces to the East. In the conclusion to *Understanding the Sick and the Healthy* Rosenzweig writes: 'Man, chilled in the full current of life, sees, like that famous Indian prince, death waiting for him. So he steps outside of life. If living means dying, he prefers not to live. He chooses death in life. He escapes from the inevitability of death into an artificial death.'[207] The famous Indian prince is, of course, Siddharta Gautama or Buddha. The Buddhist desire to break the chains of reincarnation and the Confucian cult of ancestors are for Rosenzweig a 'two-fold abandonment of the world'.[208] It implies either a view on the afterlife as a Nirvana, or, as with Confucianism, the perpetuation of the chain of ancestors who rule over the living as a form of spectres.[209] These idols are not part of the messianic war between polytheism and monotheism upon which *The Star* is erected: 'The living "gods of Greece" were worthier opponents for the living God than were the phantoms of the Asiatic East. The godheads of China and India are immense edifices built from the blocks of ancestral times; like monoliths, they still tower up to this day in the cults of the "primitives".'[210]

It is the conflict with honourable enemies that forces Rosenzweig's warrior God to the Occident, to Hellas, for 'only where there is life, be it a life intoxicated by the gods or one that is hostile to God, only there does the voice of the Living One find an echo'.[211] Here the biocentrism of his argument becomes once again visible, for the mythological gods of Hellas 'did not live beyond their realm surrounded by walls', but in contrast to the gods of the East, 'they still lived' and it is from the struggle for life that revelation begins.[212]

At the same time, Rosenzweig underlined in his lecture on the concept of world history in Kassel in 1920, that every modern human *is* the primitive, prehistorical human that God created as Adam. This human was neither Christian, nor Jewish nor pagan, but rather the primitive being made of earth that the cultures in the East discover: 'The primordial human, the prehistorical human – they do not merely excavate his traces, they recognize him not merely in the parable of the savage, the child. They themselves are savages, are children, are primordial humans.'[213]

Rosenzweig includes himself and his audience in this *they* which modern life resurrects, for he continues: 'They themselves know all about life, which stands at the limit of animality, which knows only the moment and of no past or future ... It only knows about its own life. Who among us does not know this life?'[214]

India and China are, he says, the two regions that have made the life of primordial humanity, in other words the prehistorical and precultural existence of humanity, into a culture.[215] The East is stuck in the origin of life, and not even part of history, since it denies rather than affirms death: '*Beyond* the mountains of Punjab begins the world history. There the human discovers the death.'[216] It is, according to Rosenzweig, the Western notion of death that creates history and that produces the need in Judaism to subtract itself from the course of this world in order to reveal God and live beyond the causal order of beginning, present and end.

Still, there is another movement in history that is something of a sign for peace and which opens the world to a community beyond the polytheism of cultures and nations. This is the movement of expansion identified in *The Star* with the spread of Christianity over the world. If the path of revelation commences in the West this is because the double path of revelation can take us out of the course of history and confront the problem of death and thereby this trajectory, paradoxically, comes close to end in the world before history that Buddha represents in Rosenzweig's system.

The ethnos of immortality

Rosenzweig's insistence that world history commences on the Western side of Punjab is not as controversial as it may seem, since the origin of the West is Mesopotamia, the cradle of civilization and the birthplace of written history.[217] In the lecture in Kassel on the course of world history, Rosenzweig contrasts Buddha with Gilgamesh, who is described as 'the prototype of the tragic hero . . . bordering between the divine and the human'.[218] Gilgamesh – according to legend the Mesopotamian king of Uruk – is the ideal figure of the Westerner that God seeks to challenge, whereas Buddha overcomes death through self-delusion and he is therefore, according to Rosenzweig's chauvinist logic, not a worthy opponent for Judaism and Christianity.[219]

The *Epic of Gilgamesh*, first written in Akkadian about 4,000 years ago, is, from Rosenzweig's perspective, a testament to the rise of civilization depicting the relation between death and life that he identified as the beginning of Western subjectivity. The epic tells the story of the king Gilgamesh who leaves his people in search for a plant of immortality after his beloved friend Enkidu's death. This commences the path of revelation, where Gilgamesh, due to the death of a loved one – the savage and wild warrior Enkidu – craves immortality and confronts death.[220]

After much struggle, Gilgamesh finds the plant of immortality, but loses it when he falls asleep and a snake steals it from him. Unsuccessful and depressed, he returns to his kingdom of Uruk as a mortal whose 'entire existence' has been 'glimpsed in the friend's death, as the sole content. . . . It is all the same to him that death ends by taking even himself; the essential thing is already behind him; death, his own death, has become the event that dominates his life.'[221] By leaving his kingdom, and returning from his unsuccessful adventure as a man destroyed by his angst for death, Gilgamesh 'has entered into the sphere of pure and sovereign muteness, the sphere of the Self'.[222] This is the primordial self that in the second book of *The Star* is opened for the other, whom Rosenzweig so famously portrays and whom every human is called to love. Ethically this implies a doctrine of neighbourly love, and politically it motivates his geopolitics of an international community beyond the limits of the nations and even empires. Humanity must become one even to the cost of war and imperialism.

The alienation of the self that the story of Gilgamesh tells is, to use the Hegelian jargon that Rosenzweig often comes quite near, an epic of the rise of self-consciousness craving existence to the point that freedom is born from a struggle with death.²²³ For, Hegel wrote, 'it is only through staking one's life that freedom is won; only thus is it proved that for self-consciousness, its essential being is not [just] being, not the immediate form in which it appears, not its submergence in the expanse of life.'²²⁴ Hegel traced the rise of self-consciousness to what he called the struggle between the slave and the master, and as Mohammed Bamyeh has argued, the slave is the slave 'because he refuses to sacrifice himself in the struggle against the master'.²²⁵ The slave dwells in the fear of death, for in the struggle against the master he discovers his finitude and sacrifices his freedom in order to avoid death.

The slave is bound to the fear of death, but, Bamyeh notices, the story of Gilgamesh 'is a story of a master, not his subjects, fearing death. Neither is there any indication of such a dread by his savage comrade Enkidu, who had died earlier and never ruled anyone. Gilgamesh's return back to [the] safety of a well-fortified city is an outcome of a lost battle for immortality.'²²⁶ Bamyeh claims, contrary to Hegel, that the master is more afraid of death than the slave since this fear of mortality is most intense at the *summit* of society.²²⁷ In a coincidental confirmation, but transvaluation, of the opposition between Buddha and Gilgamesh posited by Rosenzweig, Bamyeh depicts Buddha as the historical antithesis to Gilgamesh for it is with the latter that 'the life instinct wins out . . . Political history begins not with Siddhartha – who actually abandons the palace – but with Gilgamesh.'²²⁸

If world history arises beyond the mountains of Punjab, among Gilgamesh's subjects, rather than Buddha's primordial followers, this is because it is in Mesopotamia where the human discovers the meaning of death and begins to crave immortality. Buddha teaches that death is a nothing. With Gilgamesh, life becomes the ultimate value of existence, and this affirmation of life over everything else is for Bamyeh the essence of political power: all power is the power to be alive. The story of Gilgamesh reflects the desire of immortality among the ruling classes in Mesopotamia, whose tombs were filled with treasures, provisions and sometimes even sacrificed serfs and workers that should serve them in the afterlife.²²⁹

Rosenzweig had a similar view of history since he traces the origin of the world of politics to the life instinct of the self that craves existence, and that reaches its culmination in the King Gilgamesh's desire for immortality. It is from such a perspective that he emphasized the relation between politics and immortality when he discussed the story of Gilgamesh: 'Enkidu is not being lamented. . . Here the young dead man is the hero himself . . . the acclamation and fame survive him.'[230] In 'Paralipomena' he contrasted this pagan view on immortality with the Judaic idea of eternal life: 'The path to glory leads through death, that is to survival [*Weiterleben*] in time. But *never*: death leads the way to eternity.'[231] Immortality, from this perspective, is fame and this idea of the afterlife as a *Weiterleben* through worldly glory permeates not only the Mesopotamian world but also the Hellenic culture according to Rosenzweig.

In contrast to Bamyeh, Rosenzweig argued that the Greeks did not fear death but only exalted life: 'The Greeks know from the beginning that they will die. And they do not fear death. . . . The Greek . . . loves life, he does not fear death – there is something that survives him; what is this something? / Not himself, not his life. He does *not* believe in eternal life. But the beauty survives him and the glory.'[232] This description of a specifically pagan idea of immortality as the afterlife of glory is strengthened by Hannah Arendt who has claimed that mortality was the hallmark of human existence in the Greek cosmos, where all other forms of life were seen as immortal since animals and plants primarily exist as members of an eternal species.[233] The human individual is distinguished from everything else in the domain of nature by the rectilinear course of its life: human life begins and ends and does not take part in the circular immortality of animals and plants.[234] Yet, Arendt declared, by their capacity for immortal deeds the citizens of the Greek city-state could through their political life 'leave non-perishable traces behind' and overcome 'their individual mortality' by attaining 'an immortality of their own and prove themselves to be of a "divine" nature' in the *polis*.[235]

Arendt's idea of a political immortality is a perfect example of what Rosenzweig understood as pagan immortality. It is, Arendt would argue, as political beings that humans, or rather the citizens of the *polis*, become immortal by participating in the immortality of the *polis* through the liturgical acts of the community. This political and liturgical form of immortalism is transformed with the crisis of the Greek city-state, which the philosophy of Plato reflects, and it is according to Arendt completely lost with the victory of Christianity, and the decline of the Roman Empire. This made 'any striving for an earthly immortality futile and unnecessary' and, Arendt lamented, not even the reversal of the 'traditional hierarchy between action and contemplation sufficed to save from oblivion the striving for immortality which originally had been the spring and center of the *vita activa*'.[236]

The loss of the political sense of immortality, which for Arendt is a tragedy prefiguring the modern world and its reduction of humanity to an *animal laborans*, is not something that Rosenzweig mourned. He viewed this decline as a part in the providential plan of the warrior God. The destruction of the ancient world gives humanity the opportunity to liberate itself from the enclosed world, the *oecumene*, which he described in 'Globus' and *The Star* and which can move his philosophy beyond its fetish of the West.[237]

The eclipse of this world is for Rosenzweig not, as Bamyeh helps us notice, the disappearance of life as the ultimate value of existence, which Gilgamesh can be said to represent.[238] On the contrary, Rosenzweig claimed, the primordial urge to stay in life and fight for survival is a transhistorical trope and something that ties the modern human, liberated from all pagan myths, to the subjectivity that Gilgamesh represents.

I have already argued that Kjellén pondered the possibility of a political immortality in 1916, and how for Rosenzweig this was to entrust life to those 'eternal gods of paganism . . . the State and the arts', which can obtain no immortality since they belong to the order of history and therefore to the passage of time which ends all life.[239] Rosenzweig can rhetorically ask in a lecture in 1920, alluding to Spengler, if what we are moving towards is 'really only the decline of the morning land? not the rising of the earth?'[240]

In his criticism of Cohen's nationalist tractate *Deutschtum und Judentum*, Rosenzweig wrote that '[a]ll peoplehood – all true peoplehood – has its ground in history'.[241] The peoples of the world, since the rise of civilization in Mesopotamia, live in the cycle of empires and states that constitutes world history. In sharp contrast, the Jews have been elected to live outside this world and thereby reveal to humanity the possibility of an existence beyond history and even beyond the state: 'Even in his "classical" times, even in his own country . . . the Jew has never been a human of the polis [*Polismensch*] or a slave of the state [*Staatssklave*], as the ancient man.'[242] The modern word 'state', Rosenzweig argued, does not even exist in Hebrew, and for him the Jewish kingdoms during the biblical period were either ruled by 'an antipolitical priesthood' or 'a metapolitical prophethood'.[243] They were, paradoxically, not political kingdoms.

The diasporic life of Judaism reveals the possibility to live in another relation to life and history than to cling to politics as an instrument for survival, since the Jews reveal – for Rosenzweig – 'that the end can also be reached by living'.[244] The world is finished for this 'eternal people' since it dwells among the nations as something else than a *Polismensch* who is bound to the course of history. The Jews, as the ethnos of immortality, wait for a future they already incarnate by being the people who 'preserves itself by [their] subtraction' from world history.²⁴⁵

This is certainly a normative description of Judaism, for what Rosenzweig wanted his people to do is that it would try to take up the task of God and teach humanity how life can be lived as 'if the world were finished; it celebrates in its Sabbaths the sabbatical completion of the world'.²⁴⁶ By doing so Judaism reveals its 'eternal life, that is to say, [it] constantly anticipates the end and makes it therefore into the beginning'.²⁴⁷ The anticipation of the end is the reversal of beginning and after that the redemption of the world entails.

If the political liturgy of the Greek city-state was related to the idea of immortality as remembrance and fame, then the Jewish liturgical act is not – or rather should not be – part of the world of political glory. The spiritual weeks and years of Jewish liturgy manifest the remembrance of the promise of a coming messianic order beyond the state. The eternal people remind the world that the sabbatical end of the week shall be given to the world as such, and thus move all nations out of the secular chronology of nations and wars that for Rosenzweig was identical with world history.

The Sabbath as the end of the week, and the eternal Sabbath as the coming completion of the world, has the same structure as Rosenzweig's theology of death as the law of unity in life. For him, the 'Jewish people is in itself already at the goal toward which the peoples of the world are just setting out' since they lack state, nation and empire, and this means that 'by living the eternal peace, it stands outside of a warlike temporality; by resting at the goal that it anticipates in hope, it is separated from the march of those who draw near to it in the toil of centuries'.²⁴⁸ But this living that 'withdraws from toil, action, fighting for the world' must be practically verified in a diasporic life.²⁴⁹ Judaism is a task that, paradoxically, the gentiles must take up by moving towards the eternal life that the Jews represent in history by lacking state, nation and empire.

The Star was not a neutral historical description of Jewish life. It was a suggestion of how it could or rather should be enacted in the modern world. Rosenzweig's geopolitical theories of a multicultural empire were directly related to his hope for an order that could shelter the Jewish community from racism and hate. He believed that a multicultural world beyond the nation would imply an order where the Jews were given the opportunity to live diasporically in peace. In *The Star* he took a step further and claimed that we need a world beyond even the limits of empire – a world that is instead grounded in 'the silent work of creation' that all humans, be they from East or West, belong to. This, what we can call, empire of creatures is a world for 'All'. This 'All' is a new 'All'.

It is a new totality; the We that can emerge out of the forces of Christianity and Judaism.

Christianity, as the religion born out of Jewish life that converts the pagans to Israel, is part of the world history, but it transforms itself by revealing the goal of history as a coming unity of all nations, tribes, and states in a new human community: 'All worldly history is about expansion. Power is therefore the fundamental concept of history, because in Christianity Revelation has begun to spread over the world, and so all will for expansion, even the consciously and only purely worldly expansion, has become the unconscious servant of this great movement of expansion.'[250] The catastrophes and miseries of history are the field on which the new life of Christianity can emerge. But, Rosenzweig insisted, this also implies that Christianity must grow out of its old existence into a new form that is foreign to state and empire.

Once again, revealing his reliance on Schelling who hoped for a transformation of the church, Rosenzweig borrows the philosopher's triadic and Joachimite notion of the church as developing from its Petrine origin, through its Pauline centuries, into a Johannine community.[251] Petrine Christianity is for Rosenzweig the birth of Christianity as a movement that 'went out and taught all peoples'; it had 'no longer . . . any outer limits for itself as the empire did; it is on principle not satisfied with any border, it has no knowledge of renunciation'.[252] It created, through its visible and public body, an institution uniting humanity beyond the nations, perhaps best exemplified by the Roman Catholic Church. However, this unity was bound to what Rosenzweig came to define as the eternal gods of paganism – the state and the arts – which threatened to transform Christianity into 'a body without a soul'. The church in this period was cast into sectarian conflicts and driven by what Rosenzweig calls 'the Christian's eternal hatred for the Jews' to antisemitism and racism.[253]

The rise of the Pauline Church in the period of Reformation and Counter-Reformation, an age when the Christian spirit was freed from its institutional fetters, was organized around '"faith alone" . . . It was the soul alone that lived it'.[254] The church could easily exist in the world without overcoming or radically transforming the eternal gods of paganism, the state and the arts, since it primarily formed the inner life of the human, namely, what Rosenzweig defines as the soul. The Church of the Reformation and Counter-Reformation spurred an idea of the human being as an interiority, a pure soul. This interiority is the weakness of the Pauline Church according to Rosenzweig, and for him it is a sign that the Christian world is still tied to the separated and alienated self that he traced back to Gilgamesh's fear of death.

If the Petrine Church for Rosenzweig is a body without a soul, and the Pauline Church a soul without a body, then there must come a new Christian community where the soul and the body, the inner and the outer of life of the human, are mediated in a Johannine community. This new Christianity, Rosenzweig writes, 'unites the little paganisms of body and soul with the great paganism of life; and already this union, thus the mere emergence of the pagan, signifies his conversion. The Johannine completion does not have a specific form; it is simply not a piece anymore, but only completion of the till now incomplete work.'[255]

The Johannine community moves the pagan world, the cycles of nations and empires, towards the end which Judaism reveals through its existence outside the state and therefore, potentially, outside the struggle for existence that Rosenzweig comes close to equate with world history. This Johannine completion, emerging out of the simple but global revelation of 'the great paganism of life', entails the task to move our species out of the struggle for survival since it is this struggle that makes existence incomplete. We should work for a community that has no borders and is identical with the world as such: the natural world that paganism, rightly, exalts as a kind of god. It is therefore that the spherical form of the world corresponds to the possibility of a resurrection of the past in a new form. Yet, Rosenzweig argues, the pagans can only worship the gods of nature through the communal forms of tribe, state or nation that the Jews abandon by being a kind of non-people whose task it is to reveal the unity of the world: a unity beyond the borders and struggles that imprison the human species in the history of civilization and, before it, in the prehistoric world of tribes.

The reason why the revelation commences in Western civilization, and not with the wisdom of the Asian peoples, is because the expansion of Christianity is a movement out of the desire for life as survival, just as Judaism is the subtraction from the same longing. The revelation must begin where life is first and foremost understood as an affirmation of survival even in a religious sense: 'For the gods of antiquity are also living, and not only He whom today we call the living one. They are even, if you will, much more alive. For they are nothing but alive. They are immortal. Death lies beneath them.'[256] Here, in the pagan Occident, the two forces of revelation – the emergence of a Johannine community through Christianity's worldly expansion and its subsequent self-transformation, and Judaism as the diasporic subtraction from world history – find their worthy enemies in the biocentric forces that affirm life, and nothing but life.

The world is not finished, according to Rosenzweig, and death is the completion of the world, so the pagan cry of the fear of death is the beginning of an adequate relation to death since to live is to reproduce life. A culture that clings to life in an uncompleted world, full of tears and laughter, threatens to reduce existence to the work, activity and struggle of history which Rosenzweig equates with the fight against death. The gospel of Christianity and the teaching of Judaism are therefore the revelation of the coming completion of a life that still struggles in a Darwinian manner for its continuing existence. If the common sense of all life is the finitude of existence, then the revelation is the scandalous disclosure that death is the completion of life since God is neither living nor dead.

> God is not life, God is light. He is the Lord of life, but he is as little alive as he is dead; and to state one or the other about him, as the ancient man states, that 'he lives,' and as the modern man states, that he 'is dead,' betrays equal pagan partiality. Only that neither-nor of dead and alive, only that fine point where life and death touch and melt into one does not forbid the typical terminology. God neither lives nor is dead, but he gives life to what is dead, he – loves. He is the God of the living as of the dead, just because he himself is neither living nor dead; we experience his existence immediately only in the fact that he loves us, and awakens our dead Self into the beloved soul that loves in return.[257]

God is the mystery beyond death and life that pours out his light and love on the past that no human remembers but which through his light is embraced in his eternity, although it lacks all worldly glory. By being neither dead nor alive God is that which can resurrect that which is dead in the past as a new life, a life that is beyond the tears or for that matter laughter of spatial and temporal existence. This is why the work of 'the God of the living as of the dead' is the work to redeem time itself from the death that change and causality imply for life.

Blumenberg argued, as we saw in the introduction, that for the modern discussions on immortality it is no 'longer God who is the primary "object" of one's attention in the "beyond". On the contrary, that attention continues the theoretical interests and moral obligations of this world; that is, it loses its quasi-worshipful character so as to satisfy, instead, what one's finite individual life denies to one.'[258] Rosenzweig's idea of eternal life can to an extent be seen as a continuation of what he views as the prime theoretical interest – the cognition of the All – and the moral obligations of this world – the struggle for a human community and the love for the neighbour. But his notion of eternal life cannot be said to be based on the satisfaction of what is denied to the finite individual. Eternal life is, as I have shown several times, 'the life beyond life'. Accordingly, Judaism and Christianity must become communities that seek the 'neither-nor of dead and alive' which neither ancient nor modern paganism can understand.

What Christianity and Judaism should teach is the strange gospel that humanity is the species which can live outside the economy of normal life that creation itself is moving away from. Still, the human who seeks to live beyond the parameters of a normal life, a life equated with the struggle for existence, does not do so in order to give up life, since all life necessarily clings to existence. Such a human opens her life for an exteriority that the modern and the ancient humans, in their enclosed existence, do not grasp as they only can understand life and death and not the reality beyond this dichotomy that Rosenzweig calls God.

I argued before that Rosenzweig describes how 'God completes himself' by becoming 'the One and the All'. I can now add that Christianity and Judaism – if only by transcending themselves as what they are now – should be answers in the field of creation to this self-completion of God.[259] Even if this implies that world and humanity 'fade out into Redemption' they still exist as that which once was, and they exist radiantly as parts of God, as something redeemed, as something that lies outside the confines of both death and life and therefore as something which is not God.[260] God does not subsume us into his oneness. His unity is the revelation of the relation, but not the identity, between the singular and communal, the eternal and the temporal, of the We. Before the completion of the world this relation is the experience that transforms 'our dead Self into the beloved soul that loves in return'.[261] This is why the movement from the primordial world to the supra-world is the completion of the All that humanity yearns for. It is the revelation of why death is common to all.

Braiterman's suggestion, that 'Rosenzweig's writings reveal a radiant view of death that strikes a discordant note in the post-Holocaust world', is true.[262] Yet, it was the horror of modern German life that prompted him – as he wrote – not to love life, but to hope that all life, present, past and coming, is loved by the God beyond all life. If God loves both the dead and the living, and liberates the self from its desperate desire for survival so that it instead can live as a loving and beloved soul, then the revelation is something of an exodus out of the tragic and alienated subjectivity whose origin he finds in the story of Gilgamesh. The hope for eternal life is not a desire for survival. It is the hope that the dead are redeemed in the past and that we, the living, can live with them in a community that is neither dead nor alive.

In a letter to Eva and Victor Ehrenberg from 1926, Rosenzweig describes what such a community beyond death and life may look like by contrasting the idea of the immortality of the soul with the idea of the resurrection of the dead. He writes that already Tertullian saw that 'the dividing line between paganism and Christianity . . . [is] between immortality and faith in the resurrection . . . more precisely: between immortality of the soul and resurrection of the flesh.'[263] Immortality in the Bible is a description of God's eternity and given to the creatures by God: 'To receive an eternal life, they must of course enter into the world day of the Lord. Immortality happens for them only in God.'[264] All lost life, or, as Rosenzweig would say, all martyred life, is part of God's eternity. When life ends it is made eternal, and therefore united in the immortality of the past that makes it possible to hope for the redemption of the dead. Those who are gone wait in the sabbatical rest of eternity for the completion of God and it is this divine past that for Rosenzweig is the systematic completion of life and therefore the answer as to why there are tears and laughter in the world. Evil exists since God is not yet all in all.

The yearning for a system is the yearning for eternal life for only a life that is redeemed through the eternity of God is a life that can see 'the All' beyond experience and even cognition: 'The All must be grasped beyond cognition and experience, if it is to be immediately grasped.'[265] This is the vision of the prophets and just as the Protestant and the Catholic no longer should be different in the cross of Christ, the difference between Judaism and Christianity can be relativized 'when they return to the prophets'.[266] Since revelation is the revelation of 'the paganism of creation' it seems that even Christianity and Judaism have to move beyond themselves. The world Rosenzweig sought was, in the end, '*überjudisch*' and at the same time '*überchristlich*' – supra-Jewish and supra-Christian – since it was the *Überwelt* where life as we know it fades out.[267]

Life is now close to the quietude and vegetative existence of all existence blessed by the joy of cessation and reflects paradoxically the primordial life at the Eastern side of Punjab that Rosenzweig criticized. God is completed not only because humankind has saved the world, but because 'the silent work of creation' has saved Christianity and Judaism from being simple identities with no connection to the task of God's own redemption. Even if the unity that Rosenzweig seeks does not subsume the dead in an undifferentiated Nirvana, but rather resurrects that which was in a strange existence beyond life and death, it is still a world that is, as we have seen, completed in a happiness that Rosenzweig at least once described as an almost Buddhist end of the karmic cycle of life: 'The eternal cycle of the world-law is ruptured by the promise of the *happiness* of peace (Nirvana, death).'[268]

According to Bamyeh, Buddha's trajectory is the opposite of Gilgamesh's, 'for Gilgamesh it is the human that triumphs over the divine, creating thereby a political animal. In Siddhartha's case, the political in him dies with the human

– in fact, Siddhartha himself is there no longer at the end, there is only the Enlightened One.'[269] The question thereby arises: does Rosenzweig's messianic theory contradict his imperialistic defence of the West? Is the goal that his providential world history is moving towards a recapitulation of the prehistorical life that he thought was not worthy of God's opposition? The latter seems to be the case since the revelation – and thus the knowledge of the All – is a revelation of the unanimity of the manifold of life. It is only at this point, when God himself is completed, and when time has become history, that one can say that there is a cognition of the All.

The end brings forth the knowledge of the All, for to know the All, one must not only die away from one's self, and through the judgement of death become part of the unity of creation. The world itself must be completed and the manifold of life be given unity through its completion in death: 'In the last judgement, which God himself makes in his own name, the whole universe enters into His Universality, every name enters into His Oneness without name.'[270] Judgement is the day when '[a]ll name fades away' into the We of existence that Rosenzweig called the supra-world.[271] This existence beyond all names is the eternal and completed life that has nothing in common with the immortality of glory, politics and arts. At the same time, it is the resurrection of the manifold that for Rosenzweig is the world. God does not become all in all. But this divine warrior creates a unity that binds life and death into a We that can start to grasp the All. It seems that Rosenzweig's system, when it reaches its completion in the supra-world, affirms a world beyond the civilization which commences with Gilgamesh. Happiness is Nirvana. But it is a happiness where the dead are made eternal by fading away into God: the world is revealed as a unified manifold where the I and You are related to, but not subsumed by, the We that Rosenzweig finds in the revelation of the primordial world as a world beyond the world and, therefore, beyond tribe, state and empire.

Adam, Rosenzweig wrote, was neither Jew nor pagan. He was a human: a part of nature fearing death and urging completion. But what is completion? Completion is the construction of a world where the human no longer struggles for life but has become sabbatical.

Rosenzweig's political eschatology does neither commence nor end in religion or, for that matter, culture. It begins in the fear of death common to all and ends in the supra-world beyond all present civilizations, cultures and religions since it is simply a common home to everything mortal.

His call to everyone to stay in life does not in any sense contradict that at least the eternal people should live as if the world was already completed and seemingly has entered the Nirvana of existence where life is moving beyond itself. Jewish mysticism, he argued during the First World War, transforms God's distance to an immediate closeness to the point that 'its form of understanding the relationship between God and man is the joke [der Witz], i.e. the *coincidentia oppositorum*'.[272] It is in the mad joke of life itself that Rosenzweig finds a vision beyond cognition. The world can only be grasped prophetically in the midst of our laughter and tears.

Eternal life is the acceptance that the last is also the nearest, and that the end must be lived in the here and now as an affirmation of death as something that gives unity to existence. This may perhaps seem to be a grim perspective, but it is for Rosenzweig a view of life as something urging redemption, something that exists for something other than mere productivity and survival, namely, for God's own sabbath.

In this loving rest, which reveals itself as the geopolitical struggle for a We of the species outside the cycles of states and nations, creation is completed since we are learning to live in the 'neither-nor of dead and alive' that is God. Through its deeper and deeper intimacy with God the world is given the strange existence beyond death and life, which Rosenzweig describes as the light revealing 'the great paganism of life' that is found outside the city gates of the West, in the primordial but now unified world of Adam.

2

Abundance and scarcity
Karl Barth and the struggle for existence

In 1960, Karl Barth commented in passing on Charles Darwin's *On the Origin of Species by Means of Natural Selection, or the Preservation of Favoured Races in the Struggle for Life* by writing that the 'useless, unworthy, unholy, and disastrous struggle for life can only begin in all refined, crude, and crudest forms. Christians are commanded to oppose this disorder'.[1] The struggle for existence, he exclaimed, 'is not a final reality that cannot be altered. Instead, it is a powerful phantom that is destined to disappear. Hence, even though they cannot do away with it, in all circumstances they must swim against its current'.[2] The baptized are called to resist the dominions and powers that reduce life to a struggle for survival.

Fifteen years earlier, in 1945, Barth had argued that the story of Eden in *Genesis* describes the basis of an existence which cannot be equated with mere Darwinian life. The prelapsarian life of paradise is not 'a struggle for existence to be waged by creatures among themselves. It is the sphere of the need which is met by God.'[3] Paradise is the domain of an abundant and immortal life where there is peace among the beasts, and '[w]hether or not we find it practicable and desirable, the diet assigned to men and beasts by God the Creator is vegetarian'.[4] The simple fact of killing is a product of the fall, and where 'this power is used by men and animals it is used illegitimately from the standpoint of their creation'.[5]

It was this standpoint of the creation that made Barth claim that the struggle for life is a 'great disorder' and 'even though Christians participate in it and share the guilt for the resulting plight, they are at the same time born counterrevolutionaries'.[6] They are called to act against the disorder of the world which Barth described as something of a revolution against God. In their sighing, calling and crying 'Thy kingdom come', the baptized should reveal that the 'kingdom of God is God himself in the act of normalizing human existence'.[7] This normalizing is one of the queerest things visible in a world ruled by the struggle for existence: it seeks to force creation out of the logic of scarcity and selection that rules life as we know it.

The feeble and seemingly vain attempts of human creatures to mould themselves to this abundance are at the centre of the theology of eternal life that Barth develops in his writings from 1914 to 1945. In 1960, he stated that the 'Christian too is engaged in the struggle for existence in the broadest sense, and he has to endure a particular part of the pain of the creaturely world and especially of humanity'.[8] This is because he already had come to the conclusion that Scripture describes the long history of our cosmos as an 'interim period', which following the fall 'is the only time when the peace between creature and creature is broken and replaced by the struggle for existence'.[9] Eternal life is an end to the struggle for life through a new and abundant metabolic relation to creation.

God and species-being

On 5 February 1922, Barth made a short presentation of Ludwig Feuerbach's critique of theology to a small audience of colleagues and friends.[10] He began by underlining the necessity of Feuerbach's message: 'He does not write because he wants to *write* something, but because something and in fact just that *must* be written; it is not literature, it is rather a proclamation, that he offers his readers.'[11] The fact that Barth used the word *Verkündigung*, 'proclamation' or 'preaching', was a clear expression of his admiration for the lapsed theologian.

Feuerbach's *Verkündigung* was that religion alienates this-worldly and human appetites and drives – our desires, fantasies and wishes – to something extraworldly and divine. 'The essence of religion', he postulated, 'its latent nature, is the identity of the divine being with the human; but the form of religion, or its apparent, conscious nature, is the distinction between them.'[12] Religion alienates the species-being, *Gattungswesen*, of humanity to an exteriority, an object outside the human, by producing the idea of God as an ideological fantasy denying the corporal and natural basis of human life. The task of Feuerbach's anthropology was to unravel how religion does not describe God but the species-being of humanity in alienated, supernatural terms.[13]

Alluding to Anselm of Canterbury's *Proslogion*, Feuerbach wrote that 'only in its highest degree is thought truly thought, reason. Only when thy thought is God dost thou truly think, rigorously speaking; for only God is the realized, consummate, exhausted thinking power.'[14] God is for Feuerbach, just as for

Anselm, that '*quo nihil maius cogitari potest*' – that-than-which-nothing-greater-can-be-thought.[15] We believe, Anselm wrote in *Proslogion*, that God is that-than-which-nothing-greater-can-be-thought and since 'it is one thing for an object to exist in the mind, and another thing to understand that an object actually exists' it might be deduced that that-than-which-a-greater-cannot-be-thought 'cannot exist in the mind alone. For if it exists solely in the mind, it can be thought to exist in reality also, which is greater.'[16] The basic structure of Anselm's proof is that if we define God as not existing, we do not conceive him as *quo nihil maius cogitari potest* since existence for Anselm is greater than non-existence. Reality is greater than imagination.

Feuerbach admired Anselm but argued that the *Proslogion* was not in any sense a proof of the existence of the divine. God is the alienated description of the human capacity to think and imagine, and the only reality the divine denotes is the *Gattungswesen* of an animal gifted with speculative reason. The species-being of the human animal can be identified with our unique capacity to imagine and even more reason theologically. When a believer conceives God, he understands human reason 'as it truly is, though by means of the imagination he conceives this divine nature as distinct from reason, because as a being affected by external things he is accustomed always to distinguish the object from the conception of it'.[17] Humanity must understand that its powerful capacity to produce abstractions implies that reality easily turns into a screen where the human projects her desires, fears and wishes as beings with a life of their own. The idea of God should be transformed to an idea of humanity as a species of animals gifted with imagination and reason. Feuerbach desired 'to transform friends of God into friends of man, believers into thinkers, devotees of prayer into devotees of work, candidates for the hereafter into students of this world'.[18]

However, religion had been a powerful instrument for the human race. With the idea of God, our species has confronted and even transcended the finitude of life. 'Not for life', Feuerbach wrote, 'but only for (or rather, against) death do we need a God. In fact, death – as the most perceptible expression of our finitude and dependence upon another being outside us; namely, nature – is the only ultimate basis of religion.'[19] Religion is a desire for 'the abolition of death' and why does 'the Christian need a supernatural means to conquer death? Because he begins by assuming an unnatural presupposition, the presupposition that death is a consequence of sin, a punishment, a destiny brought about by an angry, evil God.'[20] The inability to accept death is the anthropological origin of religion and the time has come for us to understand that we will die since we, like all creatures, are mortal. Yet, Feuerbach argued, we have a form of immortality through our *Gattungswesen* which survives in the continuation of the life of the species.

By underlining neglected parts of the Christian tradition such as its anthropological realism, its emphasis on the bodily character of human life and its hope for economic and social justice, Feuerbach's critique of religion was a prolegomenon to any serious theology, according to Barth.[21] More important, however, was the persistence on the anthropological necessity of religion as a distorted description of human dependence on nature. Religion is something of an innate and natural capacity for the human species. In his lectures on Schleiermacher, Barth insisted that the great theologian argued that 'we are born with a religious disposition'.[22] For Schleiermacher, religion is a feeling that arises through 'the influence exerted on us by the totality of things. If we view it as the influence of the whole, the infinite totality, the universum, we have religion'.[23]

From Barth's perspective, the geniality of Feuerbach was that he developed Schleiermacher's discovery of religion as a feeling of dependency on the universe by interpreting our religious disposition as a reliance on nature rather than as a discovery of God.[24] Behind all religious mystifications lies the necessity of nature or what Feuerbach called nature religion. 'In nature religion I recognize neither more nor less than what I recognize in all religion, including the Christian, namely, its *simple fundamental truth*. And this truth is only that man is dependent on nature'.[25] The insistence that religion is a dependency on nature is Feuerbach's gift to theology since it forces the theologian to understand revelation as that which puts our feeling of dependency in a crisis. But what does such a crisis imply?

We can begin to unravel an answer to that question by turning to Barth's lectures on dogmatics in Göttingen that he began to conduct in 1924. There he stated that 'if we are not to fall into the arms of Feuerbach at the very first step . . . we must think of God as the subject'.[26] The only way to surpass Feuerbach was to make theology to a *Nachdenken*, a thinking that views God as the subject rather than the object of theology by commencing with the data of revelation.[27]

Barth's understanding of theology as a thinking that *post factum* reflects over the revelation as it is presented in Scripture has been increasingly emphasized in recent scholarship.[28] However, theology is not only an ordering of thinking that 'signals a form of creaturely knowing mirroring the divine self-knowledge in human concepts and propositions'.[29] This *Nachdenken* entails a *Nachfolge*, a following of Christ, and even a *Nachleben*, since life as such has been given its final yet veiled meaning in the incarnation, resurrection and ascension of Christ. The ontic – the fact of existence – precedes the noetic – what can be known

– since God is before the human world and everything that exists and can be thought or believed.[30] Theology entails a view on the cosmos as the site for the revelation of God and an understanding of the creature as something that has to be mirrored in the life, death and resurrection of Christ.

During the Second World War Barth stated explicitly: 'This, then, is how we must describe what the creature can do. It serves God's self-glorification in the same way as an echoing wall can serve only to repeat and broadcast the voice which the echo "answers".'[31] The creature that graciously echoes this call 'becomes an image, *the* image of God' and the 'whole point of creation is that God should have a reflection in which He reflects Himself'.[32] *Nachdenken*, the capacity to 'think along with the biblical texts', is ultimately practical by making us to echoes of the divine.[33] Through theology we can seek to 'accommodate ourselves, not to the dominion of any power (history or fate, for instance), but to that of the One to whom alone there belongs right and finally might'.[34] Theology commences with the subjectivity of God so that we can follow him instead of some other power, such as history, fate or nature.

How can we commence with God? God reveals himself according to Christian tradition in time and space as a human creature who is born, dies and is resurrected. His eternity is embedded in the concrete life of a human being just as 'the preaching office that God has instituted is still a historical, human, conditioned entity. The instruments that are put in its hands, the audible and the visible Word, are still a human word, with the implied concealment of the divinely posited reality.'[35] God is a hidden God, a rumour told by humans so, once again, how can we begin with the subjectivity of God and not with a religion which says that God has spoken in the human Jesus?

In the second book of *Church Dogmatics* published in 1938, Barth turned to the problem of religion and here we may find an answer to our question on how we can commence with God and why this beginning puts our religious inclination in a crisis. Five years after the parliamentary victory of NSDAP, which Barth had attacked to the point that he in 1935 was deported from Germany after refusing to sign the Oath of Loyalty to Adolf Hitler, he insisted that humans by necessity feel that they are confronted by powerful, natural forces 'which stand over their own life. . . . As a result, the representation of the object and aim of the striving, or of the origin of the event, has always and everywhere been compressed into pictures of deities.'[36] Religion is born, Feuerbach would say, from our feeling of dependency on nature.

Atheism, Barth continued in an even more Feuerbachian manner, is not a way out of this sensation of dependency since it 'is the contemplation of the universe and the creative power of the individual feeling which gropes after it in its nameless and formless and unrealized oneness. It is the power to be in the world and as a man.'[37] Barth was not primarily criticizing contemporary atheist philosophies with their tendencies to pantheism and monism with this attack on religion as a sensation of oneness and therefore feeling of dependency on nature. He was making a bolder claim directed against the religious constitution of the human being as such. Our dependency on nature is religious and constitutes us as creatures that mistake their being, what Barth called 'the power to be in the world', with worldly purposes or temporal categories, such as the nation, the family or for that matter the human species.

Following Max Stirner's nominalist critique of Feuerbach in *The Ego and Its Own*, Barth insisted that Feuerbach never understood 'the fictitious nature of the concept of humanity in general. He would then perhaps have refrained from identifying God with human beings, real beings, that is, who remain when the abstraction has been skimmed off.'[38] Stirner noted that the romantics 'were quite conscious what a blow the very belief in God suffered by the laying aside of the belief in spirits or ghosts, and they tried to help us out of the baleful consequences not only by their re-awakened fairy world, but at last, and especially, by the "intrusion of a higher world", by their somnambulists, visionaries of Prevorst, etc.'[39] However, the abstraction of humanity was another spectre, a secularized deity that haunted our species and even made Feuerbach one of 'the possessed'. Only by exorcizing this last ghost, the human could become an individual that owned his life and destiny.

A world with no ghosts was the basis for the ego or the individual, *der Einzige*, that Stirner hoped would emerge through a radicalization of the disenchantment that modernity implied. This exorcism made it possible for Barth to argue that Feuerbach's failure was his refusal to acknowledge 'the wickedness of the individual' and 'the fact that this individual must surely die' by clinging to the abstract concept of a humanity in general that even promised Feuerbach a form of immortality.

This does not imply that Barth accepted Stirner's nominalism. For how can the life of the concrete individual only be its own when it has not created itself? Certainly the individual can evolve out of the contingencies of the nature that we as concrete embodied beings belong to. But can an individual being be the ground for its own existence? Can nature as such be its own ground? Perhaps Stirner's ego is – just like humanity and nature – an abstraction and therefore a simple phantom? Perhaps the ego is a creature and nature a creation? And perhaps it is theology that can give notions such as humanity, nature and the individual the concreteness they tend to lack as the abstractions Stirner sought to exorcize?

Barth did not take the path of natural theology and did not argue that the finite existence of both humanity and the individual by necessity pointed to a creator. That would be religion. He emphasized instead that Christianity is bound to a historic contingency, the life and death of a concrete individual called Jesus, and not to general concepts such as nature, matter and time. In 1927 he even said that '[t]heology bows to the contingency of truth. The truth encounters it as a concrete authority. Theology is obedience [*Gehorsam*]. Its investigation is not free speculation, but a reflection [*Nachdenken*] on a given word'; and, for Feuerbach, the fact that humans accept theological authority as a revelation of something that is exterior to creation is a clear proof that religion is a mystification of our capacity for speculative and imaginative thinking.[40] For Barth, however, the limit of our life and knowledge is a mystery that can lead us to believe that there is something more than both Feuerbach's species-being and Stirner's individuals. Not, as stated, in the sense that the limit of what we can know is in itself a proof or even indication of anything more than the limit itself, but rather since it is possible to question if temporal and spatial concepts, and even abstractions like Feuerbach's humanity or Stirner's ego, are absolute, ultimate or self-identical.

This is what the Christian faith should do, according to Barth. It should relativize the power of the world by telling the rumour that the eternal has touched the temporal in the contingent life of an individual human being who, by being God, is something more than the world and the human. Nature itself, and therefore both the life of the human individual and the world it belongs to, has changed through 'the contingency of truth' since if truth is bound to a contingent life, then perhaps contingency (in the form of a free act of God), rather than necessity, is the ground for existence. To feel that existence is contingent, and that life could be otherwise than what it is, can lead to a crisis that opens us for the seemingly miraculous event that God is incarnated in Christ and thereby disrupts our feeling of dependency on nature that Feuerbach identified with religion.

Barth's description of religion as the feeling of oneness with the world was not a critique, but a verification, of Feuerbach's insistence that the human has a religious disposition. Nevertheless, this religious drive can be put into crisis through the discovery of the contingency of creation and theology has the means to conceptualize this disruption of human subjectivity. It does so, Barth argues, by listening to the rumour that says that the eternal has become implicated with the temporal, the necessary with the contingent, in the life and death of a singular individual who, according to the Christian faith, reveals the contingency of creation as such. The modern world may be freed from ghosts, as Stirner hoped, but human life is still the life of concrete individuals who live and die, and the relativity of our existence is a sign that creation itself shall pass. Christianity proclaims the end of things, even the end of what Feuerbach called nature religion, by pointing to something absolute and at the same time contingent that even relativizes death: the incarnate God.

This is why Barth could write that the 'real crisis of religion can only break in from outside the magic circle of religion and its place of origin, i.e., from man' and underlined that this crisis 'is what happens in the revelation of God'.[41] Revelation is the abolition of religion or, in what would be a more exact translation of the German *Aufhebung*, its sublation, and therefore the sublation of the forces – be they social or natural – that religion ties us to.[42] For, we must remember, religion is simply 'the power to be in the world'.

Aufhebung, which literally means lifting up, does not only denote a destruction or an annihilation but a preservation and conservation of what is negated in a new form. It is, for Barth, a renewal or resurrection. The sublation of religion is the transformation of 'the power to be in the world' to what Barth came to call true religion in accord with Augustine's *De vera religione*, and which he conceptualized as the event that can disclose itself in every phenomenon as something that makes it true.

'No religion is true', Barth insisted, it

> can only become true, i.e. according to that which it purports to be and for which it is upheld. And it can become true only in the way in which man is justified, from without; i.e., not of its own nature and being, but only in virtue of a reckoning and adopting and separating which are foreign to its own nature and being.[43]

This becoming true is the revelation of the finite and relative character of every power in the world. In other words, the natural and temporal categories that religion binds us to are legitimate if they are understood as what they are: finite and relative powers. Powers that could be otherwise than what they are. The relativization of religion as a secular and finite phenomenon is also a relativization of Christianity, which like every other religion has to become true from without and which therefore can change and be reformed. At the same time, Barth's theology of religion is based on the revelation of the divine in the contingent life of the human Jesus Christ and in this sense it becomes an apology of Christianity. It is, he wrote, 'because we remember and apply the

Christological doctrine of *assumptio carnis* that we speak of revelation as the abolition of religion'.[44] The assumption of flesh, *assumptio carnis*, is the event that makes something true by revealing the relative character of all finite things, even the relativity of nature as such, and this disclosure from without is the crisis of religion and of our dependency on every temporal power.

The incarnation, Barth claims, puts our present existence in brackets and reveals the finite character of everything worldly. If Christianity is a religion, it is 'the power to be in the world' that discloses how this life, life here and now, must be put into a crisis. It does so by reminding us that Scripture urges us to believe that life could be otherwise than what it is here and now. There exists something other, something eternal, that through a free and seemingly contingent act has touched our lives by becoming human.

Being is eating

The brilliance of Feuerbach was his simple but truthful insistence that human existence is nothing but sensual life.[45] Sensual and corporeal nature, *Sinnlichkeit*, is being and produces religion, for the divine spirit from which the human mind supposedly derives is the corporeal activity which religion has abstracted from the body as an independent being. Feuerbach, who knew the Christian tradition better than many theologians, emphasized that the theological doctrine that bread is flesh is true in a real sense. The eating of bread is an incorporation of a substance in the human body and therefore its humanization. Humans are literally bread that becomes flesh. The theological doctrine of the *Menschenwerdung* of God must be transformed to a theory of the *Menschenwerdung* of our species for the eating and drinking of God are the eating and drinking that reveal that we are animals.[46] In a review of the chemist Jacob Moleschott's study *Lehre der Nahrungsmittel* from 1822, which introduced the term 'metabolism', *Stoffwechsel*, to a more general public, Feuerbach spelled out that being itself is a metabolic process.

> Being is equal to eating; being means eating; what is eats and shall be eaten. Eating is subjective, active, to be eaten the objective, suffering form of being; but both are inseparable. It is therefore only in eating that the hollow concept of being is fulfilled and reveals the absurdity of the question: whether being and non-being are identical, i.e. if eating and hunger are identical?[47]

Moleschott was, Barth wrote in 1948, part of a group of important materialists consisting of among others Ludwig Büchner and Karl Vogt.[48] Barth was intrigued by this circle of thinkers, and clarified Feuerbach's well-known phrase, 'man is what he eats', *Der Mann ist was er isst*, by arguing that it is 'a phrase which can only be understood as brutally as is usually the case, if one overlooks (on which everything depends): that Feuerbach has simply spoken of the human stomach and human food'.[49] Feuerbach emphasized what it implies to be a human creature, namely, a psychophysical animal with social and not only biological needs.

Human existence, Barth reasoned in his lectures on ethics begun in 1928, is a life where the stomach and the sexual organs are as important as the abstract ideas of speculative theology and academic philosophy. Moral behaviour is 'conditioned by the necessity of *metabolism* and *sexuality* . . . Not everything, but a great deal in the phenomenon of man both individually and more generally may, in fact, be explained by the fact that we are continually hungry, sexually unsettled and in need of sleep'.[50] Feuerbach had ironically called his philosophy a wisdom of the anus, *Afterweisheit*, mocking the tradition of *Nachdenken* by describing it as an excrement.[51] No books might be written, no prayer might be read and no mass offered at church without satisfaction of the basic human needs to 'see, hear, walk, eat, or piss'.[52]

Like Feuerbach Barth underlined explicitly that eating, sleeping and the desire for coitus or other sexual acts are 'not ethically irrelevant'.[53] On the contrary, we have to accept that our basic metabolic existence 'is unquestionably the basic form of this will, and any deeper insight into . . . the reality of history makes it disconcertingly clear how vigorously this form of our will persists and asserts itself in every higher form by means of refined, and very refined, translations'.[54] This deceivingly Freudian description of culture as a sublimation of biological drives is in fact a Feuerbachian persistence on the ethical relevance of an embodied understanding of human history. According to Feuerbach the needs of the naked life of humanity should be satisfied in a just society where humans have become lovers of humanity rather than worshippers of gods.

Feuerbach's socialism was a political theory for the perpetuation of biological life and must be related to what Feuerbach professed as his 'hate [for] the idealism that wrenches man out of nature; I am not ashamed of my dependency on nature'.[55] This hatred for idealism was primarily a critique of Christianity which absurdly confessed 'that such dependency is contrary to my true being or hope to be delivered from it. I know further that I am a finite mortal being, that I shall one day cease to be. But I find this *very natural* and am therefore perfectly reconciled to the thought'.[56] Furthermore, he wrote that with 'intelligent egoism we forbid murder and theft among ourselves, but toward other beings, toward nature, we are all murderers and thieves'.[57] It is therefore not solely our own death that is *very natural*, also our killing of animals and our destruction of organic and inorganic nature are purely natural.

We are all murderers and thieves, Feuerbach argued, for who

> gives me the right to catch a rabbit? The fox and the vulture are just as hungry as I, just as much entitled to exist. Who gives me the right to pick a pear? It belongs just as much to the ants, the caterpillars, the birds, the four-footed animals. To whom does it really belong? To the one who takes it.[58]

It is here Feuerbach betrays his deep naïvety. By viewing life as a struggle for survival Feuerbach reveals that his hope to turn all religion to a dependency on nature easily becomes a justification of a world where we are all murderers and thieves.

Feuerbach's naturalism transforms itself all too easily to an egoism where right is built on might, according to Barth, for 'naturalistic ethics has always come under the suspicion that it is a system of radical egoism sentimentally decorated with an altruistic margin'.[59] Feuerbach's proclamation of the need to bring forth a humanity reconciled with its *Gattungswesen* was in the end a reduction of man to his self-sufficiency.

The brilliance of Feuerbach was that he sought the truth of existence in the immanence of a creaturely existence stripped of all transcendence, and therefore in bread and wine as they are. For Barth, however, this is also Feuerbach's real limit since he 'believes uncritically in the so-called sensuality as in a supposed last thing. For him God is therefore unsympathetic since quite rightly he senses in him the great troublemaker of the comfortable [*gemütlichen*] feast which we commemorate here.'[60]

The comfortable feast may be a belittling description of Feuerbach's naturalist ethics, based as it is on his view that 'in nature it is impossible to tell who is the lord and who the vassal, because all things are equally important'.[61] The organism is 'a republican community, [and] that it owes its existence to cooperation among equal beings, is the source of material evil, of struggle, illness, and death; but the cause of death is also the cause of life, the cause of evil is also the cause of good'.[62] The suffering and death that pervade nature are causes of goodness in an almost providential manner. It's a necessary product of the republic of metabolism that rules nature.

For Barth, this description of death, killing and destruction as the cause of natural goodness is worse than naïve and we can now understand what he indicated when he said in 1924 that 'if we are not to fall into the arms of Feuerbach at the very first step . . . we must think of God as the subject'.[63] Christianity should be a great disturbance of the right to pick pears and catch rabbits that no caterpillar, ant or fox can assess or understand as a right that can be questioned. Feuerbach's legitimation of the necessity of murder in nature makes us unable to question the powers that reduce life to a struggle for existence. Christianity, in contrast, should not evaluate nature from its inner economy. It should view the world from the redemption that wrests nature out of the economy of death and suffering that Barth refuses to see as something simply natural.

By arguing that Feuerbach 'believes uncritically in the so called sensual as a supposedly last thing', Barth relativized the difference between the political and the natural, the biological and the cultural, that Feuerbach could not question. Barth could, however, do this from the Christological doctrine of the *assumptio carnis*.[64] The flesh that is assumed by God in the incarnation breaks 'the continuity of factual, historical, familiar humanity' in order to 'restore the continuity of original paradisal humanity which the fall had broken, and therewith commence a new continuity of humanity'.[65] Tellingly, Barth argued that life in paradise was not only a life beyond death and killing. It was a life without religion and consequently with no need of a sublation of the religious disposition.

The human as 'paradisal man, needed no divine revelation or incarnation . . . God was not a problem for man when man was not a problem for himself'.[66] If Feuerbach conceptualized religion as an alienated yet at the same time natural attempt to deal with death, Barth insisted that God had to be described as a 'problem' or more exactly as a problematization of what we take to be the necessities of natural existence. Paradisal life was not a life beyond necessity. It was an abundant existence beyond death and scarcity. It was a necessity bound to God rather than to the struggle for survival.

In 1945, in the exegesis of what Barth called the saga of creation, Barth underlined the necessitous character of the life of all creatures in Eden by writing that the fact that the prelapsarian human 'must and may eat when he is given to eat signifies his intimate relationship to all other creatures with autonomous life, and in this way to the whole created cosmos'.[67] Being is, even in paradise, eating. Paradisal life is metabolic life. However, as I have argued, Barth underlined that 'the diet assigned to men and beasts by God the Creator is vegetarian. This makes it clear that the supremacy given to man over animals is not one of life and death.'[68] What Feuerbach saw as the *very natural* fact of killing and eating is on the one hand something deeply illegitimate and foreign to all animal life in Paradise, and on the other hand something normal in the fallen world that is ruled by the struggle for existence. It is this struggle that God seeks to challenge by revealing the possibility of a form of life no longer governed by lack or scarcity and this is why the revelation comes from without. It reveals a new economy for life by disrupting nature in its fallen form. Paradise is, for Barth, a place where our needs are satisfied by God.

Appetites, desires and even cravings are part of Eden, and Barth emphasized that when 'man finally appears at the centre of all the older circle of creation, and when it is shown in fact that everything must serve him, it must not be overlooked that man is thus revealed to be the most necessitous of all creatures'.[69] Barth concurs with Feuerbach that the human is an animal that needs other life and cannot exist without it. But the theologian insists that this dependency on creation can be redeemed from the scarcity that rules the life that must die.

All animal life, which is an almost vegetative life according to Barth – '[e]very living creature is alive because of that which it has in common with the vegetable kingdom' – must eat plants also in Paradise.[70] At the same time, Barth emphasized, '[t]he plant is undoubtedly created for its own sake as well. Only in its superabundance will it later serve that purpose', namely, the purpose to be eaten and therefore part of the metabolic but abundant economy of Paradise.[71] Paradise is a transformation of what it implies to eat and be eaten. Eternal life is a new metabolic relation to nature. It is a form of life that through its 'superabundance' does not need to make choices ruled by scarcity.

This is essential and reveals that a life satisfied by God is even beyond the need to make ethical choices. For, Barth argued during the Second World War, an answer to the violence that marks fallen nature can only be found 'by revealing in Jesus Christ the human image with which Adam was created to correspond and could no longer do so when he sinned, when he became ethical man'.[72] Our species is now compelled to partake in the differentiation between what is good and evil, and therefore between what is related to God and what belongs to what Barth would describe as the nothingness, *das Nichtige*, which the divine casts as its shadow.[73]

An economy ruled by nothingness is an economy governed by lack and scarcity, whereas the metabolic economy of Eden is still an economy of needs; but needs for creatures, that due to the 'superabundance' of their life, know no death. The proscription to eat from the tree of knowledge of good and bad gives thereby the moral or even political meaning of fallen nature. Yet, it is not a prohibition in a legal sense according to Barth since there existed no law in Paradise. It was not a juridical imperative, but an indication – a warning of what a life alienated from God would be: a life enslaved to the violence of evolution and caught in the prison house of morality with its laws, police and rules that exist as God's necessary shadow in a fallen world.

The saga of the fall is a story about the emergence of the 'ethical man' who 'wants to be like God' but instead becomes imprisoned in the new, fallen economy of scarcity that forces men and women to make the often impossible choice between good and evil.[74] The fall entails, Barth underlined, the production of '"ethics," or, rather, the multifarious ethical systems' by attempting to give 'human answers to the ethical question' and is thereby nothing but the need to give human answers to problems humans cannot fully solve.[75]

If the ethical question is the problem of the fall, and consequently the problem of birth, work and death, then it is evident that this question 'can be solved only as it was originally put – by the grace of God, by the fact that this allows man actually to *be* the answer'.[76] The answer must, once again, come from without. God must satisfy the needs of his creation. To become the answer to the problem that ethics posits, the human must not only transcend the answers given by human ethics but the whole world that makes them necessary. A step beyond the human is needed. Barth notes, however, that even if the 'grace of God protests against all man-made ethics', it does so 'positively. It does not only say No to man. It also says Yes. But it does so by completing its own answer to the ethical problem in active refutation, conquest and destruction of all human answers to it.'[77] The revelation implies what Barth calls an 'eternal yes' and an 'eternal no' by affirming the joy of creaturely existence and rejecting the nothingness of death that the fall represents.[78] This is why the grace of God can be an affirmation of human ethics only through a 'conquest and destruction of all human answers' to the problem that ethics posits since humanity as a fallen race, an animal enmeshed in death, must be destroyed through the death and resurrection of Christ so that a new answer to the problem of evil can be given.

The destruction of all human answers to the problem of creation can only be enacted by the economy of eternal life and through the production of the paradisal superabundance which does not abolish our metabolic existence but transforms it. 'Eternal life', Barth argued, is 'man's life in harmony with the life of God and all His angels, but also with that of all the rest of the elect, and, indeed, of all creation'.[79] This harmony is our world, the world of death and suffering, mirrored in the divine life of Christ that has been given to us as food and satisfaction. It is a world that has become the echo of God.

Being is still eating in such a redeemed cosmos but eating, as strange as it might seem, does not imply death. It entails as we have seen a new metabolism and we can even here and now, in our spatial and temporal existence as fallen creatures, move closer to such a new creation. For, Barth argues, '[e]ternal life is the real secret of this temporal life. We do not yet live eternal life here and now. But we are here and now made free for eternal life.'[80] To be free for eternal life is to be liberated from the constitution of human life as an ethical existence through the curse of death that constantly compels us to make moral choices since human life is, profoundly, unethical. Our life involves 'the cruel struggle for existence of all against all'.[81] This constitution of human existence as a being forced to become moral and, by extension, political is the tyranny of existence that Feuerbach could not criticize since nature in its current form was the horizon of his thought.

What Barth urges us to see is that the freedom that is given through the fall, the freedom to live a moral or immoral existence, is no real freedom. It is the freedom that chains us to death by reducing life to survival and that freedom makes it almost impossible for us to view life as something else than a struggle for the scarce resources that constantly produces political and ethical problems. To view freedom as the often impossible choice between good and evil is to understand freedom as something that is only given together with the possibility of death and killing. It is the inability to believe that there is a 'secret of this temporal life' and therefore something yet unrevealed, something that is not told, something that is fundamentally outside us.

Fractures in reality

The 'feeling of a nameless, formless and unrealized oneness', as Barth described the religious core three years after he had been expelled from Germany in 1935 for his staunch anti-fascism, found without doubt one of its most electric manifestations in Nazism which had many defenders in the church.[82]

In the early 1930s, the so-called *Deutsche Christen* championed a nationalist and soon openly racist interpretation of the Christian gospel. They embraced the Aryan paragraph, which had been implemented in 1933 by the new regime in order to exclude all non-Aryans from posts in public institutions.[83] The theologian Emanuel Hirsch wrote apropos the *Führer* that no other people in the world than the Germans have 'a statesman who takes Christianity so seriously. When Adolf Hitler ended his great speech on 1 May with a prayer, the whole world felt the wonderful sincerity of it.'[84] Barth became a leading voice against Nazism and he had already during his lectures on dogmatics in Göttingen in 1924 and 1925 criticized eugenics as something of a disguised religion by referring to the essayist Carl Christian Bry when he discoursed upon angels and demons under the heading, 'De angelis bonis et malis'.[85]

Bry had in his book *Verkappte Religionen* described the rise of antisemitism as a disguised religion, *verkappte Religion*, and a collective delusion, *kollektiver Wahn*, for a humanity that no longer believed in anything beyond the world.[86] Barth referred to Bry in passing and said that the phrenology of the eugenicist Hans F. K. Günther was a disguised demonology.[87] Barth implied that eugenics and race sciences were anything but what Hannah Arendt later would call a banal evil.[88] It was a *demonic* evil that had to be rejected. Still, the demonic is perhaps the most banal thing since it is nothingness, the privation of being, that wrests itself free from the providence of God.[89]

In 1925 Barth argued that the powers of demons are built on fantasies and that we are only touched by the demonic through our imagination.[90] He insisted that even if we must acknowledge the real existence of these fancies of imagination we should not take them all too seriously for they only accompany us 'like a tremendous shadow' and if we wander into this darkness we come under their spell.[91] The demonic is, for sure, a real shadow that haunts our existence, but it is still a shadow that falls from the power of God whose providence rules over it as over everything else.

The importance of angelology and demonology was at this stage of Barth's theological development that they gave the church the ability to view history as part of the unfolding of a drama between the fallen creation and the redemptive acts of God. By interpreting the material world from the realm of spirits, or what can be called the domain of discourses, ideas and values, one can understand how reality reflects the divine. He claimed that one can undoubtedly explain the entire world history materialistically, by the means of 'geography', 'race sciences', 'economics' and even 'meteorology', but he insisted that 'one sees how little such representations actually acquire with the purely empirical method. What happens there – I mean now apart from the will of God: world-immanently – ultimately, when a cause such as the French or Russian Revolution breaks forth, when a Napoleon dreams his Alexander dream, when a Mussolini begins and completes his path from socialist to nationalist?'[92] These occurrences, Barth argued, point to 'an independent spiritual course in the world'.[93] Thus, for him, if 'the world is not only teeming with "disguised religions" but also with disguised corresponding god-like beings, principalities and dominions, then two questions remain with us: (1) whether we in them indeed have to do with personal beings and (2) whether this realm of spirit and spirits itself is actually torn into the duality of angels and demons, that is, spirits facing God and turned away from God'.[94]

Barth answers by noting that the first question is of little importance since he accepts that our modern world has made it impossible to give a definitive answer to the question if demons are personal beings. He acknowledges that it was the archaic world with its polytheism that gave Christianity its angelology and writes that the belief in these powers implied a spiritual seriousness which modernity lacks.[95] Martin Luther would not be the great reformer without his struggle with the devil, and even a recent theologian such as Johann Blumhardt experienced the world of angels and demons as a domain of personal powers.[96]

The personality that can be given to angels and demons is perhaps solely the personification of the struggle that the Christian is called to partake in. By viewing the individual who struggles with the banality of nationalism, or for that matter the evil of antisemitism, from the point of view of demonology, the stakes in the struggle are personalized and turned to something of theological and not only existential importance. Twenty-five years later Barth would argue that '[o]ne form of the triumph which nothingness can achieve is to represent itself as a mere appearance with no genuine reality'.[97] Nothingness exists, not least as death, and it exists in a form that has profound theological consequences. In this sense, and perhaps only in this sense, demons can be said to be personal beings even if they are only mythical representations of the power of nothingness.

The second question as to whether there are fallen angels is easier to answer since Scripture differentiates the old cosmos from the redeemed world. The angels are *eudemonic* by bringing happiness, whereas the demons are *kakodemonic* by causing evil and unhappiness. Angels and demons can be seen as something of good or evil consequences for what Barth terms, using an expression by David Friedrich Strauss, 'the concrete life' of the human.[98] Strauss viewed angelology and demonology as unnecessary for modern theology, which should demythologize Scripture and reveal its nature as a moral teaching. He used the concept of 'the concrete life of humanity' in order to describe angels and demons as ideal existences that were produced by human thought as meaningless abstractions. Barth agreed with Strauss that angelology and demonology are part of a *parergon*, a marginal note, to the real subject of dogmatic theology: the doctrine of God and the explanation of humanity's relation to the divine.[99] Nevertheless, Barth emphasized in a Lutheran manner, just as the human exists as a sinner and as a redeemed creature, the world of spirits is divided between *eudemonic* and *kakodemonic* beings which endow creaturely existence with specific meaning.

Angelology, Barth affirms with Strauss, is 'a duplication of the doctrine of man'. Angelology reads human life from the perspective of the world of spirits as it is described in the Christian tradition.[100] Angelology duplicates human life by interpreting it from its concrete facticity and from the *eudemonic* and *kakodemonic* powers that reveal how human affects and values point to the world of the invisible.

What is the world in every point of its constitution, Barth asked in 1925, if not visible *and* invisible, nature *and* spirit, earth *and* heaven?[101] Creation itself is torn apart by the abstract and concealed forces that move us nearer to God or nail us to the world. There is a *mysterium iniquitatis* according to Barth and tellingly he asked, '[i]s the mystery of Judaism and the mystery of antisemitism perhaps explained by this, is the question of this mystery not rather only asked when we are shown the structure of the form of the skulls of those involved on both sides?'[102] The reason why the mystery of Judaism and antisemitism might be explained when we are shown the structure of the form of the skulls of those involved on both sides, a statement that today seems quite disturbing as well as sadly prophetic, is because death – as the force that moves human existence into the eternal life of God – proves the evil character of all racial theories. Death itself will reveal for later generations that these race theories are fantasies, phantasms, figments of imaginations bordering on nothingness and casting the world deeper into the fall by being lies.

At the same time as Barth developed his demonology, he eschewed occultism and warned against the superstitious belief in angels and demons by saying that even Catholic dogmatics has pointed out that demons cannot be seen as forces that, for example, cause human illness or disease.[103] The only theological meaning angelology and demonology can have is as a hermeneutics that suggests how human actions are duplicated eschatologically. Yet, Barth asks, '[c]an we think of this second side as empty? Is it really just passive?'[104] The invisible world, that is the world of imaginations – but still a world of *real* imaginations, *real* abstract powers that seem to have a life of its own – is not passive. It does not only mirror that which is in the eyes of eternity: it contains the abstract forces that possess history by such demonic lies as eugenics and race theories.

If angelology is only a parergon for Barth, it is still a marginal note that can help him discuss the invisible sense of the visible world and especially the sense of the sufferings and violence of creaturely life in the modern period. This is why he implied that Mussolini's abandonment of socialism is not only a human choice but a demonic event affecting the course of world history.[105] Mussolini's actions fed the demonic power of fascism that haunted and still haunts human life. This political aspect of Barth's theory of the invisible can be discerned when he underlines that only demons have a hierarchic structure and a king in Satan, whereas the order of the angels is egalitarian and democratic: 'There is *no* such *monarch* in the world of *obedient* angels. Much has been tried to be said about a ranking of *these* angels as well, but it never occurred to anybody to contrast the devil with a counterpart in the world above. The erection of the *monarchic* principle is characteristic of the demonic world as such.'[106] God is majesty, but Barth argues that the Catholic division of the angels as a hierarchical order in three spheres – (1) Angels, Archangels, Principalities (2) Powers, Virtues, Dominions and (3) Thrones, Cherubim and Seraphim – has no counterpart in Scripture.[107]

The rule of the angels is democratic and the tasks of these divine envois and heralds are never permanent duties that establish a hierarchy but transient acts involved in the eschatological unfolding of the world.[108] The duplication of the doctrine of man – angelology and demonology – is needed in order to understand that our actions and decisions are not only concrete and historical. They also implement us in the eternal in the simple sense that what we do, we do once for all. This is what it means that the human, as everything else created, belongs to the visible *and* the invisible just as to nature *and* spirit.

In a lecture on the Christian Credo in 1935, ten years after his classes on angelology and demonology, Barth would explicitly emphasize this double aspect of creaturely life when he discussed resurrection and eternal life.[109] Now he stated that the belief in the resurrection of flesh and eternal life, *Carnis resurrectionem, vitam aeternam*, indicates that 'there is with respect to human history and society, time and world, a future completely different human existence; the human, who means to know himself, shall be confronted with a mirror image of himself, in which he appears completely alien to himself'.[110] The fractures in reality between the angels and demons, and between our life here and now and our resurrected state, come from this eschatological mirroring of the visible world in the invisible, future realm where God is all in all. This mirroring is the answer as to why the 'secret of this temporal life' is 'eternal life'. Even the atheist does what he does once for all, and he does it in relation to the eternity of that which was; death transforms life to what it was and forever will be in the domain of the past. Everything we do is a decision done in relation to eternity.

Barth underlined that 'credo means decision'.[111] The one who states I believe in the resurrection of the flesh and eternal life is the one who decides to be moved by the alien self that mirrors everything that is done in eternity, and only the one that decides to reflect this future state – paradoxically revealed in death – can be said to be a believer that hopes that even the past can be redeemed from what it was reduced to in time and space. Yet life is always more than what it was: it is unfulfilled dreams, wishes never acted upon and actions never taken. By belonging to eternity life is more than what it was in time since both what we do and neglect to do, what we want or fear, are mirrored in the eternal.

And, Barth underlined ten years earlier in his angelology, '[w]hat is called decision by us, is there decisiveness, decisive being'.[112] Angels and demons are the real abstractions that we, for example, call good and evil, joy and suffering, and which we constantly have to differentiate in order to – consciously or not – decide which lord to serve.

Angels are the decisive beings, the powers of imagination and abstraction, that are good by moving creation nearer its eschatological completion where life becomes abundant and is no longer ruled by the economy of scarcity that separates life from the Edenic nutrition of God. In contrast, demons are the fantasies that embed us in the nothingness that has made the human a creature which must make a decision since our species is imprisoned in the fallen world of ethics that forces us to become moral or immoral or, more likely, to live in the grey area of mundane life.

Barth continued in 1940 to stress the double aspect of creaturely life by arguing that the incarnation has divided the temporal being 'between yesterday and tomorrow, that which lies behind and that which lies before us, what is above and what is'.[113] But now he also underlined that what perhaps can be called the decisive being of Christ himself reveals how this division is unified in God's eternal life. God is not only *after time* – 'post-temporal' – or *before time* – 'pre-temporal' – nor solely *beyond time* – 'supra-temporal'.[114] God is *with and in time* – 'co-temporal' and 'in-temporal' – for '[t]ime itself is in eternity. Its whole extension from beginning to end, each single part of it, every epoch, every lifetime, every new and closing year, every passing hour: they are all in eternity like a child in the arms of its mother.'[115] The fractures in reality, best expressed by the division between time and eternity, is healed in a movement that embeds the temporal order of finite creatures in God's life since 'God *lives* eternally'.[116]

There is what Barth calls 'a turning' and 'to have time and to live in time means to live in this turning', so the human can make the decision, consciously or not, to follow the movement that pushes creation itself to the point where life turns into God's eternal life.[117] Here, when creation enters eternity, the great divide which the *eudemonic* and *kakodemonic* powers represent in our life is reconciled. Now, or rather after time, we no longer solely believe in God but experience him. We are made into decisive beings. For, Barth writes, '[a]fter time, in post-temporal eternity' we humans are liberated from the 'fluctuation' between the forces that constitute us as ethical beings that have to make a decision.[118] Yet, we are not transformed to decisive beings since finite life has been actualized as what it forever will be by dying into the past, but because all the dead have been resurrected and now live in relation to the abundant life of the eternal. Through the resurrection we have decided to live outside the death and scarcity of the fall.

In an important sense, this decision to mirror eternity has according to Barth already been made for us in Christ. He is the turning point, the ultimate decisive being, which both produces and overcomes the antithesis between the angelic and demonic that marks existence in time. Eternity has become co-temporal and even more personal since it has a positive content in the life and death of Jesus, who is the revelation of what belongs to eternity and what remains on the side of nothingness. Moreover, if demonology is political for Barth, his doctrine on eternity and time is a political kairology since the revelation of Christ is the *kairos* of eternity in time.

Eternity, Barth postulated in 1940, had for German theology become completely alienated from the revelation of God. Eternity was 'little more than an exclamation mark which had no positive content, so that it could be placed not only behind the word "God" but behind any word at all denoting a supreme value, even in the very last analysis, as we have seen under National Socialism, behind the word "Germany".[119] This is nothing but religion, the attempt to use God to exalt that which should be relativized, judged or even destroyed, whereas eternal life must be given through that which is and, even more, dies in time.

For, Barth wrote, '[e]ven sin, death, the devil and hell – works of God's permissive will which are negative in their effects – even these works do not constitute any exception to the general rule. . . . Even the enemies of God are the servants of God and the servants of His grace'.[120] If theology is *Nachdenken*, a thinking that begins *post factum*, this is because it commences *post Christum*, and this thinking after the death and resurrection of Christ is a thinking that must view life and death as phenomena that have changed through the incarnation, crucifixion, resurrection and ascension. The simple fact of death – even the most horrific death – is not something that refutes eternal life, since the eternity of life is not the abolishment of natural death. Eternity is the transformation of the sense of finite and mortal existence from something scarce to something abundant, and it is by following this transformation that theology becomes

Nachdenken. By following the logic of God it is possible to disclose how death itself reveals the new economy of being and this is what theology seeks to do. It reveals how eternity can be the answer to what Barth called the 'secret of this temporal life'.

The sense of nonsense

Theology, Barth wrote in the first volume of his *Church Dogmatics* from 1932, is something of an 'abnormality' and it 'cannot think itself as a link in an ordered cosmos, but only as a stop-gap in a disordered cosmos'.[121] By being dogmatics it is a *Nachdenken* that seeks to express the positive content of the revelation, as it is understood in the Christian tradition, and everything that mirrors this content can be conceptualized theologically. God may, Barth famously insisted, 'speak to us through Russian Communism, a flute concerto, a blossoming shrub, or a dead dog. . . . God may speak to us through a pagan or an atheist, and thus give us to understand that the boundary between the Church and the secular world can still take at any time a different course from that which we think we discern.'[122] In a secular way this can be understood as how the data of revelation – such as the life and death of Christ – structure temporal thought. Barth's reading of Feuerbach is a good example of how he thought theology could be expressed outside the Christian tradition. Yet, theology is not simply a historical examination of the afterlife of religious ideas. It is an attempt to discuss how the world as such posits theological questions by being disordered.

Barth's insistence on the abnormality of theology in 1932 was not that dissimilar from his suggestion in the second edition of *The Epistle to the Romans*, published ten years earlier, that theology is an 'abnormal, irregular, revolutionary attack' on the human world.[123] Then Barth argued explicitly that theology must interpret the unfolding of history and the whole order of creation 'as a parable of a wholly other world'.[124] What Barth sought to emphasize in 1922 was how the world could be interpreted as an analogy for the revelation. Even in his most dialectical and crisis-centred period, analogical arguments can be found and the parable, *Gleichnis*, has for Barth the same form as the analogy.[125] Both indirectly convey a meaning by giving witness to something that is outside the world, describing 'similarities and likeness within ever greater dissimilarities or differences'.[126]

The analogical dimension of Barth's dialectical thinking is evident if we turn to an important passage in *The Epistle to the Romans* where theology and faith are described as 'the sense that is in nonsense . . . for there is no direct communication from God, and therefore the appropriation of sense in the nonsense of the world of religion can only be by faith'.[127] In German it is even more powerful: *wenn dem Unsinn tatsächlich Sinn innewohnt* – 'when sense is factually inherent in nonsense' – then faith is needed as that which seeks to understand the God which shows himself analogically in every being as '*des Sinns im Unsinn*' – the sense of nonsense.[128] Thus, even if there is no analogy of being – which Barth famously attacked as 'the invention of the Antichrist' – there is an *analogia fidei*: an analogy of faith.[129]

If faith is the possibility to interpret the nonsense of the world – and even the nonsense of pagan religions as Barth was discussing when he examined faith as the interpretation of the sense of nonsense in *Der Römerbrief* – this is because the revelation is what he later would define as a sublation of religion. By being immersed in a world of magic and superstition 'the Gospel of the Unknown God is competent to understand the mystery religions better than they do themselves, and, avoiding their dangers, is free to gather up the sense in their nonsense'.[130] All worldly phenomena can be said to duplicate human life by indicating humanity's relation to the *eudemonic* or *kakodemonic* return to God: the process of redemption or damnation that Barth came to identify with God's eternal yes and eternal no in Christ. The *analogia fidei* is the vision of the world through this duplication.

Even if we can find an analogical dimension in *The Epistle to the Romans*, Barth also wrote in 1921 that theology is 'not a system of dogmatics'.[131] The analogical structure that gives sense to the nonsense of the world was not something that could be turned into a dogmatic science that expresses the content of the abnormality of faith – revelation was a crisis, a shock, an attack on the creation. However, only three years later Barth had begun to work with a dogmatics aiming to explicate God's own speaking.[132]

Referring to Anselm, he underlined now that all 'reflection on how God can reveal himself is in truth only a "thinking after" of the fact that God has revealed himself'.[133] Dogmatics from the Greek *dogma*, which means 'that which one thinks is true', was originally a philosophical concept that referred to the main tenets of the ancient schools such as Epicureanism or Stoicism. It was in this sense that dogmatics was a *Nachdenken* for Barth. It was a critical reflection of what one thinks is true. Yet, Christian dogmatics sought to think after and thereby follow an event that had not been fully completed: the resurrection of the dead. Its *Nachdenken* was eschatological and historical since its authority as a mode of thought came from a historical figure, Jesus of Nazareth, and a historical movement: the Jews, and later gentiles, who thought Jesus was Christ.

In 1927, Barth explicitly affirmed 'that true faith is belief in authority, that the human cannot invent religion, not conceive [it] but only follow it in thought [*nur nachdenken kann*]'.[134] For Barth, this was not a subjection of reason to blind obedience. It was a participation – '*tanquam in speculo*', as in a mirror – in the reason and thinking of God that is revealed in the tradition that teaches that Christ is the positive content of eternity.[135]

Following Sigurd Baark and Manfred Josuttis, I argue that it was in Barth's book on Anselm, *Fides Quaerens Intellectum*, written in 1931, where Barth developed this speculative mirroring to a programme for his theology. Here he once again affirmed faith as belief in authority – '[f]aith is always belief in authority!' – and laid the basis for a true speculative theology.[136] 'Not all "speculative" theology says the truth', he wrote, '[b]ut also theology, that says the truth, is "speculative" theology.'[137] Anselm's speculation – his theological mirroring of God's being in his proof – was based on the postulation that the adequate name of God as that-than-which-nothing-greater-can-be-conceived implies his necessary existence.

Barth had already stated in the *Göttingen Dogmatics* that only God is '*a se*' whereas all other existence is contingent in the sense that it could also not exist.[138] By using the concept existence for God, Anselm took a category adequate to describe the presence and reality of a contingent phenomenon in the world of time and space and applied it to God as something or someone that is.[139]

However, in contrast to the species or the person, God has necessary and not only contingent existence. He cannot not be since he is not only being, but necessary being, the being that gives contingent existence the possibility to exist. In a qualified sense, God is even beyond existence and even necessity since he is what gives what we know as existence the possibility to exist. God, Barth writes in his book on Anselm, bursts every *syllogism*. 'But', he continued, 'like everything that is not God, would be nothing without God, but is something through God . . . so can statements that in reality are only adequate to objects not identical to God . . . be true statements.'[140] There is an analogical relation between everything that has contingent existence and the being that makes them exist since God is the event that gives them being or non-being. Inadequate terms like 'existence' and 'necessity' can be used to describe God as the necessity that reveals the contingency of being and, as we have seen, incarnates himself in the contingency of his creation.

Eva T. H. Brann has strengthened this reading of Anselm by analysing how the medieval theologian gave God the name that described him as the 'being which by reason of *not* being exceeded by anything *cannot* be conceived as *not* existing'.[141] Anselm conjured a borderline intuition which can be used to envision a 'negatively delineated maximal being – negatively delineated because that absolves us from facing God as a positive, definite bound'.[142] The genius of Anselm was that by defining God negatively as the only being which cannot *not* exist, he turned this negativity to a positive proof that shows why 'the God who is conceived as exceeding everything is a being, and the only being, that must exist'.[143] God's being is this wondrous and terrible cannot–not–be–being.

It was from a similar perspective that Barth argued that the one who accepts the profoundly negative name of God as the being than which nothing greater can be conceived is also the one who can openly give witness to the existence and positivity of God as that which transcends everything that is: 'The question of the existence of this and this thing can be revoked. No thing exists with such a necessity, that knowing it not also could have exemption, since no thing exists really and for the first time. The per se necessary object of knowledge is God as *the* existing.'[144] God is the only being that must exist and everything else is contingent on his will. Yet, the real value of Anselm's proof was not to show how the human intellect might form an idea of God as a being that exists by necessity. *Proslogion* was 'an aspiration of the human will to strive to *enter into* [*Hinein*streben] God, and therefore also a participation, although creaturely limited, in God's mode of being'.[145]

Barth's reading of the medieval theologian's prayer as a *Hineinstreben* into God – a striving that reveals that faith is an ethical and theological work – clearly reveals that his interest in Anselm was not intellectualist or rationalist in a reductive sense. He used *Proslogion* to reveal the contours of a life that seeks to mirror the life of God in a world of contingent rather than necessary existence. The *Nachdenken* that Anselm's theology entailed is a *Nachleben* and a *Nachfolge*. By following the thought of God we can learn to follow God as a form of life. It is not surprising that Barth in 1940 almost copied his argument of a limited *Hineinstreben* into God from his book on Anselm by insisting that when we name God adequately we participate indirectly in his self-knowledge and therefore in his eternal life.[146]

This name of God, which he identified with Christ, is the highest name in an Anselmian manner, and Barth had already at the beginning of his career understood that the one who seeks to participate in the being which this name indicates must be able to name the relativity and contingence of all other powers. Christ is the name that can revoke all other powers and God is the name for a being that transcends all beings. A being that cannot not be which Barth in his famous Tambach lecture from 1919 already had described as an authority that even questions the powers of eating, drinking, sleeping and growing old:

> However clearly we may see that the brutal prerequisites of social life – the state and the economic system, art and science, and even the more primitive necessities of eating, drinking, sleeping, and growing old – all have their own laws of mass and movement; however definitely we may reckon upon the necessity of enduring these laws; however certainly we may be convinced of the absolute folly of biting upon granite – one thing is still more certain, more serious, and clearer: we can no longer submit ourselves to these laws as *ultimate* independent authorities. And the reason is *not only* because we have been shamed into becoming wise by the outward events of our times; it is *not only* because we have become spiritually tired, tired to the point of exhaustion, of our pantheon of independent divinities. . . . It is *rather* because our souls have awakened to the consciousness of their immediacy with God.[147]

What Barth described was not a world which had ended and where the human is liberated from the biological, economic, political and even metabolic powers that Feuerbach identified with being as such. He underlined that the Christian tradition should reveal that these powers – even the powers of eating, drinking, sleeping and growing old – are not ultimate authorities. They are, Barth would insist late in life, phantoms, something passing that should be resisted as metaphysical powers since they too prolong the fall if we think they are deities that cannot be dethroned.

The souls that have 'awakened to the consciousness of their immediacy with God' are the souls that can interpret the time of revolutions, wars and catastrophes during which Barth was preaching as a period that no longer has any independent authorities. The immediacy of God is revealed in this world as the 'categorical challenge to all the authorities in life; we cannot but test them by that which alone can be authoritative'.[148] The essential meaning of Barth's early eschatology was to insist that in 'all the social relations in which we may find ourselves, we must perceive something ultimate in the mere fact of their being and having to be'.[149] If Barth in the 1930s repeatedly would state that theology is a *Nachdenken* this is because he already had come to the conclusion that everything that is can be viewed – negatively or positively – as an analogy for the God that is Christ.

What Barth accentuated with his analogical theory was, Eberhard Jüngel has argued, the notion of God's word as the *verbum externum*.[150] Barth's theology of analogy has not only its precondition in the paradigmatic event that constitutes faith: the subjectivity of God. It is, according to Jüngel, more important to stress that analogy implies the constitution of a form of life willing to give witness to God: 'Analogy means correspondence . . . *God speaks – the human answers.* Thus he is *imago dei*. Thus theological anthropology is possible.'[151] Barth's theory of analogy implies a theological anthropology through an act of interpellation. God calls the human to follow his life in order to make him capable to question the powers of this world.

Human subjectivity as something that is constituted by an exterior event can be understood through the lenses of what Louis Althusser has called interpellation: the calling or hailing of a specific subjectivity into existence.[152] Althusser uses the example of a police officer who shouts 'Stop!', where the man or woman who submits to this interpellation is thereby subjectified as an obeying subject. Similarly, the man who knocks at his friend's door and asks, 'Are you there?' interpellates the friend to constitute herself as a subject that, for example, says: 'Yes, I am.' This call or interpellation is the basic structure of ideology and, significantly, something that Althusser explicitly insists both Feuerbach and Barth failed to understand.[153]

For Barth, though, the Word of God is not an interpellation that forces the human into the order of a specific ideology. This word is the *verbum externum* that questions every structure and even every human command as something relative. It is a call to the human from a God than which nothing greater can be conceived. This is not an argument that would convince anyone without faith. But for Barth faith entails an unknown freedom, namely, the freedom to hope for an existence liberated from the struggle for survival and such freedom cannot come from the world ruled by death and scarcity. It has to come from without.

Interestingly, Althusser emphasizes that the process of interpellation is a necessary structure of all human life and the fact that ideology works by calling human subjects into existence does not entail that all ideologies are merely ideological. Truth can also call a subject into existence. If one reads Barth from this perspective, it can be stated that the interpellation he seeks to explicate calls the human into question or, on the other hand, validates every worldly power, including Christianity, from the vantage point of revelation. And, we remember, this revelation is not a religion that discloses our real dependency on nature. It is a sublation that reveals the deep fractures in reality and indicates that the world, as a contingent phenomenon, has an exteriority in that which cannot not be and which questions, rather than simply upholds, our existence by revealing that it could be otherwise than what it has become through the fall.

By arguing in 1919 that every social relation is something of a parable for that which conditions its existence, Barth affirmed that everything that is – even the most destructive power – must in some sense be related to God and his providence. Ten years later, in his important lectures on ethics, he explicitly defended a theory of the orders of creation.[154] It is true that he abandoned this approach to creation when several of his colleges and friends avowed Nazism only a couple of years later, using a theology of the orders of creation to justify the new regime. Nonetheless, five years after NSDAP took power, Barth argued that 'we have no right to do as Augustine liked to do, and straightway identify the *civitas terrena* with the *civitas Cain*'.[155] Clearly alluding to the Nazi state Barth wrote that no 'representatives, office-bearers and citizens' can protect the state 'from becoming the State of Cain'.[156] 'But', he continued, since 'the heavenly Jerusalem is also a State, and every State, even the worst and most perverse, possesses its imperishable destiny in the fact that it will one day contribute to the glory of the heavenly Jerusalem, and will inevitably bring its tribute thither' all states testify to the power and providence of God.[157] Not as a manifestation of God himself. Only as a sign that no power – not even the power of despots and dictators – is absolute. Everything in this world is relative and contingent and thereby an analogy for the divine. The *Third Reich* itself is power that only in a matter of time, albeit a time that is too long for all its victims, reveals itself as a parable. A horrific parable, a parable of hell and that which should not be, but still what Barth late in life would call a secular parable.[158] There is a necessary existence, an existence that even turns 'sin, death, the devil and hell-works' into 'servants of God' and therefore to powers that seek to bestow eternal life or eternal damnation on creation.[159] But how and in what sense do the relative, contingent, powers of the world – like eating, drinking, sleeping and growing old – participate in this, what I have called, duplication of the world in the eternal?

Naming death

If I return to Eva T. H. Brann's discussion of Anselm, it can be noted that she claims that human beings like all other embodied and temporal creatures are intrinsically qualified by existence. When humans begin to exist 'they not only gain in the vivacity of the impressions they can make on other existences and in the increased completeness of their incidental features. They also gain the negative capacity for nonexistence, that is, for that specific individual nonbeing called mortality.'[160] Humans are by necessity confronted with mortality 'which accounts in life for being insufficiently there', and through death, which stands 'for not being there at all', they are given the possibility to not be that which God, as necessary being and eternal life, cannot be.[161]

In a manner that reminds of Barth, Brann argues that Anselm's proof has existential and ethical consequences by positing that the intrinsic human qualification to exist is relative by necessity. This contingence of life is visible in the simple fact that humans, like all creatures, can die. Something happens, however, in her discussion of Anselm. Conveying her profound admiration for the Austrian philosopher Alexius Meinong, who developed a philosophy for non-existing beings, and revealing the implicit theory of immortality which seems to lurk in her work, Brann makes the point that death marks the human with 'the negative capacity for nonexistence' and 'once dead, mortals achieve as well the nonexistence attributed to fictional objects, especially at memorial services'.[162] Death perhaps only accounts for not being there at all *in life* or rather in the domain of time and space that the living equate with life.

Fictional objects – such as Don Quijote or Ignatius J. Reilly – do not exist as lifelike normal living beings but subsist, as Meinong would call it, in the sense that we can refer to them and talk about them appropriately.[163] Ignatius, for example, is a dunce in New Orleans and not a prince in Copenhagen, whereas Don Quijote is a hidalgo from La Mancha in love with Dulcinea and not a captain of the whaling ship Pequod, and Brann writes that it could be possible 'that the being of fictions is a matter for divine rather than secular science'.[164] Anselm therefore, Brann implies, is prompted to develop a theory of non-existence by arguing that the necessary being that cannot not be endows the dead with its strange *not–not–being*. The dead are in the eyes of God.

In an equivalent manner, Barth wrote in his book on Anselm that by following the trail of thoughts that prompted the monk to designate God as the being than which nothing greater can be conceived, the one who accepts the logic of the proof might acknowledge that there is an authority greater than death itself, since a being that exists necessarily transcends the two-dimensionality of death and life. If mortality has not been abolished by God through the resurrection it is because creaturely finitude is a parable, an image, an echo and thereby given a new content in the life of God. Barth affirms openly that even 'the non-being to which we turn, and into which we can fall, actually is before God even though He turns away from it. In the form of His turning away from it, it is no less the object of the divine knowledge than that which is before Him.'[165] Even nothingness is in front of God something that is.

Commenting on Lk. 20.38, which famously states that God is not the God of the dead but of the living since everything for him is alive, Barth writes that for this God 'all men are alive in their time. As such they will be revealed in the resurrection, and with their death the necessary cares which now lie like a cover over their lives will be lifted and left behind.'[166] One can see here that resurrection is the abolishing of 'the necessary cares' that we almost identify with life, such as the toil of survival, but what is more important is that by living eternally God is co-temporal with past, present and future, and lives with the dead as well as the living. It would not be an exaggeration to interpret Barth as arguing that it is the fact that the dead are alive for God that makes them subsist in a Meinongian sense for those who remember them. Otherwise, there would be no point in praying for the dead or hoping for their coming resurrection.

Theology, from this perspective, is the science of designating and naming what we with Meinong might call 'ideal Objects which do indeed subsist (*bestehen*), but which do not by any means exist (*existieren*) and consequently cannot in any sense be real (*wirklich*)'.[167] The resurrection, for instance, is from Barth's perspective real even if it is not here as a fact for all the dead and as Meinong stressed, 'the totality of what exists, including what has existed and will exist, is infinitely small in comparison with the totality of the objects of knowledge'.[168] It is easy to identify many objects that can be conceptualized, grasped and understood but which neither exist in space and time nor can be said to be real in a simple sense. These are mathematical abstractions, nonsensical objects such as golden mountains, square circles or perhaps resurrected dead, and similar non-existing phenomena which are, Meinong argues, outside being but still in a sense subsisting. These impossible, fictional or at least non-temporal and non-spatial objects reveal according to Brann the relation between Anselm and Meinong.[169]

The Mexican Calvinist theologian Adolfo García de la Sienra has similarly praised Meinong for criticizing 'the prejudice men have in the favour of the actual, a prejudice that favours the exaggeration consisting of treating the non-real (*Nichtwirkliche*) as a mere nothing (*bloßes Nicht*)'.[170] With the help of Meinong, García de la Sienra claims that Anselm rightly can deduce that existence is a property, since this is what differs a subsisting conceptual phenomenon, such as a golden mountain, from a phenomenon that is not only a figment of imagination but inherently real. By defining the reality of God as a necessary being, something that cannot not be, God is differentiated from all existence marked with contingency and the potential of non-being, and he becomes the force which can give reality to that which is possible since he is, as Barth would say, the *actus purus et singularis*: the only being that is by its own accord.

Tellingly, Barth's description of God's omniscience in 1940 as the knowledge which 'includes even non-being, even the merely possible and the impossible, even evil, death and hell, all things in their own way – but still all things' can almost be interpreted as a Meinongian idea of absolute knowledge.[171] An absolute omniscience does not know solely everything that is but all that could or for that matter could not be. God is not only that which gives being but also the being that makes everything that exceeds being possible since even that which does not exist in some manner is for him: 'Non-being also exists in its own way, not as something infinite, but as something finite, conditioned by the fact that God knows it. . . . and . . . there does not exist any being or non-being independent of Him, any object which is not an object of His knowledge, and therefore anything hidden from Him.'[172] If creaturely cognition by definition is finite and temporal, the cognition of God is something that includes what Meinong would call the world of *Aussersein* such as ideal objects like numbers or propositions or other – what we falsely or not think are non-real, non-existent objects such as the dead.[173] But what if death itself bestows the dead with that strange existence that cannot not be and which therefore transcends the two-dimensionality of life and death?

During the chaos of the Second World War, when Barth tried to express the content of eternity as the life, death and resurrection of Christ, he underlined that God elects not only our life but also our death as something that participates in his eternal life. 'Our being or non-being, our life or death', Barth wrote, 'is foreordained in the light of it. It is the predestination which in one way or another we must all fulfil. Everything else that happens to us is openly or secretly characterized by the fact that first and fundamentally this election has already taken place.'[174] The election, the fact that God has begun to redeem the world through the election of Christ, transforms death and non-being to something that participates in God's life. This argument was for Barth neither a denial of the brutal reality of the 1940s nor of the long violent history that humanity is still living in. It was, however, a denial that the disordered world of Nazism that Barth's theology of eternity challenged was the last word in the eschatological drama that, according to him, the Christ event meant.

God has not liberated creation from death or finitude as such – and therefore not from the tragedy of war or even human evil – but from what Barth called 'eternal death'.[175] This 'eternal death' is the death that forever separates the creature from God. We can only reach eternal life by dying away from time. Our finite and mortal existence, Barth clarified after the cataclysm of the Second World War, 'signifies something supremely positive if it is the case, as we have seen, that we come from God. It can be negative and evil only if our end means passing not only into non-being but into the negation of being.'[176] Life lives on outside the domain of what we falsely take to be being as such, namely the sphere of contingent existence in time and space. This argument reflects the doctrine of death that is developed in the *Göttingen Dogmatics*, where Barth returned to the classical theological typology of three forms of death: *mors corporalis*, bodily death; *mors spiritualis*, spiritual death; and *mors aeterna*, eternal death.

Death does not imply *annihilation* of being. It is *destruction* of a life and Barth writes that '[i]t is true that the *soul* cannot die in the same manner as the body, it cannot dissolve because it is not a composite. Its death is that undressing of the participation in the life of God, to which it is destined.'[177] Yet, even if the immortal soul cannot die a bodily death it can be dead in sins – and this is quite concretely also a *destruction* for Barth. The *mors spiritualis* separates the soul from God which is the source of all life. However, Barth continued, if the soul can be said to be immortal it is in fact, at the same time, abstracted from the life of the body through the bodily death which signifies the end of the human.

> Therefore, death as *mors corporalis* is the enemy of man, certainly the last enemy. Not even here is it advisable to ideologically transfigure reality. What it is in the light of the redemption must be learned from what it is in the light of the fall. The natural primitive shudder face to face with the dying is nearer to the deepest insight than a dialectic that transforms dying too quickly, at least in words, into life.[178]

The Christian should understand immortality as a resurrection of the flesh and bodily death as an end to the human as a psychophysical being. But *mors aeterna* is still the fundamental enemy to life. For, Barth continued, if one can say that we are dying the *mors spiritualis* and *corporalis* forever here and now by being fallen and mortal creatures, '[i]t is different with the third concept, the *mors aeterna*, in which the first ones are completed. It is as strictly eschatological as the opposing concept of eternal life. Eternal death is the existence of the whole spiritual-physical man in the absolute separation from the communion with God.'[179]

It is, for Barth, only the eternal death, *mors aeterna*, the death that annihilates not only life but the trace of life itself in the memory of God, which is death as such since it is only God that, in the end, is life – the being which cannot not be – and only the eternal dead are separated from God. The differentiation of spiritual and bodily death implies a thanatology that complicates the reading of Barth as a theologian who denied the immortality of the soul and defended a so-called *Ganztodtheorie*.[180]

At least in the *Göttingen Dogmatics*, Barth postulated that by dying the bodily death the soul has entered the subsisting world of non-existence and, arguably, joined the jungle of fictions and ideal objects that the living can refer to, be interpellated by and even hope for as they can be remembered.

This may seem to be a perspective foreign to Barth but in his book on prayer from 1949 he came close to arguing that his theology did not only imply a *Nachfolge* of Christ but a *Nachleben* of the dead. He explicated that it was common doctrine among Protestants during the sixteenth century that

> the saints of the Church and the faithful departed had no power to come to our aid. We may now perhaps add a question mark to such a categorical statement. I am not so sure that the saints of the Church are unable to help us.... We live in communion with the Church of the past, and from it we receive aid.[181]

He underlined 'that neither the living nor the dead can be for us what God is to us'.[182] But he accepted the relevance of prayer not only for but to the dead – and also, interestingly, to 'the saints who are alive on earth today' – since they have become the echoes of God that every creature is destined to become even if only negatively, as that which God not is.[183] And that which seems to not be can still interpellate us, such as fictional beings or those dead whom we remember and who thereby still touch us as the decisive beings they are.

Theology follows the mode of thought that Scripture reveals, and by doing so it seeks to open the believer to belief in 'the invisible side of the reality of the world [*die unsichtbare Seite der Weltwirklichkeit*]'.[184] Theology must become an investigation of this invisible world to which faith posits that the visible world is related. Our world is a duplicated world, where the difference between the dead and the living is not abolished but relativized since the resurrection has begun to put an end to eternal death.

The creature interpellated by the *verbum externum* is not in any sense a creature liberated from natural death.[185] It shall die but its death is a corporeal death, not an eternal death, since the dead do not enter nothingness but the eternity of God. Yet, since the meaning of death 'must be learned from what it is in the light of the fall' then the 'natural primitive shudder face to face with the dying is nearer to the deepest insight than a dialectic that transforms dying too quickly, at least in words, into life'. Death can still be hellish and seemingly eternal. Death is still a problem. It is the problem that reveals how humans are related to non-being.

In fact, Barth underlined in his lectures in Göttingen, that the reason why God did not 'conceal his deity in some other being, in a star or stone or animal, so as to be objective to us, so as to be comprehensible to us, so as to enable him to encounter us, to reveal himself as the hidden God' is because 'all the distinction, objectivity and nonrevelation comes into focus and becomes unambiguous only in the problem of man'.[186] This problem of the human, *Problem des Menschen*, is the problem of death since our species reveals the vastness and power of the domain of non-being that can be called hell.[187]

The problem of the human

All creatures are caught in the dialectic of life and death, and non-human animals mourn, feel grief and recognize loss. However, our species has privileged access to the domain of the non-existing by being able to conceive its almost absolute character. We are the creatures that have eaten from the tree of knowledge of good and evil and oscillate between truth and falsehood, goodness and evil, being and nothingness since to know the difference between good and bad is to know the difference between life and death, being and nothingness. The problem of the human is the ethical problem produced by our proximity to nothingness and death.

When Barth in 1945 turned to the saga of the creation in order to explicate the possibility of a sabbatical life that is not forced to die nor to struggle for its existence, he wanted to show that the prelapsarian human was a problem neither for God nor for himself. It was, as I have argued, when the human became aware of the problem of death that the human turned into a fallen being, since with 'this knowledge he will necessarily die, i.e., the process of his life will be changed into a process of death, and his return to dust, the removal of the soul and life given to him, will be irrevocably introduced'.[188] God created a world of creatures with autonomy from him and warned the humans what would happen if they left their innocent and paradisal life. The creator wanted 'to safeguard man against the threat connected with the doing of what is prohibited'.[189] Here Barth stressed that the human had the opportunity to leave his innocence in order to become like a god. However, since the human is a creature and not a deity, the attempt to become a god makes him mortal and banishes him from the abundance of life in 'paradise where there were no schools and no police' since human life did not know death and did not live in a world governed by death and the goodness and evil it creates.[190]

George S. Hendry has underlined the Kantian origins of Barth's theory of the fall as the birth of freedom and evil, and points to the Prussian philosopher's description of Genesis as 'a springboard for an inquiry into the conditions or presuppositions of the possibility of history, the subject of which he saw as freedom'.[191] In a satirical text, which Kant described as 'a movement of the power of imagination' the philosopher asked how freedom can arise out of the realm of nature and necessity.[192] Barth in his turn used the saga of creation to explicate the possibility of another form of life. He read Genesis not as a mythological explanation of how the world was created, but as an eschatological saga of the meaning of a life that is reduced to a struggle for existence in a world ruled by scarcity.

Myth has a narrative form and is often more dramatic than the biblical saga of the creation but, from Barth's perspective, it only reproduces the eschatological structure of creation that Scripture posits if it is sublated by the word of God.[193] Myth, in other words, belongs to the dependency of nature that the sagas of the Bible put in crisis. For myth, Barth argues, has a 'non-historical and timeless and abstract sense. Genuine myth makes use of the form of creation saga, but it only makes use of it'.[194] Myth belongs more to science and philosophy than theology since it does not describe the temporal transformation that nature is said to partake in according to the biblical tradition. It seeks to describe nature as such, rather than its transformation.

Kant's turn to the power of imagination has its correlation in Barth's argument that the saga of creation is a product of truthful imagination that the 'middle-class habit of the modern Western mind which is supremely phantastic in its chronic lack of imaginative phantasy' cannot apprehend.[195] For Barth, '[i]magination, too, belongs no less legitimately in its way to the human possibility of knowing. A man without imagination is more of an invalid than one who lacks a leg.'[196] His theology is an affirmation of imagination since the revelation is given to us as a poetic saga and not as a philosophical doctrine or scientific system.

Kant came close to Barth's understanding of the creation story as a saga when he notices how the Bible depicts the anthropogenesis of our species as the emergence of a fully developed humanoid in a garden with the ability to '*stand* and *walk*; he could *speak* . . . even discourse, i.e. speak according to connected words and concepts, hence *think*'.[197] Unlike us, however, our primordial forefather lacked one crucial thing: freedom. 'Instinct, that *voice of God* which all animals obey' ruled Adam and 'allowed him a few things for nourishment, but forbade him others'.[198] The fall of Adam and Eve is an exodus from a life fully ruled by the natural drive, and implies the emergence of reason because 'with the assistance of the power of the imagination it [reason] can concoct desires not only *without* a natural drive directed to them [Adam and Eve] but even *contrary* to it [the natural drive]'.[199] The fact that the first human couple did not listen to the instinct or natural drive, in other words God's command, that impelled them to avoid the tree of knowledge led them out of the garden and made them free from the bondage of nature.

This flight from the necessity of nature was, Kant stressed, the 'first attempt of a free choice' and, beautifully, he wrote that '*[r]efusal*' is the birth of a human freedom as 'a faculty of choosing . . . a way of living and not being bound to a single one, as other animals are'.[200] The human as we know our species is born and this humanoid is not only a creature exiled from the blissful state of abundant life in the Garden of Eden. The human is also an animal that can differentiate right from wrong. Our species is a race of animals *forced* to choose in a world of scarce resources and therefore *forced* to struggle for its existence. The human has become an ethical being in the quite tight room for manoeuvre of postlapsarian life with all the external and internal burdens, pressures and limits that constitute it.

Tellingly, Barth argued in a similar way that 'Adam and Eve before the fall had no conscience to the extent that the ethical question was very simply posed by the command of life itself, not by a judicial voice in themselves which is in fact to be distinguished from this command which we call conscience'.[201] Ethics, in the form of an almost impossible choice between what may be good or bad, was not needed by the prelapsarian humans since the abundance of life made such choices meaningless. We have morality due to the simple fact that we have erected a world where life has become a problem to be solved.

As we have seen, Barth would later insist that he did not believe in 'the attempted human answers to the ethical question' since the problem that ethics seek to answer can only be solved 'as it was originally put – by the grace of God, by the fact that this allows man actually to *be* the answer' to the problem of the human.[202] Before the fall humanity was the answer to the ethical question since there existed no differentiation between what Barth called 'the command of life' and 'the command of God'. Freedom was not the ability to take a decision in a world of scarce resources. It was the freedom to live in relation to God's abundance.

If the fall was produced by Adam and Eve's wilful disobedience then human will reflects the disobedience of the fall. Our will is potentially a will to refuse the command of God which, for Barth, primarily implies an inability to understand life as something eternal. It is a free will as it is a will to refusal or what Friedrich Nietzsche called a will to power, which Barth interpreted as an evolutionary capacity for survival in a Darwinian sense. To 'be powerful', he wrote, 'means to be successful in maintaining one's life by using whatever help the creaturely life around us affords, and overcoming the obstacles it poses. This will for power is the will to succeed in this way.'[203] It is important to note that this will is not in itself problematic for Barth. It is a necessity for survival in a fallen world: 'The simple affirmation of life, the will to satisfy our natural needs, the will to be healthy, the will to be happy, and the will to be individual all mean that I also have the will for power.'[204] The will for power is the biological will to survive and our 'life-act', Barth argued, is 'neither good nor bad . . . but reveals itself to be good or bad in the encounter with God's command'.[205] Once again, it is by being related to something outside our own life, to the 'alien life', 'the life of another which only the other, not I, can will to live', that our life is put into question and we are given that which Adam and Eve lacked: conscience.[206] Only if 'there is a concrete fellowship with God the Redeemer, then and only then there is such a thing as conscience' for this gift is only given to us if we understand that life can be lived for something else than the simple perpetuation of our existence.[207]

Attacking Herbert Spencer's Darwinian theory of morality and the rise of a naturalistic ethics grounded on the struggle for survival, which only four years later would find one of its political expressions in the parliamentary victory of NSDAP, Barth stated that our will to live 'changes when we understand the command of life as the command of the Creator of life. Thus understood the command implies – and this already makes impossible the ringlike arrangements of Spencer's ethics – a radical relativizing of my will to live as the will to live my *own* life.'[208] For, Barth continues, 'if in my attention a space has been created for a life that is not my own, this liberated attention, which we cannot direct to the life of God as such' is opened for 'the *creaturely life outside and alongside us*.'[209] While Barth claimed in 1924 that it was the human subject that posited the problem of human life, he argued five years later that all living beings can question our will. The human is the animal that can understand the ethical importance of all life, not only or even mainly, human life.

Pointing to what the Swiss theologian and physician Albert Schweitzer called 'reverence for life', Barth wrote that 'a person is truly ethical only when he follows the compulsion to help all life that he can, and is hesitant to do harm to anything living. He does not ask how far this life is valuable and deserves sympathy nor does he ask whether or how far it is capable of feeling. Life as such is sacred for him. He does not pluck a single leaf from a tree or break a flower and is careful not to crush insects.'[210] Barth stressed that Schweitzer included the whole region of life, from plants to animals, in his eschatological ethics and wrote that 'those who can only laugh' at the theologian's care for 'the insect that has fallen into a pond ... are themselves a little deserving of our tears.'[211] At the point where one could believe that Barth would argue for radical veganism, he concurred that it 'is certainly not an accident that Schweitzer himself did not take up service in an animal hospital but did the work of a native doctor in Central Africa.'[212] We are finite beings, and our moral choices are relative and embedded in the economy of sin that first of all reveals itself in this world as scarcity and lack, for life 'is always life *and* death, becoming *and* decaying, in virtue of which the big fish does not greet the little fish but eats it.'[213] Barth did never deny that being, in this fallen world, is eating, as Feuerbach would say. We are forced to choose whom we want to help, and our actions often imply destruction. Yet, our conscience will necessarily contradict our choices and ask us if we did the right thing and thereby point to the need of a freedom beyond the choice between good and evil. We are haunted by the undone and the possible, since we live not only in the order of being but in the domain of what could be, and this is the real meaning of the problem of the human: we have become free to live in and for eternal life and therefore for the Edenic superabundance that death turns into something scarce and finite. Only eternal life can give us a freedom that liberates us from choice.

Kant had argued that if the 'history of nature ... begins from good, for that is the *work of God*' then 'the history of freedom' commences with 'evil, for it is the *work of the human being*'.[214] Nature, the order of creation, commences from good because it is the work of God, but history begins with the fall and therefore with the radical evil of humanity. Barth agreed with this mythological interpretation of the problem of the human. But he insisted that 'the command of God' interpellates the postlapsarian existence – the being who does evil as well as good deeds – from its future, resurrected state.

What we do as humans can, at best, be a mirroring of God's yes or no and often this doing is nothing but evil in the most banal sense. But this '*work of the human being*', or 'the command of life', is contradicted by 'the command of God' that Barth describes as 'a radical *relativizing* of my will to live as the will to live my own life'.[215] To read 'the command of life' in relation to 'the command of God' is to understand that when 'we have a conscience we are not on our own'.[216] When 'my conscience speaks to me, I am *addressed*' and therefore interpellated from something that comes from the outside.[217] Conscience is '*syn-eidesis, con-scienta*, our human knowing of what, not merely according to our own presuppositions, God alone can know as he who is good'.[218] We evil, or, as what Barth would call us, ethical beings are interpellated by that which is not ourselves and that which is most foreign to us – and at the same time most close to us – is God.

Our conscience has the same structure as the limited *Hineinstreben* of our will into the life of God, which Barth discussed in his work on Anselm just a couple of months after he finished his second lecture series on ethics. To have a conscience is to be mirrored and questioned in the life of God through the encounter with the 'alien life' that is outside and alongside us and which makes our life a problem: 'An alien life is the life of another which only the other, not I, can will to live. But more important than what we will is *how* we will.'[219]

I can now deduce that Barth's theology of eternal life as a victory not over *mors temporalis* but over *mors aeterna* implies the transformation of the modus of the life instinct, the how of our will. It may be impossible for the human to overcome biological and natural death. But it is possible to believe that there is no eternal death and that the meaning of our often nonsensical existence is something other than mere creaturely survival or for that matter something more than a sophisticated cultural or learned life.[220]

Life is necessarily finite life since it is temporal. Yet, as a mortal, temporal and even more metabolic existence, life is also eternal since eternity is that which is *with* time and this is, for Barth, the reason why all life should be revered, even if we cannot live without consuming, destroying and even eating other living beings. We cannot end death. But we can transform the modality of our life – the how of our will – by seeking to open us for the 'alien life'.

Our actions and inactions embed us not only in time but in the divine life that forces itself upon us postlapsarian creatures as a 'reverence for life' for we humans are addressed by the problem of death and non-being as something that should not be. Eternal life intensifies, rather than devalues, this life, finite and present life, by forcing us to accept that what we do, we do once for all. The insect that we kill is killed forever and the undone action is never done. Still if non-being for God is something that exists in front of him as something finite, as something that is, then life is more than temporal, spatial and even actual. It is embedded in the eternal that can resurrect the life that should have been and remake that which was. There is, in other words, no resurrection without the possibility of retrocausality: the transformation of the past.

It is this eternal dimension of our finite actions that reveals that we are duplicated in the invisible life of God. By dying away in time, we are written into the eternal, since even non-being is something that is for God, and in this sense our dreams, hopes and wishes – and even more all our unlived lives – are as important for God as our actions.

Human life is not only the deeds and actions that took place in space and time. The vaster domain of life is what never happened. Thus, faith – and consequently hope and love – is as important as our actions since many of us are unable to do anything more than to regret what we have done, lament over how we have lived and despair over what has happened to us.

The disordered world reduces us often to a state of hope that we could be otherwise than what we are, and it is this hope that is more than us. It is the need for the other that is human, and even more, eternal life. Life from this perspective is never only the 'command of life', the 'simple affirmation of life' or 'the more primitive necessities of eating, drinking, sleeping, and growing old'. Life is the eternal in which even non-being, perhaps especially non-being, is entangled, since the redemption of existence is also the resurrection of all unlived, dreamt, unsatisfied and too short lives into the eternity of God. God desires to save that which should have been, the abundance of our lost paradisal existences, from the world of death through the resurrection of all those actions and inactions that have been lost in time. Yet, we must ask, what does this abundant modality – the how of the eternal will – imply here and now, in a world ruled by mortality, scarcity and the struggle for survival?

Political thanatology

In a sermon on death just a couple of months after the outbreak of the First World War in 1914, Barth said to his congregation, '[t]hrough war, death has suddenly become an important matter for millions. In endless rows, they already lie out there tucked up under foreign grass, and endless rows will still have to follow them.'[221]

Barth did not preach to his flock that they should avoid the finality, or even necessity, of death. He asked them to view life as something that has death as its prerequisite even when no war, pandemic or other global catastrophe haunted them. Nature is a boundless vanishing of the living and even a destruction of the dead through the destruction of cities and erosion of mountains: 'Every plant, every little animal, but not only they, the stars of the heaven, the sun as well as our earth, they have their existence for some time, and after that all is at an end for them.'[222]

Life itself is enmeshed in this death that encapsulates the cosmos as such and commenting on Heb. 9.27, which states that all creatures shall perish, Barth turned dying to the culminating point which gives life a specific content: 'Our physical life waits for us to give it a spiritual content, then it dies out like everything in the world. God does not die.'[223] These words, to an extent echoing what he later would call our spiritual death, *mors spiritualis*, which awaits our physical life, entail that 'life emerges out of death' in the sense that death opens us for the eternity of God.[224]

This is from Feuerbach's perspective a good example of the unnatural idea that death can be abolished. But Barth wanted his fellow Christians to understand that the hope for the resurrection of the dead is something else than an intellectualization of a primordial human urge to overcome the finitude of life.[225] Resurrection is a transvaluation of the nonsense and meaningless of death to something that gives sense to the eternal, and the eternal is the redemption of that which was. This retroactive change of the past is what the resurrection promises. By promising to release us from the shackles of being, understood as that which happened in time and space, and give life the abundance it has lost by being trapped into the scarcity and finitude that force us to choose, moralize and valorize, the resurrection can make us understand how life is more than a biological existence. Life is what could, or even more should, have been and life is related to other life as something that should be revered and even accepted as the possibility for my own existence. Life is eternal and, therefore, paradoxically necessitous. It is implicated in the web of life that emerges from the outside: from the life outside life that is God.

In another sermon from 1914, Barth addressed the theological debate on immortality and resurrection by painting the Christian as a stoic virtuoso with the power to relativize the difference between life and death. Using Meister Eckhart's idea of serenity or tranquillity, *Gelassenheit*, he depicted an existence that can laugh in the face of death. But Barth underlined, '[s]erenity is however not the highest and final word against death. We hear of the contempt for death amongst the ancient Romans or the modern Japanese, we admire them, but we do not trust them to have the right value and the right depth.'[226] They can teach us that death has to be accepted as the limit that makes life possible. Yet, for Barth, this indifference is insufficient and is not even the right attitude towards death.

> We observe also often among us a certain indifference to death, which is more similar to the boredom of life and fear of death than to the fine, majestic manner

in which God stands above death. . . . Does God then despise death?, we must ask. One despises an enemy: death, however is not God's enemy. Death just as life are after all the same in God's hands, yes, they are for him like dear children, both with their special vocation.[227]

The right attitude towards death is not stoic serenity, but the belief that death is one of God's creatures, an occurrence which, just as life, has a mission in the providential plan of God. Death is related to God's eternal no, but this no is part of the eternal yes. 'There is', Barth stated in 1921, 'no such thing as death in itself; there is only death in relation to God.'[228] *Post Christum* there is only the death of death, a death of the two-dimensionality of existence and non-existence, being and non-being, past and future, that God transcends by being that which cannot be conceived not to be. Everything, even death and non-being, is in God's hands, something that labours for eternal life, for life is no longer our present life. Just as death is death only in relation to God, life is also only life in relation to God, and eternal life is the life of not only that which was but of what could be; a life for all those who are crushed or killed by the world of the fall.

Consequently, if the hope for resurrection is something else than fear of death this is because the cultivation of the individual human as a creature partaking in the eternal life of God is a transformation of this fear to an acceptance of death as one of God's creatures. One finds here a transmutation of the theme that, according to Feuerbach, produces religion: the desire to abolish death and this is what it means to transform the how of our will. The one who sees that life is more than 'the command of life', best visible in the struggle for survival – which in our world easily can be sublimated to the struggle for a good life – transforms his view on death.

Barth's search for a transvaluation of death and his Paulinian insistence that death *post Christum* has lost its sting have made some of his critics claim that he views 'death as a natural phenomenon. *Thanatos* becomes an ally who resolves one's life and escorts one to the eternal mode of life. Even if God alone grants immortality, death has become His chief servant. In Barth's schema, the Christian hope for eternal life is barely distinguishable from a longing for death.'[229] This is a comment on Barth's view on death and immortality during and after the Second World War, but it seems to be a valid criticism of his sermons on death in 1914.

In 1944, he returned to these themes of death as an obedient servant and said that '[e]very man, also every great, important, good man, has his totally determined circle of life, his room, his time, his power and his opportunities, but therefore also his limit, that he cannot exceed'.[230] Barth turned death into a servant of God that takes us to eternal life, but only because he wanted to underline the finite character of creaturely existence. Death is part of life. Without mortality there would not be eternal life for the mortals since eternity is the redemption of those destroyed and unlived lives that follow us finite beings as the infinite set of worlds that never was. This abundance is what eternity must imply: the redemption of all that which could or did not take place in space and time, but which nevertheless is in the eyes of God just as the actions never taken or the words never said can stay in the hearts and minds of men and women. For life, as we know, is longing, desiring and imagining. It is sometimes solely a hope in a vale of tears: a scream that this cannot be all or, more desperately, should not be.

In 1948, Barth would explicitly argue that '[t]here is a dying which throws no doubt on man's participation in the resurrection and life of Jesus Christ. Death in this sense is not ruled out by man's hope in a resurrection' for when 'he is freed for eternal life, he is also freed for natural death'.[231] The Christian must remember death, *memento mori*, since this remembrance of death is *memento Domini*, remembrance of the Lord, and a celebration of creaturely life as a limited existence that by being finite can live in the eternal.[232]

This may seem to be an outrageous message in a world which experienced the cataclysm of two world wars and the horrors of the Holocaust. However, Barth clearly understood that faith in God is not a simple refutation of death, and to proclaim that in a period when the lives of millions were sacrificed on the altars of the nation and state would in the end be a proclamation of ideological nonsense. War, extreme poverty, Nazism, fascism, the atom bomb and the Holocaust did not move Barth to abandon his political thanatology – for him these horrors could only be succumbed by the hope that death would be conquered by God.

God has not abolished natural death; we live in a world where everything – even the universe as such – one day shall come to an end. But God has, in Barth's opinion, revealed that we can live for something else than 'the command of life'. Not because present life is not worth living, but because the modality of life can be given another form than the struggle for life, and we can therefore enter a kind of mad joy that makes us question what is most natural for life. Yet, only if we are able to really flourish and live a good life.

We have to be given the possibility to become something other than what we are since redemption, as Barth understood it, comes from the outside and a life that is only struggle, only misery, only sorrow – or for that matter only the attempt to fulfil one's own desires here and now – closes itself too easily for the new and that which could be. Consequently, for Barth, the victory over eternal death becomes a political demand that society should be organized according to the principle *suum cuique*, to each its own, so that every limited creature is able to meet death in peace as that which joins us with eternity.

> Where does our life come from? From its beginning, i.e., the beginning of its time, before which it did not exist. Where is it going? Towards its end, i.e., the end of its time, after which it will be no longer. Why not? Because it is creaturely life in its creaturely dimension. Because by acquiring creaturely time it acquires as its time the dimension appropriate to it as a creaturely life. The life of God requires and has a different dimension. For the life of God is not only unfathomable and inexhaustible, but self-grounded and self-creative, welling up from within itself. That is why it is eternal life, and why eternity is its dimension. In clear distinction from His, our life too acquires the dimension it needs, a dimension which fits and suits it like a tailor-made garment. *Suum cuique*![233]

These words are from 1948, but Barth had already in the 1930s pointed to the political principle *suum cuique*, which can be translated into 'to each his own' or 'may all get their due' as a hermeneutical key to his notion of death as a necessary limit to creaturely life. Barth traced the principle of the *suum cuique* to Jean Calvin and Frederick the Great, and it was interpreted by John Locke as the principle 'that there can only be justice where there is property, and even private property'.[234] The equation of that which is mine with private property is, Barth's friend and theological adversary Emil Brunner comments, 'comprehensible, but none the less a fallacy. It is true that justice is always concerned with mine and thine, and for that very reason, never the person qua person, but with the person in view of "something." That mine and thine, however, does not necessarily need to be a material object, a thing owned or possessed.'[235] The *suum cuique* may be the limited existence between life and death, or for that matter the whole interim period between the resurrection and the second coming which marks the time of the creation as a time that one day shall end.

Here Barth and Brunner agree, for thine and mine are our common destiny, it is a life limited by death and in the end by eternity itself. The principle that governs Barth's ethics is this eschatological *suum cuique*, the boundary that God has posited for every creature through death as the culmination where life and eternity merge into an eternal life. The new modality of our will has this *suum cuique* as material condition: every creaturely life should be given its allotted time in order to live in peace and thereby reflect the eternal life of God in time, if only through the unlived life it casts as a shadow. The *suum cuique* is the time and space needed to turn the scarce resources of the world to an instrument that can form a way of life that is capable of giving without asking anything in return.

In this sense our finite life can become abundant by beginning to share God's promiscuous love to everything that was, is and will be. This is the only way for the human to become the answer to the problem of ethics. We must make ourselves capable of solely living by eating the food that is God.

The *suum cuique* should be the basis for a life that is able to question the borders between mine and thine and see what we have in common with all life: our mortal and finite existence, our scarce resources, our allotted time. Thus, just as 'life emerges out of death', abundance emerges out of scarcity and perhaps even more poverty, for it is only a life that can transform that which is finite to something infinite that can turn poverty to affluence. The abundance of eternal life is not that which is; it is the richness of the paradisal which we can equate with the eternal since eternity is the life of everything lost that is found in God. It is not a coincidence that Barth in 1938 concluded one of his attacks on Nazism by putting the *suum cuique* in relation to the passing away of life into death: 'in the midst of this "world that passeth away," in the midst of the great, but temporary contrast between Church and State, in the period which the Divine patience has granted us between the resurrection of Jesus Christ and His return: [there is the] *Suum cuique*.'[236]

The *suum cuique* with its postulation of a limit to our life, a limit brought forth by death itself, is in the end the vast chasm that posits the creature as creature and God as God, and this has according to Barth ethical and political consequences. By being limited and furthermore mortal every human *should* be able to live a life redeemed from the choices that the fall forces upon us. Only thereby, in this freedom from choice, can it mirror the rest and joy that define God's eternity. The human *should* be given the right to be a creature bordering to death in peace. The *suum cuique* was for Barth an appraisal of a democratic and egalitarian society that could, in some manner, exist as a secular parable of God's abundant life.[237] Nonetheless, even with that democratic and republican ideal in mind, Barth's defence of the *suum cuique* can give a bitter taste if it is remembered that the Nazis put the motto *Jedem das Seine*, to each his own, on the main gate of the concentration camp Buchenwald in 1937.[238]

The Marxist architect Franz Ehrlich, who was imprisoned in Buchenwald, made the sign which mockingly described the lives of all the people who supposedly were given their dues in the hell of Buchenwald. Still, it must be underlined, for Barth the *suum cuique* signalled that God, and not the powers of the world, is the ultimate authority over the limited existence that is bestowed on the human as the space-time where she has the potential to enjoy her creaturely existence.

Life cannot always be affirmed – Barth was no pacifist, and he surely understood the need to fight against Nazism with military means – and he did not naïvely believe that everyone was given its own. The fall did not only give the human, but nature as such, the ability and even need to kill and take life.

Death itself makes life something scarce that has to differentiate mine from thine. Still, if death is also that which makes everything that we do eternal by moving us into the past, where that which was rests with all our unlived lives, then we can try to understand how we are duplicated by the *eudemonic* and *kakodemonic* powers that write us into the saga of God. The *suum cuique* is the place and time where we encounter the invisible by dying away from a life that has been freed from the obedience of God to become a living hell. Thus, death is God's obedient servant only if we humans struggle to erect a political order that makes us capable of revering all creaturely life, and therefore to resist the powers of the fall by seeking to make finite life dignified.

Only a life that is given the chance to mirror the innocence, joy and rest of God is a life that reflects his eternity as something else than his no to fallen existence. The creature that is given the space and time needed to mirror the divine is what Barth came to call 'the strange saint' who, with tears and laughter, provokes God and in this provocation is obedient to the election that transforms death into life.[239]

Quite beautifully, Barth wrote, '[t]he total seriousness of decision on face of God's command can reach a climax in our having to laugh and not just cry and gnash our teeth, in our having to make the best of a bad job.'[240] The nonsense of life is this bad job that we are allotted as fallen creatures and the sense of our nonsensical lives is perhaps the ability to laugh and enjoy our lives as long as they last.

We laugh since we know that there is another sense to life beyond the command of life which only can end if life, as we know it, ends. The *suum cuique* is the space and time given to the creature so that it can live for something else, something more mysterious than human existence, and by doing so participate in the transformation of the world into eternal life. Yet, such a *suum cuique* is never one's own existence; it is the vast world of 'alien life'. The human, as the most necessitous of creatures, needs an abundant life to exist. But it also necessitates everything that is not life. It needs death and death is not only the eclipse of the human individual. Everything living in time is destined to die and thereby enter the eternal.

The logical conclusion of Barth's theology of eternal life, is that everything – even evil, even death and hell itself – labours for the kingdom of God by dying away from time. The *usus* of theology, the practical application that biblical *Nachdenken* entails, is to help the one with faith to follow this labour that releases us from the seriousness of life by interpellating us with the belief that life should not be lived for the struggle for power and survival. Instead, by mirroring God we shall participate in the strange future after both death and time which prompts us to become ready to exist as something more joyful than the ethical beings who, governed as we are by the economy of the fall, lack the imagination to understand how life emerges out of death just as abundance can arise out of scarcity. For Barth, a new creation can emerge out of our dying world.

Barth's theology can be read as a prolegomenon to a theology of extinction, a contemporary theology that confronts the cosmological problem of the end of not only the human species but of the coming destruction of the universe as such. The *suum cuique* could then be seen as the vast eon of the cosmos itself, and the sense of this world, which one day will vanish, may be the joyful but at the same time painful insight that because the cosmos is temporal and finite it is also eternalized as that which once was. This does not entail that the eternalized world shall forever be what it became by dying and vanishing into the past. Barth urges us to hope that the cosmos shall be resurrected as what it should have been from the standpoint of its creation: a world undisturbed by the death that the resurrection has made God's servant. Life, from this perspective, entails the imperative that we should not only live in relation to the world of the dead and the living but even more seek to reflect the abundance of the unlived and the paradisal.

3

The animal of the infinite
Oskar Goldberg and the science of evil

When Jacob Taubes searched for information about the Oskar Goldberg circle after the Second World War, he received a letter from Isidore Hepner, who professed his admiration for the forgotten Jewish mythologist:

> My loyalty to OG is of a purely factual nature. Through him I have found the way back to Judaism as many others have.... And the crucial point is in fact this: the problem of theodicy.... He is the only one who could give a satisfactory answer to why there is suffering in the world, from where evil comes, from where the imperfections [woher die Unvollkommenheiten].[1]

Already before the Shoah, Goldberg had interpreted the Torah as a ponerology – a science of evil. The five books of Moses described how God sought to implement a covenant with his creation to counter the evil of suffering and death that was a necessary product of a finite world.

Goldberg emphasized in *Die Wirklichkeit der Hebräer* that the Hebrew *tov* and *ra*, good and evil, should not be understood in a moral sense. They signify what is positive and negative, or even pleasurable or not, for biological organisms. They constitute the conflict – *Zweispalt* – that is nothing but the 'biological principle' which rules life as a contradiction that casts death as its necessary shadow, and it was this natural fact that the Torah tried to transform.[2]

Referring to the American rabbi Simon Greenberg, Hepner wrote to Taubes:

> Should I be satisfied with an answer that I have received from Dr. Simon Greenberg from the theological seminary in New York, namely, that we do not know if death is an end? Certainly, immortality, re-incarnation, reward and punishment are open problems, but according to Gr. the Nazis in Nurnberg could have argued that they wanted to create a better, higher world for the gassed Jews.[3]

Most classical philosophy and theology gave, according to Hepner, unsatisfactory, incoherent and even contradictory answers to the question of why there is death and suffering in the world. The theological genius of Goldberg was that he had understood that the problem of immortality was related to *this* world and *this* life, and therefore to the presence of God here and now.

Goldberg's main thesis was that the myths and rituals in the Pentateuch were centred on a God who has to be differentiated from the God of the rest of Tanakh who rules as a mysterious power in heaven. The story in the Torah about the *mishkan*, the tabernacle of God, depicts the physical presence of a deity that seeks to overcome the misfortunes of the world without abolishing the world as a world in time and space. Thus, when God was, as Goldberg puts it in one of his essays, 'banished to heaven' he was no longer dwelling as a finite being in the temporal and spatial world that we humans live in and could only promise a hope of salvation after death. This absent God – whom the world religions Judaism, Christianity and Islam worship – cannot redeem his creation from the violence of a world that, from Goldberg's perspective, ultimately made the Shoah possible, without becoming present.

In this chapter I shall follow Hepner's suggestion and ask if *Die Wirklichkeit der Hebräer* can give us a 'metaphysics after Auschwitz'.[4] It was Theodor W. Adorno who insisted that through 'Auschwitz – and by that I mean not only Auschwitz but the world of torture which has continued to exist after Auschwitz and of which we are receiving the most horrifying reports from Vietnam – . . . the concept of metaphysics has been changed to its innermost core'.[5] These catastrophes made the notion 'that existence or being has a positive meaning constituted within itself and orientated towards the divine principle' to a 'pure mockery in face of the victims and the infinitude of their torment'.[6] One could ask why not the idea of a God could be a way to judge this evil as an absolute evil since religion has been said to arise from both wonder and dismay.[7] More importantly, Goldberg's reading of the Torah did not give being meaning by relating it to the divine. Hebrew metaphysics sought not primarily to explain reality but transform it.

Adorno dismissingly scorned 'the powers of Oskar Goldberg' in *Negative dialectics*, and mentioned the Jewish scholar and his follower Erich Unger in his lectures on the sociology of music.[8] Despite that, he never engaged with the Goldberg circle in a serious manner. This is unfortunate since the Jewish mythologist disclosed another path to metaphysics than the one Adorno chose.

Beginning with Aristotle, Adorno insisted that metaphysics 'starts out from an everyday, rational, sensible consciousness and attempts, by reflecting on what is given directly by the senses, to attain insight into true being – instead of presupposing this existence of an essential realm, as was the case in archaic thought'.⁹ In contrast, Goldberg read the Torah as an axiomatic system that defended a metaphysics based on the disjunction between what is and what could be that archaic thought made possible. There existed an 'essential realm', namely, the infinite domain of the possible.

> The world, as the epitome of all that exists, consists of a finite and an infinite part. By finitude is to be understood everything that is in space and time, that which is *real* [was *wirklich* ist]; by infinity, on the other hand, that which is not in space and time, but which will or can reach the spatio-temporal part of the world. Infinity is thus the epitome of everything that can be described as possible.¹⁰

The metaphysics of the Torah arose from the differentiation between 'the revealed, finite reality' and 'the unrevealed, infinite part of reality', and the rites in the Torah were ways to open the world to the vast realm of possibility that in the end is God himself: the *Elohim IHWH*, who revealed himself for Abraham as the Lord of lords: the God of all gods.¹¹ Abraham gathered a tribe worshipping this foreign God on the outskirts of civilization by calling men and women to abandon the mythical gods, the other *Elohim* described in the Torah.

The Torah was according to Goldberg part of an 'epoch of myth' when humanity lived with their gods in a manner that is close to the American psychologist Julian Jaynes's controversial theories of the rise of modern subjectivity.¹² Jaynes argued that the I-centred and self-reflective consciousness of the modern period was not older than about 3,000 years. This introspective consciousness, laying the basis for the Greek philosophy which Adorno argued was the beginning of metaphysics, originates in the emergence of linguistic capacities, mainly the development of metaphorical language. These new skills reflect the workings of our mental life as something that does not only express the demands of the external world.¹³ Humanity had, Jaynes wrote, lived most of its life without a modern self-reflective consciousness. Our species had, in the period of myth, a much more porous existence since the limit between inner and outer life was not as distinct as it would become later.

'Consciousness', Jaynes insisted, 'is a much smaller part of our mental life than we are conscious of, because we cannot be conscious of what we are not conscious of.'¹⁴ Consciousness is for Jaynes not experience. It is identical with the self-consciousness needed for self-reflective thought. The majority of our mental and physical activities is not conscious in this sense; everything, from walking to playing piano, is normally done without conscious knowledge, and when we reflect on what we are doing, we have to stop acting and begin to contemplate.[15] The growth of this form of self-reflection, Jaynes argued controversially, makes the left hemisphere of the brain more active and produces a psychophysical change in the human condition.

Slowly, through new cognitive acts and linguistic capacities a self-reflective consciousness gradually emerged that replaced the bicameral mind, in which the left hemisphere of the brain obeyed the right hemisphere that spoke to it in a hallucinatory manner.

For the bicameral mentality, or what Goldberg called the mythical mind, acts such as volition, planning and initiative were supposedly 'organized with no consciousness whatsoever and then "told" to the individual in his familiar language, sometimes with the visual aura of a familiar friend or authority figure or "god", or sometimes as a voice alone'.[16] The bicameral mind was hallucinatory and experienced the presence of what Goldberg described as gods.

The ancient mythological literature, such as the Torah, seldom refers to the mental life of its characters. Divinities and demons command, and the people listen, since, Jaynes stipulates, a self-reflective consciousness with an adequate mental language is lacking. Thus, he argued controversially, in the period of the bicameral mind humans felt that they lived in a world where divinities and spirits determined their actions and ruled over their lives, and in this sense Jaynes's theories strengthen Goldberg's hypothesis that there existed an age of myth when gods lived together with human tribes.

Without accepting Jaynes's theory as anything other than a heuristic device, I shall use it to interpret what Goldberg called 'the epoch of myth' as a period when parts of our species believed that they lived with their gods as present and real powers. If for Jaynes this presence could be explained biologically and linguistically as the lack of an introspective consciousness, Goldberg insisted that these deities should be understood anthropologically and psychophysically as collective life forms.

Jaynes thought that this mythic mentality gradually began to change around 1200 BC with the Bronze Age collapse. The decline and fall of civilizations such as the Kassites in Babylonia and the Hittite Empire in Anatolia spurred mass migrations and slowly created the need for a more self-reflective consciousness in a new environment. This new mentality is reflected in the Hebrew Bible which according to Jaynes describes a gradual 'loss of the bicameral mind, and its replacement by subjectivity of the first millennium B.C.'[17] For Goldberg, the Torah is part of this transformation of human mentality, but not primarily by laying the ground for the modern self-reflective consciousness. The emergence of this civilizational subjectivity was part of, if we believe Goldberg, state structures unable to live for something else than the '*animal* drive for self-preservation [*animalischen* Selbsterhaltungstrieb]'.[18]

The Hebrews discovered another way to break with the world of myth than through the emergence of modern subjectivity. By living in relation to the command of a deity that the Hebrews saw as the God of all gods, this people separated itself from the rest of the mythical peoples and their polytheistic pantheons. Still, the life of the Hebrews as it is told in the Torah was part of the mythical cosmos. The Torah implied a mutation of the mythic consciousness by positing a God who revealed that what Adorno described as myth's 'essential realm' did not imply a static universe of ruling powers. It showed the radical contingency of nature and why the parameters of biological life itself could change.

The 5,000-year-old world system

Taubes was fascinated by Goldberg as a young student of philosophy and religion.[19] He had met the Jewish mythologist as early as 1938 through his father, the rabbi Zwi Taubes, and wrote a critique of the Kabbalah in the spirit of *Die Wirklichkeit der Hebräer*.[20] The spell seems to have broken after the Second World War. In his article on Goldberg for the Partisan Review from 1954 he took Thomas Mann's position and exclaimed that 'Goldberg's philosophy of myth . . . threatens to usher in that tabula rasa of civilization for which conservatives today like to blame the "tyranny of Progress"'.[21]

It was Goldberg's insistence that the messianic potential of Judaism was found in the ritualistic origin of the Hebraic Scriptures, the Torah, rather than in the tradition of the prophets, which had made Mann base his portrait of the Jewish fascist Dr Chaim Breisacher in *Doctor Faustus* on him.[22]

Breisacher dreamt of a return to the world of ancient Hebrewdom, and was used by Mann as a symbol of the dangerous archaism that according to him had made Nazism possible. One might question why Mann, who himself had flirted with militarism and German nationalism, felt the need to use a Jewish thinker to depict the rise of Nazism. Especially since the critique of civilization that Goldberg and his circle defended was a violent rejection of fascism and the whole world that – according to them – ultimately had spawned this movement.

Fascism and similar totalitarian ideologies were not in any sense a regress to a cultic past for Goldberg. They belonged to the modern, European civilization that in spite of all his critique of Western civilization he saw his work as part of. He underlined explicitly that the emergence of modern, industrialized capitalism was the economic basis for the historical hermeneutics used in *Die Wirklichkeit der Hebräer*, and we will see that his work is related to the classics of modern anthropology.

Taubes acknowledged this to an extent and wrote that 'no modern philosopher has been so deeply influenced by the spirit of technology as Oskar Goldberg. For his interpretation of myth and ritual is given in a totally unsentimental and unliterary language, which could be taken from a textbook on electromagnetism.'[23] The God of the Hebrews, the *Elohim IHWH*, was portrayed in *Die Wirklichkeit der Hebräer* as an electric generator which produces currents of metaphysical energy pulsating through the cosmos.[24] However, Goldberg was a fierce critic of the industrialized world; what was modern in his work was his insistence on the experimental character of myth. Mythology, he claimed, was 'not a science of ancient times [*Altertumswissenschaft*] but transcendental research of current reality [*aktuelle transzendente Realitätsforschung*] – the people themselves are the objective for the scientific experiment: it is an ethnological experimental science.'[25]

In his article 'Die Bibelkritik', Goldberg compared the Torah with the pyramids by describing it as a ruin from a world long gone.[26] The classical theological reading of the Torah, both Jewish and Christian, which saw the five books of Moses as part of the Hebrew Bible, had to be replaced with an archaeological excavation of a world that must be distinguished from the rest of the Tanakh. The Torah depicted *Urjudentum*: 'the doctrine, which is contained in the oldest part of the Bible – the five books of Moses. . . . The Bible is not an ideological unit. Its books extend over a period of 1,500 years.'[27] Goldberg argued that the life world that the Torah described made it possible to discern two religious systems, which in turn can be differentiated in even more detailed periodizations, during this vast time period: 'the old religion of manifestations and miracle where God is on earth and engages in the fate of the people – and the late religion of faith that banishes God to heaven.'[28] Traditional theology belonged to the religion of faith in and worship of an omnipotent and absent God that, paradoxically, could not help his people since he was not present, whereas *Urjudentum* belonged to the mythical epoch where religion was based on ritual and the presence of the gods.

'Myth', Taubes argued in his dissertation *Occidental Eschatology* from 1947, 'is the "narrative" of origin. Myth answers the question of *whence*. The questions of whence and whither coincide in the eternal return of the same.'[29] Echoing Hermann Cohen's description of myth in *Ethik des Reinen Willens* as an 'incessant change in the birth and death of the world', an 'eternity of change' with 'no standstill and no duration', Taubes stipulated a necessary relation between myth, order and nature.[30]

Cohen had differentiated myth from religion, which he related to Plato's critique of mythology and the tradition of Hebraic prophets, by arguing that 'myth has no picture of the future; it places the peace of humans and of nature in the past, in the golden age. The prophet, in contrast, projects his ethics on the future. *The concept of the future distinguishes religion* from myth.'[31]

This religion of the future emerged with the prophets of the Tanakh, whom Cohen differentiated from the more mythical oriented Torah with its animal sacrifices and strict rituals.

Many myths have an eschatological structure by proclaiming an end – the myth of Ragnarök is a good example – and most eschatologies can be understood only through myths, such as the myth of the fall in Genesis. The difference between myth and religion was for Cohen structural, philosophical and political. The eschatology of myth embeds life in the cyclical order of nature and promises only justice through this eternal repetition or return to the beginning.

In contrast, the eschatology of religion transcends the self-closed cycle of nature by viewing history as the domain for the infinite task of correlating an unjust world with the divine justice of God.[32] Myth and religion are, as Jaynes would say, two distinct subjectivities. Religion represents the origin of modern subjectivity, whereas myth points back to the unreflective and even unconscious mentality of the bicameral mind. It lacks the hope of an evolution towards a future justice.

Cohen's criticism of myth was not only a philosophical and religious explanation of Judaism as a religion of reason which discerned a way out of the mythical world at the same time as it upheld the messianic promise in modernity. It was also part of his critique of capitalism. Cohen saw socialism as emerging from the tradition of the prophets, and viewed myth as an ideology that delegitimized the hope of a better world by exalting an archaic origin. Cohen's political understanding of myth as a contemporary phenomenon made it possible for Taubes to interpret *Die Wirklichkeit der Hebräer* as the 'test case for all myth-enthusiasts' in the modern era.[33] The philological brilliance of Goldberg was that he underlined the historical fact that the Torah belonged to a world full of deities, *Elohim*, that the Hebrews sought to abandon. For Taubes, Goldberg was the first modern scholar after G. W. F. Hegel and F. W. J. Schelling to develop a philosophic interpretation of polytheism, and in a world full of gods there was no unified, abstract humanity united in a common world but only a myriad of ethnicities and peoples.[34]

Different gods belonged to different peoples, and when this polytheistic world was lost, the historical context that could make the rites of the Hebrews meaningful disappeared. Yet, Taubes insisted, even if Goldberg's ethnology of the Torah was vindicated by later anthropological research, his work signalled how myth re-emerges in the modern era. Taubes saw our times as an age of technological polytheism. Goldberg, on the other hand, described our world as belonging to the subjectivity that was foreign to what Jaynes called the bicameral mind by distinguishing the epoch of myth from our contemporary world with its roots in the old civilizations of the land of the two rivers.

In an article written for Thomas Mann's anti-fascist review 'Mass und Wert' in 1937, Goldberg analysed modern myth as a dangerous *Kunstprodukt* that had nothing to do with the ancient period which he investigated.[35] He attacked the rise of Nazism by writing, apropos Friedrich Nietzsche, that 'when he calls the peoples of an age marked by the absence of metaphysics . . . to intoxicate themselves to tragic heights, then it is not the old and true myth . . . it is rather the *"Myth of the twentieth century"*, which is destined to no other success than to push the masses to pseudobacchanalian rage'.[36] Referring to the anti-Semitic propagandist Alfred Rosenberg's *The Twentieth Century Mythos* from 1930, Goldberg made clear that the rise of Nazism was not a regress to a pre-modern, archaic, cultic world, where 'the old and true myth' could be found – it was a sign of the dangers of the modern period. In fact, 'the old and true myth' is, as I will show, much younger than the course of the fixated world that Nazism and other modern totalitarian movements belong to. Still, the mythic world was long gone.

The eclipse of the mythical epoch had, according to Goldberg, catastrophic consequences since it transformed the psychophysical constitution of humanity to the point that our species no longer could live in a covenant with God. Instead, we humans have to find shelter in what Goldberg simply described as 'the state' in *Die Wirklichkeit der Hebräer*.[37]

In a manner reminiscent of world-system theorists, such as André Gunder Frank and Barry K. Gills, who have argued that 'the contemporary world has a history of at least 5,000 years', Goldberg identified the origin of the state with empires such as Akkadia, Babylon and the long history of different Egyptian civilizations.[38] These empires were the political context of the Torah, and by emphasizing that *Urjudentum* was an interim phenomenon between a mythological order of archaic tribes and a world of imperial states Goldberg described ancient Hebrewdom as a break with the Mesopotamian and Egyptian empires. The Torah also described a confrontation between the Hebrews and the other mythical tribes that tried to live in relation to a specific *Elohim*, such as the Amalekites who, as Exod. 17.14 declared without doubt, the *Elohim IHWH* wanted to eradicate after their attacks on his people.

Goldberg differentiated between peoples [*Völker*], namely, the non-state archaic peoples of the world, such as the Hebrews and the Amalekites, and the non-peoples of the states [*Staate*], who were identified with the sedentary city civilizations in the *Torah*.

Cohen's project was a defence of a Judaism adapted to these sedentary civilizations that according to Goldberg did not lead humanity into a better future. They embedded our species in the reality that Cohen argued myth glorified: nature in the sense of what is embodied in time and space. For just 'as the people is an instrument of *sublation [Aufhebung]*, the state is an institution for the *stabilization* of "nature" and also for maintaining of the natural laws of normality'.[39] The state was based on the '*animal* drive for self-preservation' – for this is what normal human nature is reduced to by its normal evolution, its striving for survival – whereas the people was the life form that sought to transform its natural existence by becoming part of the world of the gods.

When Taubes shivered over the fact that Goldberg thought that '[i]n order to establish the union between gods and men or to recover the potency of the sacral act man must first abandon or destroy the entire history of culture' he did not bear in mind that Goldberg first of all criticized a civilization that according to him had not domesticated the human animal's most base instincts, our struggle for power and survival, but rather radicalized it.[40] It was, from Goldberg's perspective, our '*animal* drive for self-preservation' that forced the human to become a political animal in the first place and it is this biological tendency that the state stabilizes as a principle of governance with, Goldberg argued after the horror of the First World War, catastrophic consequences.

Since the biological basis of the 5,000-year-old world system is the '*animal* drive for self-preservation', this non-mythical order is paradoxically older and more natural than myth, and Goldberg stressed explicitly that the Torah describes a rather recent exception in the life of our species. The Torah is radically new.

Goldberg viewed modern subjectivity as the normal anthropogenesis of the human as a toolmaking and political animal that implied a 'process of fixation' which turned our natural drives to whole civilizations.[41] This 'process of fixation' had its roots in the world that Cain initiated according to the Torah and which the metaphysical system of the Torah hoped to alter by producing a new kind of humanity: 'The fixation is rather ancient, as it stands in the beginning of the history. *It is even older than metaphysic itself.* That shows the birth of Cain, at whose arrival Eve believes that she has born . . . an IHWH-human, whereas she in reality has received the "first born of the *fixation*", the "property"-human "Cain".[42] In contrast, Abel represented the Hebraic metaphysics and myth – Goldberg used these concepts interchangeably – that Abraham took upon himself as his task to build a collective life form that broke with the order of the state and the world of the mythological tribe.

The Torah depicted a possible separation from the cycles of civilization that Cain, the toolmaker and *homo faber*, represents and it is important to note that the individuals in the Torah signified 'a technology for the construction of a people', according to Goldberg.[43] Consequently, the characters that can be found in the myths of *Urjudentum* – such as Adam, Eve, Cain, Abel, Abraham and Sarah – are anthropological principles and not primarily historical individuals. They lay the basis for an 'aprioric ethnology'.[44]

Cain was an anthropological principle denoting 'the whole generation of "Cainites", the farmers, *technicians*, and city builders' who surrounded the Abrahamic people with the civilization that finally subsumed also this nomadic tribe.[45] Abel, the first nomad and the first victim of Cain, was in contrast described by Goldberg as the incarnation of the metaphysics that represents God in the world.[46]

When the Chaldean Abram abandoned Ur with his family and became Abraham in the desert, he took up the metaphysical task of Abel by freely opening himself to a path beyond both tribe and state leading to the *Elohim IHWH* – the God who said he was the Lord of all lords. Abram did thereby something that according to Jaynes was revolutionary. He consciously chose to forsake his old identity in order to become a Hebrew and create a community whose God was a chosen God, a *Wahl-Gott* that one had to forsake the rest of the world for.

Jaynes described the Hebrews as one of the tribes that lived on the outskirts of the empires and, in a manner that strengthens Goldberg's argument, he insisted that the citizens in the Mesopotamian and Akkadian empires saw these groups of nomads as desperate outcasts or dangerous robbers. They survived by stealing 'the grapes which the vine-dressers scorned to pick, or as whole tribes raiding the city peripheries for their cattle and produce, even as nomadic Bedouins occasionally do today. The word for vagrants in Akkad, the language of Babylon, is *khabiru* and so these desert refugees are referred to on cuneiform tablets. And *khabiru* softened in the desert air, becomes Hebrew'.[47] For Jaynes, just as for Goldberg, the emergence of this people of nomads, robbers and vagrants called the Hebrews represented a new moral consciousness in a polytheistic world. Yet, for Goldberg, Abraham did something that was impossible according to Jaynes:

he chose consciously to live with God rather than lay the basis for the modern self-reflective consciousness that knows no gods.

Jaynes wrote that 'one particular group of the *Khabiru*, as the prophetic subjective age was approaching, was following only the voice of He-who-is, and rewrote the *Elohim* creation story in a much warmer and more human way, making He-who-is the only real *elohah*'.[48] This is not a very fanciful suggestion, and to an extent it does not contradict Goldberg's investigation of the Torah. But the Torah was for him not in any sense a classical source for our civilization. It depicted an escape from the world of cities, states and civilizations and described how a non-sedentary tribe discovers their God, the *Elohim IHWH*, in the refuge of the desert.

The world that broke with the bicameral mind was not founded by the Torah, but rather by the Cainite struggle for survival which Goldberg saw as the basis for the 5,000-year-old world system. The Hebrews had to leave the ancient cities of Egypt and Mesopotamia where the deities that the creator God, *Elohim IHWH*, urged his people to abandon dwelled: 'Therefore in the times of Moses, that is *before* the conquest of Canaan, all metaphysical events take place in the *desert*, and therefore, as soon as he wants to speak with IHWH, Moses must . . . *leave the city*, that is the sphere of power of the Egyptian Elohim.'[49]

The city was the sphere of Egyptian and Babylonian gods, whereas the wilderness of the desert was the domain where the creator God could become present and help his people to confront the hardships that threatened them. However, the exodus from Egypt was a flight not only from slavery but also from the anthropological constitution of the human as an animal embedded in the world of fixation and its political form: the sedentary state. But this was not only a political reading of the Torah. As problematic it may be, Goldberg meant that the catastrophic politics of his times – *Die Wirklichkeit der Hebräer* was published in 1925 – had to be understood in relation to the normal course of human evolution that he called the fixation.

The industrialized world has been evolving out of the banal and contingent effect of the violence inherent in nature, visible, for instance, in ageing, death and even the pain and danger of birth. In order to survive our species has become a creature that dwells in states, families and other institutions that – as Goldberg argues – stabilize the catastrophic tendency of nature, which, through a long process of coercion, exploitation and violence, has coagulated as capitalism in modern times.

From Goldberg's point of view, this stabilization of nature through the state is not in any sense an eradication or sublation of natural phenomena such as ageing, droughts, epidemics, the simple fact of biological death or for that matter sexual difference, but their equilibrium. With the advent of capitalism, it may seem as if humanity has mastered nature, not least due to the process of industrialization and the erection of a fossil-based civilization on the earth crust. But this stabilization of nature implies as we know today a violent pressure on the biosphere itself to the point of global catastrophes.

This fact is visible in the proliferation of entropic processes driven by technological development, and more importantly for Goldberg, it can be seen in the reduction of humanity to a species of proletarians entrapped in the industrialized world that workers are erecting all over the planet.

What Goldberg emphasized with his theory of the state as a stabilization of nature was that every territorial state is tied to the natural resources that constitute the material basis of its economy. The state is an economy determined by scarcity, whereas the people is an economy that seeks to create a form of abundance by – as we will see in the next section – modifying nature. This is something that neither Mann nor Taubes mentioned in their critiques of Goldberg. They did not relate his work to his two most close friends and collaborators, the earlier mentioned philosopher Erich Unger and the economist Adolf Caspary, and it may be the latter's examination of Karl Marx's concept of machinery that makes this current especially worth returning to in our time of climate catastrophes, planetary pandemics and economic crises.[50]

The rites and rituals in the Torah aimed to free the species from the economy of scarcity which Goldberg thought was the impetus for the civilization that found its most visible form in the fossil-based states he argued would lead to a series of catastrophes. Caspary had written in his seminal work *Die Maschinenutopie: das Übereinstimmungsmoment der bürgerlichen und sozialistischen Ökonomie* from 1927 that '[t]he way of life of the masses, within an economy that produces by means of machines, must be proletarian, since even today the machine and not the "order" [*die "Ordnung"*] maintains the relation of capital. If the way of life of the masses remains as it is now then that means: justice is impossible. The relation between justice and machines is a utopia.'[51]

For Caspary, the machine was more than a mere instrument consisting of different parts that – taken as a whole – uses mechanical power to make particular tasks easier to perform. It was a social mechanism bound to a specifically capitalist mode of production, which even produces a kind of 'machine utopia' – *Maschinenutopie* – for an existence that could envision neither an economy nor a life beyond the factory.[52]

Ten years after the Russian Revolution, Caspary argued that 'the capitalist system is the necessary and adequate form of production with machinery, economically as well as politically. No revolution changes the imperialist politics of states or the proletarian way of life of the masses, since both are grounded in the coercion that the machine exerts.'[53] Socialism and capitalism were two facets of one and the same industrial world forming our species into a race of workers.

From this perspective, if a way out of capitalism is really being sought out, then the question of whether or not it is possible to move beyond what Joshua B. Freeman recently has called the Behemoth of industrialism, and even more its distinct anthropological form, is of utmost importance.[54]

The Behemoth, Freeman writes, creates perhaps 'not exactly a new man at one with the automatic machinery and industrial processes of the giant factory as envisioned, in their own ways, by Henry Ford, Alexei Gastev, and Antonio Gramsci. But a new man and a new woman nonetheless, with a time sense dictated by the needs of mass, coordinated activity and the rhythms of machinery.'[55] Goldberg argued that this capitalist anthropogenesis had to be disrupted in order to make a way out of our factory world imaginable. In fact, he predicted that life under capitalism would be put into crisis by the catastrophic development of the machine world of capital itself.

'The proletariat', Goldberg wrote two years after the parliamentary victory of NSDAP, 'is politically and biologically the weakest of classes.'[56] It is a supplement or surplus population, a *Zusatzbevölkerung*, 'which lives due to the perfection and expansion of the machine, because only during the time of prosperous technical means of production more people can marry, more people can stay alive, and more people can be fed.'[57] This proletarianization of humanity has a clear limit in the finite natural resources needed for the reproduction of the capitalist mode of production. It was with this in mind Goldberg asked:

> What happens to the many, many millions of the technical surplus population when the machine catastrophe is here, when the factories stand still and the means of subsistence are withdrawn from the masses? In this case, these many millions will go under due to starvation since they are produced by technology's increased leeway of life [*Lebenspielraum*]. We can predict how it will end: the raw material of the earth will end in the foreseeable future.[58]

This has not happened, since, for instance, shale oil extraction has kept the price of oil low. But the development of these kinds of technologies could, from the perspective of Goldberg and Caspary, only strengthen their thesis that there is no machine-based solution to the social problem of capitalism. The continued use of fossils would, for instance, increase the catastrophic tendency in nature that capital unleashed. The Goldberg circle meant that the looming machine catastrophe would show that the psychophysical condition of the human being did not coincide with the social function it was given as a worker, citizen, consumer and so on. Beyond and outside the *noosphere* of the capitalist production and consumption lies the primordial world of biological nature, and it was this world that the Torah tried to alter by, on the one hand, breaking the 'process of fixation' and, by the other, challenging the world of myth through a new anthropogenesis.

Myth and technology

Goldberg differentiated, as we have seen, the state as the stabilization of the '*animal* drive for self-preservation' from the peoples of the mythical period who sought to sublate and transform nature. Nature denoted in the Torah the finite part of reality, the domain of time and space ruled by causality and even more scarcity, and did not coincide with the abundant and infinite part of reality which myth sought to channel as a rapture with the normality of the finite domain. Goldberg's notions of state and people entailed two distinct metabolic relations to nature, or to be more precise, two different economies of nature.

The state is an economy of scarcity since it is fixated on the finite part of reality – the spatio-temporal realm of normal causality – whereas myth is a way to produce a kind of abundance out of the scarce and finite resources of nature by moulding the finite part of reality in relation to the infinite realm that precedes it.

Myth implies a new understanding of the possible and the aim of *Die Wirklichkeit der Hebräer* was to systematize the Torah as a metaphysical system that discerned the modality of myth. In the cosmological introduction to the book, Goldberg declared that '[u]ntil now *"possibility"* had only a formal meaning, until now possibility and reality have only been differentiated in the sense that the real is present, while the possible is considered as not present'.[59] This is what the metaphysics of the Torah radically changes. The possible is the unrevealed part of reality that can become revealed in the form of what Goldberg called a mythic occurrence or manifestation:

> myths are reports of the occurrence of foreign laws of nature within the world in which we live. The empirical is the area of application of the laws of nature, which

are always and everywhere the same. But if this uniformity is broken at one point on the Earth, then a system of natural laws unknown to and directed against our empirics [*unsere Empirie*] will arise, and then a mythical occurrence is present.[60]

Mythical occurrences are defined as miracles in *Die Wirklichkeit der Hebräer*, such as the parting of the Red Sea, or when the Hebrew people are given manna in the desert to survive their exodus from Egypt.[61] In difference to the many attempts of modern theologians to reconcile the miracles reported in the Bible with the laws of nature, and even more differentiate them from unbelievable events recorded by other religious and mythical traditions, Goldberg argued that miracles are ways to alter the normal laws of nature.[62]

Miracles are the disruption of the normalcy of nature and mythical ways to describe how the world is fractured between what in contemporary cosmology is called the domain of *res extensae*; the natural domain of everything material, spatial and temporal; and the domain of *res potentiae*; the infinite domain of everything that could be.[63]

The possible or the domain of *res potentiae* is the larger part of reality, whereas the order of the actual – *res extensae* – is the surface of this vaster reality that exists as a pure modality. This implies, as I will discuss later, that possibilities exist in themselves and therefore pre-exist their actualization in time and space. There is a fullness of possibilities: the infinity or eternal life which Goldberg described as 'the state of consummation [*Vollendungszustand*] of time, events, and possibilities. From this follows the illusory nature of movement in general'.[64] The temporal and spatial domain of reality is the place of manifestation of the possible as something real and actual.

However, Goldberg underlined that 'space, time, and causality are in opposition to Kant not forms of intuition [*Anschauungsformen*] but the constitutive forms of finite reality'.[65] Movement may be an illusion from the perspective of the infinite but in the finite part of reality time, space and causality are real. They are the modes of existence for finite beings. Still, there is the possibility to produce 'a system of natural laws unknown to and directed against our empirics' by tapping into the possibilities that pre-exist time and space and these transformations of our world are what myths describe in a poetic manner: the miraculous emergence of foreign laws of nature.[66]

By insisting that foreign laws can be implemented in different regions of the earth Goldberg wanted to emphasize two things. *First*, there is the order of the empirical where the laws of nature are always and everywhere the same. This is the normalcy of nature and the fixated world of the state. Nature, from the perspective of what Goldberg calls *unsere Empirie*, is impossible to change in this world. It has become fixated to something uniform that always and everywhere is the same. Time flows in one direction and logic is ruled by the laws of non-contradiction, the law of identity and the law of excluded middle. Each thing is identical with itself, a is a and b is not a since a is a, and causality rules the world with iron law.[67] This is the domain of finitude or the *res extensae* that myth seeks to challenge, and this also explains why disruptions in the time–space fabric are increasingly uncommon. They need a form of life to become manifest as ruptures of the ordinary ontology of nature and these occurrences are what the 'process of fixation' undoes.

Second, beside this uniformity there are or at least have been the foreign laws of nature which myths document and which indicate that there indeed are ways to defy the normalcy of nature. In this sense, myths reveal the absolute contingency and plasticity of nature, and most of all the plasticity of human nature, by indicating that the finite realm is simply the surface of a vaster domain of possibility.

Thus, for Goldberg, reality in its totality is not one but differentiated in a series of planes with distinct and heterogeneous ontologies. The 'process of fixation' flattens this world of worlds and produces the homogeneity of nature that we modern humans think is identifiable with the real, whereas myths describe variations of the laws of nature through the opening of a part of the world for a mythical occurrence. This is the metaphysical doctrine of the Torah: potentiality precedes actuality and time is the plane that actualizes a specific set of potentialities in space as a specific world – a world that myths describe as a way of life for a specific people. 'Time', Goldberg wrote in *Die Wirklichkeit der Hebräer*, 'is nothing but the form for the entrance of possibilities from the infinity into the finite. Each moment of time corresponds to a given moment of the world – the world seen as a *totality* – which presents itself as a constellation or a possibility.'[68] But, as we have seen, with myth there are different worlds, different laws of nature, different totalities and therefore different possibilities and ways to live. Myths differentiate the spatial and temporal order of the world by changing the ontology of nature.

There are therefore forms of life, or rather sets of actions and behaviours, that make the infinite present in the finite domain. This '*finitization* of the infinite' occurs through what Goldberg called 'the realization of the *contradiction*', namely, the cultivation of a 'transcendent organism' that challenges the normalcy of nature.[69] These transcendent organisms are the tribes of the mythical era that seek to live in relation to a god by producing new ontological possibilities in the region of finite nature. A mythical form of life – with all its rites and rituals – is a contradiction, a challenge of nature, that often is concretized as an ascetic practice that may seem foreign to what, from the perspective of the 'process of fixation', is seen as a healthy or good life.

In the chapter of *Die Wirklichkeit der Hebräer* aptly entitled 'The equation: Peoples = Gods = Worlds', Goldberg postulated a relation of identity between peoples, gods and worlds and writes that a people enacts the life of a god as its life world.[70] *The people* is the community which cultivates *a world*, which can be identified with its symbolic representations and ritual habits, according to the rules and laws of their *god*. The god, in turn, acts as the ancestry, *Abstammung*, or point of origin, *Abstammungszentrum*, of a specific people.[71] These ancestries must be kept alive through specific ways to live in a specific region since, Goldberg stresses, 'every Elohim has a limited area, i.e. its specific place' in the world where it can become manifest as a 'contradiction' of normal nature.[72] A mythical people capable of living in relation to a god of the desert can, for instance, find an abundance of possibilities in seemingly desolate regions of the world. This, for Goldberg, is a variation of the ontology of nature.

In an article on totemism from 1927, Caspary described how a tribe develops natural qualities corresponding to their totem god: 'They who come from a water-totem can live in water. For this is the biological special ability of the fish. But mankind has the capacity to develop all biological abilities – also this one.'[73] By accepting different totems as their deities, the tribes can alter their psychophysical constitution in relation to the natural element – the *Abstammung* or *Abstammungszentrum* – that the gods are connected to. These ancestries are, we have to remember, not ways to be grounded in finite region per se. They are alterations of the scarcity of actual nature that produce new ontological possibilities for life to develop and survive in a specific region.

Referring to ethnological evidence which shows that shamanic and totemistic rituals and myths often involve the donning of animal skins and performing dances in imitation of animals, Caspary wrote that these rites can be interpreted as the channelling of the power of the gods into human nature so that it becomes transformed.[74] The cultivation of a totemistic life is essentially psychophysical since '[t]he core of totemism . . . consists in a relation of man to the animal – his totem', and this implies a transformation of life in relation to the animal that the tribe imitates.[75] These ways of life are different finitizations of the infinite and distinct variations of 'the realization of the *contradiction*' that Goldberg called myth.

Goldberg underlined that the world of the Torah is full of gods that dwell as ways of lives in specific parts of the world since nature is differentiated in numerous divine habitats. There are the gods belonging to the animal or plant world, who challenge and variate living nature. Then there are the divinities belonging to the world of dead matter which seek to contradict this part of the finite domain. All these deities are variations of natural forces that cannot exist without a people which enacts their presence in time and space by adopting them as their totems.

This does not imply that the deities of the mythical period lack independent existence. They exist as an abstract pattern, the 'totality' or 'constellation' of a specific set of the infinite possibilities that precede the finite world, that makes it possible to identify a people with a specific world and the world with a specific deity.

Margarete Susman underlined this quasi-autonomous nature of the gods or what Goldberg also called 'transcendental organisms' in her reading of the Jewish mythologist by arguing that '[t]he peoples are instruments, possibilities of the realization of metaphysical potencies: of gods against the pure powers of nature. Thus, every people is only living as long as it possesses its connection with its god, with its centre of life and power.'[76] It is not a coincidence that Susman chose the Schellingian concept of potency to describe Goldberg's mythology as a theory of the realization of metaphysical potencies since Goldberg was influenced by the Schellingian understanding of myth.[77] Schelling used the term 'potency' in his famous lectures on mythology in order to reject an understanding of myth as simple fiction.[78]

Schelling viewed myth, Ernst Cassirer explains, as 'the odyssey of the pure consciousness of God, whose unfolding is determined and mediated in equal measure by our consciousness of nature and the world and by our own consciousness of the I.'[79] Myth, in this sense, 'becomes a second "nature"' for the human, or what Goldberg calls a world or a reality, *Wirklichkeit*, in time and space.[80]

Cassirer strengthened this realistic understanding of myths and wrote that they 'are not originally "allegorical"; they do not merely copy or represent but are absolutely real; they are so woven into the reality of action as to form an indispensable part of it'.[81] When a dancer enacts a mythical drama he recapitulates and lives it in a real and even biological sense as his second nature: 'the dancer *is* the god, he *becomes* the god' and by becoming a god nature – at least human nature – is challenged and transformed.[82]

Culture and nature, biology and history, are intertwined in myth to a single ontological reality. Even death and life are entwined with each other 'as two similar parts of the same being. In mythical thinking there is no definite, clearly delimited moment in which life passes into death and death into life. It considers birth as a return and death as a survival.'[83] In myth 'all phenomena are situated on a single plane. Here there are no degrees of reality, no contrasting degrees of objective certainty.'[84] Myths reveal, as Goldberg said, that there are 'threads of connection', *Verbindungsfäden*, between humans and gods and, a fortiori, between death and life.[85] It is when this intercourse between heaven and earth ends that the mythical age eclipses and humanity becomes fixated to the normalcy of nature.

The divinities of myth are potencies as they can be said to possess and alter the world of nature, the spatio-temporal domain, by turning a dancer into a god or a people to a host in time and space for the divine. This implies for Goldberg, in sharp contrast to Cassirer, that myth does *not* depict an absolute immanence where there is no depth or transcendence. Myth is rather the capacity of a people to transcend the normality of nature in the sense that a dancer can become a god. Without this thread of connection even the God of all gods is absent. He is someone we pray to because he is not present as a manifest and visible force.

Goldberg's studies in medicine as a student and his interests in anthropology had led him to Bhutan, Nepal and Kashmir, where he conducted research for his dissertation on yogi practices and rituals, *Die abnormalen biologischen Vorgänge bei orientalischen Sekten*, such as the reduction of respiration and heart rates.[86] These experiences had a profound effect on his understanding of the Torah and when Unger explained his mentor's interpretation of mythical occurrences he mentioned 'healing by touch, immunities of every sort, real or illusory phenomena of fakirs and of sects of Asiatic religions, controlling non-conscious functions of the body such as the heart rate, breathing, etc' as examples of how the normalcy of nature can be altered through mythical occurrences.[87]

Goldberg was not alone in understanding myth as a biological or psychophysical problematic. His theories were close to the ideas of the etiologist and philosopher of myth Tito Vignoli. Vignoli argued in *Mito e scienza* from 1879, translated into German one year later, for a transcendental understanding of myth based in biology, and tried to show that animals had a mythical intelligence in the sense that they could mistake dead matter for animated beings and discern meaningful patterns in their environments.[88]

Vignoli clarified that he only used 'the term transcendental because' myth 'is actually the primitive condition of the fact [of intelligence] in its inevitable beginning, whatever form the mythical representation may subsequently take. This fact is not peculiar to any individual, people, or race, but is manifested as an essential organism of the human character, which is in all cases universal, permanent and uniform.'[89] Myth is, in short, the capacity to understand the world as something that has sense. Consequently, myth cannot be understood as a passing tendency in the life of our species. It is the transcendental and even biological basis for human intelligence since myth can be identified with the possibility of sense making: it is our way to make reality meaningful.

Vignoli almost identified myth with meaning by arguing that science and myth have the same source 'since perception is the condition of both' and for him this implied that 'the problem of myth, which includes every achievement of the human understanding, and fills all sociology, is transformed into the problem of civilization. Thought has run its course in the vast evolution from myth to science, which is rendered possible by the permanence and duration of a powerful and vigorous race.'[90] Like Goldberg, Vignoli understood that the origin of myth posited the question of the origin of civilization.

Vignoli emphasized that many peoples have become extinct through the evolution of civilization, whereas others have remained in what Vignoli describes as a savage and barbarous condition. However, what he terms '[o]ur own race, originally, as I believe, Aryo-Semitic', has 'persisted without interruption in spite of many adversities and revolutions, and has displayed in successive generations the progress of general civilization' by moving from myth to science.[91] In Western civilization humanity has evolved beyond the animal intelligence of myth. At this point it is easy to notice the vast abyss that separates Goldberg from Vignoli.

Myth according to Goldberg is as for Vignoli a biological and transcendental problematic, but it is not an animal intelligence that can be understood as the genesis of our species as a scientific or toolmaking species. Myth is 'a technology for the construction of a people'. Today, in the modern period, there are only remnants of the mythical peoples left, small pockets of archaic tribes who arrange their daily life in relation to the rites and rituals which prospered during the period of myth. Myth, from this perspective, is not something that should or even could be understood teleologically as the first step in the development of a scientific and industrialized civilization. Goldberg was closer to the perspective that Claude Lévi-Strauss later would defend in his investigations of bodily technologies among archaic peoples.[92]

Lévi-Strauss stressed the potential of so-called primitive peoples to change the psychophysical constitution of their existence and wrote that when it comes to 'the connexion between the physical and the mental, the East and the Far East are several thousand years ahead; they have produced the great theoretical and practical *summae* represented by Yoga in India, the Chinese "breath-techniques", or the visceral control of the ancient Maoris'.[93] His argument that the 'West, for all its mastery of machines, exhibits evidence of only the most elementary understanding of the use and potential resources of that super-machine, the human body' echoes Goldberg's critique of the world of fixation as a loss of a metaphysics of the body that shamans and yogi masters have developed during the ages.[94]

This is also why Goldberg described the rise of civilization as the age of fixation and argued that Cain, the builder of Enoch – the first city and state in the mythological world of the Torah – symbolized the fixated human, the *homo faber*, who cannot transform his body like the archaic peoples of the mythical period. He is nailed to the normalcy of nature and compensates his lack of what Goldberg terms metaphysics with state building.

Consequently, the eclipse of myth represents a decline to normality, *Verfall zur Normalität*, and Vignoli's description of the rise of science as a victorious evolution of the Aryan-Semitic race is an apt portrayal of the regression of the mythical order to the status quo of the fixated world. For Goldberg, this is a terrible event since the decline to normality is the triumph of the anthropological form of Cain over the metaphysical possibility that Abel represents, and which Abraham took upon himself as the task to make not only a god of nature but the God of all gods present. What Abraham sought was a new anthropogenesis: the emergence of a humanity that broke with both the state and the tribe, and therefore not only with the normalcy of nature but with the myriad of mythical gods that could not ground their tribes in the infinite domain as such. The deities who had their ancestries in specific parts of nature were not the God of the infinite and the eternal, the *Elohim IHWH*, but gods of the finite world. They belonged, in this sense, to nature in its spatial, temporal and embodied sense.

Goldberg claimed that those taboos and rites in the Torah which designate what is pure, *taharah*, and impure, *tumah*, must be related to the totemistic systems of the archaic peoples and civilizations from which the Hebrews initially gathered their members. Thus, if James George Frazer insisted that totemism was neither universal nor possible to discern in ancient Semitic religion but 'an institution peculiar to the dark-complexioned and least civilized races of mankind', Goldberg included *Urjudentum* in this order of so-called uncivilized and barbaric tribes.[95] He separated, however, the rituals and taboos of the Torah from the totemistic rites of surrounding peoples. The taboos against other gods in the Torah were necessary for the constitution of the Hebrews as the people of the one and only God who created the world and therefore all other gods, namely, the potencies of nature. In Deut. 13.6-8 one can for instance find the following taboo:

> If your brother, the son of your mother, or your son or your daughter or the wife you embrace or your friend who is as your own soul entices you secretly, saying, 'Let us go and serve other gods,' ... you shall not yield to him or listen to him, nor shall your eye pity him, nor shall you spare him, nor shall you conceal him.

This demand for separation was for Goldberg an indication that the God of all gods – unlike the other *Elohim* – did not belong to the domain of nature, and the *Elohim IHWH* could not become present if the Hebrews did not sever themselves both from the world of the tribe and from the world of the state. The eternal and true God needed a people to enact his specific mode of life which entailed the contradiction with nature and its potencies. Therefore, this God also stood in a contradiction with all other gods. He was even forced to wage a war against that which contradicted him in time and space. The exodus from Egypt is a good example when *Elohim IHWH* came into conflict with other deities.

> The whole Exodus from Egypt is nothing else than the struggle of Elohim IHWH with the elohim of the Egyptians, a struggle from which the Elohim IHWH emerges victorious. It is not alleged in the Pentateuch that the Elohim IHWH is the *only* Elohim and that there is no other Elohim, rather should all such passages that refer to ideas like that be interpreted as follows: among all Elohim who exist, and who all belong to the world structures there is *one* Elohim who in himself contains exactly that element of the world design which makes him *superior* to the other Elohim.[96]

The superiority of the *Elohim IHWH* is that he, as the principle that contains 'the element of the world design', belongs to the pre-biological and pre-historical principle of the spirit, *Geist*, to which humans can open themselves by searching for the power of creation that expresses itself in the world as the transcendence of life.

The Torah was an essentially anti-totemistic myth, a system of laws that did not give the Hebrews the ability to imitate life in a specific natural habitat, personified by a totem. The *Elohim IHWH* was a discovery of the principle, the spirit, that sought to alter nature rather than adapt the Hebrews to a specific habitat. This implied that unlike the other deities the *Elohim IHWH* needed a form of life that challenged the existing world in its totality.

Goldberg described the confrontation with the current world totality in his book on Maimonides, published as a critique of classical Judaism in 1935, on the 800th anniversary of the medieval theologian, by arguing that the covenant between God and his people was the divine endeavour to produce perfection: '*God* has a world-purpose: that is the perfecting of the world. He has this purpose independently from living beings, solely on the grounds that he must make the world equal to himself.'⁹⁷ What does this mean? The world as a composite of temporal beings is a world plagued by death and destruction and other imperfections since only God is that which cannot die. Finitude and scarcity are the basis of the totality of the finite world that must be questioned.

By creating something outside him, the infinite and eternal God brings forth a cosmos – the finite domain of time, space and causality – lacking his perfection. This also creates the potencies that in mythical language are called gods since the eternal life of God is not fully present in the finite domain of the world. The gods are, from this perspective, alienated forms of the eternal that through the creation earn quasi-autonomous existence just like the rest of the world. The *Elohim IHWH* is also the God of all other *Elohim* that can alter the normalcy of nature. Yet, the finite gods do not have the power to make the world perfect and immortal. Perfection entails immortality and by being that which cannot die the God of all gods is '*superior* to the other Elohim'.

The God that is eternal perfection, the *Elohim IHWH*, strives by inner impetus to give creation what it lacks, immortality, by becoming a finite power in the tabernacle, his portable abode, and just like other mythical peoples, as Jaynes would argue, the Hebrews lived intimately with their deity as a force that ruled over them in an immediate sense. The reason why the aim of this God was not primarily to help the Hebrews survive was that his presence questioned the reduction of life to survival. Their existence was subordinated to the task of God: to make the world perfect for this perfection is what, essentially, their God is. 'The perfecting of the world', Goldberg wrote, 'can for God only be *a reserve, a task, a purpose*' that a specific people enacts and such an enaction is a gradual confrontation with the economy of a nature ruled by finitude.⁹⁸

This is what the Torah is: the task to make the world perfect and therefore immortal and this mission could fail. The presence, *Anwesenheit*, of the Godhead in the finite domain of the world can only, at its inception, be a 'partial presence' for otherwise creation would lose its integrity and become identical with the infinitude that precedes it.⁹⁹ The God of all gods needs a people just like all other gods to become present. But the mission of this people is to break through nature and that disruption has to begin in a specific time and place and with specific rites and rituals. The *Elohim IHWH* can lose his connection to the world and be banished to heaven, which we now can identify with the world of infinite possibilities, since his people can fail to manifest his presence as what Goldberg called an ethical order. Goldberg asked: 'How does the perfecting of nature relate to the presence of God? He finds a natural order that is only appropriate for him to the smallest extent.'[100] Nature resists the divine by being plagued by death and other imperfections that cannot reflect the eternal life of God. 'Thus, God has to break this resistance. He must *break through* this low, restricted, limited natural order.'[101] He must break through death and entropy.

Goldberg identified 'this low, restricted, limited natural order' with the forces that rule normal life, such as the fact that living organisms must age, die or suffer. These are the forces of evil that can make God absent since he, as the principle of abundant and eternal life, disrupts the attempt of the world to close itself from the infinite. This is why evil first of all is the finitude and scarcity that rule the economy of normal nature.

In contrast, God is the abundance and infinity that can modify life to the point that it no longer necessarily ends with death. This is important since the Hebrews, according to Goldberg, were a missionary community of men and women who had abandoned state or tribe in order to live in relation to a God that desired to modify nature by overcoming the biology of normal life. Their mission was to confront death and the life it implied. The Torah was the answer to 'the problem: how can one be freed from one's ancestry, from the biological functions, from sexuality . . . without this leading to the necessity of leaving the domain of the finite reality'.[102] It has to be remembered that during the period of the Torah, giving birth was dangerous, and the fact that what traditional Jewish and Christian theology called the fall cursed Adam with work and Eve with birth in pain reflects this violence of normal nature that is stabilized by the state. Instead of grounding its people in a specific ancestry, the *Elohim IHWH* sought to liberate humanity from every biological ancestry and therefore from the world that fixated humanity in the production and reproduction of normal, and consequently catastrophic, life: life that kills and is killed.

For Goldberg, the cycles of birth and death were also the trajectory of the civilization that has culminated in the machine world which he and Caspary saw as a menace to the life of our species. Here we can note another similarity with modern anthropology, especially with the work of Lévi-Strauss, since Goldberg viewed the question of anthropology from the viewpoint of energy, the scarcity of resources and the imperfect conditions of life.

Behind anthropology, Lévi-Strauss insisted, there is an even more primordial entropology which shows how every human group's struggle against entropy is structured by its use and consummation of energy.[103] Goldberg can be interpreted as arguing that it is this entropological origin of civilization that the Hebrews challenged by tapping into a new source of energy: the God of gods.

This is why the Torah for Goldberg was not in any sense a classical source for our civilization. It was a critique of the catastrophic consequences of the 5,000-year-old world system.

The main enemy of the Torah was never the other gods but the fixation of humanity to the normality of nature that Goldberg identified with the struggle for survival that rules the world of scarcity. This stabilization of life as an entropic process was an imprisonment of humanity in what Goldberg called 'technology' and defined as 'the replacement of metaphysics', in other words the psychophysical techniques that modify human nature discussed earlier.[104] It is easy, even natural, for the human to live without gods and instead become subsumed by the process of fixation. This is the ordinary evolution of human life.

The Hebraic experiment to take part in God's task to turn the world into an order that represents his perfection was an anomalous and literally miraculous exception in the long and very violent history of humanity: 'The human can also, without joining the divine purpose, make nature serve him. Then he transforms the normal natural order, he creates technology. However – thereby the human does not become its *master*; he does not lead the natural order beyond itself.'[105] Technology fixates the human to the normal course of nature that, ultimately, can only create catastrophes since it produces scarcity rather than abundance, death rather than life, by stabilizing and even amplifying the entropic processes that pervade nature.

Myth is also a technology. Yet, it is a technology that sublates rather than stabilizes the scarcity of nature with other means than what Lévi-Strauss described as the 'mastery of machines'. The essential meaning of the metaphysics of the Hebrews was to perfect the world by moving humanity away from the technological civilization whose entropological processes, Goldberg prophesied, would escalate and produce more and more catastrophes like the First and Second World Wars that he had experienced. 'If man does not fulfil his ethical demand which is to become the enemy of technology in the *same* way that the Godhead itself is, then there will arise all the natural catastrophes, economic crises, and sociological monstrosities that are part of the inventory, as hard as iron, of the unethical world order', Goldberg wrote in his book on Maimonides.[106] It is only by becoming immortal that the world can be said to become ethical, and by becoming ethical it has to evolve beyond the process of fixation which imprison life in the entropic processes of nature. But what does it mean to become an enemy of technology? In what sense was Goldberg's critique of the modern factory world related to his hope to wrest humanity free from birth and death?

The flight from the Behemoth

Goldberg thought that the course of technological development would inevitably produce natural catastrophes and human misery since it escalated the instability inherent in a finite nature determined by a struggle over scarce resources.[107] Referring to Caspary's *Die Maschinenutopie* from 1927 in his book on Maimonides, he underlined even more how his work on myth was a critique of a civilization that stabilized the entropic processes of nature.

Caspary described capitalism and socialism as two machine utopias that could not solve the entropological problem. *Die Maschinenutopie* prefigured contemporary discussions of what the geologist M. King Hubbert famously has called peak oil, or even, to use Richard Heinberg's concept, peak everything, in the sense that a multitude of resources are finite and will end if the economic principles which rule production and consumption do not radically change.[108]

Caspary argued that capitalism is an agrarian revolution; a process of industrialization stratifying humanity into divergent and antagonistic classes; a Behemoth as much as a Leviathan whose 'occupation of the world' certainly should be related to the West and therefore, Goldberg argued, to a form of 'Europeanization' of the planet. This Europeanization, Caspary insisted, would entail the globalization of class struggle since 'the existence of a proletariat questions the current social order theoretically as well as practically' and, through the deepening of the contradictions of capital, 'the *legal question* of the distribution of goods' is transformed into 'the *question of existence for* the current existing society'.[109] The revolution was now at the horizon.

This hypothesis was founded on the experiences of the Russian Revolution in 1917 and the uprisings in Germany around 1919 which influenced Goldberg and Caspary's work. Contrary to the positions of the traditional left, Caspary stated in the opening sentence of *Die Maschinenutopie*: 'We only want to make one single fact known: that the mass misery of the proletariat is necessarily posited by means of production through machinery – but without the proletariat itself being able to dispense with the machine as a means of production.'[110] This was an unambiguous declaration of the political programme of the Goldberg circle: collective ownership and planned production of the factory civilization would not in themselves surpass the world of capital.

What had to be questioned both practically and theoretically was 'the point of reconciliation between bourgeois and socialist economy' – *das Übereinstimmungsmoment der bürgerlichen und sozialistischen Ökonomie* – which could be identified with the material infrastructure of capitalism and consequently, what Caspary with Marx called machinery. The expansion of the modern machine system, in other words the modern factory system, is inseparable from proletarian immiseration, entropic disorder and class conflicts that move societies towards revolutions, wars and other catastrophes.

One must tread carefully when stating this, since a machine is not a tool [*Werkzeug*], a 'means of production' used since 'it saves time'.[111] It is 'not, like the tool, a simple means for the production, but also at the same time its *motor*'.[112] The machine is an apparatus created together with and even for the world market. It is a mechanism that makes the industrial world with its factory systems possible. This is important, because the machine, as the physical motor of the specifically capitalist mode of production of surplus value, is not produced because it saves time but 'since it can produce *more* products' than a tool in a specific period of time.[113]

'The machine', Caspary clarified, 'also saves time – for each single product that can be produced faster with machines than without them', but that is 'not its utility'.[114] Its utility is to make an industrialized world market possible and the time saved by the machines produces, according to Caspary, the need for new labour in order to uphold this expanding factory system. Thus, Caspary continued: 'If the demand remained the same, that is, if the production figure remained the same, the machine would not be profitable, because it saves too much time for the individual product. The machine produces so fast that in the case of constant demand, the production of the machine itself would take more time than the non-mechanical production of goods.'[115] This implies (1) that the machine is impossible without a global infrastructure that has the market and the explicit goal of accumulation for accumulation's sake as its condition of possibility. (2) The machine is not built to make work easier for workers per se, even if this may be its indirect consequence, but in order to be the motor for the production of more and more commodities in a specific time period, such as the working day.

These two points are essential, for they imply that Caspary's argument diverges in significant ways from those who primarily view the machine as an instrument that saves necessary labour. Against this position, he wrote that

> the machine is produced economically as surplus value, that is, the production of machines does not have the character of 'necessary' but surplus labour. The machine did not emerge due to the pressure to save necessary labour, it emerged because the army of free workers that was not used for the necessary labour [for the reproduction of the goods needed for survival of the proletariat as such], was at free disposal and therefore could be hired to build machines and operate them.[116]

The machine is an instrument for an economy based on surplus labour that cannot continue to exist as a machine, that is, as a motor rather than simple means for capitalist production, without necessarily reproducing the division of labour that characterizes capitalism and that is produced through the primitive accumulation of capital.

With the rise of capitalism, more and more workers and means of productions were liberated from their shackles and turned to wage labour or capital, and at this state of the primitive accumulation there existed no machines and machine-like complexes such as modern factories. But the transition from feudalism to capitalism was made possible due to a kind of agrarian capitalism in which, Caspary argued, a surplus population in relation to the older mode of production could emerge. Workers were employed not only to produce food and similar commodities needed for immediate survival but also to produce machines.[117] This, Caspary continued, entails three things concerning the development of industrialized capitalism:

First, the extraction of surplus value is made possible without specifically capitalist machinery, since it is produced through primitive accumulation; for instance through the production of absolute surplus value, that is, long days of work on the field with the help of pre-capitalist tools. Capitalism was initially an agrarian economy primarily composed of landlords, free tenant farmers and agricultural wage workers.

Second, this implies that the wage is reduced to the societal cost of what is needed to reproduce the life of the worker so that there can be a difference between necessary and surplus labour in the process of production in order for surplus value and profit to be possible.

Third, Caspary continued, 'with the primitive accumulation of capital, surplus value is already posited: for the first machine is "coagulated surplus value", i.e., since the first machine can only be built if the total labour power in society (the proletarian *class*) can produce more than is needed for its own preservation.'[118] The enclosures that made land private and that forced people to find employment on the growing market of jobs in order to survive made it possible to employ some workers for the production of machines since others could produce their means of subsistence.

The division between proletarians producing consumer goods (*Verbrauchsgüter-Proletarier*) and proletarians producing machines (*Maschinen-Proletarier*) structures the life of capitalism into the world of production of surplus labour and, through the population rise, of more workers. This is the advent of the industrial Behemoth and, if we believe Goldberg, the reason why capitalism pushes the world into irreversible entropical processes that threaten the biosphere itself.

To summarize my argument so far, machinery for Caspary is the industrial infrastructure of the capitalist mode of production that produces not for the sake of needs but for the accumulation of profit. Machinery is neither 'the means of production' that satisfies existing needs nor a mere 'tool', however advanced or complex, useful for the production. The machine is 'the *motor* of production' that posits capital by producing new needs adapted to the capitalist economy. However, by doing so machinery creates a humanity whose needs imply the need for the continuation of capitalism as a machine civilization.

Caspary noted,

> in this way, the machine – which has arisen as a surplus product [*Mehrprodukt*] above and beyond necessary labour – becomes the means of production necessary for life. If indeed the machine does not serve to satisfy existing and necessary societal needs but rather implies their amplification; if the machine is not determined to be used in a specific economic sector but rather to develop a new economic sector, if the machine does not follow the need that it satisfies, but rather precedes it – then it only fulfils its essential determination in the cases when it produces needs whose satisfaction are necessary, but which cannot be satisfied without the machine.[119]

Here we find another crucial difference between the tool and the machine: the tool is produced to satisfy a pre-existing need, such as making labour easier, whereas the machine produces needs that can only be satisfied through the continuation of the use of machinery – the need to take a cheap flight did not exist before the airplane was used for tourism for instance – and it is in this sense that the machine according to Caspary produces a distinct form of life with specifically capitalist needs. It fixates humanity to the world of factories which is the latest, and perhaps ultimate, epoch of the 5,000-year-old world system.

This also explains why 'both the capitalist and the proletariat have an economic interest in the machine: it produces either their profit or their means of existence'.[120] The proletariat as a proletariat, that is as a class enforced to sell its labour in order to survive, and the capitalist as a capitalist, that is as an owner of capital, have immediate interests in the continuation of the capitalist machine complex since this is the infrastructure that guarantees the survival of the poor and the luxury of the rich.

If this diagnosis is true, then it is not strange that the development of capital according to the Goldberg circle did not move towards a classless society as the Marxists argued. There is for Goldberg and Caspary no real movement laying the basis of a society free from exploitation through the development of the productive forces. This is the machine utopia of Marxism that must be demystified so that the social question can be delinked from the infrastructure of capital that capitalism according to Caspary cannot be abstracted from.

However, the Goldberg circle's critique of capitalism and socialism as two forms of machine utopias reveals a proximity to those Marxists who already at the beginning of the 1920s attacked Leninism and the development in the Soviet Union as totalitarian. These currents of so-called left communists, famously denounced in V. I. Lenin's *Left-wing Communism an Infantile Disorder*, argued that the Russian Revolution showed that the working class had to find other forms of organization than the traditional Communist Party.[121]

Goldberg, Caspary and Unger were close to the left communist Simon Guttmann, who was enthralled by Goldberg's religious genius and saved his writings after his death in 1953, and Karl Korsch went to their meetings with the *Philosophische Gruppe*.[122] Guttman was one of the founders of KAPD (*Kommunistische Arbeiter-Partei Deutschlands*), which for a couple of years organized tens of thousands of workers in an organization that combatted what it saw as both Western and Soviet capitalism.

The Goldberg circle's hope for an anthropological transformation of the human species and their theoretical work on myth, philosophy and religion may seem foreign to the nexus of Marxist intellectuals belonging to the KAPD. Yet another founder of the party, the author and economist Franz Jung, defended an explicitly biological theory of revolution. In *Die Technik des Glücks*, published in two parts in 1921 and 1923, he elaborated a theory of 'the stream of life', arguing that the individual exemplar of the human species had become separated from the totality of biological existence.[123] Similar to the ideas of others in his circle, such as Ernst Fuhrmann and Raoul Hausmann, Jung wrote that '*property and capital are the compromise of life, the living consciousness of the isolated* [*des Vereinzelten*]' and posited that the struggle against capital even showed that 'the last motoric power source of human life is not yet released' since capitalism was an obstacle to the biological evolution of humanity.[124]

It was in relation to these currents and discussions that Unger already in 1921 had argued that the

> assault against the 'capitalist system' is forever in vain *at the site of its validity*. Capitalism is the most powerful and unfathomable of all systems, and can integrate every objection in the *domain* of its *power-to-be*. To raise anything against capitalism, it is first of all imperative *to go outside its field of activities* [*Wirkungsbereich*] because inside it can answer all counteraction.[125]

The field of activities of capital was the machine world that Caspary examined, and the logic behind Unger's idea of a secession from the capitalist system through mass migration – Völkerwanderung – was based on the wager that the forced proletarization that capitalism implied could produce a need for an exodus of all those urging for a life beyond the factory. It was Walter Benjamin who had summarized Unger's project as an exodus from civilization: 'Overcoming of capitalism through migration [Wanderung], Unger, *Politik und Metaphysik*.'[126] This was, in fact, the politics of the Goldberg circle.

Goldberg, Unger and Caspary sought a secession from capital's 'field of activities [Wirkungsbereich]'.[127] In practice this withdrawal implied the struggle for a 'non-catastrophic politics' adequate to the tasks needed for survival in a world that had been ravaged by the first industrialized world war and now was moving towards new disasters.[128] This might seem highly esoteric, but their ideas of an exodus from the West were part of the general discussion on Zionism that the Goldberg circle openly criticized.

Unger argued for the constitution of a Jewish community beyond the confines of the state in his book *Die Staatslose Bildung eines Jüdischen Volkes* from 1922.[129] On the basis of Goldberg's theory of the state as a stabilization of nature and therefore a normalization of its destructive character, Unger wrote that it would be dangerous for the Jewish community to become part of the nation states that belong to the whole European world 'which is nothing but an intermediate catastrophe'.[130] He insisted that building such a state would subsume the Jews under the course of history that had entrapped many other peoples in its catastrophic form of life. It would sever the Jews from their relation to the prehistoric and archaic peoples and tribes of the world which also lacked territorial states: 'The Jews should not overlook their singularly favourable position, namely, that since two thousand years they have materially been a people without history, the only one that can be free from being defeated by the fetters of the past and the reality of an empirical state existence that all other peoples have been defeated by.'[131]

Instead of building a state in the European sense, Unger proposed the construction of philosophical schools that would train Jews to develop a metaphysics for a stateless existence and seek to produce alliances with the non-Western, archaic communities scattered around the world. This was a suggestion that Unger had already defended in *Politik und Metaphysik* from 1921. There these, what he called 'metapolitical universities', were open for everyone who sought to abandon the politics of catastrophe whose centre the Goldberg circle found in the industrialized world.[132]

Today, the knowledge of how easily capital has subsumed its enemies leads even dependency theorists to argue for the impossibility of a delinking strategy: it is impossible to live outside the world market. In this sense, any secession from capital may seem hopelessly naive. Not least because millions of the wretched of the earth today are searching for a future in what is perhaps falsely deemed to be the core regions of capital such as the United States and Europe. But Goldberg, Caspary and Unger were not oblivious to the blatant fact that the masses who abandoned the poverty of the old world during the first decades of the twentieth century did so in order to find jobs and survive as proletarians in a world market that made global migration possible. However, many of those who migrated also searched for ways to live outside the confines of the industrial system of capitalism, such as in phalansteries in the United States or the kibbutzim in Palestine.

At the same time, their theory of flight from the world of civilization was based on the belief that the fundamental yet inner exteriority to capitalism, namely, the living labour that must be subsumed as work in order for capital to be accumulated, would increasingly be expelled from the world of factories due to the development of the productive forces. For, as we have seen, even if machines constantly produce the need for new labour in mining, extraction of fossil fuel and so on, they also produce unemployment and precarity, today visible in the rust belts of the world, through the production processes which they revolutionize. This was the double process of capitalist development that Caspary examined, subsumption and expulsion of labour, and both facets of this process would imply catastrophes that could produce a need for a life outside the Behemoth of the industrialized world.

The Goldberg circle came close to describing a situation in which the proletariat had to confront its own condition as a surplus population [*Zusatzbevölkerung*], a class whose survival as a class was tied to the continuation of the machine world of capitalism, since the catastrophic politics of the capitalist system would clash with the interests of the workers as biological beings.[133] Goldberg interpreted, as we have seen, Caspary's reading of Marx as indicating that capitalism is less a totality subsuming everything in its midst than an anarchic, catastrophic system expelling workers from the immediate process of production. It was a system that, like the whole history of the 'process of fixation', produced what Goldberg called – with his dense jargon – 'individuals isolated from the "people's totality" [*Volksganzen*]'.[134] These alienated and atomized individuals were fixated to the development of technology which was an *Ersatz* to the metaphysics of myth and a product of the anthropogenesis of the Homo sapiens as a toolmaking and state-building animal.

The reason why the *Elohim IHWH* is 'an enemy to technology' – and needs a people that chooses metaphysics over the machine in order to become present – is because the metabolic relation ruled by technology make the gods absent. The technology of modern machinery binds humans to the world that closes itself off from the domain of the possible and the abundance that it implies. It creates the world of fixation which is ruled by scarcity. In contrast, the gods of myth seek to alter a specific part of nature whereas the *Elohim IHWH* wants to disrupt the entropic processes that the 5,000-year-old world system can only stabilize.

When the gods no longer are present in the world, life is caught in its own destructive process, and embedded in the cycles of birth and death that the Hebrews attempted but failed to alter. And, Goldberg underlines, this absence of the gods is not only a catastrophe for life. It is a crisis for the *Elohim IHWH* himself who, as we will see, is life as such. For 'God justifies himself when he brings the lower order of nature into a higher one. That is the essence of the righteousness of God, to proceed from God himself. The Torah has known that.'[135]

This is essential, for the detailed descriptions of rites and rituals in the Torah explained not only how the Hebrews made God manifest in the world. These rites depicted how God sought to liberate himself from the imperfections that he had made possible by giving finite and temporal beings the joy and suffering of existence. By creating something outside him the perfect Godhead has created an imperfect world but by being eternal life he wants to become finite so that he can increasingly share his immortality to the realm of time and space.

Goldberg's radical claim was that the Torah was a manual for the immortalization of creaturely existence through the mythical acts that can make the infinite and eternal God present as a finite, spatial and temporal power so that he, himself, could be liberated from the imperfections of his creation. Therefore, Goldberg wrote, God has to become 'the enemy of technology' and the whole factory world which, when Caspary published *Die Maschinenutopie* in 1927, was rapidly moving towards the global crisis of 1929.[136]

In such a situation, when the economy is in a deep crisis and the metabolic and irreparable rift between humanity and the rest of nature will divide the life of the proletariat itself, a secession would not only be possible but necessary from Goldberg's perspective. But if Unger was right that in order 'to raise anything against capitalism it is first of all necessary *to go outside its field of activities*' one must ask what these fields of activities are in order to envision the Goldberg circle's desired exodus out of the Behemoth of industrialized capitalism. We can find the answer in our metabolic relation to nature.

New needs and desires for change have to be created on the basis of needs and desires specific to the anthropological form of the proletariat, namely, the workers inhabiting the factory world that Caspary sought to decipher. According to the Goldberg circle, such a feat was possible because of the radical plasticity of human life.

Caspary enigmatically claimed that even if there is no prospect of building a just society on the world of existing machines, and at the same time no possibility of returning to an agrarian idyll (a primitivistic option the Goldberg circle explicitly refused), there '*is the power of organic life*. But this power is not accessible to contemporary humanity [*der gegenwärtigen Menschheit*] in a conscious way, it belongs to the capricious nature that has been withdrawn from humanity.'[137] What contemporary humanity has no access to is a conscious cultivation of our natural, psychophysical needs and desires into a process of sublation and negation, rather than into the simple stabilization of nature that the world of fixation entails.

In order to understand the aforementioned quote on the power of organic life, we have to remember that history, for the Goldberg circle, was the history of different ways of cultivating the needs of human life. This is less fanciful than it may seem since it implies that different anthropological configurations entail different relations to nature or, once again, specific economies of nature.

It was by stressing the plasticity of human needs that Goldberg thought – probably vainly – that the particular community described in the *Torah*, grounded on the power of organic life or what he called *Geist*, could reveal a universal task to the millions whose lives were destroyed by the First and Second World Wars. The paradoxical construction of a particular political community that would express this organic openness of a species without a specific natural habitat was the basis of the work of *Die Wirklichkeit der Hebräer*, and indicates what for Goldberg was the most fundamental problem: What kind of anthropological form would be able to produce such a community?

Behind every anthropology there is, as we have seen, an even more primordial entropology, and therefore an economic order that explains how we can live, either as a species that stabilizes the entropic tendency of nature or sublates it. Contemporary humanity, or what Goldberg with his aprioristic ethnology would call the breed of Cain, is the humanity that is fixated in civilization and thereby alienated from the power of organic life. In contrast, the Torah depicts, as I have argued, an exception in the course of normal history: the attempt of Abraham and his people to flee the tribe and the state. But does this not imply that Goldberg came close to a theory of races or to a Manichean dualism between Abel and Cain as two distinct breeds? Goldberg certainly thought that the Torah belonged to a world full of gods and peoples who lived according to the rules of their deities. This theory of polytheism prompted Goldberg to develop an understanding of myth as belonging to a period when our species was differentiated in a vast multitude of peoples or what he also called races. But – as we will see in the next section – this theory of race was not a defence of the normalcy of nature that Nazism would exalt. It was a 'biological universalism' that sought to transform rather than preserve existing life by wresting everything living out of its biological and natural ancestry.[138]

Biological universalism

The groups of humans that live outside the process of fixation represent different races in the Torah, and if these tribes are submerged by the states, they lose their ability to make their deities present. The orders of fixation 'consist in the dissolution of the *peoples* into the formation of their antipode of the *state*' for 'every people that progresses in the destructive process of separation from its god finds itself inevitably at the stage of decline'.[139] This is the decline to normality that, Goldberg argued, had stabilized itself to a world where there were only remnants of races and peoples left.

It is only in the brief period of myth depicted in the Torah that humanity is fractured in distinct races. Yet, this differentiation of our species in diverging races is latent in the human since a people or a race – they are synonyms for Goldberg – is a way to open the world to the domain of the possible that precedes time and space and that is visible in all life. Life is possibility and divine life is the possibility to alter the normality of biological life.

To belong to a race implies to belong to a deity through the production of a collective life form: a people. Theoretically, humans can still form a race that abandons the world of fixation, since our species – according to Goldberg's interpretation of the Torah – is a compromise between God and nature that can be revoked. The human is not created by God but by God and nature or, rather, by God and the gods of nature.

The plural form of the subject that creates the human in Genesis is a sign that the *Elohim IHWH* needed help when he made our species: 'Let us make man in our image, after our likeness' (Gen. 1.26). Our species was produced by God and the evolution of nature, or what in the Torah is called the slime of earth (Gen. 2.7). God created the human after a world full of cosmic potencies had been brought forth. The human is therefore made after the likeness of both God and the nature that came before our species. Since nature for Goldberg can be interpreted as the animation of potencies that humans mythologize as gods, the human is constituted as an oscillation between the domain of finite deities, the potencies of nature, and the infinite divinity that is superior to the other gods: the *Elohim IHWH*.

The fact that God and nature created the human together indicates that our species exists in a state of disjunction between the finite and the infinite parts of reality. The human oscillates between the gods of temporal nature, and the God of eternal life and can easily, like Cain, follow the normal path of human evolution and become fixated in the finite realm. This implies that the human signifies 'a freedom of choice that has a *political* meaning, . . . it [humanity] should be understood as a "*compromise*", that must be sealed between the Elohim IHWH and the other Elohim, since both parties were participating in the fabrication of the human'.[140] A compromise implies a latent conflict and contradiction and this is what Adam entails: a potential conflict between the finite and infinite.

Our species can, under very specific conditions, choose to act against the tendencies that stabilize it to a toolmaking animal by following the gods, or it can even follow the God of all gods, and this implies a conflict with both the tribe and the state. It is here that Goldberg's theology of race differs from Jaynes's conceptualization of the archaic peoples as composed of beings that lack consciousness.

Consciousness for Jaynes is, as I mentioned before, self-reflectivity and ultimately the ability to make conscious choices; this is what according to him is lacking in the mythical period. In contrast, Goldberg argued that a set of conscious choices emerges in the mythical period since the mythical peoples can abandon their deities and choose to live with the *Elohim IHWH*.

The Goldberg circle was defending a new anthropogenesis, and they saw such a production of a new human as a conscious political task that not only separates our species from the material community of capital but also aims to change the basis of humanity's entropic structure. When Goldberg, Unger and Caspary predicted schematically that humanity has three anthropological choices – fixation, myth and the Torah – they envisioned three different political modes of combating the entropy that disrupts every organization of life with chaos and decline.

First, humanity can live in relation to specific parts of nature, with all its finite creatures, in a totemistic manner, and become a species of peoples who have their ancestries outside themselves in some region of nature. This is certainly better than life in civilization. But it is not enough. The totemistic divinities are, Goldberg argues, described in the *Torah* as archetypes of different biological behaviour that modify and sublate specific parts of normal nature. Still, they cannot alter nature as nature: 'The archetype of normal biology goes . . . far back, it is established in the world structure: in this way, however, the normal "biological" organism arises. Hence, there can be no true new creations based on biology.'[141] This is why the archaic life forms of prehistoric cultures were, ultimately, unable to solve the problem of scarcity.

In sharp contrast to Marxists and other radicals, Goldberg did not seek an alternative in any primitive communism or what Marshall Sahlins has called 'an original affluent society'.[142] These – what Sahlins also called – 'stone age economies' were too easily led into the path of coercion and violence that could not counter the emergence of the state as a stabilization of the entropic tendency of nature.

Second, humanity can, just as it has done, decline to the normality of property owners and city builders. It thereby ends the period of myth by becoming the *homo faber* that stabilizes the entropic destruction of human life inherent in nature through the advent of capitalism as an industrialized system that moves humanity to the peak everything situation that the Goldberg circle had already warned of in the 1920s. This is nothing but the normal, and most likely, course of human evolution.

Third, humanity has the possibility of opening itself up to a new anthropogenesis, hinted at in the life that the Hebrews took on as they set out to sublate the normal course of nature and produce a new human community. This would, Goldberg argued, entail a form of economic abundance needed in order for humanity to survive beyond the capitalist mode of production, which lays the ground for a coming 'machine catastrophe'. The hope of the Goldberg circle was ultimately that this new kind of existence, withdrawing itself from the civilizational basis of capital, would restructure the entropological constitution of human life through an abundance that even promised eternal life.

Die Wirklichkeit der Hebräer traces the third choice, but this turn away from both totemism and the fixated world has the mythical period as its condition of possibility. The rites and rituals of the Torah can only be implemented by a people able to visualize the presence of the gods. To return to Jaynes once again, it is only a people with a bicameral mind that can feel the presence of the divine in the world and thus make the *Elohim IHWH* present.

It is still theoretically possible to make the divine present, for the human is still Adam: a compromise between the finite and infinite. Our species is constituted by the likeness of both God and the potencies of nature. Yet, practically it seems impossible, since there are only remnants of the mythical peoples left in the world. The gods have withdrawn from the spatio-temporal realm and been replaced by technology.

Abraham's people became subsumed under the order of the states – already slowly beginning with the conquest of Canaan – and their mythical religion was turned to 'the form of religion of the fixation: the *world religion*. Whereas the national religion represents the *real*, transcendental and lawful regulated relation between the people and its biological centre, the God of world religion (when the true people no longer exists) is no reality but an *abstraction*. The world religion is therefore the expression of a *fictive* relation between man and God.'[143] The mythological deities had to become real as a communal life form that manifested the plasticity of human existence and thereby produced a myriad of distinct life forms or, what Goldberg called, races.

I can now deduce that race for the Goldberg circle is the mythical and ethnological relation between a people and the deity which acts as its *Abstammung*. To belong to a race is to have one's ancestry outside oneself. The mythological races are communities seeking to contradict nature. Mythical peoples or races can often adopt new members willing to live in relation to the ancestry which these communities find outside themselves in totems that break sections of humanity free from the biological and cultural ancestries that the world of the states is built upon. The metaphysical races were, Susman insisted by underlining the anti-racist logic of Goldberg's metaphysics, never 'unities of *nature, blood* and *soil*.'[144] They were communities open to the abnormal and transcendental forces of the divine.

Only a few years after Adolf Hitler's electoral success, Goldberg could, for example, write: 'Life is just a barren rest, rudimentary are also the contemporary *groups* of life. What meaning have peoples and races today? The truth is: none at all.'[145] All contemporary peoples are 'born out of geopolitical and economic interests' rather than grounded in the ancestries of deities and gods which open the world for something transcendent.[146] There are, however, remnants of mythical communities among the archaic peoples of the world, and Unger implied that there are traces of another form of humanity even in Europe.

> It is possible (to a small extent even probable) that there are elements of a more genuine unity within one or the other of these historical entities, England, France, Russia, Germany, Italy, Czech Republic, Ireland, or whatever they are called, but these [elements] would not fit into one of these covers, as they today

– tremble – over the remnants of the once living primal archetypes of all these phenomena.[147]

These words from 1921 were written in a period of hyperinflation in the Weimar Republic that had begun in 1918, and in March 1923, the republic plunged into a deep economic crisis heralding the great collapse of world capitalism in 1929. This was as a period of starvation and hunger riots.[148] The mark could no longer be saved, and inflation rose drastically. Retail business began to hoard their inventories and refuse payment in paper marks. The stores in Berlin and in several other cities were first only open two or three days a week, and then, all over Germany, only on an hourly basis, and stock remained insufficient.

Goldberg, Caspary and Unger's harsh critique of European civilization was formulated in this dramatic period. They sought an alternative in the life forms that existed outside the world of modern, industrialized states, which during their lives produced planetary wars and imperialistic and totalitarian regimes that killed millions of humans. But they also thought that beyond and outside the noosphere of the capitalist production and consumption lies the primordial world of biological nature. This world shows itself in every hunger riot, in every struggle for a better life and in the flight over every border. These conflicts are clashes of biological life against the political institutions that mediate it politically and economically.

What Unger called 'the elements of a more genuine unity' that the modern nation states tremble over, and which do not 'fit' the nation states, are the psychophysical existence of the citizens of the states and the masses of refugees who gathered in millions in Europe after the First World War. Yet, as citizens they could, according to Unger, never constitute a real people. This is not possible since these national conglomerates were bound together to 'unreal presences', formations that constituted them as a species separated into atomistic individuals and forced together in states.[149] Still, Unger and Goldberg wagered, a politics based on the biological reality that all members of the human species have in common, the fact that we are animals oscillating between finite nature and the infinitude of spirit, could be produced if communities that severed themselves from the industrialized world arose.

This could be a repetition of the flight from the 5,000-year-old world old system that the Hebrews initiated and which made them a race that separated itself from the normal course of human evolution just as they broke from the totemism of the mythical period. The originality of the Torah was that it sought to transcend the ancestries that the mythical races found in their gods by creating a community based on the human ability to be open to every region of nature. The *Elohim IHWH* comes into the world '*from outside [von außen]*' and reveals that the human does not belong to any specific place, region or culture.¹⁵⁰ The human, and Goldberg meant every human, is potentially an animal of the infinite. This transcendental homelessness is what the 'biological universalism' of the Torah implied; and it explains why the Hebrews were a kind of non-race; an existence that affirmed what disturbingly came to be called life unworthy of life, *Lebensunwertes Leben*, by living against the normalcy of nature that Nazism would exalt.

Contra naturam vivere

Biological organisms such as animals, plants and fungi are ruled by heredity and doomed to become slaves under the evolution. The mythological peoples who tried to live in relation to the gods of nature could sublate, but not overcome, the fixation process that ruled life. In contrast, the Torah was not based on nature but on the realm of possibility that precedes it and the rites, rituals and systems of taboos – such as what is impure, *tumah*, and pure, *taharah* – were attempts to liberate nature from the cycles of birth and death so that the God of all gods could become present.

For, as we remember, the revelation of a deity can happen only through the life world of a mythological people. A good example of a rite conducted against the normality of life, and therefore the necessity of death, is the sacrifice of the red heifer (Num. 19.2). The ashes of the sacrificed red cow were used for the purification of those Israelites who had come into contact with a corpse which is *tumah* for the deity who seeks to bestow immortality upon his creation.¹⁵¹

Goldberg interpreted this and other rituals as indications that 'the metaphysics of the Pentateuch' puts 'the death-tumah in work *against itself*' for through the sacrificing of the red cow is 'an *antigen against the death-tumah* created'.¹⁵² The rules of Lev. 12.2-5 that a woman after childbirth is impure is another sign that the cycle of birth and death that constitutes normal life must be purified so that God can dwell with his people.¹⁵³ Birth and death are not problematic or impure from a moral perspective but rather because they are the natural forces that tie organic life to the finite nature that God seeks to alter.

Death is 'the ancient source and prototype of the *impurity* (abi abot hatumah)' for God, since 'the Elohim IHWH is the "this-worldly" Elohim', the God of the living, the God of this world, whereas the other gods that the *Elohim IHWH* calls the world to abandon are what the Torah calls the *Elohim Metim*, the gods of death.¹⁵⁴

The deities that the God of the Torah seeks to separate humanity from are, from the perspective of humans, personifications of the nature which God wants to transform. This is why *Elohim IHWH* has to confront the other gods as foreign rulers – Goldberg calls them 'forces of occupation' and 'world powers' – since he is the uncreated and infinite reality that transcends the reality of matter, time and space and only can enter it from the outside as something that seeks to contradict it in its totality.[155]

The mythological deities are autonomous from their creator since nature is something else than God and, it is important to note, these natural forces can both open humanity to God, the infinite source of finite nature, and embed our species in the entropic process of the cosmos that threatens life itself with extinction.

Besides these gods of death, there are also the gods of biological birth that chain organic life to what in the Torah is called the *nepesh*: 'the "vegetative life"' identifiable with the simple biological need that can be discerned as the craving for hunger, thirst and sexuality in every living organism.[156] However, even vegetative life, which can be identified with striving for survival in all life, is an expression of the modality of what Goldberg calls spirit. But it is a spirit that is subsumed by the normal nature of biological ancestry that the Torah seeks to liberate creation from by adjusting the *nepesh* in relation to the spirit, *nechamah*, which in turn is related to the eternal life of the creator God.

The Torah sought, ultimately, to push humanity out of the domain of finite nature and to turn our species into an animal of the infinite: a creature that first of all belongs to God by being elevated to his domain. Read from this perspective, the reality of what Jaynes described as the bicameral mind is the reality of a God whom men and women could consciously choose to follow by abandoning all biological ancestries. This is why the Hebrews were anything but a race in the modern, or even biological, sense. It was a community that wanted to sever itself from all ancestries by living in relation to the exteriority to time, space and matter that is God.

Abraham was 'the progenitor' and 'the founder of a new community of life vigorously opposed to ancestral biology . . . He is prepared to sacrifice all that comes with it. He adopts the circumcision, is ready to slay his son, and does far more by sacrificing his former *Elohim*.'[157] By sacrificing the heavenly ram, instead of his son Isaac, Abraham offers not only his own, original totemistic god. He breaks the taboo of his original people and institutes a community which abolishes human sacrifice and seeks to bind nature to the God of eternal life. The circumcision symbolizes how Abraham wrested himself free from all ancestral biology, including the transcendental biology of the totemistic peoples. Thereby he invites everyone to join his new people and worship him who is '*in principle enemy to all orders of nature*' – the God that calls creation away from all biological and historical ancestries.[158] But, as we have seen, this enmity to the normality of nature must begin in time and space. It implies a gradual reshaping of the world through the actions of a people. These actions are the rites of the Torah, and, it is important to note, it was not God who chose Abraham. There is no election in the Torah according to Goldberg.

God did not in any sense elect Abraham. It was Abraham who found a way to open a part of creation for the divine which, in principle, could be done by everyone since God belongs to all. Abraham was willing to adopt the task of God to liberate nature from the frailties and death of normal life: 'It is the special facet of the old Hebrew metaphysics that it, despite its this-worldly nature, is an action which is *hostile* to nature in the most radical sense, and whose principle of morality is: contra naturam vivere, *to proceed against nature*.'[159] To proceed against nature is to proceed against the normalcy of a life that has become so fixated that no new creations can be found on the level of what Goldberg called 'normal biology'.[160] But how can Goldberg reconcile his claim that Hebrew metaphysics is based on a 'biological universalism' with this interpretation of the Torah as a life *contra naturam*?

The answer is that the Torah is the doctrine of how the people of God separates the infinite power of life from the powers of normal biology, through a complex system of taboos and rites that is open to others. These rites point to the different layers of the world that can be channelled against the cycles of birth and death. There is the infinite economy of life, the source of nature where life is abundant and immortal, which Goldberg called *Geist*. There is the finite economy of matter which is ruled by entropy and scarcity and which nails spirit to nature, and there is the layer of both these principles being at play in what we call life and, especially, human life. The infinite and the finite even constitute the compromise that characterizes the human as a being that is part of both spirit and matter.

Tellingly, spirit is identified as the source of biological life as such in *Die Wirklichkeit der Hebräer* and Goldberg postulated an inner 'divide' between the dimensions of life and matter in nature.[161] Life, which in its form of potentiality is identifiable with spirit, is '*the transcendence of matter*' which means that all living, biological organisms exist in an ecstatic state.[162] They have some feeling of what is outside them, and it is this transcendence that reveals that all life exists in an ecstatic state and therefore, ultimately, are related to the *Elohim IHWH*.

The sycamore tree and the fruit fly do not know that in the eyes of humans they are trees and flies. Still, they can register information from their surroundings and in different manners adapt and survive and thereby take part of what is outside them.[163] Spirit as 'the transcendence of matter' is the inner feeling of exteriority that pervades every organism: the feeling that reality is more and other than oneself or even itself. Spirit is non-identity. It is the opposite of that nature which is fixated to itself.

From this perspective, even plants and simple biological organisms such as amoebas can be said to feel in some rudimentary way that there is something outside them that they must absorb in their metabolic processes or avoid if they are threatened by it. This feeling of the organism is the disjunction between spirit and matter that constitutes it as a living, biological being: 'The divide is . . . the category of the organic or of *biology*.'[164] This means that just as spirit is not anti-material but 'the transcendence of matter', organic life cannot be reduced to its material constraints, since the divide of life is spirit and spirit is possibility.

Life is the power of potentiality visible in the efforts of every organic being to survive and this potency was, according to Goldberg, harnessed during the mythical era as life forms that modified the normalcy of nature to the point that life was not only, as it is during the course of normal human evolution, a struggle for survival. God, for Goldberg, is life, but life is not only or primarily biological life. Life is possibility and the exteriority to the world of time, space and matter. Life is what belongs to the outside. The origin of biology is pre-biological.

In this sense Goldberg was an 'extreme vitalist', as Unger called him, and a profoundly biocentric thinker who attacked the industrialized world for destroying the potency of life. The modern machine world and its industrial civilization may seem to have transformed existing nature radically and given rise to modern self-reflective consciousness. But according to Goldberg, this world can only perpetuate life as an entropic and self-destructive phenomenon, and it can only fixate life to biology as a material process that easily could become extinct.

The idea of extinction is of crucial importance in Goldberg's corpus, and he underlines that '[w]hoever believes that there *must* be life on Earth is wrong'.[165] This is why God is not only the enemy of nature and technology but even more radically 'the *enemy* of death' according to the Torah.[166] There is a conflict between life and matter, where life is the principle of transcendence and potentiality, and matter the principle of necessity and inertia, and this conflict can easily be won – in an imperfect world – by the powers of death.

God can be defeated by the imperfections of the creation that he has brought forth in the sense that he can become banished into his mysterious infinitude and eternity. He needs a covenant with a people in order to dwell in time and space as a force that increasingly shares his immortality with the world.

The *vivere contra naturam*, which is taught by the Torah, is a practical solidarity with human life against the powers of death, and this is why the Hebrew metaphysics, as a 'biological universalism', is directed against the injustices that inhibit and suppress life.

Commenting on Deut. 10.18 which states that God 'defends the cause of fatherless and the widow, and loves the foreigner residing among you, giving them food and clothing', Goldberg underlined that this is not so much a moral demand as a description of what the *Elohim IHWH* is, 'because "the defense of the fatherless and the widow", i.e. for the oppressed in general, explicitly belongs to the "attributes" of the Elohim.'[167] God is the defence of the oppressed and this is what the Hebrews must reflect to make life itself, the *Elohim IHWH*, present: an abundant life that gives without the need to ask for something in return.

A life *contra naturam* is a life against the scarcity of resources that rules normal nature. That is what, Goldberg stressed, 'Eheje ascher Eheje, that is "I am, who I am"' entails and such a life against nature is profoundly ethical.[168] The one who is himself is identical with being and therefore identical with the abundant and eternal life that the Hebrews took upon them as the task to defend 'the oppressed in general'. Justice is the totem of the Torah since justice is the life of God. Goldberg's amoralism becomes, by necessity, ethical.

Goldberg hoped, against all odds, for a new messianic Judaism open for everyone willing to live against the normality of nature that makes it so difficult to live in solidarity with other humans. There may be no hope for a new tabernacle. But he wagered that the Torah could be used for the creation of a new revelation, it implied a new possibility to live against the normalcy of nature, by men and women once again willing to follow God in his mission to redeem life from the entropic processes that threaten it.

Missionary Hebrewdom

In a letter from 1933 to the theologian Hans Kosmala, one of the organizers of the *Schwedische Israelmission* in Vienna, Goldberg emphasized that the Hebrews fought to include new members in their midst and expand the domain belonging to *Elohim IHWH*.

Goldberg pointed to the intermingling between Edomites, Egyptians and Hebrews as an evidence and wrote to Kosmala:

> You are mistaken when you write that the permission to intermingle with the Edomites and Egyptians is an exception to a general prohibition of intermingling with other peoples. There is no such thing. On the contrary: the Egyptians and Edomites are paradigmatic to show the fact that access to Hebrewdom also for other peoples . . . is open in principle.[169]

Everyone willing to live according to the taboo system of the Torah could join the Hebrews before Judaism had become part of the world of fixation. In fact, all the archaic tribes could have taken up the Torah by abandoning their gods and turn themselves to an instrument that made the infinite present in the finite realm.

> Originally the Hebrews are a people like all other peoples. Every people had the same chance to obtain the Torah. According to old, oral tradition, it has been offered to *all* peoples of the world in the same manner. . . . Because, to get in contact with the God coming from infinity, one cannot take any patent or monopoly. But historically only the Hebrews have accepted the Torah.[170]

It was a historic coincidence that it was the Hebrews who formed a covenant with the *Elohim IHWH*. However, by being related to the people who opened themselves to God the modern ancestors to the ancient Hebrews have an advantage. They are still, potentially, connected to the metaphysics of the Torah, at least as long as they try to live without a state, since the state fixates us to normal nature and undoes the people as an instrument that can make a deity manifest. It was this that gave Goldberg the hope – although he knew that the world of myth was long gone – that Judaism could renew its messianic tradition by opening itself for new members and tie itself to other remnants of the mythical tribes.

Consequently, Goldberg taunted Kosmala, and urged him to abandon his faith: 'Give up Christianity and take on Hebrewdom! Throw away the illusion and seize the original. Christianity wants to unite the peoples in "humanity". But: that which is common to humans in "unmetaphysical time", that, which extinguishes all differences to nothing, is the misfortune in the world. In misfortune, and only in that, humanity is one.'[171]

A real human community could not be based on the hardship and misery of contemporary humanity which only six years later would be cast into a new planetary war and, Goldberg wrote in his letter to Kosmala, Christianity is a religion that '*needs* the presence of misfortune in the world, because without it, it would lose its right to exist'.[172] The suffering Messiah perpetuates the miseries of the world rather than seeking to end them here and now.

Goldberg's attack on Christianity was a rejection of what he saw as all forms of false universalism. He considered the Christians to be reproducing the structure of the Cainite race, which knows no totemistic differences, but rather undoes itself through the chimeras of nationalism, fascism and Nazism.

This belief in the urgent need of a missionary Hebrewdom made Goldberg a controversial figure. Gershom Scholem described Goldberg's doctrine as a new demonology.[173] In 1925 he even called *Die Wirklichkeit der Hebräer* 'the classical work of Jewish Satanism', and after the Second World War he portrayed Goldberg and his circle as a group of 'metaphysical magicians'.[174] They turned God's law to magic.

Goldberg, on the other hand, refused to see himself as a magician. He separated prophecy, which he defined as a labour with the infinite, from magic and emphasized the prohibition of sorcery in the Torah.[175] However, Scholem was not alone in describing Goldberg as a magician. A keen reader of his work, the theologian Erwin Reisner, who attempted to have *Die Wirklichkeit der Hebräer* republished after the Second World War, analysed Goldberg's metaphysics as a 'magical messianism' in a review of his book on Maimonides.[176]

If Scholem accused Goldberg of being a reactionary, Reisner underlined the progressive and even moralistic tendencies in Goldberg's magical thinking: 'This metaphysical utopianism stands much closer to the humanistic ideology and the ideology of the enlightenment than the author believes. . . . Out of the dynamic of Judaism, Goldberg wants to proceed from a simply philosophical-theoretical to a practical-ethical Romanticism. But practical Romanticism is always magic.'[177] Behind Goldberg's harsh critique of modern civilization and his romantic view on the tribal life of *Urjudentum*, Reisner discerned a desire to make the justice of the Abrahamic God present in a world of global wars that were leading to the Shoah.

Reisner clearly admired Goldberg, but he could not accept what he saw as a reversal of the order of revelation:

> The revelation remains the primary, the action of the human is the secondary. With Goldberg this relation is reversed, there it is the human who through his cultic action makes the revelation possible at all, yes, virtually causes it. The man speaks and God answers. . . . Goldberg holds himself approximately in the middle between paganism and belief in the revelation.[178]

Reisner's critique was too Christian to be serious for Goldberg. He saw himself as an ethnologist who consciously placed himself between paganism and revelation in order to situate the revelation in its polytheistic context. It was among totemistic gods that the *Elohim IHWH* could become present since the tribes of that epoch were open to the divine forces of nature, whereas humans today view gods as hallucinations or ideological fabrications. They have lost the ability to understand the possibility of a politics on the level of nature: a politics against nature through the presence of a deity that unifies power and justice.

> God and man have the same purpose: *the making of the ethical world order.* The benefit that is given to man consists of two things. First – in relation to nature – in the elimination of the coercion that nature has imposed on him by its persistence and inertia, i.e. in all the shortcomings of the body and its frail laws of life. Second – sociologically – in the unification of might and right. Without the participation of God, the ethical world order cannot be achieved, because otherwise humanity disintegrates into opposed and conflicting interest groups. The present God is the guarantor of the ethical world order, *which unifies power and justice.*[179]

This demand of the institutionalization of an ethical order echoes Hermann Cohen's suggestion in his posthumous work, *Religion of Reason: Out of the Sources of Judaism* from 1919, that 'monotheism reaches its summit in Messianism. Messianism, however, means the dominion of the good on earth.'[180] But, if for Cohen, the origin of messianism was given by the prophets and continued in the modern world of the nation state through, for instance, the workers' movement, Goldberg wrote in *Die Wirklichkeit der Hebräer*, published six years after Cohen's posthumous masterwork: 'One has placed the "ethos of the prophets" above the Pentateuch. As a matter of fact, it is not only no "progress" but rather a "retrogression."'[181] In the Torah, the *Elohim IHWH* is present, he dwells as a principle of morality in the tabernacle, whereas with the rise of the prophets God has been turned into an abstraction that can only give us a hope for the future.

If I now return to Hepner's suggestion that Goldberg sought to develop, what I would like to call, a science of evil it is obvious that his argument is that a traditional theodicy never can answer the question why God needs help in order to become present in the world. God's revelation must be answered by a community which lives according to the rules and laws that make him manifest.

Traditional theodicy implies that there is a moral meaning with pain and suffering that will be revealed at the *eschaton*. The God of the Torah is a task that we have to take upon us so that he can live in our midst as a power that can confront the biological and sociological injustices that plague life. Goldberg defended, in the end, a politics of revelation that sought to alter nature by making God present as a force against death and entropy.

This strengthens Reisner's description of Goldberg's Judaism as a magic messianism. For magic, Lévi-Strauss has argued with much elegance, is primarily a '"gigantic variation on the principle of causality" as [Henri] Hubert and [Marcel] Mauss called it', and it 'can be distinguished from science not so much by any ignorance or contempt of determinism but by a more imperious and uncompromising demand for it'.[182] Magic is a system of correspondences that is overdetermined and, interestingly, Goldberg defined Hebrew metaphysics as 'the control of causality and contingency'.[183]

It was in their classic anthropological study *A General Theory of Magic* that Mauss and Hubert argued that magic is 'a type of ritual that presumes to cause an effect on *y* through the ruled actions performed on *x*, under the basic assumption that *x* and *y* are or can be essentially related because of certain universal "natural laws"'.[184] Read through Mauss's theory of magic, the biological miracles that the Hebrews supposedly enacted through their rituals can be seen as manifestations of a justice that counters death and liberates the dead by trying to alter the normal causality of time. The Torah was a mechanism for the resurrection since it was the way for finite, spatial and temporal reality to be formed by the atemporal and aspatial abundance of life. It aimed to alter the laws of life by tapping into the infinite possibilities that precede actual and temporal existence.

The moralization of magic that Reisner detected in *Die Wirklichkeit der Hebräer* was, for Goldberg, the reality of God when he was made present in the world. The *Elohim IHWH* sought an ethical correspondence with creation in order to share his immortality with the living and even the dead. The reality of the Hebrews – *Die Wirklichkeit der Hebräer* – is essentially God's reality – *Die Wirklichkeit Gottes* – and by defining the Torah, the law of the Hebrews, as the rituals that almost magically correspond to the divine, Goldberg comes surprisingly close to Cohen's view on immortality as an infinite task. They both defended a politics of immortality.

The politics of immortality

The ethics of the Torah was driven by a refusal to view life and death as invariable powers that could not be changed. The normal evolution of life could be transformed and, for Goldberg, immortality was the explicit goal of the God of the Torah. Not as an afterlife but as part of a this-worldly justice that sought to make, what Cohen called 'the dominion of good' present here and now.

> The fact of 'immortality' is ... *no* solution to the theodicy problem, (which is why this 'solution' is omitted in the Pentateuch). The fair compensation of the fate of the *individual* (for example, the *normal* 'Karma of the rebirth', which is always a consequence of 'bygone' deeds) provides no solution, because what it is about, a *presence of justice on earth*, that is a justice of the totality, is a *political* conception of justice. It follows: absolute justice is only given once God is present, and indeed only for the area of manifestation to which God's presence is extended. But since he is *not* there, in other words, that this world – as it is – is *not* 'the best of the worlds', that is because he [God] *cannot* be present 'just like that', this means that it is a task of the people, that is a task of a transcendental political action, to *provide* God with this power, that is to *enforce* both his liberation and his presence (which is identical with 'divine power'). This world *can* thus be 'the best of all worlds', it has ... the possibility to be that ... but only once it becomes *transcendent*.[185]

By providing God with the power to act in time and space, the world is transformed into the best of all worlds, Goldberg wrote alluding to Gottfried Wilhelm von Leibniz and this is not only the manifestation of God but his own liberation. For God, as an eternal life that creates something else than himself, the domain of finite reality, a world where life is not abundant but damaged by the frailties of spatial and temporal existence, seeks to redeem himself from the imperfections he has created by producing a world that is not him.

There is a direct correlation between immortality and God's presence, or for that matter between immortality and justice, that needs to be enacted in the world through cultic acts that manifest the ethical order that God essentially is. This seems to prove Reisner's argument that the order of revelation is turned on its head by Goldberg. But Reisner misses the fact that God, as 'I am who I am', is a reality that is before Abraham and before everyone who tries to follow his way.

Goldberg is close to orthodox Judaic teaching by insisting that there is a God of gods who creates a world independent from him and who, by being eternal and just, desires that his creation can freely turn to him in order to make his infinitude present. What might be heterodox is that Goldberg stressed that it is 'a task of transcendental political action' to '*provide* God with the power' to make the world transcendent and unfettered from the cycles of birth and death by elevating it to the realm of abundant life.

Such a liberation of the world from the imperfections of death and suffering is a liberation of God himself. God is caught in a loop that he seeks to break himself free from since he desires to be an intrinsic part of the suffering of the world. The reason why God needs a covenant with a people is that he can only be present in creation by becoming finite, and thereby share the violence of nature, in order to correlate the world to his eternal life without making it identical with his eternity. This implies that God also needs to break through the loop that he is caught in by creating something else than his infinity. God's omnipotence is restricted by the finite and temporal creation that he has brought forth. It is this restriction that he wants to overcome without destroying the autonomy of the world of time and space by making the world transcendent and part of his eternal life.

It is helpful to turn to Cohen's investigation of messianism as the 'the correlation of man with God' in order to understand Goldberg's circular conceptualization of immortality as a presence of justice on earth.[186] For all his implicit critique of Cohen, Goldberg is quite close to the idea of messianism as 'the dominion of the good on earth'. Roland Goetschel has rightly insisted that *Die Wirklichkeit der Hebräer* is a hyper-rationalization of Judaism only possible after Cohen's rereading of the Judaic tradition as a rational religion in a Kantian sense.[187] However, there is an important difference that must be acknowledged.

The danger with Cohen's perspective on history as an evolution towards a future messianic ideal is from Goldberg's perspective that it too easily misidentifies the emergence of a moral order with historical development *tout court*. Cohen wrote *Religion of Reason* against the prevailing climate of materialism and Darwinism. Nevertheless, he came close to identifying messianism as something that evolves from a process of hereditation when he criticized a too sharp and dualistic contrast between the soul and the world: 'From the world beyond it is difficult to throw a bridge to matter, which is the necessary condition for the development of the dispositions of the soul, the dispositions *heredity* has to assume and nurture.'[188] Heredity, the passing of traits from parents to their offspring, is a fitting description of Cohen's notion of immortality as the infinite task of implementing justice in the course of history.

Historical change can be used to demystify the illusion, Cohen writes, that 'everything has been and always will be the same'.[189] The idea that nothing can change is 'rooted in the psychological error that hatred is an ordering power in the economy of nature, as is the struggle for existence which destroys countless germs in order to eliminate them from the contest'.[190] Even if one cannot 'deny the tendency to destruction, as little as we deny the elimination of the inferior germs, we distinguish the animate from everything material, even in the organic, and we reject the analogy between the two spheres, between that of nature and that of the moral world, as a will-o'-the-wisp'.[191] It is here Cohen and Goldberg differ. The latter postulates a direct analogy between nature and the moral world.

From Goldberg's perspective, it is logical to argue that the simple destruction of life forms like germs is a proof of the violence and evil of nature that God wants to change; not in order to save so-called inferior germs but since evil is a product of the struggle for existence that pervades all life as long as it is fixated to the normalcy of nature. Nature can be stabilized, even normalized, as the modern state and the whole cycles of empires it belongs to. But the struggle for survival pervades it and its consequence is death, and not seldom mass death. As I stated at the beginning of this chapter, the Hebrew *tov* and *ra*, good and evil, should not be understood morally. They denote what is positive and negative, or even pleasurable or not for biological organisms but, in this sense, they become ethical for those who desire that everyone should be bestowed his or her good.[192]

Goldberg's ethics is not an infinite task that structures time as an evolutionary process towards a messianic future. The task of the infinite is to break through the evil of suffering here and now. Therefore, immortality, from Goldberg's perspective, is not possible through an evolution of moral traits in the course of history. This would postpone justice to a coming world that is not present among those who need it. God, and in extension the justice for biological life that he is, must be made manifest as an immediate and even physical reality. Thus, if the infinite is something that one inherits through the process of time according to Cohen, Goldberg views the infinite as something like a mutation of existing life. The infinite is what elevates the finite to the realm of the eternal by making the world transcendent.

With this said, Goldberg argued as we have seen at the same time in an almost Cohenian manner that God's eternal life only gradually can become present in the spatio-temporal realm of causality that we live in – the Torah is something of a transition period between the order of fixation and the eternity of God – and even more; Goldberg can be said to concur with the conclusion of Cohen's argument. Both made a distinction between the animate and the material. The animate, or what Cohen also calls the soul, is for Goldberg the transcendence of matter, and they both insisted that animation, the principle of life, is more than a biological concept. Life is a moral and political phenomenon and furthermore also a concept of possibility in an ontological sense. Life is the elevation of matter to the realm of the infinite. One could argue that by making the world transcendent God is aiming to make everything alive and therefore eternal. Yet, to succeed with this form of panpsychist politics, death must be overcome and the frailties and injustices of life combatted by a tribe that chooses to live the divine task.

Inherent in life, at least in human life, is the potential to address that which is not but could or should be. The world of the given can be correlated to the world of what should be, the domain of the possible, that exceeds everything that is in the spatio-temporal realm of matter and causality.

Cohen defended the concept of correlation in *Religion of Reason*. The basis of his theory of correlation can be found in the Kantian distinction between being, *Sein*, and what ought to be, *Sollen*, which he developed in *Ethik des Reinen Willens*. There Cohen wrote that the distinction between what is and what ought to be is the essential truth of idealism and critical philosophy: '*In this slogan, Kant agrees with Plato. It is the path of idealism that frees itself from the bondage of nature and from the tyranny of experience.*'[193] That which *ought to be* is the future messianic kingdom, 'the dominion of the good on earth', that the tradition of the prophets articulated and which transcends the present world. It is in this emphasis on *modality* that Cohen and Goldberg, for all their important differences, converge.

When Goldberg argued that 'God is not satisfied with what is given' it is hard not to read this as a comment on Cohen's messianism.[194] 'Messianism', Cohen wrote, 'degrades and despises and destroys the present actuality, in order to put in the place of this sensible actuality a new kind of supersensible actuality, not supernatural, but of the future. The future creates a new earth and a new heaven and, consequently, a new actuality.'[195] This new actuality is for Cohen addressed as prayer and longing, which for him is the ability to exceed that which is.[196] The one who is praying makes sure that he is not 'engulfed in the stifling present' or 'deprived of the ability to anticipate the future and to make if effective. This power of anticipation is, in general, the power of the consciousness of time'.[197]

Prayer awakens the soul which for Cohen is the 'principle of life', and we remember that life cannot be fully subsumed in the given or the material.[198] The soul is a messianic concept, tied to the work for a future justice, and this is why every prayer should be an articulation of a coming messianic kingdom that binds together the souls of the living with the souls of the dead in acts of remembrance and love for the oppressed and murdered.

Life is surely a biological phenomenon – '[t]he soul of man needs the biological individual' – but Cohen defined life as something that exceeds the confines of biology in a manner that reminds of Goldberg's argument that life is 'the transcendence of matter'.[199]

Turning to the first chapter of *Die Wirklichkeit der Hebräer* it becomes evident, with the distinction between *Sein* and *Sollen* in mind, that Goldberg's reading of the Torah is based on a disjunction between infinite possibility and the finite realm of time, space and matter in a Cohenian manner. 'Space, Time, and Causality' constitute, as we have seen, the domain of finite nature according to Goldberg, whereas the infinite part of reality is the realm of possibility which precedes the realm of finite space and time and contradicts the laws of classical logic by revealing being as a pure modality.[200]

Read in relation to Cohen, Goldberg's ontology can be interpreted as a naturalization of the Kantian difference between what is and what ought to be, since the imperfections of nature, such as death and suffering, give witness to how creation should be redeemed from the evil that plagues it.

Goldberg's science of evil is a doctrine of the modality of being. God is what should be and, as we have seen, what should be *is*. It is the realm of the infinite where life is eternal. Absolute potentiality is being. Being itself is thereby not actual but modal. It is the eternal and infinite life, the reservoir of abundant possibilities, that has to become finite in order to transform the world to the point that the suffering of natural evil, such as ageing and death, can be overcome.

The *El Olam*, the uncreated source of everything, is the vast potentiality which precedes the world of actual time and space, and the Hebrews are the people living in relation to this uncreated potentiality of existence as their God. It is important to remember that this eternal abundance cannot know death since life, and only life, is potentiality, whereas death is fixation and simple actuality. It is the corpse that no longer lives that God, as eternal life, can resurrect. Goldberg had already in his essay 'Ontologie' underlined that ontology and logic must begin with the possible rather than the actual and this argument prefigured his idea in *Die Wirklichkeit der Hebräer* that potentiality should be understood as the wider, infinite, part of the real.[201]

Although Goldberg wrote 'Ontologie' at a very young age sometime between 1903 and 1908 – at the same time as he was conducting and presenting his research on the Torah – this dense essay is through its originality a serious critique of the basis of Aristotelean logic. The classic tradition of logic has regarded ontology and the laws of logic as fixed and admitting no conceivable alternatives. The structure of the universe and the nature of human reason have been posited as unable to change. Traditional ontology and logic know nothing outside its realm, and they cannot, to use Cohen's words, help us become free from the 'bondage of nature' and 'the tyranny of experience'.

For Goldberg, ontology must encompass the field of imagination as an order of reality, and 'Ontologie' is a development of Kant's idea of a transcendental imagination. Kant investigated the productive function of imagination by differentiating it from the reproductive imagination which, in his categorization, belonged to the domain of psychology rather than transcendental philosophy.[202]

Transcendental imagination orders and relates the manifold of appearances as something that is possible to associate, compare, and experience: 'it is only by means of this transcendental function of the imagination that even the affinity of appearances, and with it . . . experience itself becomes possible; for without them no concepts of objects at all would converge into an experience.'[203] Transcendental imagination is more than an aid for knowledge: it structures and even makes experience possible.

The transcendental imagination produces a capacity in us to understand the structure of reality which, for Goldberg, points to the modality of being as such: the absolute potentiality that only imagination can adequately conceptualize since it is with imagination we grasp that which could be. Thus, for Goldberg, imagination is related to immortality and the 'transcendental political act' that can provide God the means to liberate himself since an eternal life is an eternal potentiality. But how and why?

Goldberg insists that imagination is not only the means to conjure a new experience of reality. It is also an instrument that can be used to produce a new form of being since being is the domain of the potential and imagination the link between actual and potential being, the realm of the finite and the domain of the infinite. Actual being is on the one hand the given, and on the other that which can be invented, *erfunden*, and therefore imagined. Goldberg's logic of imagination is a form of contradiction, *Widerspruch*, with the given order, and at the same time a conceptualization of that which is since everything in its deepest form is potentiality: it is something that could be and therefore could be otherwise than what it is.[204]

Contradiction comes before identity, just as possibility comes before actuality, in this paradoxical system since being is not only that which is but potentiality. By being alive being exists in a state of contradiction. This implies, as we have seen, that the given is the potential revelation of the unrevealed world of possibilities that precedes the spatial, temporal and material part of reality that we easily mistake for reality as such, and that rules the ordinary logic determined by the law of non-contradiction, the law of identity and the law of excluded middle. However, a true logic, Goldberg insisted, must begin with the fact that being is modality and therefore that everything finite, as something possible, could be otherwise than what it is. Being can contradict itself since only a being that is fixated to itself is determined by the law of non-contradiction and the law of identity and such an actualized being is, in a sense, dead. Life necessitates a logic of contradiction since life is change.

In *Die Wirklichkeit der Hebräer* the principle of contradiction is the revelation of deities in the order of time, space and matter as that which transforms the normalcy of nature, and in 'Ontologie' contradiction is the way imagination can produce new means to exist in the world. Imagination is an anticipation of a new state of being and this makes it possible for Goldberg to define being as 'the being generating principle' which in *Die Wirklichkeit der Hebräer* is described as the *El Olam* and the *Elohim IHWH*.[205] This is why life is the best expression of something that constantly is in contradiction with itself. Life is something that transcends itself by being in becoming.

Only death is actual and identical, and something that cannot be otherwise than what it is. But is not God, as that which is who he is, 'I am who I am', actual according to Goldberg? Yes, but only as the absolute and eternal modality of everything that could be, and therefore as eternal life and immortality. God is actual as eternal life and therefore as that which generates possibility. This is why life is the clearest expression of the logic of contradiction that Goldberg defended and which he also termed revelation: if life is potentiality, it is also that, at least in its human form, which can open itself to the realm of the possible and transform the given.

Mythologically this implies the action to make the world transcendent, and therefore – as Cohen would argue – to force the world to correlate with the divine so that it can be given immortality. It is in this sense Goldberg's logic of imagination converges with his politics of immortality and why his critique of Aristotelean logic is a critique of the mode of thought determined by the process of fixation.

If I return to the postulation in *Die Wirklichkeit der Hebräer* that '[u]ntil now "*possibility*" had only a formal meaning, until now possibility and reality have only been differentiated in the sense that the real is the present, while the possible is considered as not present', it is evident that Goldberg sought to construct an ontology of life as pure modality.[206] The mythical life forms that harness the organic power of life tamper with the modality that for Goldberg has its ultimate source in God's eternal life, and this life is in the end a logic of pure forms that does not ground as much as it challenges the realm of matter and time and space. Imagination is the revelation that life contradicts the given by being connected to something that is not spatial, temporal or material but rather immortal. Thus, like Cohen, Goldberg's system led to a conceptualization of the possible but in contrast to the author of *Religion of Reason* Goldberg argued that being itself is *what ought to be* since being is possibility.

The number of the soul

Before *Die Wirklichkeit der Hebräer* was published in 1925, Goldberg had in 1908 become famous in Jewish circles for a numerological reading of the Torah, *Die fünf Bücher Mosis – ein Zahlengebäude*, that traced the strange and supposedly divine combination of numbers that the Hebrew letters represent in the Torah.

This rather forgotten book finds contemporary readers. The scholar of religion Tomasz Sikora argued as late as 2014 that there are only two answers as to from where the complicated mathematical structure Goldberg found in Torah can originate: 'Either the structure is of divine inspiration, supporting its transcendental character, or it results from the conscious or unconscious activity of the human brain.'[207]

One should perhaps add that this construction could also be the product of pure chance, but for Goldberg the mathematical structure around series of 3, 7, 12, 13 and 26 signified that the Torah had a divine origin. He praised the mathematical kabbalism of the medieval rabbi Jakob ben Ascher and argued that this kind of Jewish speculation was not a mystic doctrine where the individual submerges himself into the reality of God through numerological speculation. It was a metaphysical praxis that sought a connection point between the divine and the finite.[208]

However, by defending a mathematical reading of the Torah, Goldberg was not only inscribing himself in an old tradition of gematria and numerology, he was commenting on the Schellingian philosophy of nature that he and Unger developed in their respective works.[209] Lorenz von Oken had argued in his *Elements of Physiophilosophy* that '[p]hilosophy, as the science which embraces the principles of the universe or world, is only a logical, which may perhaps conduct us to the real, conception.'[210] He even insisted that the 'universe or world is the reality of mathematical ideas, or in simpler language, mathematics.'[211]

Oken's philosophy of nature described nature as the manifestation of mathematical ideas which he related to the concept of spirit: 'Spirit is the motion of mathematical ideas. Nature, their manifestation.'[212] These mathematical ideas have a culmination point in the number zero which Oken used as the concept for the condition of the possibility of being: 'The ideal zero is an absolute unity, or monas; it is not a singularity, such as one individual thing, or as the number 1; it is an indivisibility, a numberlessness, in which neither 1 nor 2, neither a line nor a circle can be found; in short, a unity without distinction, a homogeneity, brightness, or translucency, a pure identity.'[213] This nothing is the eternal that 'succumbs to no definitions of time and space, [it] is neither finite nor infinite, neither great nor small, neither quiescent nor moved; but it is and it is not all this. That is the conception of eternity.'[214] The reason why nothing or zero is eternal and infinite is because if it is something, and therefore a positive or negative number, it would have a boundary in time and space. A number is not indivisible or infinite since it is impossible to count the eternal. Number has a fixation point in the world of the actual, whereas the infinite exceeds the actual. God is not a finite something or an arithmetical value, amount or quantity. God is nothingness since he is innumerable. But he is also the zero that makes positive and negative numbers possible. Thus, for Oken, the mathematization of nature in relation to the idea of zero as eternity was related to what he called the divine science, namely, theology, the science which is 'arithmetic personified'.[215]

Arithmetic, the study of number and the operations between them symbolized as addition, subtraction, multiplication and division, can from Oken's perspective be used to grasp the structure of the world that has arisen from the nothing of eternity. Theology can personify or use myths as means to discuss these processes of the world as forces that have meaning for the human, such as the totemistic gods that structured the world of the mythical peoples according to Goldberg.

In a similar manner Goldberg – who read Oken and was influenced by Schelling – described the attempt of the Hebrews to adapt their life to the rules of their God as a 'personal science of nature', *persönliche Naturwissenschaft*, related to the concept of number: '*number*' is 'the basis of both physics and (in terms of content, "esoteric") at the same time metaphysics'.[216] Mathematics binds physical reality to the infinite realm that it emerges out of. It is, in this sense, a science that connects the finite realm of the actual to the infinite domain of what could be and this is why the study of God is necessary numerological and even implies a 'personal science of nature'.

Goldberg's description of this 'personal science of nature' is frustratingly vague. He postulates a mathematical relation between physical and psychical phenomena by implying that for example a yogi's lowering of the heart rate through concentration and meditation can be mathematized and discerned scientifically.[217] But for all its vagueness, the argument is less mysterious than it seems. Goldberg alluded to Gustav Fechner, whose so-called Fechner's law or Weber-Fechner's law is still used in psychology to trace the mathematical relation between the actual change in a physical stimulus and the perceived change in the one who is affected by it.[218]

Fechner was influenced by Oken, and Goldberg fuses Fechner's idea of the possibility to mathematize psychophysical phenomena with Oken's insistence that every philosophy of nature commences with the mathematical principle of zero as a concept of creation, into a form of mathematical ontology: 'Mathematics is based upon nothing, and, consequently, arises out of nothing... Out of nothing, therefore, it is possible for something to arise, for mathematics, consisting of propositions, is a something in relation to 0.'[219] For Oken, this implied a platonic pantheism: 'the universe', he wrote, 'is only an analysis of the self-consciousness of God.'[220] In contrast, but through a similar description of the condition of possibility of the world as a zero or nothing, Goldberg found a chasm between the infinite possibility of the zero, and the finite mathematical numbers that arise from this creative nothingness which exceeds all numbers and cannot be counted.

Goldberg called the nothingness of God 'the pre-real nothingness [*das vorreale Nichts*]' and 'the pre-worldly God, [*der vorweltliche Gott*]', in order to denote the infinitude that came before spatio-temporal reality, and argued that the Hebrews developed rites that sought to repeat this miraculous creation of something out of nothing in time and space.[221] This theory was, according to Hepner, the most important aspect of Goldberg's theology besides his critique of theodicy, namely, 'the principle of repetition', *das Wiederholbarkeits-Prinzip*.[222] The ritual of Yom Kippur was such a rite of recapitulation of the infinite source of life and the possibility to begin anew.[223]

Yom Kippur, the day of atonement, indicated for Goldberg that the moral and ethical structure to atone and remember must be used against the normal order of nature, such as the irreversibility of time. The Hebrews did not only struggle to create a just society. They worked for the liberation of nature from the injustice of death, and they could do this only by taking part in the creative act that created the finite world out of nothing. This creativity is God himself. The reason why God could create something out of nothing was that he created a finite world out of the infinite nothingness that he is by being that which exceeds every finite boundary and numerological value. God may therefore be understood through numbers but he transcends mathematics by being that which is uncountable.

Oken's idea of nothing as the concept of a numberless eternity sheds light on the *ex nihilo*-logic which Goldberg found in the Torah by examining the *El Olam*, the uncreated world of potentiality, as the primordial and pre-worldly nothingness of creation. Oken had argued that the '[e]ternal is the *nothing* of Nature. As the whole of mathematics emerges out of zero, so must everything which is a Singular have emerged from the Eternal or nothing of Nature.'[224] This is, from Goldberg's perspective, the primordial or pre-worldly nothingness, *das vorweltliche Nichts,* or the *El Olam*, the pure potentiality of existence which Oken described with the concept of zero as the infinite ground of every other number.

The numbers or combination of numbers designate, for Oken, the structure of reality as the evolution of mind and the possibility of the human species to mathematize the world as a form of platonic system. Once again, one can see a striking similarity with Goldberg as he related *das Seelische* to his enigmatic theory of numbers.[225] The soul has a number and the soul is another name for life. Goldberg discerned a mathematical and numerological relation between the soul – the principle of animation– and the pure potentiality of spirit that animates matter. The numbers are not existing in themselves. They denote the region of pure potentiality and modality that, as we have seen, comes before matter, time and space and therefore, and only in this sense, can be said to not be since it exceeds every finite boundary. Numbers disclose the pre-biological world of the *El Olam* and indicate that there is a realm outside spatial, temporal and causal being: the exteriority of pure potentiality that is the pre-worldly God.

The origin of life is a library of pure potentialities that can be mathematized and traced beyond the order of matter, time and space, according to Goldberg.[226] Life is an abstract pattern of forms, a pure potentiality, and it is this creative nothingness that the Torah teaches the Hebrews to tamper with in the world of time and space. Unger rightly described Goldberg's philosophy of life as a Semitic Pythagoreanism in his important study on ontological imagination, *Gegen die Dichtung,* from 1925.[227]

Unger read Goldberg's philosophy of life as a meontology, a study of non-being, based on the concept of a creative nothingness, and he argued that it could be used in order to grasp the genesis of what Plato called forms and what Unger described as universals: 'In short, Plato did what "philosophy" always does: he gave the "lowest" and the "highest" – the "last" (the empirical) and the "first" (the absolute reality) – and he left out that which is . . . worthwhile knowing: the real intermediate, the genesis, the concretion.'[228] Plato, Unger argued, aimed 'to stabilize the reality of the universals' rather than grasp the production of new forms that can structure the world.[229] Plato did not conceptualize the realm of universals as a domain of possibility that could contradict, and therefore change, the world of the given.

One can argue if this is a correct reading of Plato or not, what is important to note is that the unfolding of being, identifiable with the potentiality of change, is not hierarchical according to Unger's interpretation of Goldberg. There is in Goldberg's system a sharp difference between the idea and the real, the ideas and corporeal life, but the potentials or universals are modalities of the real, sensory world. The infinite and the finite form one whole: reality as such. The infinite is certainly better and greater than the finite by being immortal but the infinite cannot exist without the finite. The finite arises out of the infinite, and the latter, in the form of God, needs aid to become part of his creation as something that can exist in time and space as what one perhaps can call a number. The infinite produces the finite in order to create a world of living beings and is thereby the infinite and the eternal. God can only be before the world by creating a world. Unger helps us therefore understand that Goldberg's numerology implies a biological Platonism, where the universals, or what Goldberg called worlds, are related to the unfolding of creaturely and finite life as something else than the nothingness of God.

The world of pure potentialities is immortal. It is the *El Olam*; and since this world cannot die, it has, from the perspective of the human, an ethical character by being 'the enemy of death'. There is, if we believe Goldberg, a form of calculus of life that ultimately has a political meaning for mortal life: immortality is a principle of justice since it can only give without asking for something in return. It is a call that life should be a life against death and for the dead. This is why a this-worldly immortality is the ultimate goal of the Torah. Since such an immortality can only be given to a life that wrests itself free from the cycles of birth and death by viewing them as impure, Goldberg's wager of a this-worldly immortality is a suggestion that life must be liberated from the struggle for existence. Immortality is, as strange as it might seem, a way to make us unadapted to the normal laws of evolution.

It should be noted that Goldberg was not alone in defending numerological theories during the Weimar Republic. The Jewish anarchist Gustav Landauer, perhaps most famous for his participation in the short-lived Bavarian Soviet Republic, might help us understand the creative drift in Goldberg's numerology. Landauer developed an eschatological philosophy of numbers in his *Skepsis und Mystik,* a work that was read in the circles of radicals and revolutionaries that Goldberg was close to.[230] Numbers, Landauer argued, are not only means to mathematize the spatial world of things. They are instruments to understand becoming and change.[231]

Praising the realists of the medieval period and criticizing what he saw as a modern form of nominalism, Landauer concluded that the number signifies the potential of change and infinity as there is no last number, no last becoming, but only an eternity of possibilities. For both him and Goldberg this had immense political and ethical consequences. All that exists are the forms and forces, what Landauer called communities, that unfold towards a new totality or even a new covenant.[232] Numbers were a way to address the reality of the possible that precedes the world of time, space and causality.

With the help of Landauer's political numerology, it is possible to postulate that for Goldberg the number of the soul is life's participation in the pre-worldly and immortal nothingness – the domain of *res potentiae* – that according to Oken is the potential of all numbers and thus of finite nature.

If the soul can be described as a number, perhaps even a self-moving number as an old tradition of Platonism has suggested, this is because life belongs to the immortal nothingness of God himself which according to Goldberg can be recapitulated through the rituals of repetition that the Torah teaches in order to make *das vorweltliche Nichts* present.[233] The number, not in itself but as the symbol or pattern which in time and space can visualize the domain of *res potentiae*, is the condition of possibility of the resurrection of the dead in Goldberg's theology, because the number is a sign of a transcendental existence that reveals that the dead live on as a vestige of the past. His work became after the Second World War literally a hauntology that sought to liberate the dead.[234]

If God as 'I am who I am' is the infinite set of possibilities, and therefore eternal life, that can be mathematized, he is also the transcendental life that contains every finite possibility and every finite life. In this sense everything living, and everything that could be, rests in the life of the eternal. This is, by necessity, a theological argument based on Goldberg's belief that the Torah revealed the numerological structure of the God of all gods. But it is a theological argument based on the belief that mathematics disclose a universe of Platonic forms or, what Goldberg called, the infinite and immortal domain of the possible.

Goldberg did not call his system theology, but Caspary described aptly his work as 'the theology of the righteousness of God himself'. For since God is eternal life, he is a God that does not only live but is willing to act against the imperfections of his creation by seeking those who are ready to enforce his eternity. God seeks to make himself righteous by elevating finite life to the realm of the infinite without destroying its autonomy from the divine.

Caspary's interpretation of Goldberg's work as a theology of God's own liberation from the imperfections of evil strengthens Reisner's suggestion that Goldberg's magical messianism is a profoundly ethical doctrine based on the defence of biological life against the forces of death and extinction.

Goldberg's ontology of *res potentiae* even raises the hope that if life perishes and becomes extinct it can rise forth again since the origin of life is something other than biological existence and since every possibility and, therefore, every life, pre-exist its actualization in the atemporal and aspatial realm of the potential. For, we have to remember, God is the abundant and eternal possibilities that, when they become manifest in time and space, we name and even more count as life.

God is 'the being generating principle' and, according to Goldberg, this vast and eternal otherness to finite and biological life yearns for a reflection of his eternity in the world which he has created out of the nothingness that he is. This is what it means to perfect the world: it is to liberate life from the scarcity that reduces it to a struggle for survival, and for Goldberg this implied the need to confront the 5,000-year-old world system which fixated life to the entropic processes whose last manifestation Caspary analysed in *Die Maschinenutopie*.

In spite of the archaic primitivism that Mann and Taubes reacted against, Reisner, Caspary and Hepner were right when they interpreted Goldberg as a great, modern moralist: a philosopher of myth who urged every human to live a life against death yet for the dead. It is true that Goldberg described his reading of the Torah as amoral, and he did not criticize the brutal commands to, for instance, kill the Amalekites who attacked the Hebrews when they were fleeing from Egypt. Goldberg was no pacifist. He thought that the Torah was constituted as an assembly for all men and women who were willing to abandon their old gods, and more importantly forsake the whole region of fixation that is normal life, in order to live in the realm of the possible rather than in the domain of actual. But if the human as the animal of the infinite is a covenant between God and the gods, an amalgam of the infinite and the finite, one must ask if the Torah could be interpreted as a way to open, rather than eradicate, polytheism to the monotheistic impulse of abundant and eternal life.

Could not the potencies of finite nature be saved by the *El Olam* just as the humans and all other forms of life can be redeemed by this God of all gods? Can the 'transcendental political act' that seeks to make the world the best of all worlds liberate the gods of nature since they too are living and part of the world that God wants to make perfect?

If God is the this-worldly God, the *Elohim IHWH*, he must seek to redeem the potencies of nature which he himself has brought forth as parts of his creation. In the end, the Torah seeks to save us from all ancestries, and thereby decouple humanity from the totem gods that ground us in the world as well as from the process of fixation that embeds us in the state. The gods may thereby lose their old lives, but they might instead – like every other part of the cosmos – become transcendent just as the God of all gods.

Is this not the ultimate mutation, and redemption, of life: a redeemed pantheon that now serves the abnormal and abundant economy of life rather than fixates the human species in the scarcity and finitude of normal existence? It seems to me, that this is a logical reading of the metaphysics defended in *Die Wirklichkeit der Hebräer*. If God seeks to redeem all life, he must logically also save the gods from the entropy that even threatened the *Elohim IHWH* to fail in his attempt to liberate himself from the imperfections of his creation.

Goldberg's theology pushes the human imagination to its limits and uncovers at least for us modern sceptics who are bound to find his thought absurd and magical that the impossible and seemingly irrational can say something true about history and human life. It can unveil a yearning for a justice that does not stop at the limits of human society but rather pervades so deep into the order of being that it desires to liberate God or, at least, the idea of the divine. It is in this sense, and probably only in this sense, Goldberg's work can be said to be a metaphysics for the world after Auschwitz since it does not seek to legitimize that which is but rather save the Godhead from the evil of his own creation. According to Goldberg, if we can learn something from the period of myth, when the gods lived with tribes of men and women, it is the truth that there exist greater things than the economic and political development that has entrapped humanity in the prison house of fixation. Goldberg termed the power that was greater than civilization life and urged us to understand that everything living is part of a world of pure modality that, by being infinite, eternal and pre-biological, cannot die but also, sadly, easily can be banished from the world populated by those animals oscillating between finitude and infinity that we call humans. This is the choice that forces itself upon the animal of the infinite: to follow the cycle of catastrophes that is the evolution of normal life or take up the quixotic task of making the world eternal.

4

Life outside life
Theology and resistance

'It appears', Hans Blumenberg wrote in *The Legitimacy of the Modern Age*, that 'contemporary Christianity, around the world, scarcely mentions immortality in its rhetoric any longer, and thus unintentionally has abandoned a principal element of its historical identity'.[1] Different historical periods do not only give different answers to seemingly universal problems. They pose distinct metaphysical and philosophical questions. When a new period commences, older problems and questions die away. 'A striking example', Blumenberg continued, 'is the fact that people have not always inquired about immortality and apparently will not always be inquiring about it in the future.'[2]

Immortality in its occidental form, Blumenberg argued, arose with 'the biblical text after the Babylonian exile' and survived at least 'all the way to Kant's postulate, it was a position that, while it could be changed in many ways, every new system had to occupy'.[3] This seems, at first hand, to no longer be the case. The hope of overcoming death is not determining our lives. It is a thought that does not stay if it crosses our minds. Yet, Blumenberg emphasized that discussions on immortality did survive in the modern era even if they were increasingly uncommon. They were related to this life, to our hopes here and now, rather than to what he described as the 'beyond'.[4] Today, for instance, immortality is often viewed as a technological problematic emerging out of theories of life extension, reversal of ageing and transhumanism.

The same tendency can be seen in philosophy. The Yale philosopher Martin Hägglund seeks, for instance, to translate the theological desire for eternal life to a longing for survival as a mortal being. If 'one did not affirm mortal life, there would be no desire to save anything from death, since only life can be threatened by death'.[5] Life is temporal and consequently mortal. An absolute life that knows no death is 'the same as an absolute death, an absolute evil, or an absolute violence' since, by being mortal, life has to die.[6] The only meaning immortality can have, from this perspective which severs eternity and time as two entities that never meet, is temporal survival for a mortal being since eternal life is nothing but eternal death.

The Princeton philosopher Mark Johnston's idea of immortality as the afterlife of the good we do – good philosophy, good works, good music and so on – in the remembrance of coming generations is evidently less self-interested than Hägglund's interpretation of immortality as a perpetuation of this life. For even if Johnston's idea of how one can survive death rests on an idea of immortality as survival, he states explicitly that 'there are no persisting selves worth caring about'.[7] Johnston insists that if life is necessarily mortal, the good we do for posterior generations can survive death since 'the good' according to him has 'a collective interest in making the human world a better world, a world in which it is easier for individual personalities to become open to goodness'.[8] The perpetuation of the openness for goodness produces a certain survival beyond death in the good we do, even good persons can be said to survive in the manner that perhaps the good deeds by Violet Gibson, who tried to kill Benito Mussolini, or Giorgio Perlasca, who saved thousands of Jews from the Nazis in Budapest, live on in future generations.

Johnston's suggestive theory of the afterlife is almost an archetype of the inner logic of the modern discussion on immortality, as Blumenberg understood it, since it is based on a refusal of any exteriority to the nature that creaturely life is said to be exhausted in. This transforms immortality into survival, and it complicates ideas of eternal life and the resurrection as a hope for the dead.

The perspectives that I have studied in this book represent a resistance to the reduction of immortality and even more of life to survival by questioning time, space and matter as first principles that fully determine biological existence. Rosenzweig, Goldberg and Barth wagered that the time which is no longer present to human eyes is not annulled in nothingness. It is embedded in the eternity that lives in the strange world of that which forever was and which they identified as God.

Rosenzweig's suggestion that the present always exists after itself, that the now is always already preceded – a time no longer present but embedded in the eternity of the past – gave him the hope that death itself endows creatures with eternal life. God is neither dead nor alive but an existence beyond death and life.

Barth's proposal that eternity does not cancel time, but rather is its pre-temporal and post-temporal condition of possibility, rests on his view on immortality as a new economy of life based on abundance rather than scarcity. Immortality is not a simple preservation of mortal existence. It is a transformation of life.

Goldberg interpreted the Torah as a modal ontology that described how the possible precedes the actual and it made him insist that living organisms are bound to the infinite and eternal realm of what could be that exceeds the reality of time and space.

Thus, for all of them, life could not be fully identified with present life and the human animal, gifted as it is with imagination, can even hope for the resurrection of the dead. As Walter Benjamin, who went to the meetings with Goldberg's *Philosophische Gruppe*, remarked apropos 'the hope of redemption that we nourish for all the dead. This hope is the sole justification of the faith in immortality, which must never be kindled from one's own existence.'[9]

This is essential, since the politics of immortality that I have examined is neither a hope for the perpetuation of mortal life in Hägglund's sense, nor a work for the good that survives death in the manner that Johnston argues. It seeks to transform the economy of life by refusing to view it as being destined to be governed by scarcity and by developing ethical and political strategies that counter the reduction of life to a mere struggle for survival. Not, as we have seen, by denying death – Barth and Rosenzweig came close to affirming death as death – but by arguing that life is not identical with its biological, material, spatial or even temporal form.

What is at stake in the challenge against the biocentric order that I have examined is ultimately the possibility of a ponerology, a science of evil. The subjects of this book interpreted life and death as indications of a moral and political universe rather than solely a biological or mortal existence. They interpreted life not only from the perspective of what it is biologically. They sought to understand what life could be if it was redeemed from death or rather what it would mean ethically and politically if life was determined by another understanding of death than as the simple cessation of mortal existence.[10] What would it imply if life is tied to the eternal and thereby immortal?

Life and death are still infested with an ethical and political meaning in our late-capitalist era. Life and death govern policies and rule quotidian life. We moderns, or whatever we are, know that life has some form of meaning. Yet, life and death, existence and non-existence, are coupled with ideas of survival rather than redemption. The legitimization of the modern age is, just as Blumenberg understood, an illegitimization of eternal life as a belief in a redemption connected to the 'beyond'. Blumenberg can thereby help us understand why a life related to such a beyond is less abstract than it seems since it first and foremost clashes with the view of life as only or even primarily an evolutionary process governed by fitness and adaptation.

What Blumenberg described as the moralization of immortality was parallel with an immanentization and biologization of life that in the period between 1914 and 1945 was politicized with catastrophic consequences. Rosenzweig, Barth and Goldberg sought to surpass this biocentric definition of life, if only by challenging it from within, by legitimating the hope for a change that would transform the Darwinian economy of survival beyond recognition. This is why immortality did not primarily mean a life after death for them. Immortality signified a fundamental alteration of the sense of life, mortality and survival. It revealed the need to reconceptualize life as something that was not identical with its biological facticity since it pointed to the otherness that they all named God.

The question that Blumenberg insisted that the modern age eclipsed through its 'second overcoming of Gnosticism' – the question of an exteriority to the human cosmos – was raised in the work of Rosenzweig, Barth and Goldberg. The modern project, Blumenberg argued, was not based on a secularization of theological themes. It rested upon the legitimization of 'human self-assertion' against 'theological absolutism'.[11] For Blumenberg, this 'human self-assertion' was related to a problem that the Christian world had grappled with and that he almost described as a biological problematic inherent in human life. This was the problem of evil in its most banal sense: death and suffering – the problem that became so acute in the years between 1914 and 1945.

The term Gnosticism in *The Legitimacy of the Modern Age* denoted the philosophical and religious currents that recognized the evil in creation – death, pain, oppression and exploitation – or even identified it with the existing world, and like Marcion of Sinope promised something other, something beyond, as a path to salvation. Gnosticism was the doctrine that argued that the evil of our world 'could only be destroyed from *outside*, by the superior strength of the transcendent principle, or "overcome" by a move *toward the outside*. Human hope had its vanishing point beyond the world.'[12] Western Christianity overcame this mode of thought by chastening its own eschatological impetus and by making the human (and one should add the angels) the cause of evil through the fall.[13] The apocalyptic dimension of faith was interiorized as a doctrine of the last things and bound to the life and fate of the individual.

Salvation was now promised as a distant good or as a redemption that only could be given at the other side of the gates of death and since evil was our own fault, perpetuated as original sin, there was no salvation in this world. This, Blumenberg noted, was why immortality became such an important preoccupation in Western thought. The end was postponed and turned inwards. It would necessarily come even if it was waiting in a distant future or banished to the land of the dead. The important message was that salvation and judgement were not here. The redemption was far away. Our final destiny was in the beyond. But what we do, we do in relation to this end. The chastening of the apocalyptic and messianic desire implied thereby a Gnostic residue. The Christian and the Gnostic agreed that our salvation and judgement, ultimately, come from the beyond that denotes an ethical and political universe that give evil meaning. We must 'move toward the outside' by living in relation to the fullness and goodness which is not fully here, in this vale of tears, but that one day will reveal itself in all its splendour. Immortality was, as Hans Kelsen rightly noticed, a political concept that governed life here and now and produced complex political and ethical theologies.

The confrontation with evil and the hope for a blessed life threatened thereby to unleash the desire for another world, and to once again challenge the order of the cosmos as being unjust. Under specific circumstances Christianity ushered Gnostic movements since it could not free itself from the residue of the otherworldly without abandoning its faith in God.

Gnosticism needed a second overcoming. Through the gradual emergence of 'human self-assertion', perhaps best exemplified with the rise of modern science and technology, which was 'laid upon' the modern European human a solution to the Gnostic problem, and therefore the problem of evil, was found.[14] The collapse of the Medieval political and spiritual systems initiated a profound existential shift visible in the understanding of evil, according to Blumenberg. 'The bad aspects of the world no longer appear as metaphysical marks of the quality of the world principle or punishing justice but rather as marks of the "facticity" of reality.'[15] Life was seen as a contingent phenomenon determined by the evolutionary process of survival. There was no outside or beyond.

This cosmological 'indifference' took many other forms than Darwinism. However, it was often centred around the sense of life as something grounded in the immanence and facticity of existence, and thereby it could produce new forms of almost religious ecstasy. 'Thus', Blumenberg emphasized, the rise of the modern age as a period of 'human self-assertion' should not be reduced to

> the naked biological and economic preservation of the human organism by the means naturally available to it. It means an existential program, according to which man posits his existence in a historical situation and indicates to himself how he is going to deal with the reality surrounding him and what use he will make of the possibilities that are open to him.[16]

For Blumenberg it is 'science [that] has broken the brutal mechanism of the "survival of the fittest": it gives more life to people who are less "fit" for life and keeps them alive longer'.[17] Triumphally he exclaimed after the Second World War that we no longer 'live in a Darwinian world, or at any rate we live in a world that is less and less Darwinian' since (what he simply called) 'science' has transformed the world in an irreversible manner.[18] This is of crucial importance, for the 'self-assertion' of our species is identical with the growing capacity of the human to modify nature to the extent that evil can be seen as a technological problem.[19]

'Technique', Blumenberg noted, 'is a product of human impatience with nature', and a scientific age structured around the growing capacity to mould earth in relation to human needs does not know how to treat the question of immortality as something else than as a metaphor for the reproduction, transformation and survival of the human species.[20] Evil, or what in the English translation of *The Legitimacy of the Modern Age* is called the bad, is something that reveals the universe's indifference to life. For the modern human, Blumenberg argued, 'the indifference of the self-preservation of everything in existence lets the bad appear to him as whatever opposes his own will to live'.[21] Evil is that which hinders the flourishing of human life or even life as such.

But what is life? From a biological perspective, life can be delineated as a general concept for organisms that metabolize, process chemicals and bring energy into their bodies in order to maintain a homeostatic order and, therefore, survive. It is a network of complex organizations of cells composed of atoms that reproduce themselves, and through acts of reproduction, such as copulation or splitting, secure the survival of the species.[22]

The biologist Peter Ward has described these reproduced forms of life as copies, which develop and are marked by a process of senescence.[23] Such ageing and growing organisms have an autonomy that gives them a specific self-determination and capacity to respond to both inner stimuli and influences from the outside world. All life is governed by hereditation, and a necessarily evolutionary process of natural selection that many Darwinists have described as a struggle for existence. In sum, an organism that adapts to its surrounding environment, responds to stimuli from the outside world, reproduces itself metabolically and secures its survival by being fit within its inner and external environment is alive, and even a 'Darwinian life'.[24]

Blumenberg's insistence that our era no longer is 'Darwinian' appears to be wishful thinking from this perspective. But the German philosopher rightly noted that '[s]elf-preservation is a biological characteristic, and insofar as man stepped onto the world's stage an imperfectly and adapted organism, he had need from the start of auxiliary means, implements, and technical procedures for securing the satisfaction of his elementary needs'.[25] Technology and science are certainly such means and therefore something that belong to a species that like all other species, Ward argues, 'is a slave to a process called evolution, Darwinian evolution, in fact, for Charles Darwin got the process spectacularly correct even without understanding how any characteristic could be heritable. Along with replication and metabolism, evolution is one of three tripods that defines life on Earth.'[26]

This 'Darwinian life' is, if we believe Ward, so inherently destructive and unstable that 'it is life that will cause the end of life itself, on this or any planet inhabited by Darwinian life, through perturbation and changes of either temperature, atmospheric gas composition, or elemental cycles to values inimical to life'.[27] One does not need to agree with this 'Medea hypothesis' in order to accept the view of life as something that adapts, evolves and is ruled by a metabolic economy that involves competition and struggle as well as cooperation and mutual aid. However, we do know that the world of 'human self-assertion', tied as it is to our fossil-based economy that tellingly is not analysed in any detail by Blumenberg, has pushed us into a new extinction event and thereby this 'self-assertion' of the modern age reflects the catastrophic dimension of life that Ward underlines.

Our species has recently been described as 'an unsustainable "super predator," which – unless additionally constrained by managers – will continue to alter ecological and evolutionary processes globally'.[28] The origin of this dangerous animal can be found in the First and especially the Second Industrial Revolution. The latter was the socio-economic context for the theories of immortality and eternal life that Rosenzweig, Barth and Goldberg defended, and this industrialization of Europe became the economic basis for the generalization of the existential sentiments that Blumenberg analysed with such precision.

Traditionally dated from the beginning of the Franco-Prussian War in 1870 until the outbreak of the First World War in 1914, the Second Industrial Revolution dramatically altered the face of the world and embedded the planet in the technological infrastructure that we now take for granted: telegraph and later telephone lines, gas and water supply, modern sewage systems and railway networks laid the basis for a whole new world and, even more, a new life. Parallel with the industrialization of the planet biological existence became understood as something in need and, as Blumenberg has reminded his readers, 'man has not [always] seen his situation in the world as one of fundamental want and physical need.'²⁹ The idea of scarcity arose around the same time as economics and biology were intertwined in the capitalist economy that is the motor of Blumenberg's 'human self-assertion'.

When this 'assertion' is 'laid upon' the species its existence is caught in the catastrophes that formed Rosenzweig, Barth and Goldberg's life. Now economy was related, in fact, to the biological properties of the human species and labour was seen as 'the only means of overcoming the fundamental insufficiency of nature and of triumphing for an instant over death'.[30]

It is these two processes of biologization and economization– perhaps best exemplified by the network of industrialized and capitalist nation states that arose with the First and Second Industrial Revolutions – that Rosenzweig, Barth and Goldberg resisted. Their theologies of immortality cannot be separated from the nation state which Rosenzweig sought an exodus from nor from the industrial Behemoth that Goldberg already in the 1930s argued was moving towards a catastrophe for the biosphere. Immortality was a way to question the fall of our species into the cycles of a civilization that knows of no other life than one that, ultimately, is ruled by scarcity, need and the technological means to solve these problems. But by relating life to an exteriority, and refusing to view it as fully identical with its material facticity, Rosenzweig, Barth and Goldberg delineated another form of life and even pushed for a new anthropogenesis. What was needed was another Adam. They revived, in this sense, the Gnostic residue by insisting that the problem of evil could only be solved by God.

By being temporal psychophysical beings, Rosenzweig meant that humans cling like all other living organisms to survival. Humans even do this at the cost of war or, he insisted, for the hope of a glorious afterlife. Discussing what he saw as pagan theologies of immortality and their modern afterlife in the collective life of the nation, he revealed that there are forms of life, primarily identified by Rosenzweig with Christianity and Judaism, that move beyond this logic. These religions seek – or to be more precise should seek – to find the meaning of life beyond the temporality of mortal existence and in the completion of existence in a sabbath that undoes life as something destined to labour for survival.

The goal of his magnum opus, *The Star of Redemption*, was to describe a form of life transcending the two-dimensionality of death and life, past and future, that constitutes every creaturely existence and therefore was anchored in a 'life beyond life'. But what could legitimize such an eschatology in a modern world where, as Rosenzweig thought, theology had lost its legitimate authority?

It is in the concrete, factual existence of the individual, the life that must die, that philosophy and theology must commence in order to be legitimate for a modern human. Rosenzweig's philosophy was an examination of the mortality and finitude of human life and a search for what he called the All. Mortality produces the possibility of philosophy and gives rise to the idea of immortality as a desire for satisfaction and survival in an almost Blumenbergian sense. This is reflected in Rosenzweig's examination of the emergence of civilization in Mesopotamia, and his interpretation of Gilgamesh's search for immortality as the *Urquelle* of Western subjectivity that Jewish and Christian existence should challenge in order to free life for something vaster than temporal and political glory.

Immortality as a longing for survival was not a modern phenomenon according to Rosenzweig, which Blumenberg comes close to arguing by insisting that immortality in the modern period no longer is related to a divine life beyond the temporal domain. Gilgamesh's fear of death was examined by Rosenzweig as an individual desire to avoid death. He traced the origin of the biocentric paradigm of modernity back to the rise of Western civilization and naturalized this desire to live on as a necessary aspect of life: *life is a struggle against death* and ideas of immortality are ways to cope with our mortality.

Thus, for Rosenzweig, Christianity and Judaism transformed the idea of immortality to something that is not born from the will to survival. Immortality must be the hope of the redemption of the dead and the whole realm of the past. Since what we do we do forever, we do it once for all in relation to the past that – Rosenzweig wagered – does not enter nothingness. It is written into the eternity of what was as that which is given completion. Death eternalizes life and life is related to the otherness of God.

No final judgement can be given among those blessed with life since life is a manifold of relative and finite perspectives. Rosenzweig called life polytheistic and defined revelation as the disclosure of 'the paganism of creation'. The cognition of the All, the monotheistic unity of the polytheism of creation that Rosenzweig searched for, was possible only from the perspective that knows no difference between the living and the dead and that in a sense transcended the religious categories that structured Rosenzweig's thought since the revelation of *The Star of Redemption* was the revelation that death is common to us all.

This perspective is the monotheistic unity of eternal life which Rosenzweig called God: a God who, in contrast to the dead deity of the moderns and the living gods of the pagans, is neither alive nor dead. The God of all gods is the light that discloses the unity that death brings to all life since in life existence is fractured in differing experiences, contradicting viewpoints and antagonistic perspectives. The land of the dead belongs to all of us, and Judaism as a religion of the diaspora should be unfettered from the nation and teach the species that a home that, just like death, is common to all must be beyond state and nation. Rosenzweig's proposal became an anti-statist geopolitics – which at the same time, in a troubling manner, legitimized death, war and religious conflict – and those who affirm such a strange sabbatical existence beyond both life and death must do the impossible and begin to transcend the struggle for life.

The affirmation of death as a path beyond a life reduced to a labour for survival was radicalized by Barth. He argued in an almost disturbing manner that death is labouring for the providence of God. The whole order of creation mirrors the life, death and resurrection of Christ which for Barth was the sign of the inexistence of nothingness. Death itself takes part in God's eternal life that, by being revealed in a human creature, has been given a historical, spatial and temporal form. This strange, abundant and divine life has been born as a human who ages, lives and dies.

Blumenberg heckled Barth's reading of Feuerbach in *The Legitimacy of the Modern Age* and interpreted it as a way to translate the problem of the human condition to theological jargon and this 'detour' raised the question what is the need of God? '[W]ould it not have been better . . . if He had not existed at all?'[31] Yet Blumenberg failed to see what Barth was trying to do when he translated the meaning of human life to theology. He sought to mirror everything in the life of an individual who transformed our 'command of life' by living in relation to an economy that was not built upon survival but on a capacity to win life through sacrifice.

The eternal life that Christ shares with creation through his resurrection has not abolished natural death. It has transmuted nothingness by embedding the dead in God rather than in the *nihil* of non-existence, and by urging us to understand that life could be an anti-economy, a capacity to live for something else than all finite powers – be they only 'the powers of eating, drinking, sleeping, and growing old' – that possess us.

It is hard, perhaps impossible, not to read this domestication of death as a phenomenon that mirrors the revelation of God as exactly what Barth did not want it to be: the basis of a myth and a religion. But, for him, the saga of creation – and this saga was the saga of Christ – did not give meaning to life in a mythical or religious manner. Revelation puts our existence into a crisis by disclosing that life itself, especially human life, can only become meaningful if the nonsense of creaturely life that Barth equated with Darwinian existence is revealed to have a limit in death. But this limit is as every limit a sign of an exteriority. It points beyond itself by being a border and Barth identified this beyond with Christ: the Word of God.

The one who is interpellated by this *verbum externum* can be habituated to use the power of imagination to challenge the authorities that force organic life to be a struggle for survival: 'In principle each of us is capable of divination and poetry, or at least capable of receiving their products. In principle each of us can be open to the actualities of pre- and post-history; each of us can produce saga and prophecy or at least perceive them when they come from others.'[32] Such an imaginative animal is, potentially, open for the gospel that life can be lived for other principles than creaturely survival or worldly glory. Barth sought to revive the Gnostic residue of Christianity by insisting that the baptized – and in the end the human – should neither fear nor desire to abolish death.

Death is the limit that proves why human life is a creaturely life, a life that is not eternal. However, by dying *post Christum* – and everything dies *post Christum* according to Barth, even that which died before Christ – all creatures mirror the life that according to the theologian is the revelation of eternal life. Not only the baptized are the echoes of the God who, strangely, can be seen as a new metabolic relation to nature, a new way to be necessitous and desiring since this God does not seek to undo life, death and need but convert their meaning in relation to the abundance of Paradise.

All who refuse to solely live for the basis of Darwinian life reflect this paradisal life given to the creation through the person of eternity named Christ, whereas all those unable to live for the alien and unknown life of this stranger mirror the demonic nothingness that eternal life challenges.

The human is a finite being – a nonsensical life in time and space that is born and shall die – divided by the exteriority that challenges the command of life. To live a life that reflects eternity is to affirm this trial inherent in our lives in order to exist for greater things than 'human self-assertion'. Thus, for Barth, the sense of the brutal and meaningless existence of a humanity caught in a world of war is the *suum cuique*. Every creature should be given its own time in order to understand the sense of factical life inside the thanatological bracket of existence that makes life necessarily finite and mortal. Only then might it have the possibility to knowingly mirror the perpetual rest of the divine. It is death, the limit of life, which opens us to the exteriority to life. One must ask if Barth's political thanatology could risk becoming a mysticism seducing us to forget life here and now? Perhaps. But such forgetting may also be the prerequisite for viewing our life as something more than present life. In the end, Barth's theology of death seeks to reveal how a new world can emerge out of a dying cosmos. It points to the need of a theology of extinction that reminds us that the cosmos itself is finite; the *suum cuique* needed for everything temporal to become eternalized in the God who Barth argued was revealed through the death and resurrection of a human creature that no longer is adapted to the world of the mortals and instead wants to give us eternal life.

Goldberg was according to Adolf Caspary a theologian who struggled with the problem of evil. In sharp contrast to traditional religion and theology, Goldberg interpreted the Torah as a teaching of a God that needs assistance to endow his creation with immortality. The complicated laws of *Urjudentum* were the acts that ultimately aimed to correlate God's divinity with the world of time and matter in a covenant. It was the Hebrews who took upon them the task to make God present in the tabernacle as a force aiming to transform the normalcy of nature; the chain of birth and death that traditional Judaism and Christianity describe as a consequence of the fall.

During the period of the Exodus from Egypt through the conquering of the land of Canaan, when the God of creation, the *Elohim IHWH*, dwelled with his people in the tabernacle, the Hebrews opened their life for the divine so that he could become present in time and space. The creator God, whom Goldberg in accord with traditional Jewish teaching described as omnipotent, uncreated, perfect and eternal life, had created a world outside himself, and therefore a finite and temporal reality damaged by imperfections such as suffering and death. Yet, since this God is perfection itself, or what traditional theology calls the good, he sought to embed his creation in his eternal life without abolishing its autonomy.

The story of God's covenant with the Hebrews, a people open to everyone willing to live against the imperfections of nature, was for Goldberg a saga of how the infinite God became a finite deity in time and space struggling for, and ultimately losing, a point of connection with the world. The *Elohim IHWH* was banished to heaven since he was forced back to the mode of pure potentiality that cannot exist in a world of actual matter in time and space without a covenant that breaks through the normalcy of a nature ruled by death and scarcity.

According to Goldberg, the Hebrews enacted their God as a form of life when they followed the rules of the Torah and he interpreted this divine presence anthropologically as the call of humanity out of the world of fixation that Cain represented in his system. Cain was the prototype of the *homo faber* who, in contradistinction to the primitive and archaic peoples of the world to whom the Hebrews of the Torah belonged, was imprisoned in a civilization that transformed the human animal into the 'super-predator' that today threatens life. Abraham, a former Chaldean who abandoned the Mesopotamian city of Ur in order to live in the wilderness with his God, was the initiator of a new anthropogenesis. He sought to decouple human life from the struggle for survival that the fixated world stabilized to the 5,000-year-old world system that today is entering a profound crisis according to Goldberg.

Immortality was for him a 'biological universalism' that through its intensification in the present would liberate mortal life from the imperfections of nature and ultimately from death itself. It is hard not to read him as a theologian of the modern period who validates Blumenberg's interpretation of immortality as a moral idea related to the unfolding of life. This is strengthened when one notices that the problem of extinction is at the centre of his work. Yet, he related life to the otherness which Blumenberg argued that the modern world's self-assertion abandoned. The problem of evil was, for Goldberg, still the problem of God. Goldberg described God as 'the being generating principle' and argued that the divine is the abnormal force that wants to break the fixation that makes life prone to extinction by enslaving it to the necessity of matter.

The difference between life and matter is the difference between freedom and necessity or better potentiality and actuality. The life that no longer has the potency to act, but is mere being, is dead, whereas the matter that is animated by the autonomous potential to act is alive. And, Goldberg insisted, what in the Torah is called *El Olam* is nothing but the name of the modality that is the origin of creation itself. This is the exteriority in Goldberg's metaphysics: the exteriority of the possible that precedes and pre-exists the actual.

If the horrors of war and the emergence of Nazism were seen by Jacob Taubes, Thomas Mann and others as a re-emergence of the cultic basis of culture, Goldberg argued that the roots of these abominations are the birth of the toolmaking animal, the *homo faber*. It was the formation of humanity into an animal entrapped in its own technological development that the Torah criticized. However, the Torah sought also to lead us humans out of the world of the archaic tribes to which it belonged since these groups did not enter the abundant and eternal life that is the *Elohim IHWH*.

Goldberg sought an alternative to both primitivism and civilization and found the contours to such an existence beyond tribe and the state in the Torah. Together with his comrades Caspary and Unger, Goldberg defended a politics of exile from the apparatuses that fixate life to the present world. What this exodus from civilization implies is frustratingly vague but his vision was nurtured by an idea of human life as the freedom to move beyond the normalcy of nature even to the point that the living can seek to live against death and for the dead. In this sense one can say that even Goldberg argued that the human must be trained to die away from this life, life here and now, in order to become another form of animal. For, in contrast to the totemistic tribes of the world, the Torah does not seek to ground us in nature but wants to free humanity from all cultural and biological ancestries.

Guided by this rejection of the normalcy of life I can tentatively summarize the ideas on immortality in this study as the following thesis: to be truly alive is, in a sense, to be dead. It is to enter the zone of indiscernibility between life and death where the spectres of the past, the unborn of tomorrow and the flesh of the living exist together in what Barth and Rosenzweig called eternal life. To be alive is to be more than living and what is common to the beings of the past and those of the future is this transcendence that we, who live in the non-existence of the present, can take part in as beings that are much more than alive. This may seem strange, but in the end it is close to what classical philosophy understood as an *ars moriendi*, albeit in a collective form. It is a political thanatology and ponerology. It is a recognition that the problem of evil cannot be solved by human self-assertion. Evil must be confronted with a new anthropogenesis, a revelation of a new form of life.

If one listens to the theologies of eternal life in this study, it is only such a life, a life not disinterested in living but in the end not only interested in surviving, that can modify the draconian and totalitarian laws of existence that Ward rightly calls Darwinian. It is in this sense that the theologies which I have studied are means to conjure a being in the world which confronts the basis of an age where 'human self-assertion' can only radicalize the entropical and Darwinian tendencies that Blumenberg falsely thought the modern world had overcome.

This new being, one could argue, is nothing but the imaginative life of the human species that I, in the chapter on Goldberg, defined as an animal of the infinite. We humans are certainly creatures who live in the order of being, but we are also always entering the sphere of what could be. Reality is divided by that which is and that which could and even more should be, and theology is an expression of this power of transcendental imagination that according to Goldberg reveals itself as a disjunction in being between actuality and modality.

However, this imagination is shaped by different ideologies, philosophies and religions and what I have shown in this study is how Christianity and Judaism were used to conceptualize life as that which wrests itself out of the confines of the actual. What theology gave Rosenzweig, Barth and Goldberg was a way to question the reduction of life to its biological, cultural and political facticity. Thus, even if one is sceptical of religion and theology, one must admit that theology gave these three thinkers a way to question the 'human self-assertion' that today is falling apart. The period between 1914 and 1945 revived the Gnostic residue that Blumenberg thought had been overcome through modernity's attempt to embed life in its own biological indifference, and perhaps this re-discovery of the outside could reveal that life could be otherwise than what it has become in a world seemingly destined to be ruled by scarcity and the struggle for glory and survival.

As William James famously said already in 1909, if nature is not ruled by God but by indifference it may be because it is more demonic than divine: 'Nature, more demonic than divine, is above all things *multifarious*. So many creatures that feed or threaten, that help or crush, so many beings to love or hate, to understand or stare at – which is on top or which subordinate, who can tell?'[33] For James, '[t]empests and conflagrations, pestilences and earthquakes reveal supramundane powers, and instigate religious terror rather than philosophy' and it is the fact of death and killing that makes the longing for a redemption of the dead still legitimate in a world where God seems absent.[34] The brutality of the world wars, and the nihilistic meaninglessness of the Holocaust, did, from the perspective that I have examined in this book, nurture the hope for redemption since it was based on an acknowledgement of the demonic character of Darwinian life.

Many contemporaries to Rosenzweig, Barth and Goldberg viewed such a perspective as a retreat to an archaic and magical worldview, but for them life was by definition not solely a biological phenomenon. Life was a force that produced a sense that transcended the domain of the factual. They argued in different ways that this transcendence can and must be understood in itself, not only from the perspective of the human. They wagered, as Rosenzweig wrote, the possibility of a perspective 'beyond experience' that in the end only can be verified before death as a form of life. Their theologies of eternal life became political theories on how life should be lived, since they all thought that a life lived for something other than survival may be the only verification that immortality can have in a world where death still rules over life. Immortality implied for them a new economy of life, a new metabolic relation to nature, not the perpetuation of life but the seemingly impossible hope that the past itself could be redeemed.

To be alive became the imperative to live for something more than the forces of production and reproduction that today perpetuate destructive processes of life, not least in the empires and nations of the world that in the period I have studied reduced human existence to material for work in factories, trenches and camps. Biological life is in the end not what is most interesting or important for the psychophysical being we call human. It is all too often a life of labour and toil, a life solitary, poor, nasty, brutish and short, and it is a life that has not much in common with the vast domain of the eternity of the past where the dead according to the subjects of this study wait for redemption.

Perhaps the good life is, after all, what a long tradition in Western philosophy has called the contemplative life, and for the theologians I have examined such a contemplative life is not an academic or isolated life. It is a life where contemplation above all is a rest from the struggle for existence: a form of life that seeks to uproot itself and all those following it from the cycles of birth and death that according to Goldberg has coagulated to our contemporary factory world.

Such a world also sets limits for all 'human self-assertion' and pushes parts of our species to search for that which is outside the confines of a life increasingly fixated to civilization and its inherent evolutionary drive. For Rosenzweig that implied the struggle for an existence beyond state, empire and nation; for Barth it implied the confrontation with the 'command of life' to the point that not even 'the powers of eating, drinking, sleeping, and growing old' could be seen as neutral powers; for Goldberg it implied the hope for a sublation of the normalcy of nature. These three theologians posited the need to solve the 'problem of the human' which had become identical with the survival of the cycles of civilization that Barth described as a fall into Darwinian existence and which Goldberg and Rosenzweig argued had its origin in the empires of Babylon and Mesopotamia.

In this part of the world, Judaism, Gnosticism and Christianity emerged, and if Gnosticism is the problem of evil then the Gnostic residue of both modern Judaism and Christianity may in the end be related to life itself. For, I must ask again, what is life? Life, the subjects of this study insist, is more than a Darwinian process of evolution. Life is a life outside life. Life is never only living. It cannot only be this life, life here and now, since that would be a life fixated to the present. It would be a life that forever was survival. Living, at least in its complex human form, implies the capacity to push imagination beyond the confines of what we now take to be life and thereby we can relativize the difference between life and death by remembering that the present is born from that which is dead and emerging into a future that is not yet alive.

Sections of our species have for many centuries lived in relation to not only the living but also the dead, and many of us human apes are still celebrating the cult of the dead in temples around the world. Fabián Ludueña Romandini has rightly insisted that '[t]he metaphysical tradition of the West has conceived . . .

the world beyond the senses as in essence political and, in many cases, as the ontological foundation itself of all politics. Immortality is found, within this tradition, in a form of endowment dependent upon civic virtue.'[35] What this enigmatic quote implies is that, according to this long tradition, our afterlife is made complementary to the relation that our political and ethical actions have to the world beyond the senses. This is not, as for Johnston, a suggestion that only the good we do may survive. It is an indication that everything, even time itself, exists after itself and that the world of the possible exists together with the world of that which was. Life thereby judges itself for what it does, or neglects to do, it does in relation to the eternal. It is this moral and ethical aspect of our lives that binds the world of the visible to the domain of the invisible and, to once again quote Blumenberg, inscribes 'the "facticity" of reality' with 'metaphysical marks'.

The strange quality of life – and perhaps especially human life – is that it is not self-identical with its actuality since it belongs to the realm of possibility that according to Goldberg is immortal. My life exceeds what I do; it is what I hoped, what I wanted, what I wished had happened. Life is always more than the visibility of the actual. It is the invisibility of the wished, the desired and the dreamt. This is what human life entails. It is related to the wide world of what could have been or what should have been.

At the same, life is incarnated in organisms that are finite and mortal and that according to Barth should be given their allotted time to live as something else than creatures forced to labour for their survival. This is the fundamental contradiction and impossibility of life that perhaps can give us a glimpse into the uncanny existence that, if we believe Rosenzweig, is neither dead nor alive but a light which seeks to liberate itself from the evil of its own creation by embedding it in the strange abundance that knows neither death nor scarcity.

This is theological speculation and the discussions I have examined indicate or simply postulate the existence of a life that cannot be identified with creaturely life. They are a call for the constitution of communities that long for the redemption of the living as well as of the beings dwelling in the vast world of the dead. It is in this sense the theology of eternal life is less based on what many would call reason and more on what Barth in 1945, when he considered the possibility of non-Darwinian life, described as imagination. Is not one of the greatest joys of life that which liberates our thinking from the banality of possible experience and the often-tiresome world of the merely actual? And is not the desire for eternal life and immortality worth studying even if it remains unanswered in a world still plagued by death, killing and extinction? If we listen to Rosenzweig, Barth and Goldberg they would urge us to move thought beyond the limits of what can be known; otherwise, we would lack the power to resist the forms of 'self-assertion' that only seem to perpetuate the evil of death and suffering by not questioning the confines of a world that identifies life with existent life; a life reduced to that which is here and now instead of being a life outside life.

Notes

Introduction

1. I shall discuss several attempts to define immortality as a political concept in this study. Here it is sufficient to mention four prominent examples: Hans Kelsen, 'The Soul and the Law', *The Review of Religion* 4, no. 1 (1937): 337–60; Arnold Ehrhardt, 'Unsterblichkeitsglaube und Politik im Römerreich', *Theologische Zeitschrift* 2, no. 6 (1946): 418–37; Claude Lefort, 'The Death of Immortality?' in *Democracy and Political Theory*, trans. David Macey (Oxford: Polity Press, 1988), 256–82, and Hannah Arendt, *The Human Condition* (Chicago: University Press, 1998).
2. See for instance Ray Kurzweil, 'Reinventing Humanity: The Future of Machine-Human Intelligence', *The Futurist* 40, no. 2 (2006): 39–46. Kurzweil argues that despite 'the wonderful future potential of medicine, real human longevity will only be attained when we move away from our biological bodies entirely. As we move towards software-based existence, we will gain the means of "backing our-selves up" (storing the key patterns underlying our knowledge, skills, and personality in a digital setting) thereby enabling a virtual immortality'. Kurzweil, 'Reinventing Humanity', 44.
3. Kelsen, 'The Soul and the Law'. The French original of this text, 'L'âme et le droit', was published in 1936 in *IIe Annuaire de l'Institut International de Philosophie du Droit* (Paris: Ed. Sirey, 1936), 60–70.
4. Carl Schmitt, *Political Theology: Four Chapters on the Concept of Sovereignty*, trans. George Schwab (Chicago: University of Chicago, 2005).
5. Kelsen, 'The Soul and the Law', 359–60.
6. Hans Blumenberg, *The Legitimacy of the Modern Age*, trans. Robert Wallace (Cambridge, MA: MIT Press, 1999).
7. Ibid., 444.
8. Ibid., 443.
9. Michel Foucault, *The Order of Things: An Archaeology of the Human Sciences*, trans. Alan Sheridan (London: Routledge, 2002), 303.
10. Ibid.
11. Charles Darwin, *The Origin of Species by Means of Natural Selection or the Preservation of Favoured Races in the Struggle for Life* (New York: D. Appleton and Company, 1861), 425.

12 The historian of ideas Oliver Botar, who has studied the so-called *Lebensphilosophie* during this epoch, has used the Hungarian biologist Raoul H. France's term 'biocentrism' in order to grasp the feeling of many that the 'age of biological thinking has ... just begun'. See Oliver A.I. Botar, 'Defining Biocentrism', in *Biocentrism and Modernism*, eds Oliver A. I. Botar and Isabel Wünsche (London: Routledge, 2011), 15.
13 Richard Weikart, 'The Role of Darwinism in Nazi Racial Thought', *German Studies Review* 36, no. 3 (2013): 537–66.
14 Davide Tarizzo, *Life: A Modern Invention*, trans. Mark William Epstein (Minneapolis: University of Minnesota Press, 2017).
15 Ibid., 50.
16 Michael Dillon, *Biopolitics of Security: A Political Analytic of Finitude* (London: Routledge, 2015), 77.
17 Paul Weindling, 'Weimar Eugenics: The Kaiser Wilhelm Institute for Anthropology, Human Heredity and Eugenics in Social Context', *Annals of Science* 42, no. 3 (1985): 303–18, at 304.
18 Ibid.
19 See the chapter 'Biologische Politik' in Wilhelm Schallmayer, *Beiträge zu einer Nationalbiologie. Nebst einer Kritik der methodologischen Einwände und einem Anhang über wissenschaftliches Kritikerwesen* (Jena: Hermann Costenoble, 1905), 65–150.
20 Ibid., 66.
21 Ibid., 67.
22 Sheila Faith Weiss, *Race Hygiene and National Efficiency: The Eugenics of Wilhelm Schallmayer* (Los Angeles: University of California Press, 1987), 40.
23 The polymath scientist John Burdon Sanderson Haldane, celebrated for his work on physiology, evolutionary biology and mathematics, was, for example, a herald of a biopolitical perspective from a Marxist perspective, but he also understood the danger of eugenics. In his book *Heredity and Politics* from 1938, which violently attacked the race politics of the Nazis as unscientific and irrational, he noticed that 'the English National Council of Labour Women has recently passed a resolution in favour of the sterilization of defectives, and this operation is legal in Denmark and other countries considerably to the "left" of Britain in their politics'. Haldane criticized these and similar positions but professed his loyalty to a politics of hereditation by arguing that the increase in our knowledge of genetics may 'fully justify the application to man of certain measures which have led to improvements in the quality of our domestic animals'. See John Burdon Sanderson Haldane, *Heredity and Politics* (London: Allen and Unwin, 1938), 9.
24 See Reinhard Mocek, 'The Program of Proletarian Rassenhygiene', *Science in Context* 11, no. 3-4 (1989): 609–17 and Paul Kammerer, *Lebensbeherrschung: Grundsteinlegung der organischen Technik* (Munich: Monistische Bibliothek, 1919).
25 Kammerer, *Lebensbeherrschung*, 19.

26 It is perfectly evident why one could and should call Barth a theologian. Rosenzweig was perhaps more of a philosopher of religion than a theologian, although he developed a theology in *The Star of Redemption* and argued that philosophy is crowned by theology: see Franz Rosenzweig, *The Star of Redemption*, trans. Barbara E. Galli (Madison: University of Wisconsin Press, 2005); Franz Rosenzweig, *Der Stern der Erlösung* (Haag: Martinus Nijhof Publishers, 1976). Oskar Goldberg refused to describe himself as a theologian but he developed a teaching of God, and therefore a theology which one of his followers, Adolf Caspary, rightly pointed out. See 'Maimonides' in Oskar Goldberg, *Zahlengebäude, Ontologie, Maimonides und Aufsätze 1933 bis 1947*, ed. Manfred Voigts (Würzburg: Königshausen & Neumann, 2013), 123–217; Adolf Caspary, 'Theologie der Selbstgerechtigkeit Gottes', in *Grenzbote* (Bratislava, 1936). A digital version of the transcript is available through the Leo Baeck Institute/Center for Jewish History. Available online: https://digipres.cjh.org/delivery/DeliveryManagerServlet?dps_pid =IE8265702 (accessed 17 September 2017).
27 Obviously, the subjects of this study were not alone in challenging this paradigm. See for example Liisi Keedus, *The Crisis of German Historicism: The Early Political Thought of Hannah Arendt and Leo Strauss* (Cambridge: Cambridge University Press, 2015) for a discussion on Arendt and Strauss's critique of historicism and its political implications. See also Charles R. Bambach, *Heidegger, Dilthey, and the Crisis of Historicism* (London: Cornell University Press, 1995) for a study on the philosophical implications of the crisis of historicism.
28 Blumenberg, *The Legitimacy of the Modern Age*, 442.
29 Ludwig Feuerbach, *Thoughts on Death and Immortality: From the Papers of a Thinker, along with an Appendix of Theological-Satirical Epigrams, Edited by One of His Friends*, trans. J. A. Massey (Berkeley: University of California Press, 1980), 111.
30 Lefort, 'The Death of Immortality?' 256–82.
31 Ibid., 267.
32 See for example Mark A. Noll, *Christians in the American Revolution* (Vancouver: Regent College Publisher, 2006).
33 The idea of the afterlife as the future survival of our species is defended by the moral philosopher Samuel Scheffler. See Samuel Scheffler, *Death and the Afterlife* (Oxford: Oxford University Press, 2016).
34 See Otto Petras, *Post Christum: Streifzüge durch die geistige Wirklichkeit* (Berlin: Widerstands Verlag, 1935) and Mattias Martinson, 'Towards a "Theology" of Christian Monumentality: Post-Christian Reflections on Grace and Nature', in *Monument and Memory: 4th Nordic Conference in Philosophy of Religion*, eds Jonna Bornemark, Mattias Martinson and Jayne Svenungsson (Berlin: LIT Verlag, 2014), 21–42. Jacob Taubes also uses the concept 'post-Christian' in order to describe our present world: Jacob Taubes, *Occidental Eschatology*, trans. David Ratmoko (Stanford: Stanford University Press, 2009), 193.

35 Kelsen, 'The Soul and the Law', 341.
36 Ibid., 341.
37 Karl Barth, *Church Dogmatics: Volume III:2*, trans. Geoffrey Bromiley and Thomas Forsyth Torrance (Edinburgh: T&T Clark, 1960), 384–94.
38 Ibid., 387.
39 Kjellén coined the terms 'geopolitics' and 'biopolitics'. See Rudolf Kjellén, *Staten som Lifsform* (Stockholm: Hugo Gebers Förlag, 1916). One of his readers was Franz Rosenzweig as we shall see in Chapter Two.
40 Hans Leisegang, *Religionsphilosophie der Gegenwart* (Berlin: Junker und Dünnhaupt, 1930).
41 Schalom Ben-Chorin, *Jenseits von Orthodoxie und Liberalismus: Versuch über die Jüdische Glaubenslage der Gegenwart* (Tübingen: J. C. B. Mohr, 1991).
42 Margarete Susman, 'Vortrag über Oskar Goldberg', in *Zahlengebäude, Ontologie, Maimonides und Aufsätze 1933 bis 1947*, 389–408.
43 I borrow the expression 'resisting history' from David Myers, who has examined the anti-historicist logic in the writings of Hermann Cohen, Franz Rosenzweig, Leo Strauss and Isaac Breuer, and noticed similarities between them and Karl Barth's criticism of historicism. See David N. Myers, *Resisting History: Historicism and Its Discontents in German-Jewish Thought* (Princeton: Princeton University Press, 2003), 35.
44 Mark Lilla, *The Stillborn God: Religion, Politics, and the Modern West* (New York: Vintage Books, 2008), 10.
45 Quoted in Alexander Raviv, *Was the Real Thomas Mann an Antisemite? The Jewish Issue in Thomas Mann's Non-Fictional Writings versus the Image of the Jew in Thomas Mann's Novels* (Berlin: Münster, 2007), 136–7.
46 Manfred Voigts, *Oskar Goldberg: Der mythische Experimentalwissenschaftler: Ein verdrängtes Kapitel jüdischer Geschichte* (Berlin: Agora Verlag, 1992).
47 On Barth's critique of militarism and Nazism, see: Arne Rasmusson, 'Church and Nation-State: Karl Barth and German Public Theology in the Early 20th Century', *Ned Geref Teologiese Tydskrift* 46, no. 3–4 (2005): 18–30, and Arne Rasmusson, '"Deprive them of their pathos": Karl Barth and the Nazi Revolution Revisited', *Modern Theology* 23, no. 3 (2007): 369–91.
48 Paul Mendes-Flohr, 'Messianic Radicals: Gustav Landauer and Other German-Jewish Revolutionaries', in *Gustav Landauer: Anarchist and Jew*, eds. Paul Mendes-Flohr and Anya Mali (Berlin: De Gruyter, 2015), 12–44, at 37.
49 Paul Mendes-Flohr, ed., *The Philosophy of Franz Rosenzweig* (Hanover: University Press of New England, 1988); Renate Schindler, *Zeit, Geschichte, Ewigkeit in Franz Rosenzweigs Stern der Erlösung* (Berlin: Parerga, 2007); Martin Brasser, *Rosenzweig als Leser: Kontextuelle Kommentare zum Stern der Erlösung* (Tübingen: M. Niemeyer, 2004) and Norbert M. Samuelson, *User's Guide to Franz Rosenzweig's*

Star of Redemption (London: Routledge, 1999). I also highly recommend Bruce Rosenstock, *Philosophy and the Jewish Question: Mendelssohn, Rosenzweig, and Beyond* (New York: Fordham University Press, 2010) and Elliot Wolfson, *Giving beyond the Gift: Apophasis and Overcoming Theomania* (New York: Fordham University Press, 2014), 34–89.

50 See for instance Stéphane Mosès, *System and Revelation: The Philosophy of Franz Rosenzweig*, trans. Catherine Tihanyi (Detroit: Wayne State University Press, 1992) and Stéphane Mosès, *The Angel of History: Rosenzweig, Benjamin, Scholem*, trans. Barbara Harshaw (Stanford: Stanford University Press, 2009), 17–61.

51 Benjamin Pollock, *Franz Rosenzweig and the Systematic Task of Philosophy* (New York: Cambridge University Press, 2009).

52 I borrow the term 'yearning' from Andrea Poma's description of Hermann Cohen's philosophy as a yearning for form: Andrea Poma, *Yearning for Form and Other Essays on Hermann Cohen's Thought* (Dordrecht: Springer, 2006).

53 Friedrich Naumann, *Mitteleuropa* (Berlin: Reimer, 1915). The historian Jörg Brechtefeld writes that Friedrich Naumann's ideas of a *Mitteleuropa* were related to the vision of industrialists, such as Alfred Hugenberg, the director of the legendary company Krupp AG, who in 1914 had 'organized a meeting of all economic societies in Berlin . . . regarding German war goals'. Brechtefeld continues: 'On the surface, Naumann argues for a Central Europe union in order to secure resources. But his argumentation reaches beyond the immediate needs of the war; he states that, after the war, the world will be divided into two economic super-regions (*wirtschaftliche Großräume*): an Anglo-American and a Russio-Asiatic one. The subsequent development of *Mitteleuropa* was, for Naumann, the next logical step on the path towards larger economic entities, something that Germany had been pursuing since the Zollverein and the subsequent creation of the Reich'. Jörg Brechtefeld, *Mitteleuropa and German Politics: 1848 to the Present* (Basingstoke: Palgrave Macmillian, 1996), 45.

54 Jörg Kreienbrock, 'Franz Rosenzweig's Mitteleuropa, a New Levante', in *Personal Narratives, Peripheral Theatres: Essays on the Great War 1914–18*, eds Anthony Barker, Maria Eugénia Pereira, Maria Teresa Cortez, Paulo Alexandre Pereira and Otília Martins (Cham: Springer International, 2018), 185–200, at 190.

55 Ibid., 190.

56 Franz Rosenzweig, 'Monarchie, Republik und Entwicklung', in *Zweistromland: Kleinere Schriften zu Glauben und Denken*, ed. Annemarie Mayer and Reinhold Mayer (Dordrecht: Martinus Nijhoff, 1984), 249–52; Franz Rosenzweig, 'Neuorientierung', in *Zweistromland*, 257–60; Franz Rosenzweig, 'Realpolitik', in *Zweistromland*, 261–6; Franz Rosenzweig, 'Vox Dei?' in *Zweistromland*, 267–82; Franz Rosenzweig, 'Cannä und Gorlice', in *Zweistromland*, 283–96; Franz Rosenzweig, 'Eine Erörterung des strategischen Raumbegriffs', in *Zweistromland*,

297–300; Franz Rosenzweig, 'Das Kriegsziel', in *Zweistromland*, 309–12; Franz Rosenzweig, 'Nordwest und Südost', in *Zweistromland*, 301–8; Franz Rosenzweig, 'Die neue Levante', in *Zweistromland*, 309–12; Franz Rosenzweig, 'Globus: Studien zum weltgeschichtlichen Raumlehre', in *Zweistromland*, 313–66.

57 Rosenzweig's emphasis on death is something that Zachery Braitermann and Elliot Wolfson have insisted upon, and I will follow them by relating Rosenzweig's understanding of death to his philosophy of eternal life. See Elliot R. Wolfson, 'Facing the Effaced: Mystical Eschatology and the Idealistic Orientation in the Thought of Franz Rosenzweig', *Zeitschrift für Neuere Theologiegeschichte* 4, no. 1 (1997): 39–81 and Zachary Braiterman, '"Into life?" Franz Rosenzweig and the Figure of Death', *AJS Review* 23, no. 2 (1998): 203–21.

58 Franz Rosenzweig, *Hegel und der Staat* (Berlin: Suhrkamp, 2010).

59 Rosenzweig, *The Star of Redemption*; Rosenzweig, 'Globus'; Franz Rosenzweig, *Das Büchlein vom gesunden und kranken Menschenverstand* (Frankfurt am Main: Jüdischer Verlag im Suhrkamp Verlag, 1992); Franz Rosenzweig, *Understanding the Sick and Healthy*, trans. Nahum N. Glatzer (Cambridge and London: Harvard University Press, 1999). Benjamin Pollock, 'From Nation State to World Empire: Franz Rosenzweig's Redemptive Imperialism', *Jewish Studies Quarterly* 11, no. 4 (2004): 332–53.

60 See Eberhard Jüngel, *Barth-Studien* (Zürich: Benziger Verlag, 1982); Bruce McCormack, *Critically Realistic Dialectical Theology: Its Genesis and Development, 1909–1936* (Oxford: Clarendon Press, 1995); Dietrich Korsch, *Dialektische Theologie nach Karl Barth* (Tübingen: J. C. B. Mohr, 1996); Christope Chalamet, *Dialectical Theologians: Wilhelm Herrmann, Karl Barth and Rudolf Bultmann* (Zürich: Theologischer Verlag Zürich, 2005); the chapters 'The Barthian Revolt: Karl Barth, Paul Tillich, and the Legacy of Liberal Theology' and 'Idealistic Ironies: From Kant and Hegel to Tillich and Barth' in Gary Dorrien, *Kantian Reason and Hegelian Spirit: The Idealistic Logic of Modern Theology* (London: John Wiley, 2015), 454–572; George Hendry, 'The Transcendental Method in the Theology of Karl Barth', *Scottish Journal of Theology* 37, no. 2 (1984): 213–27 and Jacob Taubes, 'Theodicy and Theology: A Philosophical Analysis of Karl Barth's Dialectical Theology', *The Journal of Religion* 34, no. 4 (1954): 231–43.

61 Nathan Hitchcock, *Karl Barth and the Resurrection of the Flesh: The Loss of the Body in Participatory Eschatology* (Eugene: Pickwick Publications, 2013) and R. Dale Dawson, *The Resurrection in Karl Barth* (Aldershot: Ashgate, 2007); Yo Fukushima, *Aus dem Tode das Leben: Eine Untersuchung zu Karl Barths Todes- und Lebensverständnis* (Zürich: Theologischer Verlag Zürich, 2009).

62 For an introduction to Barth's life and scholarly development see Eberhard Busch, *Karl Barth: His Life from Letters and Autobiographical Texts*, trans. John Bowden (Eugene: Wipf and Stock 2005).

63 Wilhelm Herrmann, *Ethik: Grundriss der theologischen Wissenschaften* (Tübingen: J. C. B. Mohr, 1901). See Johann Friedrich Lohmann, *Karl Barth und der Neukantianismus: Die Rezeption des Neukantianismus im 'Römerbrief' und ihre Bedeutung für die weitere Ausarbeitung der Theologie Karl Barths* (Berlin: De Gruyter, 2010), for a comprehensive study on Barth's relation to the Neo-Kantians. For a study on the relation between Herrman and Barth see for example Chalamet, *Dialectical Theologians*. See also Busch, *Karl Barth*, 33–60.

64 McCormack, *Critically Realistic Dialectical Theology*, 129–30. The German Barth-exegetes who have influenced McCormack, such as Ingrid Spieckermann, Michael Beintker and Eberhard Jüngel, are, together with the American theologian Kenneth Oakes, important for my reading of Barth. Their discoveries of an analogical conceptualization of God in Barth's writings already in 1919 and 1922 enable me to argue that the radical but nonetheless analogical difference between God and creation is mirrored in Barth's discussion on the ideas of immortality, eternal life and resurrection. See Ingrid Spieckermann, *Gotteserkenntnis. Ein Beitrag zur Grundfrage der neuen Theologie Karl Barths* (München: C. Kaiser, 1985), Michael Beintker, *Die Dialektik in der 'dialektischen Theologie' Karl Barths* (München: C. Kaiser, 1987). See also Kenneth Oakes, *Reading Karl Barth: A Companion to Karl Barth's Epistle to the Romans* (Eugene: Cascade Books, 2011).

65 McCormack, *Critically Realistic Dialectical Theology*, 21.

66 Timothy Gorringe, *Against Hegemony* (Oxford: Oxford University Press, 2005), 31.

67 McCormack, *Critically Realistic Dialectical Theology*, 129.

68 Ibid., 21. See also Karl Barth, *The Epistle to the Romans*, trans. Edwyn C. Hoskyns (Oxford: Oxford University Press, 1968).

69 Ibid., 21. Karl Barth, *The Göttingen Dogmatics: Introduction in the Christian Religion*, trans. Geoffrey W. Bromiley (Grand Rapids: W.B. Eerdman, 1991); Karl Barth, *Unterricht in der christlichen Religion 2 1924/25* (Zürich: Theologischer Verlag Zürich, 1990); Karl Barth, *Church Dogmatics: Volume I:1*, trans. Geoffrey William Bromiley (Edinburgh: T&T Clark, 1975).

70 For McCormack, the continuity in theological perspective between the second edition of *The Epistle to the Romans* and the *Church Dogmatics* 'so greatly outweighs the discontinuity that those who wish to read the dogmatics without the benefit of the lens provided by *Romans II* will understand everything in the wrong light'. McCormack, *Critically Realistic Dialectical Theology*, 244–5.

71 Karl Barth, *Fides Quaerens Intellectum: Anselms Beweis der Existenz Gottes im Zusammenhang seines theologischen Programms* (Zürich: Theologischer Verlag Zürich, 1981) and Hans Urs von Balthasar, *The Theology of Karl Barth*, trans. T. Edward Oakes SJ (San Francisco: Ignatius Press, 1992).

72 Manfred Josuttis, *Die Gegenständlichkeit der Offenbarung: Karl Barths Anselm Buch und die Denkform seiner Theologie* (Bonn: H. Bouvier, 1965) and Sigurd

Baark, *The Affirmation of Reason: On Karl Barth's Speculative Theology* (Cham: Springer International Publishing, 2018). Baark defends, quite controversially, a reading of Barth as a speculative theologian in the Hegelian sense. In this he was preceded by the German theologians, Wolfhart Pannenberg and Klaus Krüger. See Klaus Krüger, *Der Gottesbegriff der Spekulativen Theologie* (Berlin: Walter de Gruyter, 1970), 151 and 169 and Wolfhart Pannenberg, *Offenbarung als Geschichte* (Göttingen: Vandenhoeck & Ruprecht, 1970), 9; Wolfhart Pannenberg, *Systematic Theology*, vol. I, trans. Geoffrey W. Bromiley (New York: T&T Clark, 2004), 304; Wolfhart Pannenberg, 'Die Subjektivität Gottes und die Trinitätslehre: Ein Beitrag zur Beziehung zwischen Karl Barth und der Philosophie Hegels', in *Grundfragen systematischer Theologie: Gesammelte Aufsätze*, vol. 2 (Göttingen: Vandenhoeck & Ruprecht, 2011), 96–111, at 98.

73 See Mark I. Wallace, *The Second Naiveté: Barth, Ricoeur, and the New Yale theology* (Macon: Mercer, 1995), 52–3.

74 McCormack, *Critically Realistic Dialectical Theology*, 455–8.

75 Ibid., 22.

76 Barth, *The Epistle to the Romans*; Barth, *The Göttingen Dogmatics*; Karl Barth, *Church and State*, trans. G. Ronald Howe (London: Student Christian Movement Press, 1939), Karl Barth, *Ethics*, trans. Geoffrey W. Bromiley (Edinburgh: T&T Clark, 1981); Barth, *Church Dogmatics: Volume I:1*; Karl Barth, *Church Dogmatics: Volume I:2*, trans. Geoffrey William Bromiley and Harold Knight (Edinburgh: T&T Clark, 1956); Karl Barth, *Church Dogmatics: Volume II:1*. trans. T. H. L. Parker, W. B. Johnston, Harold Knight and J. L. M. Haire (Edinburgh: T&T Clark, 1957); Karl Barth, *Church Dogmatics: Volume II:2* trans. T. H. L. Parker, W. B. Johnston, Harold Knight and J. L. M. Haire (Edinburgh: T&T Clark, 1957), 92; Karl Barth, *Church Dogmatics: Volume III:1*, trans. J. W. O. Edwards and Harold Knight (Edinburgh: T&T Clark, 1958). These titles are shortened as *CD I:1*, *CD I:2* and so on.

77 On Goldberg, Unger, and the *Philosophische Gruppe* see Voigts, *Oskar Goldberg*, 153–72. See also Manfred Voigts, 'Jüdisches Denken im Frühexpressionismus. Oskar Goldberg und Erich Unger im Zeichen Friedrich Nietzsches', in *Jüdischer Nietzscheanismus*, eds. Werner Stegmaier and Daniel Krochmalnik (Berlin: W. de Gruyter, 1997), 168–87 and Manfred Voigts, ed., *Jacob Taubes und Oskar Goldberg: Aufsätze, Briefe, Dokumente* (Würzburg: Königshausen & Neumann, 2011).

78 Voigts, *Oskar Goldberg*, 15–19.

79 Oskar Goldberg, *Die fünf Bücher Mosis: Ein Zahlengebäude: Die Feststellung einer einheitlich durchgeführten Zahlenschrift* (Berlin: Liebmann, 1908).

80 For an excellent introduction to Goldberg, gematria and his view on mathematics, see the chapter 'Georg Cantor and the Mathematics of God' in Bruce Rosenstock, *Transfinite Life: Oskar Goldberg and the Vitalist Imagination* (Bloomington: Indiana University Press, 2017), 42–75.

81 Ibid., xiv.

82 Voigts, *Oskar Goldberg*, 15–27.
83 Gershom Scholem, *Walter Benjamin: The Story of a Friendship*, trans. Harry Zohn (New York: Schocken, 981), 98. See also Gershom Scholem, *From Berlin to Jerusalem: Memories of My Youth*, trans. Harry Zohn (New York: Schocken, 1980), 146–9.
84 Scholem, *From Berlin to Jerusalem*, 147.
85 For a detailed account of the relation between Thomas Mann and Oskar Goldberg, see Christian Hülshörster, *Thomas Mann und Oskar Goldbergs 'Wirklichkeit der Hebräer'* (Frankfurt am Main: Klostermann, 1999). See also the chapter 'Thomas Mann und Oskar Goldberg' in Voigt, *Goldberg*, 235–70.
86 Oskar Goldberg, *Die Wirklichkeit der Hebräer: Einleitung in das System des Pentateuch* (Wiesbaden: Harrassowitz Verlag, 2005 (1925)); Goldberg, *Zahlengebäude, Ontologie, Maimonides und Aufsätze 1933 bis 1947*.

Chapter 1

1 Rosenzweig, *Hegel und der Staat*, 526.
2 Ibid., 532.
3 I borrow this argument from Wolfgang D. Herzfelt who has written an excellent study on Rosenzweig and geopolitics; see Wolfgang D. Herzfeld, *Franz Rosenzweig, 'Mitteleuropa' und der Erste Weltkrieg* (Freiburg: K. Alber, 2013), 78.
4 Rosenzweig, 'Vox Dei?', 278.
5 Rosenzweig, 'Die neue Levante', 309–12.
6 Friedrich Meinecke, *Weltbürgertum und Nationalstaat. Studien zur Genesis des deutschen Nationalstaates* (Munich: R. Oldenbourg, 1908).
7 Duncan Celly, '"The Goal of that Pure and Noble Yearning": Friedrich Meinecke's Visions of 1848', in *The 1848 Revolutions and European Political Thought*, eds Douglas Moggach and Gareth Stedman Jones (Cambridge: Cambridge University Press, 2018), 293–321, at 310.
8 Ibid.
9 Ibid., 312.
10 See Petar Bojanic, 'Franz Rosenzweig's Ground of War', *Bamidbar* 1, no. 1 (2011): 35–46.
11 Quoted in ibid., 39, but modified by me. Original: Franz Rosenzweig, 'Letter to His Parents' 1 October 1917, in *Briefe und Tagebücher, 1900–1918*, eds. Rachel Rosenzweig and Edith Rosenzweig – Scheinmann (Haag: Martinus Nijhoff Publishers, 1979), 459.
12 Rudolf Kjellén, *Inledning till Sveriges geografi* (Göteborg: Wettergren & Kerber, 1900). Rosenzweig wrote in one of his letters from 1917 that he was reading Kjellén during the war: Franz Rosenzweig, *Briefe und Tagebücher 1900–1918*, 342.

13 Rudolf Kjellén, *Der Staat als Lebensform* (Leipzig: Hirzel, 1917) and Rudolf Kjellén, *Schweden: Eine politische Monographie*, ed. Friedrich Meinecke (Berlin: R. Oldenbourg, 1917).
14 See the chapter 'Rosenzweig's War' in Gil Anidjar, *The Jew, the Arab: A History of the Enemy* (Stanford: Stanford University Press, 2003), 87–98, for a critical discussion on Rosenzweig's messianic theory of war and his ideas on Islam.
15 Kreienbrock, 'Franz Rosenzweig's Mitteleuropa, a New Levante', 192.
16 See Franz Rosenzweig, 'Vertauschte Fronten', in *Zweistromland*, 235–7.
17 See Hermann Cohen, *Religion of Reason: Out of the Sources of Judaism*, trans. Simon Kaplan (Atlanta: Scholars Press, 1995).
18 Rosenzweig, *The Star of Redemption*, 9.
19 Ibid., 446.
20 See the chapter 'System as Task of Philosophy: "The Oldest System-Program of German Idealism"', in Pollock, *Franz Rosenzweig and the Systematic Task of Philosophy*, 61–5.
21 Rosenzweig, *The Star of Redemption*, 15.
22 Ibid., 18.
23 Ibid.
24 Pierre Hadot, *Philosophy as a Way of Life: Spiritual Exercises from Socrates to Foucault*, trans. Arnold Davidson (Oxford: Blackwell Publishers Ltd, 1995), 267.
25 Rosenzweig, *The Star of Redemption*, 96.
26 Ibid., 88.
27 Quoted in Giovanni Reale, *A History of Ancient Philosophy III: Systems of the Hellenistic Age*, ed. and trans. John R. Catan (Albany: State University of New York Press, 1985), 173.
28 Rosenzweig, *The Star of Redemption*, 10.
29 Heinrich Rickert, *Grundprobleme der Philosophie: Methodologie, Ontologie, Anthropologie* (Tübingen: J. C. B. Mohr [Paul Siebeck], 1934), 7.
30 Heinrich Rickert, *Die Philosophie des Lebens: Darstellung und Kritik der Philosophischen Modeströmungen unserer Zeit* (Tübingen: J. C. B. Mohr [Paul Siebeck], 1920).
31 Ibid., 59.
32 Ibid.
33 Rosenzweig, *The Star of Redemption*, 9.
34 Ibid.
35 Ibid.
36 Ibid., 10.
37 Nitzan Lebovic has noted that it was Georg Simmel, one of Rickert's students who was attacked in *Die Philosophie des Lebens*, who popularized the concept of bare or mere life in his *Lebensanschauung: Vier metaphysische Kapitel* (Munich: Duncker & Humblot, 1918). See Nitzan Lebovic, *The Philosophy of Life and Death: Ludwig Klages and the Rise of Nazi Biopolitics* (New York: Palgrave-Macmillan, 2013). See

also Giorgio Agamben, *Homo Sacer: Sovereign Power and Bare Life*, trans. Daniel Heller-Roazen (Stanford: Stanford University Press, 1998).

38 Rosenzweig, *The Star of Redemption*, 10.
39 Gérard Bensussan, 'Rosenzweig and War. A Question of "Point of View": Between Creation, Revelation, and Redemption', *The Centennial Review* 13, no. 1 (2013): 115–36, at 115.
40 Rosenzweig, *The Star of Redemption*, 414.
41 Ibid, 19.
42 Franz Rosenzweig, 'New Thinking', in *Franz Rosenzweig's 'The New Thinking'*, eds. and trans. Alan Udoff and Barbara E. Galli (Syracuse: Syracuse University Press, 1999) 67–102, at 69.
43 Rosenzweig, *The Star of Redemption*, 414.
44 Ibid.
45 Rickert, *Die Philosophie des Lebens*, 59.
46 Franz Rosenzweig, *Briefe und Tagebücher 1918–1929* (Haag: Martinus Nijhoff Publishers, 1979), 1114.
47 Rosenzweig, *The Star of Redemption*, 349.
48 Ibid.
49 Rosenzweig, 'New Thinking', 80.
50 Max Brod, *Paganism, Christianity, Judaism: A Confession of Faith*, trans. William Wolfe (Tuscaloosa: University of Alabama Press, 2011).
51 Ibid., 5.
52 Ibid.
53 Rosenzweig, 'New Thinking', 80.
54 Franz Rosenzweig, '"Germ Cell" of *The Star of Redemption*', in *Franz Rosenzweig's 'The New Thinking'*, 45–66, at 61.
55 Ibid.
56 Franz Rosenzweig, 'Paralipomena', in *Zweistromland*, 61–124, at 72.
57 Rosenzweig, 'New Thinking', 80.
58 Rosenzweig, *The Star of Redemption*, 42.
59 Rosenzweig, 'Paralipomena', 95.
60 Rosenzweig, '"Germ Cell" of *The Star of Redemption*', 50.
61 Ibid.
62 Rosenzweig, *The Star of Redemption*, 42.
63 Rosenzweig, *Briefe und Tagebücher 1918–1929*, 1114.
64 Rosenzweig, 'Paralipomena', 121.
65 Rosenzweig, *The Star of Redemption*, 96.
66 Rosenzweig, 'New Thinking', 90.
67 Ibid., 79.
68 Ibid.
69 Rosenzweig, *The Star of Redemption*, 444.

70 Samuelson, *User's Guide to Franz Rosenzweig's Star of Redemption*, 62.
71 Rosenzweig, *The Star of Redemption*, 9.
72 Ibid., 239.
73 Ibid.
74 Rudolf Ehrenberg, *Theoretische Biologie: Vom Standpunkt der Irreversibilität des Elementaren Lebensvorganges* (Berlin: Springer, 1923), 6.
75 Ibid.
76 Ibid.
77 Rosenzweig, 'New Thinking', 88.
78 Ibid., 91.
79 Ibid.
80 Franz Rosenzweig, 'Hic et Ubique', in *Cultural Writings of Franz Rosenzweig*, ed. and trans. Barbara E. Galli (New York: Syracuse University Press, 2000), 83–97, at 93.
81 Rosenzweig, *The Star of Redemption*, 443–4.
82 Ibid., 444.
83 Ibid.
84 Franz Rosenzweig, 'Jüdische Geschichte im Rahmen der Weltgeschichte', in *Zweistromland*, 539–52, at 543–4.
85 Rosenzweig, *The Star of Redemption*, 350.
86 Rosenzweig, 'Jüdische Geschichte im Rahmen der Weltgeschichte', 544.
87 Rosenzweig, *The Star of Redemption*, 297.
88 Ibid., 348.
89 Kjellén, *Staten som Lifsform*, 182.
90 Ibid., 46.
91 Ibid., 47.
92 Friedrich Ratzel, *Politische Geographie; oder, Die Geographie der Staaten, des Verkehres und des Krieges* (Munich: R. Oldenbourg, 1903).
93 Friedrich Ratzel, *Anthropogeographie* (Darmstadt: Wissenschaftliche Buchgesellschaft, 1975).
94 I borrow this argument from Christian Abrahamsson, 'On the Genealogy of Lebensraum', *Geographia Helvetica* no. 68 (2013): 37–44, at 41.
95 Friedrich Ratzel, *Physikalische Geographie und Naturcharakter der Vereinigten Staaten von Nord-Amerika* (Munich: Oldenbourg, 1878) and Friedrich Ratzel, *Culturgeographie der Vereinigten Staaten von Nordamerika: unter besonderer Berücksichtigung der wirtschaftlichen Verhältnisse* (Munich: R. Oldenbourg, 1880).
96 Kracauer's critique of Buber and Rosenzweig can be found in: Siegfried Kracauer, *The Mass Ornament: Weimar Essays*, trans. Thomas Y. Levin (London: Harvard University Press, 1995), 189–202. For Spengler's discussion on his so-called morphology of world history see Oswald Spengler, *The Decline of the West*, trans. Charles Frances Atkinson (New York: Alfred A. Knopf, 1926), 5–8. For an examination of the relation between Spengler and Rosenzweig, see Sonia

Goldblum, 'Oswald Spengler et le refus de la Révélation. Rosenzweig lecteur du *Déclin de l'Occident*'. Available online: https://halshs.archives-ouvertes.fr/hal-00463442/document (accessed 1 April 2017).
97 Rosenzweig, *Briefe und Tagebücher 1918–1929*, 629.
98 Rosenzweig, 'Jüdische Geschichte im Rahmen der Weltgeschichte', 551.
99 Kjellén, *Staten som Lifsform*, 174.
100 Franz Rosenzweig, 'Faith and Knowledge', in *God, Man, and the World–Lectures and Essays*, ed. and trans. Barbara E. Galli (New York: Syracuse University Press, 1998), 97–121, at 109.
101 Ibid., 109.
102 See Cass Fisher, 'Absolute Factuality, Common Sense, and Theological Reference in the Thought of Franz Rosenzweig', *Harvard Theological Review* 109, no. 3 (2016): 342–70.
103 Rosenzweig, 'New Thinking', 83.
104 Rickert, *Die Philosophie des Lebens*, 14.
105 Rosenzweig, *The Star of Redemption*, 235.
106 Ibid., Franz Rosenzweig, 'The Science of the World', in *God, Man, and the World–Lectures and Essays*, 81–96, at 95.
107 Fisher, 'Absolute Factuality, Common Sense, and Theological Reference in the Thought of Franz Rosenzweig', 344.
108 Rosenzweig, 'New Thinking', 69.
109 See Peter Gordon, *Rosenzweig and Heidegger: Between Judaism and German Philosophy* (Berkeley: University of California Press, 2005), 33.
110 Franz Rosenzweig, 'The Science of God', in *God, Man, and the World–Lectures and Essays*, 37–61, at 41.
111 Ibid., 42.
112 The whole third volume of *The Star of Redemption* is written against the fanatics and tyrants who want to steal the kingdom of heaven from God: Rosenzweig, *The Star of Redemption*, 284–424.
113 Rosenzweig, 'New Thinking', 94.
114 Ibid.
115 Rosenzweig, *The Star of Redemption*, 446.
116 Gordon, *Rosenzweig and Heidegger*, 86–91.
117 Ibid., 176.
118 Ibid., 177.
119 Rosenzweig, *The Star of Redemption*, 446.
120 Ibid.
121 Ibid., 446–7.
122 Ibid., 447.
123 Rosenzweig, 'Paralipomena', 95.
124 Ibid., 102.

125 Wolfson, 'Facing the Effaced', 39 and 43.
126 Ibid., 42.
127 Rosenzweig, *Understanding the Sick and Healthy*, 103.
128 Quoted in Zachary Braiterman, '"Into life?" Franz Rosenzweig and the Figure of Death', 217. Original in: Franz Rosenzweig, *Rosenzweig: His Life and Thought*, ed. and trans. Nahum Glatzer (Indianapolis/Cambridge: Hackett Publishing Company, 1998), 67.
129 Rosenzweig, *Understanding the Sick and Healthy*, 103.
130 Braiterman quotes Glatzer: 'This concluding chapter – on death – stands in a striking contrast to the final passage of *The Star of Redemption*'. See Braiterman, '"Into life?" Franz Rosenzweig and the Figure of Death', 203.
131 See note 75 in Pollock, *Franz Rosenzweig's Conversions* (Bloomington: Indiana University Press, 2014), 248.
132 Rosenzweig, 'Faith and Knowledge', 120.
133 Rosenzweig, *The Star of Redemption*, 406.
134 Ibid., 21.
135 Rosenzweig, 'New Thinking', 98.
136 Martin Kavka, 'Verification (Bewährung) in Franz Rosenzweig', in *German-Jewish Thought between Religion and Politics: Festschrift in Honour of Paul Mendes-Flohr on the Occasion of His Seventieth Birthday*, eds. Christian Wiese and Martina Urban (Berlin: De Gruyter 2012), 167–84, at 167.
137 Ibid.
138 Rosenzweig, 'New Thinking', 99.
139 For a discussion on Karl Popper's criticism of the logical positivists see Phil Parvin, *Karl Popper* (London: Bloomsbury Publishing, 2014), 14–18.
140 Rosenzweig, 'New Thinking', 98–9.
141 David Baumgardt, *Jenseits von Machtmoral und Masochismus. Hedonistische Ethik als kritische Alternative* (Meisenheim: Hain, 1977), 410.
142 Rosenzweig, *Understanding the Sick and Healthy*, 103.
143 Rosenzweig, *The Star of Redemption*, 116.
144 Ibid.
145 Nathan Rotenstreich, 'Common Sense and Theological Experience on the Basis of Franz Rosenzweig's Philosophy', *Journal of the History of Philosophy* 5, no. 4 (1967): 353–60, at 360.
146 Fisher, 'Absolute Factuality, Common Sense, and Theological Reference in the Thought of Franz Rosenzweig', 360–8.
147 Rotenstreich, 'Common Sense and Theological Experience on the Basis of Franz Rosenzweig's Philosophy', 359.
148 Franz Rosenzweig, 'Science and Life', in *God, Man, and the World–Lectures and Essays*, 123–33, at 133.
149 Rosenzweig, '"Germ Cell" of *The Star of Redemption*', 64.
150 Pollock, *Franz Rosenzweig and the Systematic Task of Philosophy*, 299.

151 F. W. J. von Schelling, *Philosophie der Offenbarung* (Frankfurt am Main: Suhrkamp am Main, 1977). For an introduction to Schelling and his philosophy of revelation see for instance: Walter Schulz, *Die Vollendung des Deutschen Idealismus in der Spätphilosophie Schellings* (Pfullingen: Neske, 1975); Xavier Tilliette, *Schelling une Philosophie en Devenir* (Paris: Vrin, 1992); Xavier Tilliette, *Attualità di Schelling* (Milano: U. Mursia, 1974); Manfred Frank, *Der Unendliche Mangel an Sein: Schellings Hegelkritik und die Anfänge der Marxschen Dialektik* (Munich: Wilhelm Fink Verlag, 1992); Tyler Tritten, *Beyond Presence: The Late F.W.J. Schelling's Criticism of Metaphysics* (Boston: Walter de Gruyter, 2012).
152 von Schelling, *Philosophie der Offenbarung*, 156. Italics in original.
153 von Schelling, *Philosophie der Offenbarung*, 159–60. Italics in original.
154 Tritten, *Beyond Presence*, 62.
155 Ibid.
156 Rosenzweig, 'Science of the World', 93.
157 Rosenzweig, *The Star of Redemption*, 115.
158 Ibid.
159 Ibid., 19. Feuerbach criticizes Hegel and the long tradition of idealism by arguing: 'Being, grounded as it is altogether on such non-verbalities, is therefore itself something non-verbal. Indeed, it is that which cannot be verbalized. Where words cease, life begins and being reveals its secret. If, therefore, non-verbality is the same as irrationality, then all existence is irrational because it is always and forever only this existence.' Ludwig Feuerbach, 'Principles of the Philosophy of the Future', in *The Fiery Brook: Selected Writings of Ludwig Feuerbach*, trans. Zawar Hanfi (London and New York: Verso, 2012), 399–551, at 486. It is in this essay that Feuerbach in a Schellingian manner differentiates his new thinking, or new philosophy, from old thinking, or old philosophy, and it might be from Feuerbach that Rosenzweig takes this distinction. For a discussion on the relation between Feuerbach and Rosenzweig see Luca Bertolino, 'Alle origini del "nuovo pensiero: Rosenzweig interprete di Feuerbach', *TEORIA* 28, no. 1 (2008): 195–206.
160 Rosenzweig, '"Germ Cell" of *The Star of Redemption*', 47.
161 Schelling, *Philosophie der Offenbarung*, 118. Italics in original.
162 Hans Ehrenberg, *Die Parteiung der Philosophie: Studien wider Hegel und die Kantianer* (Leipzig: Verlag von Felix Meiner, 1911), 79.
163 Rosenzweig, 'Science of the World', 81.
164 Ibid., 82.
165 Rosenzweig, 'The Science of God', 41.
166 Ibid., 55.
167 Rosenzweig, 'Faith and Knowledge', 102.
168 Rosenzweig, *The Star of Redemption*, 143.
169 Ibid.

170 Rosenzweig, 'The Science of God', 55.
171 Ibid., 41.
172 Ibid., 56.
173 Ibid., 55.
174 Rosenzweig, *The Star of Redemption*, 256.
175 Rosenzweig, *Der Stern der Erlösung*, 266. No italics in original.
176 Ibid., 258.
177 Rosenzweig, *The Star of Redemption*, 443.
178 Ibid.
179 Bensussan, 'Rosenzweig and War', 33.
180 Rosenzweig, 'Globus', 348.
181 Ibid., 313.
182 Ibid.
183 Rosenzweig, *The Star of Redemption*, 254.
184 Ibid.
185 Ibid., 352.
186 Rosenzweig, 'Globus', 348.
187 Hermann Cohen, *Deutschtum und Judentum: mit grundlegenden Betrachtungen über Staat und Internationalismus* (Gießen: Verlag von Alfred Töpelmann, 1923), 57.
188 Franz Rosenzweig, 'Deutschtum und Judentum', in *Zweistromland*, 169–75, at 169.
189 Ibid.
190 Rosenzweig, 'Globus', 368.
191 Rosenzweig, 'New Thinking', 91.
192 Rosenzweig, 'Globus', 313.
193 Rosenzweig, *The Star of Redemption*, 444.
194 Carl Schmitt, *Land and Sea: A World-Historical Meditation*, trans. Samuel Garrett Zeitlin (Candor: Telos Press Publishing, 2015).
195 See Vittorio Cotesta, 'Rosenzweig, Schmitt and the Concept of Europe', in *Europe in Crisis: Intellectuals and the European Idea, 1917–1957*, eds. Mark Hewitson and Matthew D'Auria (New York: Berghahn Books, 2015), 173.
196 Brod, *Paganism, Christianity, Judaism*, 252.
197 Ibid., 252–3.
198 Ibid., 253.
199 Rosenzweig, *The Star of Redemption*, 350–1.
200 Ibid., 351.
201 Rosenzweig, 'Jüdische Geschichte im Rahmen der Weltgeschichte', 552.
202 Ibid.
203 Rosenzweig, *The Star of Redemption*, 68.
204 Rosenzweig, *Der Stern der Erlösung*, 65. No italics in original.
205 Rosenzweig, *The Star of Redemption*, 43.

206 Rosenzweig describes the coming millennium as a struggle between 'Abend- und Morgenland, Kirche und Islam, Germanen und Araben'. Rosenzweig, 'Jüdische Geschichte im Rahmen der Weltgeschichte', 545.
207 Rosenzweig, *Understanding the Sick and Healthy*, 102; Rosenzweig, *The Star of Redemption*, 45.
208 Samuelson, *User's Guide to Franz Rosenzweig's Star of Redemption*, 58.
209 Ibid.
210 Rosenzweig, *The Star of Redemption*, 43.
211 Ibid., 45–6.
212 Ibid., 46.
213 Rosenzweig, 'Jüdische Geschichte im Rahmen der Weltgeschichte', 539.
214 Ibid.
215 Ibid., 540.
216 Ibid.
217 See for example Guillermo Algaze, *Ancient Mesopotamia at the Dawn of Civilization: The Evolution of an Urban Landscape* (Chicago: The University of Chicago Press, 2014).
218 Rosenzweig, *The Star of Redemption*, 85.
219 Rosenzweig, 'Jüdische Geschichte im Rahmen der Weltgeschichte', 540.
220 Rosenzweig, *The Star of Redemption*, 85.
221 Ibid.
222 Ibid.
223 G. W. F. Hegel, *Phenomenology of Spirit*, trans. A. V. Miller (Oxford: Oxford University Press, 1977), 111–19.
224 Ibid., 114.
225 Mohammed Bamyeh, *Of Death and Dominion: The Existential Foundations of Governance* (Evanston: Northwestern University Press, 2007), 8.
226 Ibid.
227 Ibid.
228 Ibid., 10.
229 Ibid.
230 Rosenzweig, 'Jüdische Geschichte im Rahmen der Weltgeschichte', 541.
231 Rosenzweig, 'Paralipomena', 112.
232 Rosenzweig, 'Jüdische Geschichte im Rahmen der Weltgeschichte', 541.
233 Arendt, *The Human Condition*, 18.
234 Ibid., 19.
235 Ibid.
236 Ibid., 22.
237 Rosenzweig, *The Star of Redemption*, 63.
238 Bamyeh, *Of Death and Dominion*, 9.
239 Rosenzweig, *The Star of Redemption*, 443–4.

240 Franz Rosenzweig, 'Der Jüdische Mensch', in *Zweistromland*, 559–76, at 572.
241 Rosenzweig, 'Deutschtum und Judentum', 173.
242 Franz Rosenzweig, 'Der Jude im Staat', in *Zweistromland*, 553–5, at 554.
243 Ibid.
244 Rosenzweig, *The Star of Redemption*, 415.
245 Ibid., 427.
246 Ibid., 443.
247 Ibid.
248 Ibid., 351.
249 Ibid.
250 Ibid., 427–8.
251 On Schelling's triadic conception of the church as a Petrine, Pauline and Johannine community, see Schelling, *Philosophie der Offenbarung*, 313–25.
252 Rosenzweig, *The Star of Redemption*, 297.
253 Ibid., 437.
254 Ibid., 299.
255 Rosenzweig, *The Star of Redemption*, 302.
256 Ibid., 41.
257 Ibid., 403.
258 Blumenberg, *The Legitimacy of the Modern Age*, 443.
259 Rosenzweig, *The Star of Redemption*, 256.
260 Ibid.
261 Ibid., 403.
262 Braiterman, '"Into life?" Franz Rosenzweig and the Figure of Death', 220–1.
263 Rosenzweig, *Briefe und Tagebücher 1918–1929*, 1115–16.
264 Rosenzweig, *The Star of Redemption*, 277.
265 Ibid., 414.
266 Rosenzweig, 'Paralipomena', 110.
267 Ibid. No italics in the original.
268 Rosenzweig, 'The Science of God', 55.
269 Bamyeh, *Of Death and Dominion*, 26.
270 Rosenzweig, *The Star of Redemption*, 414.
271 Ibid., 255.
272 Rosenzweig, 'Paralipomena', 109. No italics in original.

Chapter 2

1 Karl Barth, *The Christian Life: Church Dogmatics IV:4. Lecture Fragments*, trans. Geoffrey William Bromiley (Grand Rapids: William B. Eerdmans Publishing Company, 1981), 212.

2 Ibid.
3 Barth, *CD III:I*, 208.
4 Ibid.
5 Ibid.
6 Barth, *Christian Life*, 212.
7 Ibid.
8 Ibid., 179.
9 Karl Barth, *Church Dogmatics: Volume III:4*, trans. A. T. MacKay, T. H. L. Parker, Harold Knight, H. A. Kennedy and J. Marks (Edinburgh: T&T Clark, 1961), 353.
10 Karl Barth, 'Feuerbach', in *Vorträge und kleinere Arbeiten 1922–1925*, ed. Holger Finze-Michaelsen (Zürich: Theologischer Verlag Zürich, 1990), 6–13.
11 Barth, 'Feuerbach', 8.
12 Ludwig Feuerbach, *The Essence of Christianity*, trans. George Eliot (Walnut: MSAC Philosophy Group, 2008), 203.
13 For a discussion on Feuerbach's notion of species-being, *Gattungswesen*, see Larry Johnston, *Between Transcendence and Nihilism: Species-ontology in the Philosophy of Ludwig Feuerbach* (New York: Lang, 1995).
14 Feuerbach, *The Essence of Christianity*, 32. See also Anselm of Canterbury, 'Proslogion', in *The Major Works*, eds. Brian Davies and Gillian R. Evans (Oxford: Oxford University Press, 1998), 82–104. On the relation between Barth and Anselm see Robert D. Shofner, *Anselm Revisited: A Study on the Role of the Ontological Argument in the Writings of Karl Barth and Charles Hartshorne* (Leiden: Brill, 1974).
15 Feuerbach, *The Essence of Christianity*, 32.
16 Anselm of Canterbury, 'Proslogion', 87.
17 Feuerbach, *The Essence of Christianity*, 4.
18 Quoted in Van A. Harvey, *Feuerbach and the Interpretation of Religion* (Cambridge: Cambridge University Press 1997), 228.
19 Ludwig Feuerbach, *The Essence of Faith according to Luther*, trans. Melvin Cherno (New York: Harper & Row, Publishers, 1967), 126.
20 Ibid., 127.
21 I borrow this argument from Manfred H. Vogel, 'The Barth-Feuerbach Confrontation', *The Harvard Theological Review* 59, no. 1 (1966): 27–52, at 29. See also Joseph C. Weber, 'Feuerbach, Barth, and Theological Methodology', *The Journal of Religion* 46, no. 1 (1966): 24–36; John Glasse, 'Barth on Feuerbach', *The Harvard Theological Review* 57, no. 2 (1964): 69–96; Richard Paul Cumming, 'Revelation as Apologetic Category: A Reconsideration of Karl Barth's Engagement with Ludwig Feuerbach's Critique of Religion', *Scottish Journal of Theology* 68, no. 1 (2015): 43–60.
22 Karl Barth, *The Theology of Schleiermacher: Lectures at Göttingen, Winter Semester of 1923/24*, trans. Geoffrey W. Bromiley (Grand Rapids: William B. Eerdmans Publishing Company, 1982), 245.

23 Ibid., 252.
24 Barth, 'Feuerbach 1922', 12. No italics in original.
25 Ludwig Feuerbach, *Lectures on the Essence of Religion*, trans. Ralph Manheim (New York: Harper & Row, Publishers, 1967), 37.
26 Barth, *The Göttingen Dogmatics*, 63.
27 See Karl Barth, *Unterricht in der christlichen Religion 1: 1924* (Zürich: Theologischer Verlag, 1985), 74–5.
28 Baark, *Affirmation of Reason*, 135.
29 Ibid., 261.
30 This is something that Manfred Josuttis also has emphasized in his excellent study on Anselm and Barth. See Josuttis, *Die Gegenständlichkeit der Offenbarung*, 42.
31 Barth, *CD II:1*, 670.
32 Ibid., 673.
33 Baark, *Affirmation of Reason*, 135.
34 Barth, *CD II:1*, 674.
35 Barth, *The Göttingen Dogmatics*, 76.
36 Barth, *CD I:2*, 282.
37 Ibid., 324.
38 Karl Barth, 'Feuerbach', in *Karl Barth: Theologian of Freedom*, ed. Clifford Green (Minneapolis: Fortress Press, 1991), 90–7, at 97. See also, Max Stirner, *The Ego and Its Own*, trans. Steven Byington (Cambridge: Cambridge University Press, 2000).
39 Stirner, *The Ego and Its Own*, 35.
40 Karl Barth, 'Die Theologie und der Moderne Mensch', in *Vorträge und kleinere Arbeiten 1925-1930*, ed. Hermann Schmidt (Zürich: Theologischer Verlag Zürich, 1994), 160–82, at 169. No italics in the original.
41 Barth, *CD I:2*, 324.
42 See the paragraph 17: 'The Revelation of God as the Abolition of Religion' in ibid., 280–361. For the original see 'Gottes Offenbarung als Aufhebung der Religion' in Karl Barth, *Die kirchliche Dogmatik I:2* (Zürich: Theologischer Verlag Zürich, 1980), 304–97.
43 Barth, *CD I:2*, 325.
44 Ibid., 297.
45 Ludwig Feuerbach, 'Wider den Dualismus von Leib und Seele, Fleisch und Geist', in *Gesammelte Schriften 10*, ed. Werner Schuffenhauer (Berlin: Akademie Verlag, 1971), 122–50, at 147.
46 I borrow this argument from John Hymer, 'Verteidigung von Feuerbachs Moleschott Rezeption: Feuerbachs offene Dialektik', in *Identität und Pluralismus in der globalen Gesellschaft--Ludwig Feuerbach zum 200. Geburtstag*, eds. Ursula Reitemeyer, Takayuki Shibata and Francesco Tomasoni (New York: Waxmann Verlag, 2006), 129–44.

47 Ludwig Feuerbach, 'Die Naturwissenschaft und die Revolution', in *Gesammelte Schriften 10*, ed. Werner Schuffenhauer (Berlin: Akademie Verlag, 1971), 347–68, at 358. Barth comments this essay in 1910 in a lecture for his confirmands. See Karl Barth, *Konfirmandenunterricht 1909–1921* (Zürich: Theologischer Verlag Zürich, 1987), 65.
48 Barth, *CD III:2*, 386.
49 Karl Barth, 'Ludwig Feuerbach (1927)', in *Ludwig Feuerbach*, ed. Erich Thies (Darmstadt: Wissenschaftliche Buchgesellschaft, 1976), 1–32, at 6.
50 Barth, *Ethics*, 128.
51 For a discussion on Feuerbach and his concept of *Afterweisheit* see Hymer, 'Verteidigung von Feuerbachs Moleschott Rezeption:Feuerbachs offene Dialektik', 139.
52 Feuerbach, *Lectures on the Essence of Religion*, 356.
53 Barth, *Ethics*, 128.
54 Ibid.
55 Feuerbach, *Lectures on the Essence of Religion*, 36.
56 Ibid.
57 Ibid., 317.
58 Ibid.
59 Barth, *Ethics*, 138.
60 Ibid., 12. No italics in the original.
61 Feuerbach, *Lectures on the Essence of Religion*, 137.
62 Ibid.
63 Barth, *The Göttingen Dogmatics*, 63.
64 Barth, *CD I:2*, 297.
65 Karl Barth, *The Göttingen Dogmatics*, 211.
66 Ibid., 155.
67 Barth, *CD III:1*, 208.
68 Ibid.
69 Ibid., 143.
70 Ibid.
71 Ibid.
72 Barth, *CD II:2*, 517.
73 See the paragraph 'God and Nothingness', in Karl Barth, *Church Dogmatics: Volume III:3*, trans. Geoffrey William Bromiley and R. J. Ehrlich (Edinburgh: T&T Clark, 1960), 289–360.
74 Barth, *CD II:2*, 517.
75 Ibid.
76 Ibid.
77 Ibid.

78 Barth, *CD III:1*, 124.
79 Ibid., 773.
80 Ibid., 773-4.
81 Barth, *CD II:1*, 114.
82 Barth, *CD I:2*, 324.
83 Paul S. Chung, *Karl Barth: God's Word in Action* (Eugene: Cascade Books, 2008), 288.
84 Quoted in Gorringe, *Against Hegemony*, 130.
85 Barth, *Unterricht in der christlichen Religion 2: 1924/25*, 274 and 321.
86 Carl Christian Bry, *Verkappte Religionen: Kritik des kollektiven Wahns* (Gotha: Verlag Friedrich Andreas Perthes, 1924), 98.
87 Barth, *Unterricht in der christlichen Religion 2: 1924/25*, 321.
88 Hannah Arendt, *Eichmann in Jerusalem: A Report on the Banality of Evil* (London: Faber & Faber, 1963).
89 Barth, *Unterricht in der christlichen Religion 2: 1924/25*, 297.
90 Ibid., 341.
91 Ibid., 342.
92 Ibid., 321.
93 Ibid.
94 Ibid., 321-2.
95 Ibid., 322.
96 Ibid.
97 Barth, *CD III:3*, 525.
98 Barth, *Unterricht in der christlichen Religion 2: 1924/25*, 315.
99 Ibid., 328.
100 Ibid., 323.
101 Ibid., 323.
102 Ibid., 321.
103 Ibid., 339.
104 Ibid., 324.
105 Ibid., 321.
106 Ibid., 334.
107 Ibid., 343
108 Ibid.
109 Karl Barth, *Credo: Die Hauptprobleme der Dogmatik, dargestellt im Anschluß an das Apostolische Glaubensbekenntnis. 16 Vorlesungen, gehalten an der Universität Utrecht im Februar und März 1935* (Zürich: Evangelischer Verlag, 1948), 139.
110 Ibid.
111 Ibid., 148.
112 Barth, *Unterricht in der christlichen Religion 2: 1924/25*, 336.
113 Barth, *CD II:1*, 628.

114 Ibid., 620–3.
115 Ibid., 623.
116 Ibid., 640.
117 Ibid., 627 and 629.
118 Ibid., 630 and 631.
119 Ibid., 633.
120 Barth, *CD II:2*, 92.
121 Barth, *CD I:1*, 10.
122 Ibid., 55.
123 Barth, *The Epistle to the Romans*, 531.
124 Ibid., 107.
125 Beintker, *Die Dialektik in der 'dialektischen Theologie' Karl Barths*, 251–9.
126 I borrow this argument from Oakes, *Reading Karl Barth*, 21. Oakes and Beintker argue that the analogy and the parable have the same structure in Barth's thinking.
127 Barth, *The Epistle to the Romans*, 193.
128 Karl Barth, *Der Römerbrief* (Zürich: Theologischer Verlag Zürich, 2005), 188. Not italicized in the original.
129 Barth, *CD I:1*, xiii.
130 Barth, *The Epistle to the Romans*, 193.
131 Ibid., 527.
132 Barth, *The Göttingen Dogmatics*, 63.
133 Ibid., 151.
134 Karl Barth, 'Das Wort in der Theologie von Schleiermacher bis Ritschl, 1927', in *Vorträge und kleinere Arbeiten 1925–1930*, ed Schmidt, 183–214, at 201.
135 Ibid. No italics in original.
136 Karl Barth, *Fides Quaerens Intellectum*, 15.
137 Ibid., 47.
138 Barth, *The Göttingen Dogmatics*, 413.
139 Barth, *Fides Quaerens Intellectum*, 92.
140 Ibid., 28–9.
141 Eva T. H. Brann, *The Ways of Naysaying* (Lanham: Rowman & Littlefield Publishers, 2001), 106.
142 Ibid.
143 Ibid.
144 Barth, *Fides Quaerens Intellectum*, 101–2.
145 Ibid., 15.
146 Barth, *CD II:1*, 59.
147 Barth, 'The Christian's Place in Society', in *The Word of God and the Word of Man*, trans. Douglas Horton (New York: Harper & Row, Publishers, (1919) 1957), 289–90.
148 Ibid., 290.
149 Ibid., 300.

150 Eberhard Jüngel, 'Die Möglichkeit theologischer Anthropologie auf dem Grunde der Analogie. Eine Untersuchung zum Analogieverständnis Karl Barths', in *Barth-Studien* (Zürich: Benziger Verlag, 1982), 210–32, at 226.
151 Ibid. Not italicized in original.
152 Louis Althusser, 'Ideology and Ideological State Apparatuses (Notes towards an Investigation)', in *Essays on Ideology*, trans. Ben Brewster (London: Verso, 1984), 1–60.
153 Ibid., 37.
154 For a discussion on Karl Barth and the orders of creation see Paul T. Nimmo, 'The Orders of Creation in the Theological Ethics of Karl Barth', *Scottish Journal of Theology* 60, no. 1 (2007), 24–35.
155 Karl Barth, 'The Significance of the State for the Church', in *Church and State*, trans. G. Ronald Howe (London: Student Christian Movement Press, 1939), 37–61, at 42.
156 Ibid.
157 Ibid.
158 This shows that Barth's discussion on the so-called lordless powers in the lecture notes collected in *The Christian Life* must be related to these earlier discussions. In these lectures, he attacks the rule of money, the development of technology and even the power of the fashion industry. See Barth, *Christian Life*, 223–30.
159 Barth, *CD II:2*, 92.
160 Brann, *The Ways of Naysaying*, 107.
161 Ibid.
162 Ibid.
163 See Alexius Meinong, 'The Theory of Objects', in *Realism and the Background of Phenomenology*, ed. Roderick Chisholm, trans. Isaac Levi, D. B. Terrell and Roderick Chisholm (Atascadero: Ridgeview, 1981), 76–117, at 79.
164 Eva T. H. Brann, 'The Being of Fictions', *Perspectives on Political Science* 43, no. 3 (2014), 116–21, at 121.
165 Barth, *CD II:1*, 554.
166 Barth, *CD III:2*, 295.
167 Meinong, 'The Theory of Objects', 79.
168 Ibid.
169 It should also be noted that Eileen C. Sweeney has argued in sharp contrast to Brann that 'Anselm clearly has what Meinong called "a prejudice in favor of the actual"'. See Eileen C. Sweeney, *Anselm of Canterbury and the Desire for the Word* (Washington: The Catholic University of America Press, 2012), 160.
170 Adolfo García de la Sienra, 'The Ontological Argument', in *The Rationality of Theism*, ed. Adolfo García de la Sienra (Amsterdam: Rodopi, 2000), 127–42, at 130.
171 Barth, *CD II:1*, 553.
172 Ibid.

173 For a discussion on Meinong's concept of *Aussersein* see: Dale Jacquette, *Alexius Meinong: The Shepherd of Non-Being* (Cham: Springer International Publishing, 2015), 174.
174 Barth, *CD II:2*, 160.
175 Ibid., 774.
176 Barth, *CD III:2*, 595.
177 Barth, *Unterricht in der christlichen Religion 2: 1924/25*, 441.
178 Ibid.
179 Ibid., 442.
180 For a critique of the traditional reading of Barth as a *Ganztod*-theologian, see Fukushima, *Aus dem Tode das Leben*, 23.
181 Karl Barth, *Prayer*, trans. W. L. Jenkins (Westminster: John Knox Press, 2002), 12.
182 Ibid.
183 Ibid.
184 Barth, *Unterricht in der christlichen Religion 2: 1924/25*, 309.
185 Barth explicitly wrote in 1948 that if 'hope in Christ is a real liberation for natural death, this rests on the fact that by divine appointment death as such belongs to the life of the creature and is thus necessary to it'. Barth, *CD III:2*, 639. Almost twenty years earlier he stated, in a discussion on eternal life, that we 'are the children of God. Our citizenship is in heaven, in the Jerusalem that is above. This is no less true than we must die. It replaces that death. Where we see death coming, the Lord comes, the kingdom of God, that which is perfect. We are responsible to this future of ours.' Barth, *Ethics*, 469.
186 Barth, *The Göttingen Dogmatics*, 185–6.
187 Barth, *Unterricht in der christlichen Religion 1: 1924*, 167.
188 Barth, *CD III:1*, 259.
189 Ibid.
190 Barth, *Ethics*, 390.
191 Hendry, 'The Transcendental Method in the Theology of Karl Barth', 219–20.
192 Immanuel Kant, 'Conjectural Beginning of Human History', in *Anthropology, History, and Education*, trans. Allen W. Wood and ed. Günter Zöller (Cambridge: Cambridge University Press, 2007), 160–75, at 163.
193 On the difference between saga and myth see Barth, *CD III:1*, 84–5.
194 Ibid., 85.
195 Ibid., 81.
196 Ibid., 91.
197 Kant, 'Conjectural Beginning of Human History', 164.
198 Ibid., 165.
199 Ibid.
200 Ibid., 166.
201 Barth, *Ethics*, 476.

202 Barth, *CD II:2*, 517.
203 Barth, *Ethics*, 134.
204 Ibid.
205 Ibid., 135.
206 Ibid., 139.
207 Ibid., 477.
208 Ibid., 138.
209 Ibid.
210 Ibid., 140.
211 Ibid., 141.
212 Ibid., 143. See also the recapitulation of this discussion in CD *III*. Here Barth is openly affirming that Christian ethics begins with the care for the human creature and not the animal. But he writes: 'We may leave the general statement and ask what is to be said of the concrete demand. We certainly cannot dismiss it as "sentimental." Nor may we take the easy course of questioning the practicability of the instructions given, let alone the wider consequences and applications. The directness of the insight and feeling revealed (not unlike those of Francis of Assisi), and the constraint expressed, are stronger than all such criticism. Those who can only smile at this point are themselves subjects for tears. How do we really justify ourselves if we differ from Schweitzer in this matter? For while the problem of treating life with respect becomes very obscure beyond its human form, it does not cease to be a problem. If we are really listening in relation to the human life of ourselves and others, we cannot feign deafness with regard to animal and vegetative life outside the human sphere. It is surely to Schweitzer's credit, even if on the basis of an unacceptable general presupposition, that he has warned us so warmly and earnestly to consider this question. There always have been men who in respect of non-human life have no greater knowledge but do have deeper and more vivid presentiments and intuitions and therefore feel more acute and detailed obligations than the great majority. It is told of one of the most enlightened of the younger generation of German theologians immediately after the First World War that he once discovered near Bamberg a weir on whose grating certain snails were always being caught and perishing, and that this made such an impression on him that from time to time he felt compelled to travel to Bamberg to help at least some of these creatures. And who is to say whether this kind of bizarre action is not in the long run at least as noble and respectable as the books in which men like F. T. Vischer, J. W. Widmann and Carl Spitteler, objecting strongly to the divine activity, dilate on the suffering of animals and commend themselves as thoughtful poets?' CD *III:4*, 349–50.
213 Barth, *Ethics*, 142.
214 Kant, 'Conjectural Beginning of Human History', 169.
215 Barth, *Ethics*, 138.

216 Ibid., 477.
217 Ibid., 485.
218 Ibid., 475.
219 Ibid., 139.
220 What the resurrection signifies, Barth argues in his *Ethics*, is the death of death, the death of the eternal death: not in the sense that death as a biological and temporal fact has been abolished but that time has joined eternity through the incarnation and become encapsulated in the eternal life of God: 'What is promised, the inheritance, is that God is not only in himself the A and O, the first and the last [cf. Rev. 1.8; 22.13], but that there is for us a last as well as a first, that our temporal life does not begin with God and with death, but ends also with God, that it thus has eternity for all its temporality.' Barth, *Ethics*, 469.
221 Karl Barth, 'Safenwil, Kölliken, Sonntag, den 22. November 1914: Hebräer 4, 9-10', in *Predigten 1914*, ed. Jochen Fahler (Zürich: Theologischer Verlag, 1999), 576–87, at 577.
222 Ibid., 582.
223 Ibid.
224 Ibid., 586.
225 Ibid.
226 Ibid., 585.
227 Ibid.
228 Barth, *The Epistle to the Romans*, 512.
229 Hitchcock, *Karl Barth and the Resurrection of the Flesh*, 185.
230 Karl Barth, 'Klagelieder 3,2,1-23 (1944)', in *Predigten 1935–1952* ed. Anton Drews (Zürich: Theologischer Verlag Zürich, 1996), 293–304, at 296.
231 Barth, *CD III:2*, 638.
232 Barth relates the remembrance of death, *memento mori*, to the remembrance of God, *memento domini*, in his *Church Dogmatics*. See Barth, *CD III:4*, 591.
233 Barth, *CD III:2*, 559.
234 Emil Brunner, *Justice and the Social Order*, trans. Mary Hottinger (Cambridge: The Luttwerworth Press, 2002), 23.
235 Ibid. For a discussion on the relation and conflicts between Barth and Brunner, see John W. Hart, *Karl Barth vs. Emil Brunner: The Formation and Dissolution of a Theological Alliance, 1916–1936* (New York: Peter Lang, 2001).
236 Karl Barth, 'The Service Which the Church Owes to the State', in *Church and State*, 62–86, at 86. 'Suum cuique' is not italicized in the original.
237 Barth was probably quite close to Dietrich Bonhoeffer's use of the *suum cuique* as an anti-fascist principle that could be used to defend what the latter called the right to bodily life. See Jennifer Moberly, *The Virtue of Bonhoeffer's Ethics: A Study of Dietrich Bonhoeffer's Ethics in Relation to Virtue Ethics* (Eugene: Pickwick Publishers, 2013), 146.

238 See Jonathan Petropoulos, *Artists under Hitler: Collaboration and Survival in Nazi Germany* (New Haven: Yale University Press, 2015), 13–14.
239 On the strange saint, a concept that Barth used in 1960 against the reduction of life to a struggle for survival, see Barth, *Christian Life*, 179.
240 Barth, *Ethics*, 512. Ola Sigurdson's study on humour and theology show how humour can be a weapon for the ones that often are prompted to use laughter, satire and ridicule in order to defend their lives or just to express the ecstatic joy and love of existence that theology often describes as God. See Ola Sigurdson, *Gudomliga komedier: Humor, subjektivitet, transcendens* (Göteborg: Glänta Produktion, 2021).

Chapter 3

1 See Hepner's letter to Taubes in Voigts, *Jacob Taubes und Oskar Goldberg*, 39. All translations in this chapter are mine if not stated otherwise.
2 Goldberg, *Die Wirklichkeit der Hebräer*, 136.
3 Voigts, *Jacob Taubes und Oskar Goldberg*, 39.
4 Theodor W. Adorno, *Metaphysics: Concept and Problems*, trans. Edmund Jephcott (Stanford: Stanford University Press, 2001).
5 Ibid., 101.
6 Ibid., 101–2.
7 John Henry Newman, *An Essay in Aid of a Grammar of Assent* (Place of publication not identified: Assumption Press, 2013), 229.
8 Theodor W. Adorno, *Negative Dialectic*, trans. E. B. Ashton (New York: Continuum, 2007), 106 and Theodor W. Adorno, *Introduction to the Sociology of Music*, trans. E. B. Ashton (New York: The Seabury Press, 1976), 141.
9 Adorno, *Metaphysics: Concept and Problems*, 22.
10 Goldberg, *Die Wirklichkeit der Hebräer*, 1
11 Ibid.
12 Julian Jaynes, *The Origin of Consciousness in the Breakdown of the Bicameral Mind* (New York: Houghton Mifflin Company, 1990).
13 Ibid., 48–59.
14 Ibid., 23.
15 Ibid., 25.
16 Ibid., 75.
17 Ibid., 294. Jaynes discusses the fact that the oldest stories of the Hebrew Bible were compiled and written down in a period when the seeds of a modern self-reflective consciousness had emerged and writes: 'As I have said, most of the books of the Old Testament were woven together from various sources from various centuries. But some of the books are considered pure in the sense of not being compilations,

but being pretty much all of one piece, mostly what they say they are, and to these a thoroughly accurate date can be attached. If we confine ourselves for the moment to these books, and compare the oldest of them with the most recent, we have a fairly authentic comparison which should give us evidence one way or another. Among these pure books, the oldest is Amos, dating from the eighth century B.C., and the most recent is Ecclesiastes, from the second century B.C. They are both short books, and I hope that you will turn to them before reading on, that you may for yourself sense authentically this difference between an almost bicameral man and a subjective conscious man.' Ibid., 295.
18. Goldberg, *Die Wirklichkeit der Hebräer*, 139.
19. See Manfred Voigt's preface to Voigts, *Jacob Taubes und Oskar Goldberg*, 7–11.
20. Jacob Taubes, 'Kabbalah', in *Jacob Taubes und Oskar Goldberg*, 21–30, at 24.
21. Jacob Taubes, 'From Cult to Culture', in *From Cult to Culture: Fragments Toward a Critique of Historical Reason*, trans. Mara H. Benjamin and William Rauscher (Stanford: Stanford University Press, 2010), 247.
22. See Hülshörster, *Thomas Mann und Oskar Goldbergs 'Wirklichkeit der Hebräer'* and 'Thomas Mann und Oskar Goldberg', in Voigts, *Oskar Goldberg*, 235–70.
23. Ibid., 239–40.
24. Goldberg, *Die Wirklichkeit der Hebräer*, 74.
25. Ibid., 16. Not italicized in the original.
26. Oskar Goldberg, 'Die Bibelkritik', in *Zahlengebäude, Ontologie, Maimonides und Aufsätze 1933 bis 1947*, 287–98, at 294.
27. Oskar Goldberg, 'Die Wirklichkeit der Hebräer', in *Zahlengebäude, Ontologie, Maimonides und Aufsätze 1933 bis 1947*, 299–304, at 299.
28. Ibid.
29. Taubes, *Occidental Eschatology*, 11.
30. Hermann Cohen, *Ethik des Reinen Willens* (Berlin: Bruno Cassirer, 1904), 379.
31. Ibid., 383–4.
32. Cohen, *Religion of Reason*, 399.
33. Ibid., and Taubes, 'From Cult to Culture', 235–47, at 247.
34. Taubes, 'From Cult to Culture', 241.
35. Oskar Goldberg, 'Die griechische Tragödie', in *Zahlengebäude, Ontologie, Maimonides und Aufsätze 1933 bis 1947*, 285.
36. Ibid., 284–5.
37. Goldberg, *Die Wirklichkeit der Hebräer*, 47.
38. André Gunder Frank and Barry K. Gills, eds., 'The 5,000 Year World System: An Interdisciplinary Introduction', in *The World System: Five Hundred Years or Five Thousand?* (Hoboken: Routledge 1996), 3–55, at 3.
39. Goldberg, *Die Wirklichkeit der Hebräer*, 48.
40. Taubes, 'From Cult to Culture', 247.
41. Goldberg, *Die Wirklichkeit der Hebräer*, 44.

42 Ibid., 47.
43 Ibid., 260.
44 Ibid.
45 Ibid., 47.
46 Ibid.
47 Jaynes, *The Origin of Consciousness in the Breakdown of the Bicameral Mind*, 294.
48 Ibid., 298.
49 Ibid., 35.
50 Adolf Caspary, *Die Maschinenutopie: Das Übereinstimmungsmoment der bürgerlichen und sozialistischen Ökonomie* (Berlin: Verlag David 1927), 79–80.
51 Ibid.
52 Ibid., 77.
53 Ibid., 83–4.
54 Joshua B. Freeman, *Behemoth: A History of the Factory and the Making of the Modern World* (New York: W.W. Norton 2018).
55 Ibid., 319.
56 Goldberg, 'Maimonides', 215.
57 Ibid., 214.
58 Ibid.
59 Goldberg, *Die Wirklichkeit der Hebräer*, 1.
60 Oskar Goldberg, 'Die Götter der Griechen', in *Zahlengebäude, Ontologie, Maimonides und Aufsätze 1933 bis 1947*, 227–48, at 227.
61 Goldberg, *Die Wirklichkeit der Hebräer*, 51–2.
62 A recent example of a reconciliation of miracles and the so-called laws of nature can be found in Wolfhart Pannenberg, 'The Concept of Miracle', *Zygon* 37, no. 3 (2002): 759–62.
63 On *res potentia* and *res extensa* see for example: Stuart A. Kauffman and Arran Gare, 'Beyond Descartes and Newton: Recovering Life and Humanity', *Progress in Biophysics and Molecular Biology* 119, no. 3 (2015): 219–24 and Stuart A. Kauffman, 'Res Potentia and Res Extensa Linked, hence United, by Quantum Measurement', in *Physics and Speculative Philosophy: Potentiality in Modern Science*, eds. Timothy E. Eastman, Michael Epperson and David Ray Griffin (Boston: De Gruyter, 2016), 47–52.
64 Goldberg, *Die Wirklichkeit der Hebräer*, 3.
65 Ibid.
66 Ibid., 4.
67 Ibid., 2.
68 Ibid., 2–3.
69 Ibid., 6.
70 Ibid., 14.
71 Ibid., 41.

72 Ibid., 74.
73 Adolf Caspary, 'Was ist Totem?', *Der Querschnitt* 3, no. 7 (1927): 187–9, at 189.
74 Ibid.
75 Ibid., 187.
76 Susman, 'Vortrag über Oskar Goldberg', 398.
77 Voigts discusses a Schellingian undercurrent in the work of Goldberg; see Manfred Voigts, *Oskar Goldberg*, 122–4. Erich Unger states explicitly that he views this quite Goldbergian philosophy of life as a continuation of the Schellingian tradition, see Erich Unger, *Das Lebendige und das Göttliche* (Jerusalem: Hatehiya Press, 1966), 184. See also Rosenstock, *Transfinite Life*, 42.
78 See Edward Allen Beach, *The Potencies of God(s): Schelling's Philosophy of Mythology* (Albany: State University of New York Press, 1994), 6–8. F. W. J. Schelling, *Philosophie der Mythologie: Philosophische Einleitung* (Stuttgart: K.F.A., 1861).
79 Ernst Cassirer, *The Philosophy of Symbolic Forms: Mythical Thought*, trans. Ralph Manheim (New Haven & London: Yale University Press, 1956), 9.
80 Ibid.
81 Ibid., 39.
82 Ibid.
83 Ibid., 37.
84 Ibid., 36.
85 Goldberg, 'Die griechische Tragödie', 267–86, at 273.
86 Voigts, *Oskar Goldberg*, 28–32.
87 Erich Unger, 'The Natural Order of Miracles: I. The Pentateuch and the Vitalistic Myth', *The Journal of Jewish Thought & Philosophy*, trans. Esther J. Ehrman 11, no. 2 (2002): 135–52, 151.
88 Tito Vignoli, *Myth and Science: An Essay* (London: Kegan Paul, Trench, Trübner & Co., 1898).
89 Ibid., 6–7.
90 Ibid., 321.
91 Ibid., 322.
92 Claude Lévi-Strauss, *The Savage Mind*, trans. anonymous (London: Weidenfeld and Nicolsson, 1966), 10–12.
93 Claude Lévi Strauss, *Race and History*, trans. anonymous (Paris: UNESCO, 1958), 27.
94 Ibid.
95 James George Frazer, *Marriage and Worship in Early Societies: A Treatise on Totemism and Exogamy*, vol. IV (New York: Cosimo Classics, 2009), 14. See A. A. Goldenweiser's refutation of Frazer's view on totemism: 'Totemism, an Analytical Study', *Journal of American Folklore* 23 (1910): 179–293.
96 Goldberg, *Die Wirklichkeit der Hebräer*, 18.
97 Goldberg, 'Maimonides', 176.
98 Ibid.

99 Ibid.
100 Ibid.
101 Ibid.
102 Goldberg, *Die Wirklichkeit der Hebräer*, 274.
103 Claude Lévi-Strauss, *A World on the Wane*, trans. John Russell (London: Hutchinson, 1962), 397.
104 Goldberg, *Die Wirklichkeit der Hebräer*, 45.
105 Goldberg, 'Maimonides', 177.
106 Ibid.
107 Ibid., 214.
108 Kenneth S. Deffeyes, *Hubbert's Peak: The Impending World Oil Shortage* (Princeton: Princeton University Press, 2009), and Richard Heinberg, *Peak Everything: Waking Up to the Century of Declines* (Gabriola: New Society Publishers, 2007).
109 Caspary, *Die Maschinenutopie*, 5.
110 Ibid.
111 Ibid., 72.
112 Ibid., 71.
113 Ibid., 72.
114 Ibid.
115 Ibid.
116 Ibid., 71.
117 Ibid., 13.
118 Ibid., 15.
119 Ibid., 74–5.
120 Ibid.
121 V. I. Lenin, *'Left-wing' Communism, an Infantile Disorder: A Popular Essay in Marxian Strategy and Tactics*, trans. unknown (New York: International Publishers 1962).
122 For an introduction to Guttmann's life and work see: Nicholas Jacobs and Diethart Kerbs, 'Wilhelm Simon Guttmann, 1891–1990: A Documentary Portrait', *German Life and Letters* 62, no. 4 (2009): 401–14. Richard Whelan describes Guttman's interest in Goldberg's numerological speculations. See Richard Whelan, *Robert Capa: A Biography* (Lincoln: University of Nebraska Press 1985), 32.
123 Franz Jung, *Die Technik des Glücks; psychologische Anleitungen in vier Übungsfolgen* (Berlin: Der Malik Verlag 1921).
124 Ibid., 18 and 67.
125 Erich Unger, *Politik und Metaphysik* (Berlin: Königshausen & Neumann, 1989), 48.
126 Walter Benjamin, 'Capitalism as Religion', in *Selected Writings: 1913–1926*, ed. Marcus Bullock and Michael W. Jennings (Cambridge: Belknap, 1999), 288–90, at 290.
127 Unger, *Politik und Metaphysik*, 48.
128 Ibid., 7.

129 Erich Unger, *Die Staatslose Bildung eines Jüdischen Volkes* (Berlin: Verlag David, 1922).
130 Ibid., 19–20.
131 Ibid., 31.
132 Ibid., 52.
133 Goldberg, *Maimonides*, 214.
134 Goldberg, *Die Wirklichkeit der Hebräer*, 83.
135 Goldberg, 'Maimonides', 176.
136 Ibid.
137 Ibid., 214.
138 Goldberg, *Die Wirklichkeit der Hebräer*, 140.
139 Ibid., 47.
140 Ibid., 34.
141 Ibid., 285.
142 Marshall Sahlins, *Stone Age Economics* (London: Routledge, 2017), 1.
143 Goldberg, *Die Wirklichkeit der Hebräer*, 48–9.
144 Susman, 'Vortrag über Oskar Goldberg', 392.
145 Goldberg, 'Die Bibelkritik', 293.
146 Ibid.
147 Unger, *Politik und Metaphysik*, 37.
148 Hans Mommsen, *The Rise and Fall of Weimar Democracy*, trans. Elbog Forster and Larry Eugene Jones (Chapel Hill, NC: University of North Carolina Press, 1996).
149 Unger, *Politik und Metaphysik*, 37.
150 Goldberg, *Die Wirklichkeit der Hebräer*, 74. Italicized in the original.
151 Ibid., 322–5.
152 Ibid., 325.
153 Ibid., 281.
154 Ibid., 32.
155 Ibid., 14.
156 Ibid., 162.
157 Ibid., 79.
158 Goldberg, 'Maimonides', 174. For Goldberg's discussion on eternal life and paradise see Goldberg, *Die Wirklichkeit der Hebräer*, 34.
159 Goldberg, *Die Wirklichkeit der Hebräer*, 90.
160 Ibid., 285.
161 Ibid., 5.
162 Ibid.
163 For an examination of the senses of plants see Daniel Chamovitz, *What a Plant Knows: A Field Guide to the Senses* (New York: Straus and Giroux, 2017).
164 Goldberg, *Die Wirklichkeit der Hebräer*, 7.
165 Goldberg, 'Die Bibelkritik', 293.

166 Goldberg, *Die Wirklichkeit der Hebräer*, 67.
167 Ibid., 128.
168 Ibid., 10.
169 Oskar Goldberg, 'Missionierendes Hebräertum', in *Zahlengebäude, Ontologie, Maimonides und Aufsätze 1933 bis 1947*, 219–26, at 223.
170 Ibid., 223–4.
171 Ibid., 226.
172 Ibid.
173 Voigts, *Oskar Goldberg*, 118–22. See also the following excellent essay on Goldberg, Unger and Scholem by Manfred Voigts, 'Eine nicht ausgetragene Kontroverse: Die Beziehung Gershom Scholems zu Oskar Goldberg und Erich Unger', *Aschkenas* 25, no. 2 (2015): 313–64.
174 Gershom Scholem, *Briefe, Band I 1914–1947* (Munich: CH Beck, 1994), 230 and Scholem, *From Berlin to Jerusalem*, 149.
175 Goldberg, *Die Wirklichkeit der Hebräer*, 5 and 292.
176 Erwin Reisner, 'Magischer Messianismus', *Kirchenblatt für die reformierte Schweiz* 92, no. 5 (1936): 66–71.
177 Ibid., 68.
178 Ibid.
179 Goldberg, 'Die Wirklichkeit der Hebräer', 302.
180 Cohen, *Religion of Reason*, 21.
181 Goldberg, *Die Wirklichkeit der Hebräer*, 49.
182 Lévi-Strauss, *The Savage Mind*, 10–11.
183 Goldberg, *Die Wirklichkeit der Hebräer*, 133. Italicized in the original.
184 Marcel Mauss, *A General Theory of Magic* (New York: Routledge Classics, 2005), 78.
185 Goldberg, *Die Wirklichkeit der Hebräer*, 67.
186 Cohen, *Religion of Reason*, 399.
187 Roland Goetschel, 'Das Verhältnis von Oskar Goldberg zur Kabbala', in *Die Wirklichkeit der Hebräer*, 341–60, at 359.
188 Cohen, *Religion of Reason*, 307.
189 Ibid., 453.
190 Ibid.
191 Ibid., 453–4.
192 Goldberg, *Die Wirklichkeit der Hebräer*, 136.
193 Cohen, *Ethik des Reinen Willens*, 13.
194 Goldberg, 'Maimonides', 175.
195 Cohen, *Religion of Reason*, 291.
196 Ibid., 375.
197 Ibid.
198 Ibid., 304.

199 Ibid., 376.
200 Goldberg, *Die Wirklichkeit der Hebräer*, 3.
201 Oskar Goldberg, 'Ontologie', in *Zahlengebäude, Ontologie, Maimonides und Aufsätze 1933 bis 1947*, 69–122.
202 Immanuel Kant, *Critique of Pure Reason*, trans. and eds. Paul Guyer and Allen W. Wood (Cambridge: Cambridge University Press, 1998), B 152/257.
203 Ibid., A 123/ 240.
204 Goldberg, 'Ontologie', 109.
205 Ibid., 104.
206 Goldberg, *Die Wirklichkeit der Hebräer*, 1.
207 Tomasz Sikora, 'The Genealogy of Shem According to Oskar Goldberg', *The Polish Journal of the Arts and Culture* 9 (2014). Available online: http://www.pjac.uj.edu.pl/documents/30601109/c4018edd-0ad6-49a9-af48-6036d1ee9233 (accessed 10 August 2017).
208 Oskar Goldberg, 'Zur Einleitung in den Baal ha-Turim: Die Zahlenmystik eines Grossen Talmudisten. Zum Andenken an Bernhard Mayer', in *Zahlengebäude, Ontologie, Maimonides und Aufsätze 1933 bis 1947*, 345–9, at 345.
209 Voigts discusses a Schellingian undercurrent in the work of Goldberg, see Voigts, *Oskar Goldberg*, 122–4 and Unger states explicitly that he views his work as part of the Schellingian tradition, see Unger, *Das Lebendige und das Göttliche*, 184. See also Frantisek Novotny, *The Posthumous Life of Plato* (Hague: Martinus Nijhoff, 1977), 78, for a brief discussion on Plato and numerology.
210 Lorenz von Oken, *Elements of Physiophilosophy*, trans. Alfred Tulk (London: Ray Society, 1847), 1.
211 Ibid.
212 Ibid.
213 Ibid., 9.
214 Ibid.
215 Ibid., 29.
216 Goldberg, *Die Wirklichkeit der Hebräer*, 28.
217 See Shirley Telles 1, Meesha Joshi, Manoj Dash, P. Raghuraj, K. V. Naveen and H. R. Nagendra, 'An Evaluation of the Ability to Voluntarily Reduce the Heart Rate After a Month of Yoga Practice', *Integrative Physiological & Behavorial Science* 39, no. 2 (2004), 119–25.
218 For an excellent introduction to Fechner see: Michael Heidelberger, *Nature from Within: Gustav Theodor Fechner and His Psychophysical Worldview*, trans. Cynthia Klohr (Pittsburgh: University of Pittsburgh Press, 2004). Fechner is probably most famous for his book *Elemente der Psychophysik* (Leipzig: Breitkopf und Härtel, 1860), but he wrote also about immortality. See Gustav Fechner, *The Little Book of Life after Death*, trans. Mary C. Wadsworth (Boston: Little, Brown & Co., 1904), a book which William James wrote a preface to.

219 Oken, *Elements of Physiophilosophy*, 5.
220 Ibid., 423.
221 Goldberg, *Die Wirklichkeit der Hebräer*, 61
222 Ibid., 293.
223 Ibid.
224 Oken, *Elements of Physiophilosophy*, 9.
225 Goldberg, *Die Wirklichkeit der Hebräer*, 28.
226 The theoretical biologist Andreas Wagner has argued for a library of platonic forms as the origin of life and postulated that life is nothing but the materialization of specific mathematical combinations that can be traced in the development of enzymes and genotype networks. In the last chapter of his study, *The Arrival of the Fittest*, entitled 'Plato's Cave', Wagner summarizes his thesis in a manner that sounds a bit Goldbergian: 'These libraries and their texts differ fundamentally from the muscles, nerves, and connective tissues that an anatomist dissects and that we can touch with our bare hands. They are not even like cellular organelles visible through a microscope, or the structure of DNA revealed by X-ray crystallography. They are concepts, mathematical concepts, touchable only by the mind's eye.' See Andreas Wagner, *The Arrival of the Fittest* (New York: Current, 2015), 219.
227 Erich Unger, *Gegen die Dichtung: Eine Begründung des Konstruktionsprinzips in der Erkenntnis* (Leipzig: Meiner, 1925), 177–8.
228 Ibid., 181.
229 Ibid.
230 Gustav Landauer, *Skepsis und Mystik* (Berlin: Egon Sleichel & Co, 1903).
231 Ibid., 126.
232 Ibid.
233 It was the Syrian Platonist philosopher Numenius of Apamea who famously argued that Pythagoras and Xenocrates described the soul as a self-moving number. See Philp Sidney Horky, *Plato and Pythagoreanism* (Oxford: Oxford University Press, 2016), 74.
234 Goldberg was interested in parapsychology and worked as a ghost photographer when he was connected to Yale University. *The New Yorker* made a reportage on his search for hauntings in 1943: Ebba Jonsson, Eugene Kinkead and Russell Maloney. 'Ghost Photographer', *The New Yorker* 17 July 1943. Available online: https://www.newyorker.com/magazine/1943/07/17/ghost-photographer (accessed 10 September 2017). Goldberg reported that he had learnt the art of discovering ghosts during an expedition to Kashmir where he met the guru Shri Agamya Paramahamsa, who travelled to the United States and England and lectured on yogi practices and Eastern Mysticism. See Manfred Voigts, *Oskar Goldberg*, 294–9. It should also be mentioned that Goldberg wrote a short text on how one should conduct research on ghosts when he lived in the United States and we can see that his interest in the afterlife of the dead was motivated by a moral and

religious desire to free the ghosts from the horrors of the past: 'Having taken pictures of the ghosts, we must release them from the earthbound conditions – as our religious and ethical duty. Most of them are souls doomed to this painful destiny due to shock during the last days of their life – and they can be helped to straighten out matters troubling them, and thus be released for their proper progression. However, there are some cases where they have no desire to be released, – and if those cases are properly treated, we may expect, in the future, a close connection and permanent communication between this world and the beyond.' Oskar Goldberg, 'Rules for Research in Hauntings', in *Zahlengebäude, Ontologie, Maimonides und Aufsätze 1933 bis 1947*, 305–8, at 307. It would be interesting to examine Goldberg's interests in ghost photography and what can be called the spectrality of the dead in relation to his interest in Schellingian philosophy of nature since Schelling had an interest in ghosts and even wrote a philosophical tractate centred on the question of the afterlife: F. W. J. Schelling, *Clara: or, On Nature's Connection to the Spirit World*, trans. Fiona Steinkamp (New York: State University of New York Press, 2002). Finally, Bruce Rosenstock has written an important chapter on Goldberg's spectrology in his book on the Jewish mythologist. See Rosenstock, *Transfinite Life*, 204–29.

Chapter 4

1. Blumenberg, *The Legitimacy of the Modern Age*, 467.
2. Ibid.
3. Ibid.
4. Ibid., 443.
5. Martin Hägglund, *Radical Atheism: Derrida and the Time of Life* (Stanford: Stanford University Press, 2008), 129.
6. Ibid., 59.
7. Mark Johnston, *Surviving Death* (Princeton: Princeton University Press, 2010), 306.
8. Ibid., 336.
9. Walter Benjamin, 'Goethe's Elective Affinities', in *Selected Writings Volume 1: 1913–1926*, eds. Michael W. Jennings and trans. Stanley Corngold (London: The Belknap Press of Harvard University Press, 1996), 297–360, at 355.
10. In this sense the subjects examined in this study can clearly be said to partake in the history of messianism that Jayne Svenungsson has examined in a book on the history of Western messianism. See Jayne Svenungsson, *Diving History: Prophetism, Messianism and the Development of the Spirit*, trans. Stephen Donovan (New York: Berghahn, 2016).
11. Blumenberg, *The Legitimacy of the Modern Age*, 123.

12 Ibid., 137–8.
13 Ibid., 133.
14 Ibid., 138.
15 Ibid.
16 Ibid.
17 Ibid., 230.
18 Ibid.
19 Ibid., 34.
20 Ibid., 223.
21 Ibid., 138.
22 This is the definition of life that Peter Ward borrows from Paul Davies. See Peter Ward, *The Medea Hypothesis: Is Life on Earth Ultimately Self-Destructive?* (Princeton: Princeton University Press, 2009), 3–4.
23 Ibid.
24 Ward, *The Medea Hypothesis*, 1–14.
25 Blumenberg, *The Legitimacy of the Modern Age*, 138.
26 Ward, *The Medea Hypothesis*, xxi.
27 Ibid., 35.
28 Chris T. Darimont, Caroline H. Fox, Heather M. Bryan and Thomas E. Reimchen, 'The Unique Ecology of Human Predators', *Science* 349, no. 6250 (2015): 858–60.
29 Blumenberg, *The Legitimacy of the Modern Age*, 138.
30 Foucault, *The Order of Things*, 279–80.
31 Blumenberg, *The Legitimacy of the Modern Age*, 6.
32 Barth, *CD III:1*, 95.
33 William James, *A Pluralistic Universe: Hibbert Lectures to Manchester College on the Present Situation in Philosophy* (New York: Longman's Green, 1909), 22.
34 Ibid.
35 Fabián Ludueña Romandini, *Principios de Espectrología: La comunidad de los espectros II* (Buenos Aires: Miño y Dávila, 2016), 223.

Bibliography

Abrahamsson, Christian. 'On the Genealogy of Lebensraum'. *Geographia Helvetica*, 68 (2013): 37–44.

Adam, Mark B., ed. *The Wellborn Science: Eugenics in Germany, France, Brazil, and Russia*. Oxford: Oxford University Press, 1990.

Adorno, Theodor W. *Introduction to the Sociology of Music*, translated by E. B. Ashton. New York: The Seabury Press, 1976.

Adorno, Theodor W. *Metaphysics: Concept and Problems*, translated by Edmund Jephcott. Stanford: Stanford University Press, 2001.

Adorno, Theodor W. *Negative Dialectic*, translated by E. B. Ashton. New York: Continuum, 2007.

Agamben, Giorgio. *Homo Sacer: Sovereign Power and Bare Life*, translated by Daniel Heller-Roazen. Stanford: Stanford University Press, (1995) 1998.

Algaze, Guillermo. *Ancient Mesopotamia at the Dawn of Civilization: The Evolution of an Urban Landscape*. Chicago, IL: The University of Chicago Press, 2014.

Althusser, Louis. 'Ideology and Ideological State Apparatuses (Notes Towards an Investigation)'. In *Essays on Ideology*, translated by Ben Brewster, 1–60. London: Verso, (1969) 1984.

Anders, Günther. *Die Antiquiertheit des Menschen. Band 1: Über die Seele im Zeitalter der zweiten industriellen Revolution*. Munich: C.H. Beck, 1956.

Anidjar, Gil. *The Jew, the Arab: A History of the Enemy*. Stanford: Stanford University Press, 2003.

Anselm of Canterbury. 'Proslogion'. In *The Major Works*, edited by Brian Davies and G. R. Evans, 82–104. Oxford: Oxford University Press, (1077–1078) 1998.

Arendt, Hannah. *Eichmann in Jerusalem: A Report on the Banality of Evil*. London: Faber & Faber, 1963.

Arendt, Hannah. *The Human Condition*. Chicago, IL: The University of Chicago Press, (1958) 1998.

Baark, Sigurd. *The Affirmation of Reason: On Karl Barth's Speculative Theology*. Cham: Springer International Publishing, 2018.

Balthasar, Hans Urs von. *The Theology of Karl Barth*, translated by T. Edward and S. J. Oakes. San Francisco, CA: Ignatius Press, (1951) 1992.

Bambach, Charles R. *Heidegger, Dilthey, and the Crisis of Historicism*. London: Cornell University Press, 1995.

Bamyeh, Mohammed. *Of Death and Dominion: The Existential Foundations of Governance*. Evanston, IL: Northwestern University Press, 2007.

Barth, Karl. *Church and State*, translated by G. Ronald Howe. London: Student Christian Movement Press, (1938) 1939.
Barth, Karl. *Church Dogmatics: Volume I:1*, translated by Geoffrey William Bromiley. Edinburgh: T&T Clark, (1932) 1975.
Barth, Karl. *Church Dogmatics: Volume I:2*, translated by Geoffrey William Bromiley and Harold Knight. Edinburgh: T&T Clark, (1938) 1956.
Barth, Karl. *Church Dogmatics: Volume II:1*, translated by T. H. L. Parker, W. B. Johnston, Harold Knight and J. L. M. Haire. Edinburgh: T&T Clark, (1940) 1957.
Barth, Karl. *Church Dogmatics: Volume II:2*, translated by T. H. L. Parker, W. B. Johnston, Harold Knight and J. L. M. Haire. Edinburgh: T&T Clark, (1942) 1957.
Barth, Karl. *Church Dogmatics: Volume III:1*, translated by J. W. O. Edwards and Harold Knight. Edinburgh: T&T Clark, (1945) 1958.
Barth, Karl. *Church Dogmatics: Volume III:2*, translated by Geoffrey Bromiley and Thomas Forsyth Torrance. Edinburgh: T&T Clark, (1948) 1960.
Barth, Karl. *Church Dogmatics: Volume III:3*, translated by Geoffrey William Bromiley and R. J. Ehrlich. Edinburgh: T&T Clark, (1950) 1960.
Barth, Karl. *Church Dogmatics: Volume III:4*, translated by A. T. MacKay, T. H. L. Parker, Harold Knight, H. A. Kennedy and J. Marks. Edinburgh: T&T Clark, (1951) 1961.
Barth, Karl. *Church Dogmatics: Volume IV:3*, translated by Geoffret William Bromiley. Edinburgh: T&T Clark, (1959) 1961.
Barth, Karl. *Credo: Die Hauptprobleme der Dogmatik, dargestellt im Anschluß an das Apostolische Glaubensbekenntnis. 16 Vorlesungen, gehalten an der Universität Utrecht im Februar und März 1935*. Zürich: Evangelischer Verlag, 1948.
Barth, Karl. 'Das Wort in der Theologie von Schleiermacher bis Ritschl, 1927'. In *Vorträge und kleinere Arbeiten 1925–1930*, edited by Hermann Schmidt, 183–212. Zürich: Theologischer Verlag Zürich, (1928) 1994.
Barth, Karl. *Der Christ in der Gesellschaft: eine Tambacher Rede*. Würzburg: Patmos Verlag, 1920.
Barth, Karl. *Der Römerbrief*. Zürich: Theologischer Verlag Zürich, (1922) 2005.
Barth, Karl. *Die kirchliche Dogmatik I:2* Zürich: Theologischer Verlag Zürich, (1938) 1980.
Barth, Karl. *Die Protestantische Theologie im 19. Jahrhundert: Ihre Geschichte und ihre Vorgeschichte*. Zürich: Theologischer Verlag Zürich, (1947) 1994.
Barth, Karl. 'Die Theologie und der Moderne Mensch'. In *Vorträge und kleinere Arbeiten 1925–1930*, edited by Hermann Schmidt, 160–82. Zürich: Theologischer Verlag Zürich, (1927) 1994.
Barth, Karl. *Ethics*, translated by Geoffrey W. Bromiley. Edinburgh: T&T Clark, (1928-1929/1973) 1981.
Barth, Karl. 'Feuerbach'. In *Karl Barth: Theologian of Freedom*, edited by Clifford Green, 90–7. Minneapolis, MN: Fortress Press, (1952) 1991.
Barth, Karl. 'Feuerbach'. In *Vorträge und kleinere Arbeiten 1922–1925*, edited by Hermann Schmidt, 6–13. Zürich: Theologischer Verlag Zürich, (1922) 1990.

Barth, Karl. *Fides Quaerens Intellectum: Anselms Beweis der Existenz Gottes im Zusammenhang seines theologischen Programms*. Zürich: Theologischer Verlag Zürich, (1931) 1981.

Barth, Karl. 'Klagelieder 3,2,1-23 (1944)'. In *Predigten 1935–1952*, edited by Hartmut Spieker and Hinrich Stoevesandt, 293–304. Zürich: Theologischer Verlag Zürich, (1944) 1996.

Barth, Karl. *Konfirmandenunterricht 1909-1921*. Zürich: Theologischer Verlag Zürich, 1987.

Barth, Karl. 'Ludwig Feuerbach (1927)'. In *Ludwig Feuerbach*, edited by Erich Thies, 1–32. Darmstadt: Wissenschaftliche Buchgesellschaft, (1927) 1976.

Barth, Karl. *Prayer*, translated by W. L. Jenkins. Westminister: John Knox Press, (1949) 2002.

Barth, Karl. 'Religion und Wissenschaft'. In *Vorträge und kleinere Arbeiten 1909–1914*, edited by Herbert Helms, Friedrich W. Marquardt, Hans-Anton Drewes and Hinrich Stoevesandt, 418–38. Zürich: Theologischer Verlag Zürich, (1912) 1993.

Barth, Karl. 'Safenwil, Kölliken, Sonntag, den 22. November 1914: Hebräer 4, 9–10'. In *Predigten 1914*, edited by Jochen Fahler, 576–87. Zürich: Theologischer Verlag, 1999.

Barth, Karl. *The Christian Life: Church Dogmatics IV:4. Lecture Fragments*, translated by Geoffrey William Bromiley. Grand Rapids, MI: William B. Eerdmans Publishing Company, (1967) 1981.

Barth, Karl. 'The Christian's Place in Society'. In *The Word of God and the Word of Man*, translated by Douglas Horton, 272–327. New York: Harper & Row, Publishers, (1919) 1957.

Barth, Karl. *The Epistle to the Romans*, translated by Edwyn C. Hoskyns. Oxford: Oxford University Press, (1922) 1968.

Barth, Karl. *The Göttingen Dogmatics: Introduction in the Christian Religion*, translated by Geoffrey W. Bromiley. Grand Rapids, MI: W.B. Eerdman, (1985) 1991.

Barth, Karl. 'The Service Which the Church Owes to the State'. In *Church and State*, translated by G. Ronald Howe, 62–86. London: Student Christian Movement Press, (1938) 1939.

Barth, Karl. 'The Significance of the State for the Church'. In *Church and State*, translated by G. Ronald Howe, 37–61. London: Student Christian Movement Press, (1938) 1939.

Barth, Karl. *The Theology of Schleiermacher: Lectures at Göttingen, Winter Semester of 1923/24*, translated by Geoffrey W. Bromiley. Grand Rapids: William B. Eerdmans Publishing Company, (1923–1924) 1982.

Barth, Karl. *Unterricht in der christlichen Religion 1: 1924*. Zürich: Theologischer Verlag Zürich, (1924) 1985.

Barth, Karl. *Unterricht in der christlichen Religion 2: 1924/5*. Zürich: Theologischer Verlag Zürich, (1924-1925) 1990.

Baumgardt, David. *Jenseits von Machtmoral und Masochismus: Hedonistische Ethik als kritische Alternative*. Meisenheim: Hain, 1977.

Beach, Edward Allen. *The Potencies of God(s): Schelling's Philosophy of Mythology.* Albany: State University of New York Press, 1994.

Beintker, Michael. *Die Dialektik in der 'dialektischen Theologie' Karl Barths.* Munich: C. Kaiser, 1987.

Ben-Chorin, Schalom. *Jenseits von Orthodoxie und Liberalismus: Versuch über die Jüdische Glaubenslage der Gegenwart.* Tübingen: J. C. B. Mohr, (1939) 1991.

Benjamin, Walter. 'Capitalism as Religion'. In *Selected Writings: 1913-1926*, edited by Marcus Bullock and Michael W. Jennings, 288–90. Cambridge, MA: Belknap, 1999.

Benjamin, Walter. 'Goethe's Elective Affinities'. In *Selected Writings Volume 1: 1913-1926*, edited by Michael W. Jennings, and translated by Stanley Corngold. London: The Belknap Press of Harvard University Press, 1996.

Bensussan, Gérard. 'Rosenzweig and War. A Question of "Point of View": Between Creation, Revelation, and Redemption'. *The Centennial Review*, 13, no. 1 (2013): 115–36.

Berghahn, Volker Rolf. *Modern Germany: Society, Economy and Politics in the Twentieth Century.* Cambridge: Cambridge University Press, 1994.

Bertolino, Luca. 'Alle origini del "nuovo pensiero": Rosenzweig interprete di Feuerbach'. *TEORIA*, 28, no. 1 (2008): 195–206.

Blumenberg, Hans. *The Legitimacy of the Modern Age*, translated by Robert Wallace. Cambridge: MIT Press, (1966) 1999.

Bojanic, Petar. 'Franz Rosenzweig's Ground of War'. *Bamidbar*, 1, no. 1 (2011): 35–46.

Botar, Oliver A. I. 'Defining Biocentrism'. In *Biocentrism and Modernism*, edited by Oliver A. I. Botar and Isabel Wünsche, 15–46. London: Routledge, 2011.

Braiterman, Zachary. '"Into life?" Franz Rosenzweig and the Figure of Death'. *AJS Review*, 23, no. 2 (1998): 203–21.

Brann, Eva T. H. 'The Being of Fictions'. *Perspectives on Political Science*, 43, no. 3 (2014): 116–21.

Brann, Eva T. H. *The Ways of Naysaying.* Lanham, MD: Rowman & Littlefield Publishers, 2001.

Brasser, Martin. *Rosenzweig als Leser: Kontextuelle Kommentare zum Stern der Erlösung.* Tübingen: M. Niemeyer, 2004.

Brechtefeld, Jörg. *Mitteleuropa and German Politics: 1848 to the Present.* Basingstoke: Palgrave Macmillian, 1996.

Brechtken, Magnus. '*Madagaskar für die Juden*': *Antisemitische Idee und politische Praxis 1885-1945.* Munich: R. Oldenbourg Verlag, 1997.

Brett, George Sydney. *History of Psychology: Ancient and Patristic.* New York: Routledge, 2013.

Brod, Max. *Paganism, Christianity, Judaism: A Confession of Faith*, translated by William Wolfe. Tuscaloosa, AL: University of Alabama Press, (1921) 2011.

Brunner, Emil. *Justice and the Social Order*, translated by Mary Hottinger. Cambridge: The Luttwerworth Press, (1945) 2002.

Bry, Carl Christian. *Verkappte Religionen: Kritik des kollektiven Wahns.* Gotha: Verlag Friedrich Andreas Perthes, 1924.

Busch, Eberhard. *Karl Barth: His Life from Letters and Autobiographical Texts*, translated by John Bowden. Eugene, OR: Wipf and Stock, (1975) 2005.

Caspary, Adolf. *Die Maschinenutopie: Das Übereinstimmungsmoment der bürgerlichen und sozialistischen Ökonomie*. Berlin: Verlag David, 1927.

Caspary, Adolf. 'Theologie der Selbstgerechtigkeit Gottes'. Grenzbote (Bratislava, 1936). A digital version of the text can be found through the Leo Baeck Institute/Center for Jewish History. Available online: http://www.europeana.eu/portal/sv/record/2048612/data_item_cjh_lbiarchive_oai_digital_cjh_org_1420058.html (accessed 17 September 2017)

Caspary, Adolf. 'Was ist Totem?'. *Der Querschnitt*, 7, no. 3 (1927): 187–9.

Cassirer, Ernst. *The Philosophy of Symbolic Forms: Mythical Thought*, translated by Ralph Manheim. New Haven, CT and London: Yale University Press, (1925) 1956.

Celly, Duncan. '"The Goal of That Pure and Noble Yearning": Friedrich Meinecke's Visions of 1848'. In *The 1848 Revolutions and European Political Thought*, edited by Douglas Moggach and Gareth Stedman Jones, 293–321. Cambridge: Cambridge University Press, 2018.

Chalamet, Christope. *Dialectical Theologians: Wilhelm Herrmann, Karl Barth and Rudolf Bultmann*. Zürich: Theologischer Verlag Zürich, 2005.

Chamovitz, Daniel. *What a Plant Knows: A Field Guide to the Senses*. New York: Straus and Giroux, 2017.

Chandler, Alfred D. and Takashi Hikino. *Scale and Scope: The Dynamics of Industrial Capitalism*. Cambridge, MA: Belknap Press, 1990.

Chung, Paul S. *Karl Barth: God's Word in Action*. Eugene, OR: Cascade Books, 2008.

Cohen, Hermann. *Deutschtum und Judentum: mit grundlegenden Betrachtungen über Staat und Internationalismus*. Gießen: Verlag von Alfred Töpelmann, 1923.

Cohen, Hermann. *Ethik des Reinen Willens*. Berlin: Bruno Cassirer, 1904.

Cohen, Hermann. *Religion of Reason: Out of the Sources of Judaism*, translated by Simon Kaplan. Atlanta, GA: Scholars Press, (1919) 1995.

Cotesta, Vittorio. 'Rosenzweig, Schmitt and the Concept of Europe'. In *Europe in Crisis: Intellectuals and the European Idea, 1917–1957*, edited by Mark Hewitson and Matthew D'Auria, 169–82. New York: Berghahn Books, 2015.

Cumming, Richard Paul. 'Revelation as Apologetic Category: A Reconsideration of Karl Barth's Engagement with Ludwig Feuerbach's Critique of Religion'. *Scottish Journal of Theology*, 68, no. 1 (2015): 43–60.

Daniel-Hughes, Carly. *The Salvation of the Flesh in Tertullian of Carthage: Dressing for the Resurrection*. New York: Palgrave Macmillan, 2011.

Darimont, Chris T., Caroline H. Fox, Heather M. Bryan and Thomas E. Reimchen 'The Unique Ecology of Human Predators'. *Science*, 349, no. 6250 (2015): 858–60.

Darwin, Charles. *On the Origin of Species by Means of Natural Selection, or the Preservation of Favoured Races in the Struggle for Life*. New York: D. Appleton and Company, (1859) 1861.

Dawson, R. Dale. *The Resurrection in Karl Barth*. Aldershot: Ashgate, 2007.

Deffeyes, Kenneth S. *Hubbert's Peak: The Impending World Oil Shortage*. Princeton, NJ: Princeton University Press, 2009.

Dillon, Michael. *Biopolitics of Security: A Political Analytic of Finitude*. London: Routledge, 2015.

Dorrien, Gary. *Kantian Reason and Hegelian Spirit: The Idealistic Logic of Modern Theology*. London: John Wiley, 2015.

Durst, Dennis L. *Eugenics and Protestant Social Reform: Hereditary Science and Religion in America, 1860–1940*. Eugene, OR: Pickwick Publications, 2017.

Ehrenberg, Hans. *Die Parteiung der Philosophie: Studien wider Hegel und die Kantianer*. Leipzig: Verlag von Felix Meiner, 1911.

Ehrenberg, Rudolf. *Theoretische Biologie: Vom Standpunkt der Irreversibilität des Elementaren Lebensvorganges*. Berlin: Springer, 1923.

Ehrhardt, Arnold. 'Unsterblichkeitsglaube und Politik im Römerreich'. *Theologische Zeitschrift*, 2, no. 6 (1946): 418–37.

Fangerau, Heiner. 'Monism, Racial Hygiene, and National Socialism'. In *Monism: Science, Philosophy, Religion, and the History of a Worldview*, edited by Todd H. Weir, 223–47. New York: Palgrave Macmillan, 2012.

Fechner, Gustav. *Elemente der Psychophysik*. Leipzig: Breitkopf und Härtel, 1860.

Fechner, Gustav. *The Little Book of Life After Death*, translated by Mary C. Wadsworth. Boston, MA: Little, Brown & Co., (1836) 1904.

Feuerbach, Ludwig. 'Die Naturwissenschaft und die Revolution'. In *Gesammelte Schriften 10*, edited by Werner Schuffenhauer, 347–68. Berlin: Akademie Verlag, (1850) 1971.

Feuerbach, Ludwig. *Lectures on the Essence of Religion*, translated by Ralph Manheim. New York: Harper & Row, Publishers, (1851) 1967.

Feuerbach, Ludwig. 'Principles of the Philosophy of the Future'. In *The Fiery Brook: Selected Writings of Ludwig Feuerbach*, translated by Zawar Hanfi, 399–551. New York: Verso, (1843) 2012.

Feuerbach, Ludwig. *The Essence of Christianity*, translated by George Eliot. Walnut, CA: MSAC Philosophy Group, (1841) 2008.

Feuerbach, Ludwig. *The Essence of Faith According to Luther*, translated by Melvin Cherno. New York: Harper & Row, Publishers, (1844) 1967.

Feuerbach, Ludwig. 'Wider den Dualismus von Leib und Seele, Fleisch und Geist'. In *Gesammelte Schriften 10*, edited by Werner Schuffenhauer, 122–50. Berlin: Akademie Verlag, (1846) 1971.

Fisher, Cass. 'Absolute Factuality, Common Sense, and Theological Reference in the Thought of Franz Rosenzweig'. *Harvard Theological Review*, 109, no. 3 (2016): 342–70.

Flohr, Paul Mendes. 'Messianic Radicals: Gustav Landauer and Other German-Jewish Revolutionaries'. In *Gustav Landauer: Anarchist and Jew*, edited by Paul Mendes Flohr and Anya Mali, 12–44. Berlin: De Gruyter, 2015.

Foucault, Michel. *The Order of Things: An Archaeology of the Human Sciences*, translated by Alan Sheridan. London: Routledge, (1966) 2002.

Frank, Manfred. *Der Unendliche Mangel an Sein: Schellings Hegelkritik und die Anfänge der Marxschen Dialektik*. Munich: Wilhelm Fink Verlag, 1992.

Frazer, James George. *Marriage and Worship in Early Societies: A Treatise on Totemism and Exogamy*, vol. IV. New York: Cosimo Classics, 2009.

Freeman, Joshua B. *Behemoth: A History of the Factory and the Making of the Modern World*. New York: W.W. Norton, 2018.

Fried, Johannes. *Aufstieg aus dem Untergang: Apokalyptisches Denken und die Entstehung der modernen Naturwissenschaft im Mittelalter*. Munich: Beck, 2001.

Fukushima, Yo. *Aus dem Tode das Leben: Eine Untersuchung zu Karl Barths Todes- und Lebensverständnis*. Zürich: Theologischer Verlag Zürich, 2009.

Galli, Barbara Ellen. *Franz Rosenzweig and Jehuda Halevi: Translating, Translations, and Translators*. Montreal: McGill-Queen's University Press, 1995.

García de la Sienra, Adolfo. 'The Ontological Argument'. In *The Rationality of Theism*, edited by Adolfo García de la Sienra, 127–42. Amsterdam: Rodopi, 2000.

Gasman, Daniel. *Haeckel's Monism and the Birth of Fascist Ideology*. New York: Lang, 2008.

Glasse, John. 'Barth on Feuerbach'. *The Harvard Theological Review*, 57, no. 2 (1964): 69–96.

Glatzer, Nahum. 'Franz Rosenzweig in His Student Years'. In *Essays in Jewish Thought*, 222–30. Tuscaloosa: Alabama Press, 1978.

Goetschel, Roland. 'Das Verhältnis von Oskar Goldberg zur Kabbala'. In *Die Wirklichkeit der Hebräer*, edited by Manfred Voigts, 341–60. Wiesbaden: Harrassowitz Verlag, 2005.

Goldberg, Oskar. 'Die Bibelkritik'. In *Zahlengebäude, Ontologie, Maimonides und Aufsätze 1933 bis 1947*, edited by Manfred Voigts, 287–98. Würzburg: Königshausen & Neumann, (1938) 2013.

Goldberg, Oskar. *Die fünf Bücher Mosis: Ein Zahlengebäude: Die Feststellung einer einheitlich durchgeführten Zahlenschrift*. Berlin: Liebmann, 1908.

Goldberg, Oskar. 'Die griechische Tragödie'. In *Zahlengebäude, Ontologie, Maimonides und Aufsätze 1933 bis 1947*, edited by Manfred Voigts, 267–86. Würzburg: Königshausen & Neumann, (1938) 2013.

Goldberg, Oskar. 'Die Götter der Griechen'. In *Zahlengebäude, Ontologie, Maimonides und Aufsätze 1933 bis 1947*, edited by Manfred Voigts, 227–48. Würzburg: Königshausen & Neumann, (1937) 2013.

Goldberg, Oskar. *Die Wirklichkeit der Hebräer: Einleitung in das System des Pentateuch*. Wiesbaden: Harrassowitz Verlag, (1925) 2005.

Goldberg, Oskar. 'Die Wirklichkeit der Hebräer'. In *Zahlengebäude, Ontologie, Maimonides und Aufsätze 1933 bis 1947*, edited by Manfred Voigts, 299–304. Würzburg: Königshausen & Neumann, (1941) 2013.

Goldberg, Oskar. 'Maimonides'. In *Zahlengebäude, Ontologie, Maimonides und Aufsätze 1933 bis 1947*, edited by Manfred Voigts, 123–217. Würzburg: Königshausen & Neumann, (1935) 2013.

Goldberg, Oskar. 'Missionierendes Hebräertum'. In *Zahlengebäude, Ontologie, Maimonides und Aufsätze 1933 bis 1947*, edited by Manfred Voigts, 219–26. Würzburg: Königshausen & Neumann, (1933) 2013.

Goldberg, Oskar. 'Ontologie'. In *Zahlengebäude, Ontologie, Maimonides und Aufsätze 1933 bis 1947*, edited by Manfred Voigts, 69–122. Würzburg: Königshausen & Neumann, (1903–1908) 2013.

Goldberg, Oskar. 'Rules for Research in Hauntings'. In *Zahlengebäude, Ontologie, Maimonides und Aufsätze 1933 bis 1947*, edited by Manfred Voigts, 305–8. Würzburg: Königshausen & Neumann, (1943) 2013.

Goldberg, Oskar. *Zahlengebäude, Ontologie, Maimonides und Aufsätze 1933 bis 1947*, edited by Manfred Voigts. Würzburg: Königshausen & Neumann, 2013.

Goldberg, Oskar. 'Zur Einleitung in den Baal ha-Turim: Die Zahlenmystik eines Grossen Talmudisten. Zum Andenken an Bernhard Mayer'. In *Zahlengebäude, Ontologie, Maimonides und Aufsätze 1933 bis 1947*, edited by Manfred Voigts, 345–9. Würzburg: Königshausen & Neumann, (1946) 2013.

Goldblum, Sonia. 'Oswald Spengler et le refus de la Révélation. Rosenzweig lecteur du Déclin de l'Occident'. Available online: https://halshs.archives-ouvertes.fr/hal-00463442/document (accessed 1 April 2017).

Goldenweiser, A. A. 'Totemism, an Analytical Study'. *Journal of American Folklore*, 23 (1910): 179–293.

Gordon, Peter. *Rosenzweig and Heidegger: Between Judaism and German Philosophy*. Berkeley, CA: University of California Press, 2005.

Gorringe, Timothy. *Against Hegemony*. Oxford: Oxford University Press, 2005

Gregory, Frederick. 'Proto-Monism in German Philosophy, Theology, and Science, 1800–1845'. In *Monism: Science, Philosophy, Religion, and the History of a Worldview*, edited by Todd H. Weir, 45–70. New York: Palgrave Macmillan, 2012.

Gunder Frank, Andre and Barry K. Gills. 'The 5,000 Year World System: An Interdisciplinary Introduction'. In *The World System: Five Hundred Years or Five Thousand?*, edited by Andre Gunder Frank and Barry K. Gills, 3–58. Hoboken: Routledge, 1996.

Hadot, Pierre. *Philosophy as a Way of Life: Spiritual Exercises from Socrates to Foucault*, translated by Arnold Davidson. Oxford: Blackwell Publishers Ltd, (1987) 1995.

Haeckel, Ernst. *The Riddle of the Universe*, translated by Joseph McCabe. London: Watts & Co, (1899) 1913.

Hägglund, Martin. *Radical Atheism: Derrida and the Time of Life*. Stanford: Stanford University Press, 2008.

Haldane, John Burdon Sanderson. *Heredity and Politics*. London: Allen and Unwin, 1938.

Hart, Jeffrey. *Reactionary Modernism: Technology, Culture, and Politics in Weimar and the Third Reich*. New York: Cambridge University Press, 2003.

Hart, John W. *Karl Barth vs. Emil Brunner: The Formation and Dissolution of a Theological Alliance, 1916–1936*. New York: Peter Lang, 2001.

Harvey, Van A. *Feuerbach and the Interpretation of Religion*. Cambridge: Cambridge University Press 1997.

Hegel, G. W. F. *Phenomenology of Spirit*, translated by A.V. Miller. Oxford: Oxford University Press, (1807) 1977.

Heidelberger, Michael. *Nature from Within: Gustav Theodor Fechner and His Psychophysical Worldview*, translated by Cynthia Klohr. Pittsburgh: University of Pittsburgh Press, (1993) 2004.

Heinberg, Richard. *Peak Everything: Waking Up to the Century of Declines*. Gabriola: New Society Publishers, 2007.

Hendry, George. 'The Transcendental Method in the Theology of Karl Barth'. *Scottish Journal of Theology*, 37, no. 2 (1984): 213–27.

Herrmann, Wilhelm. *Ethik: Grundriss der theologischen Wissenschaften*. Tübingen: J. C. B. Mohr, 1901.

Herzfeld, Wolfgang D. *Franz Rosenzweig, "Mitteleuropa" und der Erste Weltkrieg*. Freiburg: K. Alber, 2013.

Hitchcock, Nathan. *Karl Barth and the Resurrection of the Flesh: The Loss of the Body in Participatory Eschatology*. Eugene, OR: Pickwick Publications, 2013.

Horky, Philp Sidney. *Plato and Pythagoreanism*. Oxford: Oxford University Press, 2016.

Hülshörster, Christian. *Thomas Mann und Oskar Goldbergs 'Wirklichkeit der Hebräer'*. Frankfurt am Main: Klostermann, 1999.

Hymer, John. 'Verteidigung von Feuerbachs Moleschott Rezeption: Feuerbachs offene Dialektik'. In *Identität und Pluralismus in der globalen Gesellschaft--Ludwig Feuerbach zum 200. Geburtstag*, edited by Ursula Reitemeyer, Takayuki Shibata and Francesco Tomasoni, 129–44. New York: Waxmann Verlag, 2006.

Jacobs, Nicholas and Diethart Kerbs. 'Wilhelm Simon Guttmann, 1891–1990: A Documentary Portrait'. *German Life and Letters*, 62, no. 4 (2009): 401–14.

Jacquette, Dale. *Alexius Meinong: The Shepherd of Non-Being*. Cham: Springer International Publishing, 2015.

James, William. *A Pluralistic Universe: Hibbert Lectures to Manchester College on the Present Situation in Philosophy*. New York: Longman's Green, 1909.

Jaynes, Julian. *The Origin of Consciousness in the Breakdown of the Bicameral Mind*. New York: Houghton Mifflin Company, 1990.

Johnston, Larry. *Between Transcendence and Nihilism: Species-ontology in the Philosophy of Ludwig Feuerbach*. New York: Lang, 1995.

Johnston, Mark. *Surviving Death*. Princeton, NJ: Princeton University Press, 2010.

Jonsson, Ebba, Eugene Kinkead and Russell Maloney. 'Ghost Photographer'. *The New Yorker*, 17 July 1943. Available online: https://www.newyorker.com/magazine/1943/07/17/ghost-photographer (accessed 10 September 2017).

Josuttis, Manfred. *Die Gegenständlichkeit der Offenbarung: Karl Barths Anselm Buch und die Denkform seiner Theologie*. Bonn: H. Bouvier, 1965.

Jung, Carl Gustav. *Mysterium Coniunctionis: An Inquiry into the Separation and Synthesis of Psychic Opposites in Alchemy*, translated by R. F. C. Hull. London: Routledge, 1970.

Jung, Franz. *Die Technik des Glücks; psychologische Anleitungen in vier Übungsfolgen*. Berlin: Der Malik Verlag 1921.

Jüngel, Eberhard. 'Die Möglichkeit theologischer Anthropologie auf dem Grunde der Analogie. Eine Untersuchung zum Analogieverständnis Karl Barths'. In *Barth-Studien*, 210–32. Zürich: Benziger Verlag, 1982.

Kammerer, Paul. *Lebensbeherrschung: Grundsteinlegung der organischen Technik*. Munich: Monistische Bibliothek, 1919.

Kant, Immanuel. 'Conjectural Beginning of Human History'. In *Anthropology, History, and Education*, translated by Allen W. Wood, 160–75. Cambridge: Cambridge University Press, (1786) 2007.

Kant, Immanuel. *Critique of Pure Reason*, translated by Paul Guyer and Allen W. Wood. Cambridge: Cambridge University Press, (1781) 1998.

Kauffman, Stuart. 'Res Potentia and Res Extensa Linked, hence United, by Quantum Measurement'. In *Physics and Speculative Philosophy: Potentiality in Modern Science*, edited by Timothy E. Eastman, Michael Epperson and David Ray Griffin, 47–52. Boston: De Gruyter, 2016.

Kauffman, Stuart. and Arran Gare. 'Beyond Descartes and Newton: Recovering Life and Humanity'. *Progress in Biophysics and Molecular Biology*, 119, no. 3 (2015): 219–24.

Kavka, Martin. *Jewish Messianism and the History of Philosophy*. Cambridge: Cambridge University Press, 2009.

Kavka, Martin. 'Verification (Bewährung) in Franz Rosenzweig'. In *German-Jewish Thought between Religion and Politics: Festschrift in Honour of Paul Mendes-Flohr on the Occasion of His Seventieth Birthday*, edited by Christian Wiese and Martina Urban, 167–84. Berlin: De Gruyter, 2012.

Keedus, Liisi. *The Crisis of German Historicism: The Early Political Thought of Hannah Arendt and Leo Strauss*. Cambridge: Cambridge University Press, 2015.

Kelsen, Hans. 'God and the State'. In *Essays in Legal and Moral Philosophy*, translated by Peter Heath, 61–82. Dordrecht-Holland: D. Reidel Publishing Company, 1973.

Kelsen, Hans. 'L'âme et le droit'. In *IIe Annuaire de l'Institut International de Philosophie du Droit*, 60–70. Paris: Ed. Sirey, 1936.

Kelsen, Hans. 'The Soul and the Law'. *The Review of Religion*, 4, no. 1 (1937): 337–60.

Kjellén, Rudolf. *Der Staat als Lebensform*. Leipzig: Hirzel, 1917.

Kjellén, Rudolf. *Inledning till Sveriges geografi*. Göteborg: Wettergren & Kerber, 1900.

Kjellén, Rudolf. *Schweden: Eine politische Monographie*, edited by Friedrich Meinecke. Berlin: R. Oldenbourg, 1917.

Kjellén, Rudolf. *Staten som lifsform*. Stockholm: Hugo Gebers Förlag, 1916.

Korsch, Dietrich. *Dialektische Theologie nach Karl Barth*. Tübingen: J. C. B. Mohr, 1996.

Koslowski, Peter. 'Metaphysische Theologie und Dogma. Erik Petersons Auseinandersetzung mit Gnosis und Mystik'. *Neue Zeitschrift für Systematische Theologie und Religionsphilosophie*, 33, no. 3 (1991): 248–61.

Kracauer, Siegfried. *The Mass Ornament: Weimar Essays*, translated by Thomas Y. Levin. London: Harvard University Press, 1995.

Kreienbrock, Jörg. 'Franz Rosenzweig's Mitteleuropa a New Levante'. In *Personal Narratives, Peripheral Theatres: Essays on the Great War 1914–18*, edited by Anthony

Barker, Maria Eugénia Pereira, Maria Teresa Cortez, Paulo Alexandre Pereira and Otília Martins, 185–200. Cham: Springer International, 2018.

Krüger, Klaus. *Der Gottesbegriff der Spekulativen Theologie*. Berlin: Verlag Walter de Gruyter & Co, 1970.

Kurzweil, Ray. 'Reinventing Humanity: The Future of Machine-Human Intelligence'. *The Futurist*, 40, no. 2 (2006): 39–46.

Landauer, Gustav. *Skepsis und Mystik*. Berlin: Egon Sleichel & Co., 1903.

Lebovic, Nitzan. *The Philosophy of Life and Death: Ludwig Klages and the Rise of Nazi Biopolitics*. New York: Palgrave-Macmillan, 2013.

Lefort, Claude. 'The Death of Immortality?' In *Democracy and Political Theory*, translated by David Macey, 256–82. Oxford: Polity Press, 1988.

Leisegang, Hans. *Religionsphilosophie der Gegenwart*. Berlin: Junker und Dünnhaupt, 1930.

Lenin, V. I. *'Left-wing' Communism, an Infantile Disorder: A Popular Essay in Marxian Strategy and Tactics*. New York: International Publishers, 1962.

Lévi Strauss, Claude. *A World on the Wane*, translated by John Russell. London: Hutchinson, 1962.

Lévi Strauss, Claude. *Race and History*, translated by anonymous. Paris: UNESCO, (1952) 1958.

Lévi Strauss, Claude. *The Savage Mind*, translated by anonymous. London: Weidenfeld and Nicolsson, (1962) 1966.

Lilla, Mark. *The Stillborn God: Religion, Politics, and the Modern West*. New York: Vintage Books, 2008.

Lohmann, Johann Friedrich. *Karl Barth und der Neukantianismus: Die Rezeption des Neukantianismus im 'Römerbrief' und ihre Bedeutung für die weitere Ausarbeitung der Theologie Karl Barths*. Berlin: De Gruyter, 2010.

Mauss, Marcel. *A General Theory of Magic*. London and New York: Routledge Classics, (1902) 2005.

McCormack, Bruce. *Critically Realistic Dialectical Theology: Its Genesis and Development 1909–1936*. Oxford: Clarendon Press, 1995.

Meinecke, Friedrich. *Weltbürgertum und Nationalstaat: Studien zur Genesis des deutschen Nationalstaates*. Munich: R. Oldenbourg, 1908.

Meinong, Alexius. 'The Theory of Objects'. In *Realism and the Background of Phenomenology*, edited by Roderick Chisholm, translated by Isaac Levi, D. B. Terrell and Roderick Chisholm, 76–117. Atascadero, CA: Ridgeview, 1981.

Mendes-Flohr, Paul R. *The Philosophy of Franz Rosenzweig*. Hanover: University Press of New England, 1988.

Milgrom, Jacob. *Leviticus: A Book of Ritual and Ethics*. Minneapolis, MN: Fortress Press, 2004.

Moberly, Jennifer. *The Virtue of Bonhoeffer's Ethics: A Study of Dietrich Bonhoeffer's Ethics in Relation to Virtue Ethics*. Eugene, OR: Pickwick Publishers, 2013.

Mocek, Reinhard. 'The Program of Proletarian Rassenhygiene'. *Science in Context*, 11, no. 3–4 (1989): 609–17.

Mommsen, Hans. *The Rise and Fall of Weimar Democracy*, translated by Elbog Forster and Larry Eugene Jones. Chapel Hill, NC: University of North Carolina Press, (1989) 1996.

Mosès, Stéphane. *System and Revelation: The Philosophy of Franz Rosenzweig*, translated by Catherine Tihanyi. Detroit: Wayne State University Press, (1982) 1992.

Mosès, Stéphane. *The Angel of History: Rosenzweig, Benjamin, Scholem*, translated by Barbara Harshaw. Stanford: Stanford University Press, (1992) 2009.

Myers, David N. *Resisting History: Historicism and Its Discontents in German-Jewish Thought*. Princeton, NJ: Princeton University Press, 2003.

Naumann, Friedrich. *Mitteleuropa*. Berlin: Reimer, 1915.

Newman, John Henry. *An Essay in Aid of a Grammar of Assent*. Place of publication not identified: Assumption Press, 2013.

Nimmo, Paul T. 'The Orders of Creation in the Theological Ethics of Karl Barth'. *Scottish Journal of Theology*, 60, no.1 (2007): 24–35.

Noll, Mark A. *Christians in the American Revolution*. Vancouver: Regent College Publisher, 2006.

Novotny, Frantisek. *The Posthumous Life of Plato*. Hague: Martinus Nijhoff, 1977.

Oakes, Kenneth. *Reading Karl Barth: A Companion to Karl Barth's Epistle to the Romans*. Eugene, OR: Cascade Books, 2011.

Oken, Lorenz von. *Elements of Physiophilosophy*, translated by Alfred Tulk. London: Ray Society, (1843) 1847.

O'Reilly, Andrea. 'Nationalism and Motherhood'. In *Encyclopedia of Motherhood, Volume 1*, edited by Andrea O'Reilly, 893. Los Angeles: SAGE Publications, 2010.

Pannenberg, Wolfhart. 'Die Subjektivität Gottes und die Trinitätslehre: Ein Beitrag zur Beziehung zwischen Karl Barth und der Philosophie Hegels'. In *Grundfragen systematischer Theologie: Gesammelte Aufsätze, Volym 2*, 96–111. Göttingen: Vandenhoeck & Ruprecht, 2011.

Pannenberg, Wolfhart. *Offenbarung als Geschichte*. Göttingen: Vandenhoeck & Ruprecht, 1970.

Pannenberg, Wolfhart. *Systematic Theology*, Vol. 1, translated by Geoffrey W. Bromiley. New York: T&T Clark, (1988) 2004.

Pannenberg, Wolfhart. 'The Concept of Miracle'. *Zygon*, 37, no. 3 (2002): 759–62.

Pannenberg, Wolfhart. *Wissenschaftstheorie und Theologie*. Frankfurt: Suhrkamp, 1973.

Parvin, Phil. *Karl Popper*. London: Bloomsbury Publishing, 2014.

Petras, Otto. *Post Christum Streifzüge durch die geistige Wirklichkeit*. Berlin: Widerstands Verlag, 1935.

Petropoulos, Jonathan. *Artists under Hitler: Collaboration and Survival in Nazi Germany*. New Haven, CT: Yale University, Press 2015.

Pollock, Benjamin. *Franz Rosenzweig and the Systematic Task of Philosophy*. New York: Cambridge University Press, 2009.

Pollock, Benjamin. *Franz Rosenzweig's Conversions*. Bloomington: Indiana University Press, 2014.

Pollock, Benjamin. 'From Nation State to World Empire: Franz Rosenzweig's Redemptive Imperialism'. *Jewish Studies Quarterly*, 11, no. 4 (2004): 332–53.
Poma, Andrea. *Yearning for Form and Other Essays on Hermann Cohen's Thought.* Dordrecht: Springer, 2006.
Rasmusson, Arne. 'Church and Nation-State: Karl Barth and German Public Theology in Early 20th Century'. *Ned Geref Teologiese Tydskrift*, 46, no. 3–4 (2005): 18–30.
Rasmusson, Arne. '"Deprive Them of Their Pathos": Karl Barth and the Nazi Revolution Revisited'. *Modern Theology*, 23, no. 3 (2007): 369–91.
Ratzel, Friedrich. *Anthropogeographie.* Darmstadt: Wissenschaftliche Buchgesellschaft, (1882/1891) 1975.
Ratzel, Friedrich. *Culturgeographie der Vereinigten Staaten von Nordamerika: unter besonderer Berücksichtigung der wirtschaftlichen Verhältnisse.* Munich: R. Oldenbourg, 1880.
Ratzel, Friedrich. *Physikalische Geographie und Naturcharakter der Vereinigten Staaten von Nord-Amerika.* Munich: Oldenbourg, 1878.
Ratzel, Friedrich. *Politische Geographie; oder, Die Geographie der Staaten, des Verkehres und des Krieges.* Munich: R. Oldenbourg, 1903.
Raviv, Alexander. *Was the Real Thomas Mann an Antisemite? The Jewish Issue in Thomas Mann's Non-Fictional Writings versus the Image of the Jew in Thomas Mann's Novels.* Berlin: Münster, 2007.
Reale, Giovanni. *A History of Ancient Philosophy III: Systems of the Hellenistic Age*, edited by John R. Catan, translated by Giovanni Reale. Albany, NY: State University of New York Press, 1985.
Reisner, Erwin. 'Magischer Messianismus'. *Kirchenblatt für die reformierte Schweiz*, 92, no. 5 (1936): 66–71.
Richards, Robert J. *The Tragic Sense of Life: Ernst Haeckel and the Struggle over Evolutionary Thought.* Chicago, IL: Chicago University Press, 2008.
Richter, Ingrid. *Katholizismus und Eugenik in der Weimarer Republik und im Dritten Reich.* Paderborn: Schöningh, 2001.
Rickert, Heinrich. *Die Philosophie des Lebens: Darstellung und Kritik der Philosophischen Modeströmungen unserer Zeit.* Tübingen: J. C. B. Mohr (Paul Siebeck), 1920.
Rickert, Heinrich. *Grundprobleme der Philosophie, Methodologie, Ontologie, Anthropologie.* Tübingen: J. C. B. Mohr (Paul Siebeck), 1934.
Rohde, Erwin. *Psyche: The Cult of Souls and Belief in Immortality among the Greeks*, translated by W. B. Hillis. London: Kegan Paul Trench, (1894) 1915.
Rohde, Erwin. *Seelencult und Unsterblichkeitsglaube der Griechen.* Freiburg: J. C. B. Mohr, 1894.
Roosevelt, Theodore. 'On American Motherhood'. Available online: http://www.nationalcenter.org/TRooseveltMotherhood.html. (Accessed 17 January 2017), 1905.
Rosenstock, Bruce. *Philosophy and the Jewish Question: Mendelssohn, Rosenzweig, and Beyond.* New York: Fordham University Press, 2010.

Rosenstock, Bruce. *Transfinite Life: Oskar Goldberg and the Vitalist Imagination*. Bloomington, IN: Indiana University Press, 2017.
Rosenzweig, Franz. 'Apologetisches Denken--Bemerkung zu Brod und Baeck'. In *Zweistromland*, edited by Reinhold and Annemarie Mayer, 677-86. Haag: Martinus Nijhof Publishers, (1923) 1984.
Rosenzweig, Franz. *Briefe und Tagebücher 1900-1918*, edited by Rachel Rosenzweig and Edith Rosenzweig-Scheinmann. Haag: Martinus Nijhoff Publishers, 1979.
Rosenzweig, Franz. *Briefe und Tagebücher 1918-1929*, edited by Rachel Rosenzweig and Edith Rosenzweig-Scheinmann Haag: Martinus Nijhoff Publishers, 1979.
Rosenzweig, Franz. 'Cannä und Gorlice'. In *Zweistromland: Kleinere Schriften zu Glauben und Denken*, edited by Reinhold Mayer and Annemarie Mayer, 283-96. Dordrecht: Martinus Nijhoff Publishers, (1917) 1984a.
Rosenzweig, Franz. *Das Büchlein vom gesunden und kranken Menschenverstand*. Frankfurt am Main: Jüdischer Verlag im Suhrkamp Verlag, (1964) 1992.
Rosenzweig, Franz. 'Das Kriegsziel'. In *Zweistromland: Kleinere Schriften zu Glauben und Denken*, edited by Reinhold Mayer and Annemarie Mayer, 309-12. Dordrecht: Martinus Nijhoff Publishers, (1917) 1984b.
Rosenzweig, Franz. 'Der Jude im Staat'. In *Zweistromland*, edited by Reinhold Mayer and Annemarie Mayer, 553-5. Haag: Martinus Nijhof Publishers, (1920) 1984a.
Rosenzweig, Franz. 'Der Jüdische Mensch'. In *Zweistromland*, edited by Reinhold Mayer and Annemarie Mayer, 559-76. Haag: Martinus Nijhof Publishers, (1920) 1984b.
Rosenzweig, Franz. *Der Stern der Erlösung*. Haag: Martinus Nijhof Publishers, (1921) 1976.
Rosenzweig, Franz. 'Deutschtum und Judentum'. In *Zweistromland: Kleinere Schriften zu Glauben und Denken*, edited by Reinhold Mayer and Annemarie Mayer, 169-75. Dordrecht: Martinus Nijhoff Publishers, (1917) 1984c.
Rosenzweig, Franz. 'Die neue Levante'. In *Zweistromland: Kleinere Schriften zu Glauben und Denken*, edited by Reinhold Mayer and Annemarie Mayer, 309-12. Dordrecht: Martinus Nijhoff Publishers, (1917) 1984d.
Rosenzweig, Franz. 'Eine Erörterung des strategischen Raumbegriffs'. In *Zweistromland: Kleinere Schriften zu Glauben und Denken*, edited by Reinhold Mayer and Annemarie Mayer, 297-300. Dordrecht: Martinus Nijhoff Publishers, (1917) 1984e.
Rosenzweig, Franz. 'Faith and Knowledge'. In *God, Man, and the World--Lectures and Essays*, edited and translated by Barbara E. Galli, 97-121. New York: Syracuse University Press, (1920) 1998.
Rosenzweig, Franz. '"Germ Cell" of The Star of Redemption'. In *Franz Rosenzweig's 'The New Thinking'*, edited and translated by Alan Udoff and Barbara E. Galli, 45-66. Syracuse: Syracuse University Press, (1917) 1999.
Rosenzweig, Franz. 'Globus: Studien zum weltgeschichtlichen Raumlehre'. In *Zweistromland: Kleinere Schriften zu Glauben und Denken*, edited by Reinhold Mayer and Annemarie Mayer, 313-66. Dordrecht: Martinus Nijhoff Publishers, (1917) 1984f.
Rosenzweig, Franz. *Hegel und der Staat*. Berlin: Suhrkamp, (1920) 2010.

Rosenzweig, Franz. 'Hic et Ubique'. In *Cultural Writings of Franz Rosenzweig*, edited and translated by Barbara E. Galli, 83-97. New York: Syracuse University Press, (1919) 2000.

Rosenzweig, Franz. 'Jüdische Geschichte im Rahmen der Weltgeschichte'. In *Zweistromland*, edited by Reinhold Mayer and Annemarie Mayer, 539-52. Haag: Martinus Nijhof Publishers, (1920) 1984c.

Rosenzweig, Franz. 'Monarchie, Republik und Entwicklung'. In *Zweistromland: Kleinere Schriften zu Glauben und Denken*, edited by Reinhold Mayer and Annemarie Mayer, 249-52. Dordrecht: Martinus Nijhoff Publishers, (1917) 1984g.

Rosenzweig, Franz. 'Neuorientierung'. In *Zweistromland: Kleinere Schriften zu Glauben und Denken*, edited by Reinhold Mayer and Annemarie Mayer, 257-60. Dordrecht: Martinus Nijhoff Publishers, (1917) 1984h.

Rosenzweig, Franz. 'New Thinking'. In *Franz Rosenzweig's "The New Thinking"*, edited and translated by Alan Udoff and Barbara E. Galli, 67-102. Syracuse: Syracuse University Press, (1925) 1999.

Rosenzweig, Franz. 'Nordwest und Südost'. In *Zweistromland: Kleinere Schriften zu Glauben und Denken*, edited by Reinhold Mayer and Annemarie Mayer, 301-8. Dordrecht: Martinus Nijhoff Publishers, (1917) 1984i.

Rosenzweig, Franz. 'Paralipomena'. In *Zweistromland*, edited by Reinhold Mayer and Annemarie Mayer, 61-124. Haag: Martinus Nijhof Publishers, (1926) 1984.

Rosenzweig, Franz. 'Realpolitik'. In *Zweistromland: Kleinere Schriften zu Glauben und Denken*, edited by Reinhold Mayer and Annemarie Mayer, 261-6. Dordrecht: Martinus Nijhoff Publishers, (1917) 1984j.

Rosenzweig, Franz. *Rosenzweig: His Life and Thought*, edited and translated by Nahum N. Glatzer, Indianapolis, IN and Cambridge: Hackett Publishing Company, (1961) 1998.

Rosenzweig, Franz. 'Science and Life'. In *God, Man, and the World--Lectures and Essays*, edited and translated by Barbara E. Galli, 123-33. New York: Syracuse University Press, (1918) 1998.

Rosenzweig, Franz. 'The Science of God'. In *God, Man, and the World--Lectures and Essays*, edited and translated by Barbara E. Galli, 37-61. New York: Syracuse University Press, (1921) 1998.

Rosenzweig, Franz. 'The Science of the World'. In *God, Man, and the World--Lectures and Essays*, edited and translated by Barbara E. Galli, 81-96. New York: Syracuse University Press, (1922) 1998.

Rosenzweig, Franz. *The Star of Redemption*, translated by Barbara E Galli. Madison, WI: University of Wisconsin Press, (1921) 2005.

Rosenzweig, Franz. *Understanding the Sick and Healthy*, translated by Nahum N. Glatzer. Cambridge and London: Harvard University Press, (1964) 1999.

Rosenzweig, Franz. 'Vertauschte Fronten'. In *Zweistromland: Kleinere Schriften zu Glauben und Denken*, edited by Reinhold Mayer and Annemarie Mayer, 235-7. Dordrecht: Martinus Nijhoff Publishers, (1929) 1984.

Rosenzweig, Franz. 'Vox Dei?'. In *Zweistromland: Kleinere Schriften zu Glauben und Denken*, edited by Reinhold Mayer and Annemarie Mayer, 267–82. Dordrecht: Martinus Nijhoff Publishers, (1917) 1984k.

Rosenzweig, Franz. *Zweistromland*, edited by Reinhold Mayer and Annemarie Mayer. Haag: Martinus Nijhof Publishers, (1926) 1984.

Rotenstreich, Nathan. 'Common Sense and Theological Experience on the Basis of Franz Rosenzweig's Philosophy'. *Journal of the History of Philosophy*, 5, no. 4 (1967): 353–60.

Sahlins, Marshall. *Stone Age Economics*. London: Routledge 2017.

Samuelson, Norbert M. *User's Guide to Franz Rosenzweig's Star of Redemption*. London: Routledge, 1999.

Schallmayer, Wilhelm. *Beiträge zu einer Nationalbiologie. Nebst einer Kritik der methodologischen Einwände und einem Anhang über wissenschaftliches Kritikerwesen*. Jena: Hermann Costenoble, 1905.

Scheffler, Samuel. *Death and the Afterlife*. Oxford: Oxford University Press, 2016.

Schelling, F. W. J. von. *Clara: or, On Nature's Connection to the Spirit World*, translated by Fiona Steinkamp. New York: State University of New York Press, (1810–1817) 2002.

Schelling, F. W. J. von. *Philosophie der Mythologie (Philosophische Einleitung), Werke XI*. Stuttgart: K.F.A., (1837–1842) 1861.

Schelling, F. W. J. von. *Philosophie der Offenbarung*. Frankfurt am Main: Suhrkamp am Main, (1841/1842) 1977.

Schindler, Renate. *Zeit, Geschichte, Ewigkeit in Franz Rosenzweigs Stern der Erlösung*. Berlin: Parerga, 2007.

Schmid, Carlo. *Mensch und Technik: die sozialen und kulturellen Probleme im Zeitalter der 2. industriellen Revolution*. Bonn: Vorstand der SPD, 1956.

Schmitt, Carl. *Land and Sea: A World-Historical Meditation*, translated by Samuel Garrett Zeitlin. Candor, NY: Telos Press Publishing, (1942) 2015.

Schmitt, Carl. *Political Theology: Four Chapters on the Concept of Sovereignty*, translated by George Schwab. Chicago, IL: University of Chicago, (1922) 2005.

Scholem, Geshom. *Briefe, Band I 1914–1947*. Munich: CH Beck, 1994.

Scholem, Geshom. *From Berlin to Jerusalem: Memories of My Youth*, translated by Harry Zohn. New York: Schocken, (1977) 1980.

Schulz, Walter. *Die Vollendung des Deutschen Idealismus in der Spätphilosophie Schellings*. Pfullingen: Neske, 1975.

Schwarz, Hans. *The God Who Is: The Christian God in a Pluralistic World*. Eugene, OR: Cascade Books, 2011.

Seeberg, Erich. *Wer ist Christus?* Tübingen: J. C. B. Mohr (Paul Siebeck), 1937.

Shofner, Robert D. *Anselm Revisited: A Study on the Role of the Ontological Argument in the Writings of Karl Barth and Charles Hartshorne*. Leiden: Brill, 1974.

Sigurdson, Ola. *Gudomliga komedier: Humor, subjektivitet, transcendens*. Göteborg: Glänta Produktion, 2021.

Sikora, Tomasz. 'The Genealogy of Shem According to Oskar Goldberg'. *The Polish Journal of the Arts and Culture*, 9 (2014). Available online: http://www.pjac.uj.edu.pl/documents/30601109/c4018edd-0ad6-49a9-af48-6036d1ee9233 (accessed 10 August 2017).
Simmel, Georg. *Lebensanschauung. Vier metaphysische Kapitel*. Münich: Duncker & Humblot, 1918.
Simmel, Georg. *The View of Life: Four Metaphysical Essays, with Journal Aphorisms*, translated by John A. Y. Andres and Donald N. Levine. Chicago: The University of Chicago Press, (1918) 2010.
Smith, Adam. *The Theory of Moral Sentiments*, edited by Knud Haakonssen. Cambridge: Cambridge University Press, (1759) 2002.
Spengler, Oswald. *The Decline of the West*, translated by Charles Frances Atkinson. New York: Alfred A. Knopf, (1918) 1926.
Spieckermann, Ingrid. *Gotteserkenntnis. Ein Beitrag zur Grundfrage der neuen Theologie Karl Barths*. Munich: Chr. Kaiser, 1985.
Stengers, Isabelle. *Cosmopolitics*, translated by Robert Bononno. Minneapolis: University of Minnesota Press, (2003) 2010.
Stirner, Max. *The Ego and Its Own*, translated by Steven Byington. Cambridge: Cambridge University Press, 2000.
Susman, Margarete. 'Vortrag über Oskar Goldberg'. In *Zahlengebäude, Ontologie, Maimonides und Aufsätze 1933 bis 1947*, edited by Manfred Voigts, 389–408. Würzburg: Königshausen & Neumann, 2013.
Svenungsson, Jayne. *Diving History: Prophetism, Messianism and the Development of the Spirit*, translated by Stephen Donovan. New York: Berghahn, (2013) 2016.
Sweeney, Eileen C. *Anselm of Canterbury and the Desire for the Word*. Washington, DC: The Catholic University of America Press, 2012.
Tarizzo, Davide. *Life: A Modern Invention*, translated by Mark William Epstein. Minneapolis: University of Minnesota Press, 2017.
Taubes, Jacob. 'From Cult to Culture'. In *From Cult to Culture: Fragments Toward a Critique of Historical Reason*, translated by Mara H. Benjamin and William Rauscher, 235–47. Stanford: Stanford University Press, 2010.
Taubes, Jacob. 'Kabbalah'. In *Jacob Taubes und Oskar Goldberg: Aufsätze, Briefe, Dokumente*, edited by Manfred Voigts, 21–30. Würzburg: Königshausen & Neumann, (1942) 2011.
Taubes, Jacob. *Occidental Eschatology*, translated by David Ratmoko. Stanford: Stanford University Press, (1947) 2009.
Taubes, Jacob. 'Theodicy and Theology: A Philosophical Analysis of Karl Barth's Dialectical Theology'. *The Journal of Religion*, 34, no. 4 (1954): 231–43.
Telles, Shirley, Meesha Joshi, Manoj Dash, P. Raghuraj, K. V. Naveen and H. R. Nagendra. 'An Evaluation of the Ability to Voluntarily Reduce the Heart Rate After a Month of Yoga Practice'. *Integrative Physiological & Behavorial Science*, 39, no. 2 (2004): 119–25.
Thweatt-Bates, Jeanine. *Cyborg Selves: A Theological Anthropology of the Posthuman*. London: Routledge, 2016.

Tilliette, Xavier. *Attualità di Schelling*. Milano: U. Mursia, 1974.
Tilliette, Xavier. *Schelling une Philosophie en Devenir*. Paris: Vrin, 1992.
Tritten, Tyler. *Beyond Presence: The Late F.W.J. Schelling's Criticism of Metaphysics*. Boston, MA: Walter de Gruyter, 2012.
Tutino, Stefania. *Empire of Souls: Robert Bellarmine and the Christian Commonwealth*. New York: Oxford University Press, 2011.
Unger, Erich. *Das Lebendige und das Göttliche*. Jerusalem: Hatehiya Press, 1966.
Unger, Erich. *Die Staatslose Bildung eines Jüdischen Volkes*. Berlin: Verlag David, 1922.
Unger, Erich. *Gegen die Dichtung: Eine Begründung des Konstruktionsprinzips in der Erkenntnis*. Leipzig: Meiner, 1925.
Unger, Erich. *Politik und Metaphysik*. Würzburg: Königshausen & Neumann, (1921) 1989.
Unger, Erich. 'The Natural Order of Miracles: I. The Pentateuch and the Vitalistic Myth', translated by Esther J. Ehrman. *The Journal of Jewish Thought & Philosophy*, 11, no. 2 (2002): 135–52.
Vignoli, Tito. *Myth and Science: An Essay*. London: Kegan Paul, Trench, Trübner & Co., 1898.
Vogel, Manfred H. 'The Barth-Feuerbach Confrontation'. *The Harvard Theological Review*, 59, no. 1 (1966): 27–52.
Voigts, Manfred. 'Eine nicht ausgetragene Kontroverse: Die Beziehung Gershom Scholems zu Oskar Goldberg und Erich Unger'. *Aschkenas*, 25, no. 2 (2015): 313–64.
Voigts, Manfred. *Jacob Taubes und Oskar Goldberg: Aufsätze, Briefe, Dokumente*. Würzburg: Königshausen & Neumann, 2011.
Voigts, Manfred. 'Jüdisches Denken im Frühexpressionismus. Oskar Goldberg und Erich Unger im Zeichen Friedrich Nietzsches'. In *Jüdischer Nietzscheanismus*, edited by Werner Stegmaier and Daniel Krochmalnik, 168–87. Berlin: W. de Gruyter, 1997.
Voigts, Manfred. *Oskar Goldberg: Der mythische Experimentalwissenschaftler: Ein verdrängtes Kapitel jüdischer Geschichte*. Berlin: Agora Verlag, 1992.
Wagner, Andreas. *The Arrival of the Fittest*. New York: Current, 2015.
Waldrop, Charles T. *Karl Barth's Christology: Its Basic Alexandrian Character*. Berlin: Mouton Publishers, 1984.
Wallace, Mark I. *The Second Naiveté: Barth, Ricoeur, and the New Yale Theology*. Macon, GA: Mercer, 1995.
Ward, Peter. *The Medea Hypothesis: Is Life on Earth Ultimately Self-Destructive?* Princeton, NJ: Princeton University Press, 2009.
Weber, Joseph C. 'Feuerbach, Barth, and Theological Methodology'. *The Journal of Religion*, 46, no. 1 (1966): 24–36.
Weikart, Richard. 'The Role of Darwinism in Nazi Racial Thought'. *German Studies Review*, 36, no. 3 (2013): 537–66.
Weindling, Paul. *Health, Race and German Politics between National Unification and Nazism, 1870–1945*. Cambridge: Cambridge University Press, 1989.

Weindling, Paul. 'Weimar eugenics: The Kaiser Wilhelm Institute for Anthropology, Human Heredity and Eugenics in Social Context'. *Annals of Science*, 42, no. 3 (1985): 303–18.
Weiss, Sheila Faith. *Race Hygiene and National Efficiency: The Eugenics of Wilhelm Schallmayer*. Los Angeles, CA: University of California Press, 1987.
Whelan, Richard. *Robert Capa: A Biography*. Lincoln, OR: University of Nebraska Press, 1985.
Wolfson, Elliot R. 'Facing the Effaced: Mystical Eschatology and the Idealistic Orientation in the Thought of Franz Rosenzweig'. *Zeitschrift für Neuere Theologiegeschichte*, 4, no. 1 (1997): 39–81.
Wolfson, Elliot R. *Giving Beyond the Gift: Apophasis and Overcoming Theomania*. New York: Fordham University Press, 2014.

Index

Abel 128, 139, 153
abnormality 92, 93
Abraham 36, 53, 54, 121, 128, 139, 152, 156, 159–60, 167
Abrahamic religion 26
Abstammung 135, 156
Abstammungszentrum 135
abstraction 73, 76, 77, 79, 87, 90, 156
Aby Warburg library 13
academic historiography 7
academic philosophy 80
Adam 57, 68, 69, 83, 106, 107, 142, 154, 155, 190
Adorno, Theodor W. 120, 121, 123
afterlife 4, 5, 24, 60, 92, 184, 190, 237 n.234
Afterweisheit 80
Althusser, Louis 97
America 32, 53–5
American Revolution 4, 5
analogia fidei 93
analogical theory 92–4, 97
Anders, Günther 12
'An die Deutschen' (Hölderlin) 15
Aneignung 11
angelology 6, 86–90
angels 86–90
animal intelligence 138
animal laborans 61
Anselm of Canterbury 11, 72–3, 93–5, 98–100, 109
anthropogenesis 105, 131, 132, 139, 150, 155, 190, 195, 196
Anthropogeographie (Ratzel) 31
anthropogeography 31
anthropological realism 74
anthropology 72, 152
anti-fascism 85
antisemitism 7, 63, 86–8
Anwesenheit 141
aprioric ethnology 128, 152
archaic primitivism 180, 195
Arendt, Hannah 5, 60, 61, 86

Aristotelean logic 171, 173
Aristotle 120
Arrival of the Fittest, The (Wagner) 236 n.226
Aryan ideologies 3
Aryan-Semitic race 139
ascension 74, 91
Asia 54
assumptio carnis 79, 82
atheism 75–6
Aufhebung (sublation) 78, 127, 129, 152
Auschwitz 120, 181
Aussersein 101
Austro-Hungarian Empire 8
autochthonic phenomenon 31
autochthonic spatiality 15
avant la lettre 56
axiology 5

Baark, Sigurd 11, 94
Babylon 122, 126, 128, 198
Balkanfront 8, 20, 36
Balthasar, Hans Urs von 11
Bamyeh, Mohammed 59–61, 67
Barth, Karl 1, 2, 4, 6, 7, 9–11, 71, 184–6, 189, 190, 192–4, 196–200, 203 n.26, 207 n.64, 224 n.158, 225 n.185, 226 n.212, 227 nn.220, 237
being is eating 79–85
CD III 226 n.212
Christian Life, The 224 n.158
Church and State 11
Church Dogmatics 11, 75, 92
Der Römerbrief 93
Epistle to the Romans, The 10, 11, 92, 93
Ethics 227 n.220
Fides quaerens intellectum 11, 94
fractures in reality 85–92
God and species-being 72–9
Göttingen Dogmatics 10, 11, 94, 102, 103

naming death 98–104
political thanatology 110–17
problem of human 104–10
sense of nonsense 92–8
Tambach lecture (1919) 96
Theology of Schleiermacher, The 10
Baumgardt, David 39, 40
Behemoth 131, 144–53, 190
being, identification of 24
being-already-there (*Schon-da-sein*) 46
being and thinking 43
being itself 8, 44, 171
being of the world 1, 46
being-there (*Da-sein*) 46
Beintker, Michael 207 n.64
Beit Hamidrash 12
Ben-Chorin, Schalom 6
Benjamin, Walter 12, 149, 185
Bensussan, Gérard 20
Beobachtung 11
Bewährung 39
Biberfeld, Abraham 12
Bible 105, 133
biocentrism 2, 4, 8, 57, 64, 185, 186, 191, 202 n.12
biological abilities 135
biological evolution 148
biological organisms 31, 119, 155, 158, 160, 161, 169
biological politics (*biologische Politik*) 3
biological theory of revolution 148
biological universalism 153–8, 160, 162, 195
biologization 3, 7, 190
biology 2, 3, 6, 8, 136, 137, 142, 155, 159–61, 171, 190
biopolitics 6, 8, 17
biosphere 146
bloßes Leben 20
Blumenberg, Hans 1, 2, 4, 5, 28, 65, 183, 185–92, 195–7, 199
Blumhardt, Johann 87
body 1, 20, 31, 36, 63–4, 79, 102, 137, 139, 165
Bonhoeffer, Dietrich 227 n.237
Botar, Oliver 202 n.12
Braiterman, Zachary 37, 48, 66, 206 n.57
Brann, Eva T. H. 95, 98, 99
breath-techniques 138
Brecht, Berthold 12

Breisacher, Chaim 7, 123
Brod, Max 23, 24, 29, 55
Bronze Age 122
Brunner, Emil 114
Bry, Carl Christian 86
Buber, Martin 12, 32
Buchenwald 115
Büchner, Ludwig 6, 79

Cain 127–8, 139, 152, 154, 194
Cainites 128
Calvin, Jean 114
Canaan 129, 156, 194
capital 146, 148, 149, 150
capitalism 3, 123, 125, 129, 130, 131, 144, 146–50
capitalist economy 147
capitalist system 130, 149, 150
Carnis resurrectionem 89
Caspary, Adolf 12, 13, 130, 131, 135, 142, 144, 145–50, 152, 154, 157, 179, 180, 194, 195
Cassirer, Ernst 17, 136, 137
catastrophic politics 129, 150
Catholic dogmatics 88
Caucasian peoples 23
Celly, Duncan 16
China 57
Christendom 56
Christian civilization 29
Christian doctrine 11
Christian dogmatics 93
Christian ethics 226 n.212
Christianity 5, 16–18, 22, 24, 26, 30, 54, 55, 57, 58, 60, 63–7, 77–82, 87, 97, 120, 163–4, 187, 190, 191, 193, 194, 196, 198
Christian(s) 5, 23, 30, 37, 55, 71–3, 87, 111, 164
Christian tradition 74, 75, 79, 88, 92, 96
Christocentrism 11
Christological doctrine 79, 82
Church of the Reformation and Counter-Reformation 63
circumcision 159
Cohen, Hermann 9, 17, 18, 52, 53, 61, 124, 125, 127, 165–70, 172–4
coincidentia oppositorum 69

colonialism 55
colonization 53
Columbus, Christopher 53, 55
comfortable (*gemütlichen*) feast 81
Communism 7
Communist Party 148
completion 47–51, 62, 65, 67, 68
'the concrete life of humanity' 87
Confucianism 56
conscience 106–9
consciousness 121–3, 136, 154, 161
Constitution of Austria (1920) 1
contemporary Christianity 183
contingency 77, 78, 94, 95, 97, 99, 101, 123, 134
corporeal activity 79
cosmology 1, 2, 5, 19, 26, 117, 132, 187
Counter-Reformation 63
counterrevolutionaries 71
creatio ex nihilo 24
creation 10, 11, 13, 26, 27, 29, 35, 37, 42, 49, 50, 54, 66–9, 71, 72, 76–8, 82–4, 86, 88, 90, 94, 98, 101, 104, 117, 120, 141, 160, 162, 191
critical philology 7
cultural history 21

Dacqué, Edgar 12
Darwin, Charles 2, 71, 189
Darwinian evolution 189, 198
Darwinian theory of morality 107
Darwinism 168, 187
das Seelische 177
Dawson, R. Dale 9
'De angelis bonis et malis' (Bry) 86
death 9, 17–29, 33–42, 44–8, 50, 51, 56–60, 62–9, 73, 75, 78, 81, 82, 84, 85, 88–92, 98–105, 108–14, 116, 117, 119, 120, 129, 136, 137, 142, 158, 162, 168, 173, 178, 183–5, 190, 191–3, 195, 196, 200
Decline of the West, The (Spengler) 32
de Gama, Vasco 53
deities 25, 27, 122, 123, 135, 136, 140, 153, 154, 156, 159
democracy 7
demonology 6, 86–9, 91, 164
demons 86–90

der Einzige 76
detheologization 2, 4, 28
Deutsche Christen 85
Deutschtum und Judentum (Cohen) 52, 61
De vera religione (Augustine) 78
dialectical thinking 93
diaspora 8, 54, 61, 62, 64, 192
diastasis 10, 11
Die Maschinenutopie: das Übereinstimmungsmoment der bürgerlichen und sozialistischen Ökonomie (Caspary) 130, 144, 151, 180
Die Parteiung der Philosophie (Ehrenberg) 45
Die Philosophie des Lebens (Rickert) 19
Die Staatslose Bildung eines Jüdischen Volkes (Unger) 149
Die Technik des Glücks (Jung) 148
die Wende der Weltgeschichte 30
disguised religions 86
divine 23–6, 28, 50, 72, 73, 78, 79, 84, 86, 99, 109, 136, 137, 142, 155, 156, 160
Döblin, Alfred 12
Doctor Faustus (Mann) 7, 123
dogmatics 74, 85, 92, 93
Dornseiff, Franz 12

early capitalism 55
East Indies 53
Eckhart, Meister 111
economization 190
Eden 71, 82, 83, 106
ego 76, 77, 81
Ego and Its Own, The (Stirner) 76
Egypt 129, 140, 194
Ehrenberg, Eva 66
Ehrenberg, Hans 45
Ehrenberg, Rudolf 23, 24, 28
Ehrenberg, Victor 66
Ehrlich, Franz 115
einen Rund 53
Eisler, Robert 12
Elements of Physiophilosophy (Oken) 174
Elohim IHWH 121, 124–9, 139–42, 151, 153, 154, 158, 159, 161–3, 165, 166, 173, 181, 194, 195

Elohim Metim 158
El Olam 171, 173, 177, 178, 180, 195
English National Council of Labour Women (Haldane) 202 n.23
entropic processes 130, 143, 144
entropological processes 142, 143
Epic of Gilgamesh 58
Epicureanism 93
Epicurus 19
epistemology 47
epoch of myth 121, 122, 126
erfunden 172
Ersatz 150
eschatological ethics 108
eschatology 17, 22, 37, 44, 47, 53, 54, 68, 89, 96, 101, 105, 125, 186
eternal being 46, 47, 51
eternal end 29
eternal life 1, 4, 5, 6, 8–11, 12, 15, 17, 18, 21, 23, 29, 30, 32, 36–8, 41, 47, 48, 49, 51, 52, 54, 60, 62, 65, 66, 67, 69, 72, 83–5, 88–90, 95, 98, 99, 101, 102, 108–10, 112–16, 141, 142, 154, 155, 159, 167–69, 171, 173, 179, 180, 183, 184, 189, 191, 192, 194, 196, 197, 199, 206 n.57
eternal people 51, 61, 68
eternity 37, 46–9, 51, 60, 65, 67, 75, 88–92, 94, 101, 103, 109–11, 113–16, 162, 169, 175, 177, 184, 193
ethical order 141 165, 167
ethics 1, 19, 39, 84, 90, 106, 114, 115, 125, 169
Ethik des Reinen Willens (Cohen) 124, 170
Ethik: Grundriss der theologischen Wissenschaften (Hermann) 10
ethnicism 29
eudemonic power 88, 90, 116
eugenics 3, 86, 88, 202 n.23
Europe 8, 13, 54, 55, 156, 157, 189
European civilization 123, 157
European community 16
Europeanization 144
Eve 106, 107, 142
evil 13, 19, 67, 73, 81, 83–6, 108, 120, 169, 180, 186, 188, 190, 194–6, 198–200

existence 19, 29, 30, 41, 50, 59, 64–6, 68, 69, 81, 94, 95, 98, 100, 112
   biological 184
   creaturely 5, 10, 11, 22–7, 35, 113, 115
   earthly 23
   embodied 20, 21
   ethical 85
   finite 15
   human 3–5, 7, 35, 60, 79, 80, 85, 88, 89, 116, 156, 197
   mortal 91, 102, 184, 185
   natural 82
   prelapsarian 11
   primordial 32
existence (*Dasein*) 46
ex nihilo-logic 177

faith 93–5, 97, 103, 110, 185
fascism 7, 23, 88, 113, 123, 164
fear 18–21, 23, 37, 38, 59, 60, 63, 64, 68, 112
Fechner, Gustav 176
Feuerbach, Ludwig 4, 6, 11, 44, 72–4, 76–83, 85, 92, 96, 97, 108, 111, 112, 192, 215 n.159
Fichte, J. G. 18
First Industrial Revolution 190
First World War 7, 8, 10, 11, 15, 16, 21, 40, 52, 69, 110, 127, 143, 152, 157, 189, 226 n.212
Fisher, Cass 34
fixation, process of 127, 129, 132, 134, 135, 143, 150, 153, 156
Ford, Henry 131
foreign laws of nature 133, 134
Francé, Raoul H. 202 n.12
Franco-Prussian War (1870) 189
Frank, André Gunder 126
Fraze, James George 139
Frederick the Great 114
freedom 59, 85, 97, 105, 106, 108, 115, 195
Freeman, Joshua B. 131
Freie jüdische Lehrhaus 9
French Revolution 4, 5
Fuhrmann, Ernst 148

Ganztodtheorie 103
García de la Sienra, Adolfo 100

Gastev, Alexei 131
Gattungswesen 72–4, 81
Gegen die Dichtung (Unger) 177
Geist 140, 152, 160
Geisterkampf 16
Gelassenheit 111
gematria 12
General Theory of Magic, A (Mauss) 166
Genesis 71, 105, 125, 153
geopolitical theology 17
geopolitics 16, 21, 31, 51, 53, 58, 62, 69, 192
German idealism 8, 18, 20, 41, 42
German Jews 53, 56
German politics 15
German Social Democratic Party 10
Germany 1–3, 6–8, 10, 16–18, 29, 54, 56, 157
Germany uprisings (1919) 144
Geschlecht 56
gesunder Menschenverstand 34
Gibson, Violet 184
Gilgamesh 58–61, 63, 66–8, 191
Gills, Barry K. 126
Glatzer, Nahum 38
Gleichnis 92
globalization 53, 55, 144
Gnosticism 186, 187, 197, 198
God 10, 11, 12, 17, 23–9, 35, 36, 38, 56, 57, 65–8, 69, 81–4, 89–95, 100, 103, 104, 112, 113, 116, 140–2, 151, 153–4, 159, 160, 162, 167, 168, 175, 180–1, 191, 192, 194, 207 n.64
   command 107, 108
   defining 95
   immediacy of 96
   kingdom of 1, 30, 71, 116
   life of 99, 101, 102, 109
   omniscience 101, 168
   power of 86
   and species-being 72–9
   unity of 47, 66
   wisdom of 42
   Word 42, 97, 193
Goethe, Johann Wolfgang von 23
Goetschel, Roland 168
Goldberg, Oskar 1, 2, 4–7, 12–13, 22, 23, 25, 27, 39, 119–23, 184, 185, 189, 190, 194–200, 235 n.209, 236–7 n.234
   5,000-year-old world system 123–32
   biological universalism 153–8
   contra naturam vivere 158–62
   Die abnormalen biologischen Vorgänge bei orientalischen Sekten 137
   'Die Bibelkritik' 124
   Die fünf Bücher Mosis-ein Zahlengebäude 12, 174
   Die Wirklichekit der Hebräer 12, 13, 22, 119, 120, 123–5, 129, 132–5, 152, 155, 160, 164–7, 168, 171, 173, 174, 181
   'The equation: Peoples = Gods = Worlds' 135
   flight from Behemoth 144–53
   Maimonides: Kritik der Jüdischen Glaubenslehre 13
   missionary Hebrewdom 162–6
   number of soul 174–81
   'Ontologie' 171–3
   politics of immortality 166–74
   'The proletariat' 131
Goldberg circle (*Goldberg-Kreis*) 12, 132, 144, 147–9, 151, 152, 154–6
Gordon, Peter 35, 37
Gotthold Ephraim, Lessing 1
Gramsci, Antonio 131
Great Depression (1930s) 3
Greek(s) 60
   gods 27
   philosophy 18, 121
Greenberg, Simon 119
Günther, Hans F. K. 86
Guttmann, Simon 148

Hadot, Pierre 19
Haeckel, Ernst 3, 6, 31
Hägglund, Martin 183–5
Haldane, John Burdon Sanderson 202 n.23
happiness 37, 47, 48, 67, 68
Harnack, Adolf von 9, 10
Hausmann, Raoul 148
heathendom 26, 29
Hebraic metaphysics 128
Hebraic prophets 125
Hebrew Bible 32, 122, 124, 228 n.17

Hebrewdom   162–6
Hebrew metaphysics   120, 160, 162, 166
Hebrews   12, 123–9, 133, 139–43, 151, 155, 157–9, 162–3, 166, 171, 175–7, 180, 194
Hegel, G. W. F.   9, 16, 18, 23, 25, 32, 59, 125, 215 n.159
Heidegger, Martin   17, 37
Heinberg, Richard   144
Hellas   57
Hellenic culture   60
Hendry, George S.   105
Hepner, Isidore   119, 120, 165, 176, 180
Heredity and Politics (Haldane)   202 n.23
Hermann, Wilhelm   9, 10
hermeneutics   35, 123
Hineinstreben   95, 109
Hirsch, Emanuel   85
historicism   6, 7
Hitchcock, Nathan   9
Hitler, Adolf   75, 85, 156
Hölderlin, Friedrich   15, 17
Holocaust   113
Homer   26, 27
Homo capitalisticus   55
homo faber   139, 194, 195
Horkheimer, Max   13
Hubbert, M. King   144
Hubert, Henri   166
Hugenberg, Alfred   205 n.53
human cognition   18, 20, 21
humanity   29–32, 47–9, 51, 53, 56, 59, 61–3, 66, 72, 73, 76, 77, 80–2, 84, 93, 101, 108, 121, 125–7, 130, 131, 137–9, 142, 143, 147, 151, 152, 154, 155, 194
humanization   79
human reason   73, 171
human self-assertion   4, 186, 187, 189, 190, 193, 196–8, 200
human subjectivity   10, 77, 97
human will   106–7
hyperinflation   157

idealism   80, 170
ideologies   97, 125
immanence   24–6, 28, 33, 81, 137, 187
immortal life   71
imperialism   16, 53, 59

incarnation   74, 77–9, 82, 90, 91, 94, 199
India   53, 57, 138
individual being   76, 77
industrialism   131
industrialization   130, 144, 189
industrialized capitalism   124, 146, 151
Institut for Sozialforschung (Horkheimer)   13
interpellation   97
invisible world   88, 89, 103
irrationality   7, 13
irreversible entropical processes   146
Islam   17, 120
Israel   30
Italy   55

Jakob ben Ascher   174
Jaynes, Julian   121–2, 125, 128, 129, 141, 154, 155, 159
Jean-Jacques, Rousseau   31
Jerusalem   98
Jesus Christ   10, 11, 30, 74, 75, 77, 78, 83, 84, 90–2, 94–6, 101, 113, 115, 192, 193
Jewish diaspora   54
Jewish liturgy   23, 50, 60, 62
Jewish mysticism   12, 69, 174
Jews   8, 30, 37, 50, 51, 55, 56, 61–4, 94, 149, 184
Johann Gottfried, Herder   1
Johannine community   63, 64
Johnston, Mark   184, 185, 199
Joseph and His Brothers (Mann)   13
Josuttis, Manfred   11, 94
Judaism   13, 16–18, 22–4, 54, 57, 58, 61–7, 88, 120, 123, 125, 127, 140, 162–4, 166, 168, 190–2, 194, 196, 198
Jung, Franz   148
Jüngel, Eberhard   97, 207 n.64
Junker und Dünnhaupt Verlag   6

kakodemonic power   88, 90, 116
Kammerer, Paul   3
Kant, Immanuel   1, 18, 43, 105, 106, 108, 133, 172
Kavka, Martin   39
Kelsen, Hans   1, 5, 187

khabiru 128, 129
Kjellén, Rudolf 6, 16, 17, 31, 32, 61
knowledge 4, 17, 18, 22, 33, 34, 37, 39, 40, 43, 44, 46, 49, 63, 68, 100, 150
Kommunistische Arbeiter-Partei Deutschlands (KAPD) 148
Korsch, Karl 12, 148
Kosmala, Hans 162–3
Kracauer, Siegfried 32
Kreienbrock, Jörg 8, 17
Kunstprodukt 126

lamentation 40
Land and Sea (Schmitt) 54
Landauer, Gustav 178, 179
law of unity 34, 62
laws of logic 171
Lebensphilosophie 19, 202 n.12
Lebensraum 31, 53
Lebensunwertes Leben 158
Lefort, Claude 4, 5
left communists 148
Left-wing Communism an Infantile Disorder (Lenin) 148
Legitimacy of the Modern Age, The (Blumenberg) 1, 183, 186, 188, 192
Lehre der Nahrungsmittel (Moleschott) 79
Leibniz, Gottfried Wilhelm von 167
Leisegang, Hans 6, 12
Lenin, V. I. 148
Leninism 148
Lévi-Strauss, Claude 138, 142, 143, 166
liberal democracy 7
liberation 29, 50, 53, 97, 101, 108, 142, 168
life 2–5, 15, 18–21, 29, 30, 33, 37, 40, 41, 46, 47, 50, 58, 66, 67, 69, 75, 79, 81, 82, 90, 102, 109, 111, 116, 117, 136, 137, 160, 166–7, 169–71, 183–5, 190, 196, 198–200
  age of 4
  alien 109
  animal 82, 83
  biological 80, 123, 160, 169, 180, 197
  contemplative 198
  creaturely 35, 36, 88–90, 107
  Darwinian 71, 188, 193
  definition of 27
  finitude of 9, 73, 111
  form of 5, 30, 60, 83, 97, 105, 140, 161, 169, 188, 190, 194, 196
  human 5, 6, 18–21, 23, 26, 60, 78, 85, 88, 93, 97, 107, 110, 152, 160, 170, 199
  Jewish 23
  of justice 36
  multiplicity of 35
  non-Darwinian 199
  paradisal 82
  postlapsarian 106
  prelapsarian 71
  sensual 79
  unity of 47, 68
'life beyond life' 35–6, 38, 56, 65
Lilla, Mark 7
living-eternally 50, 51
Locke, John 114
Loewenson, Erwin 12
love 30, 31, 36, 48, 58, 65, 66, 115
Ludueña Romandini, Fabián 198

McCormack, Bruce 10, 11
machine catastrophe 155
machinery 13, 130, 144, 145, 147
Machtübernahme 1
Magellan (Fernão de Magalhães) 53
magic messianism 166, 180
magic thinking 164
Manichean dualism 153
Mann, Thomas 7, 12, 13, 123, 126, 130, 180, 195
martyrdom 39, 40
Marx, Karl 13, 130, 145, 150
Marxism 148
Marxists 147, 148, 155
Maschinenutopie (machine utopia) 130
mass migration 149, 150
Mass und Wert 13, 126
mastery of machines 143
materialism 6, 24, 168
material world 19, 23, 86
mathematical ideas 174–5
mathematical kabbalism 174
mathematical ontology 176
Maury, Pierre 11

Mauss, Marcel 166
Medea hypothesis 189
Meinecke, Friedrich 16, 17, 29, 31, 32, 52
Meinong, Alexius 99–101
memento Domini 113
memento mori 113
Menschenwerdung 79
Mesopotamia 58–61, 129, 191, 198
messianic politics 31, 54
messianic theory 39, 40, 68
messianic war 57
messianism 165, 166, 168, 170
metabolic economy 83
metabolic relations 72, 83, 132, 151
metabolism (*Stoffwechsel*) 79–81, 84
metaphysical magicians 13, 164
metaphysical utopianism 164
metaphysics 2, 5, 41, 42, 45, 56, 96, 120, 121, 126, 132, 139, 143, 149, 151, 156, 158, 160, 162, 181, 195
metapolitical universities 149
migration 31, 32, 53
militarism 10, 123
miracles 133
mishkan 120
Mito e scienza (Vignoli) 137
Mitteleuropa (1915) 8, 15, 30, 205 n.53
modern anthropology 124, 142
modernity 2, 5, 7, 76, 87, 125, 191, 197, 198
modern machine system 145–6, 151
modern politics 16
modern subjectivity 121, 123, 125, 127
Moleschott, Jacob 6, 79
monarchic principle 89
monism 76
monotheism 57, 165
monotheistic civilization 35
moral ideology 5
morality 84, 106, 107, 160, 165
moralization 2
mors aeterna (eternal death) 101–3, 109, 113, 184
mors corporalis (bodily death) 102, 103
mors spiritualis (spiritual death) 102, 103, 111
mortality 19, 25, 34, 35, 37, 59, 60, 99, 110, 113, 191

mortal life 10, 17, 18, 41, 49, 178, 183
Moses 24, 119, 129
multicultural empire 16, 17, 53, 62
multicultural Germany 17
Musil, Robert 12
Mussolini, Benito 88, 184
Myers, David 204 n.43
myth 6, 12, 23, 25, 30, 105, 120, 123–5, 128, 150, 153
myth and technology 132–43
mythical mind 122
mythical Ouroboros 25
mythic unity 23
mythology 124, 125

Nachdenken 11, 74, 75, 77, 80, 91–6, 117
Nachfolge 74, 95, 103
Nachleben 74, 95, 103
nationalism 9, 29, 87, 123, 164
National Socialism 91
nation state 15, 16, 23, 30–2, 53, 69, 157, 190
natural death 91, 103, 109, 113
naturalism 7, 81
naturalist ethics 81, 107
natural laws 133
natural selection 2, 188
nature 4, 7, 8, 19, 23–6, 29–31, 43–6, 54, 55, 60, 64, 68, 73, 74, 132–4, 142, 151, 153, 154, 169, 195
nature religion 74, 78
Naumann, Friedrich 8, 16, 30, 205 n.53
Nazi Germany 2
Nazism 7, 13, 85, 98, 101, 113, 115, 116, 123, 126, 153, 158, 164, 195
nechamah 159
Negative Dialectic (Adorno) 120
nepesh (vegetative life) 159
New Levant 16, 17
new thinking 9, 21, 28, 33, 35, 44
New Yorker, The 236 n.234
Nietzsche, Friedrich 18, 44, 107, 126
Nirvana 56, 67–9
nominalism 76, 179
non-being 101, 103, 104, 109, 110, 112
non-catastrophic politics 149
non-existence 99, 103, 112, 185
non-existing beings 99, 101
non-identity 34, 43, 44

non-verbality 44, 215 n.159
noosphere 132, 157
normal biology 155, 160
nothingness (*das Nichtige*) 83, 84, 87, 91, 100, 176, 177, 179, 184
NSDAP 7, 75, 98, 107, 131
numerology 13, 174, 178

Oakes, Kenneth 207 n.64
Oath of Loyalty 75
Occident 55–7, 64
Occidental Eschatology (Taubes) 124
Oken, Lorenz von 174–7
Old Testament 228 n.17
'the One and the All' 49, 66
ontology 5, 34, 43, 45, 134, 135, 171–3, 180
organic life 152, 161
organic nature 28
organic technology 3
Origin of Species, The (Darwin) 2
otherness 37, 41

pagan antiquity 19, 21
pagan gods 27, 36
paganism 23–30, 35–7, 50, 55, 61, 63–7, 69, 165, 191
pagan religions 93
pagan traditions 27, 37
pantheism 76
paradise 71, 82, 83
Pauline Church 63, 64
Pentateuch 22, 120, 158, 165
Perlasca, Giorgio 184
Petrine Christianity 63
Petrine Church 64
philo-logy 42
Philosophie der Offenbarung (Schelling) 42
Philosophische Gruppe 12, 148, 185
philosophy 17–19, 27, 33, 40–2, 45, 49, 56, 190
  of being 21
  critical 170
  definition of 19
  German 18
  of life 35, 177
  modern 18, 20, 44
  of nature 43
  negative 42, 43, 45
  positive 42, 43
  speculative 41
  system of 21, 22
  theological 21
  tradition of 20, 21
  of unity 47
planetary community 53
plasticity 134, 152
Plato 20, 24, 60, 125, 177–8
Platonic idealism 24
Platonic pantheism 176
Platonism 178, 179
Platonists 19
Ploetz, Alfred 3
Polismensch 61
political discourses 6
political ideology 1, 5
political numerology 179
political power 59
political thanatology 110–17, 193, 196
political theology 11
Politik und Metaphysik (Unger) 149
Politische Geographie (Ratzel) 31
Pollock, Benjamin 8, 38
polyanthropism 19, 26
polycosmism 19, 26
polytheism 6, 19, 26, 35, 47, 49, 56, 57, 87, 125, 126, 153, 191
ponerology 13, 119, 185, 196
post-Christian world 5
post Christum 112, 193
potency 136
power of imagination 105, 106
primitives 57
primordial entropology 142, 152
primordial humanity 57
primordial individual 21, 22
primordiality 21, 25
primordial life 67
primordial world 21, 22, 24–30, 33, 35, 36, 42, 44, 49, 66, 68
prius 43
proletarians 130
proletariat 6, 144, 145, 147, 150–2
proletarization 149
Proslogion (Anselm of Canterbury) 72, 73, 95
Protestants 103

proto-totalitarian idea   24
providence   29–30, 86, 98, 112, 192
psychophysical phenomena   176
psychophysical techniques   143
Punjab   57–9, 67

race interest (*Rasseinteresse*)   3
races   152–4, 156
race sciences   86
racial hygiene   3
racial theories   31, 88
racism   3, 62, 63
racist politics   31
radical veganism   108
rationality   16, 19
Ratzel, Friedrich   31–2, 53
reality   1, 4, 11, 18, 19, 21, 23, 27, 29, 33, 39, 42–6, 85–92, 97, 100, 101, 121, 132–4, 166
redemption   13, 17, 22, 36, 40–51, 56, 62, 66, 67, 69, 82, 86, 93, 110, 111, 113, 181, 185–7, 191, 198
Reformation   63
Reformed Theology   10
reincarnation   1, 24, 25, 56
Reisner, Erwin   12, 164–7, 180
religion   5, 6, 72–9, 82, 125, 156
Religion of Reason, out of the Sources of Judaism (Cohen)   165, 168, 170, 174
religious practices   19
renewal   22, 33, 35, 46, 56, 78
renewed world   24, 26, 28, 30, 32, 36, 42, 55
res extensae   133, 134
resisting history   204 n.43
res potentiae   133, 180
resurrection   1, 3, 5, 9, 11, 38, 46, 64, 66–8, 74, 75, 78, 84, 89, 91, 93, 99, 100–3, 109–15, 117, 166, 179, 185, 193
revelation   10, 17, 18, 22, 24–6, 35–7, 41–5, 48, 50, 57–8, 63, 64–8, 74, 75, 77–9, 83, 90–3, 97, 105, 158, 164, 165, 167, 174, 191, 192
reverence for life   107
Rickert, Heinrich   19–20
rituals   22, 23, 120, 124, 130, 135, 138, 139, 151, 155, 158, 166

Roman Catholic Church   63
Roman Empire   30, 60
Romanticism   164
Rosenberg, Alfred   126
Rosenzweig, Franz   1, 2, 4–9, 12, 15–69, 184–6, 189–92, 196–200, 203 n.26, 206 n.57, 215 n.159
  'the cognition of the All'   18–22
  common sense of death   33–42
  'The Configuration or the Eternal Supra-World'   22
  creaturely existence   22–7
  Das Büchlein vom gesunden und kranken Menschenverstand (*Understanding the Sick and the Healthy*)   34
  'Die neue Levante'   16
  'The Elements or the Everlasting Primordial World'   21
  ethnos of immortality   58–69
  'Globus: Studien zur weltgeschichtlichen Raumlehre'   16, 51–4, 61
  Hegel und der Staat   15, 17
  Kriegsopera   16, 29
  'The New Thinking'   26, 54
  oecumene (*Ökumene*)   52, 54, 61
  'Paralipomena'   24, 26, 60
  'The Path or the Ever Renewed World'   22
  redemption of God   42–51
  Star of Redemption, The   8, 9, 15–18, 21–3, 28–30, 34, 35, 37–9, 41, 42, 44, 48, 50, 52, 54–8, 61, 62, 190, 191, 203 n.26
  struggle for survival   27–33
  subtraction and expansion of history   51–8
  Understanding the Sick and Healthy   9, 38, 56
  'Vox Dei?'   16
Rotenstreich, Nathan   41
Russian Revolution (1917)   130, 144, 148

Sabbath   62
saga of creation   82, 105
Sahlins, Marshall   155
salvation   186, 187
Schallmayer, Wilhelm   3

Schelling, F. W. J. von   18, 41–5, 63, 125, 136, 175
Schellingian philosophy   174, 237 n.234
Schleiermacher, Friedrich   10, 74
Schmitt, Carl   1, 54
Scholem, Gershom   12, 13, 164
Schopenhauer, Arthur   18, 44
Schwedische Israelmission   162
Schweitzer, Albert   107, 108, 226 n.212
science   41–2, 138, 139
science of evil   119, 165, 171, 185
Second Industrial Revolution   189, 190
second law of thermodynamics   46
Second World War   11, 75, 83, 101, 102, 112, 119, 123, 143, 152, 164, 179, 188
secular chronology   62
Sein   170, 171
Sein-zum-Tode   37
self, alienation of   59
self-consciousness   59
self-delusion   58
self-transformation   64
Semitic Pythagoreanism   177
sexuality   80, 159
shamanic ritual   135
Shoah   119, 120
Shri Agamya Paramahamsa   236 n.234
Siddharta Gautama (Buddha)   56, 58, 59, 67–8
Sikora, Tomasz   174
Simon, Ernst   22
simple fundamental truth   74
Sinnlichkeit   79
Skepsis und Mystik (Landauer)   178
social interest (*Sozialinteresse*)   3
socialism   80, 88, 125, 131, 144, 148
social relation   98
Society for Race Hygiene   3
Socrates   20
Sollen   170, 171
soul   5, 19, 21, 49, 50, 63, 64, 66, 67, 96, 102–4, 169, 174–81
'The Soul and the Law' (Kelsen)   1
Soviet Union   148
speculation   25, 34, 41, 77, 94, 174, 199
Spencer, Herbert   107
Spengler, Oswald   32, 33, 55, 61
Spieckermann, Ingrid   207 n.64

spirits   23, 86–7, 88, 159–61, 174–5
Staten som Lifsform (Kjellén)   6, 17, 31
Stirner, Max   76–8
Stoicism   93
stone age economies   155
Strauss, David Friedrich   87, 88
struggle for existence/survival   2, 3, 11, 27–33, 40, 47, 49, 51, 64, 66, 71, 72, 81, 82, 97, 105–7, 110, 112, 117, 129, 143, 169, 198
subhuman symbols   31
suffering   13, 28, 36, 40, 43, 48, 50, 81, 82, 88, 119, 120, 168, 200
summae   138
superabundance   83, 84, 108
supra-world   22, 26, 29, 33, 35, 44, 51, 52, 66, 68
surplus labour   145, 146
surplus value   146
survival of the fittest   188
Susman, Margarete   6, 136, 156
suum cuique   114–17, 193, 227 n.237
Swiss Social Democratic Party   10
syllogism   94

taharah   139, 158
Tanakh   120, 124, 125
Taubes, Jacob   119, 123–7, 130, 180, 195
Taubes, Zwi   123
technological development   130, 144, 198
temporality   33, 34, 39, 44, 46, 48
Tertullian   66
Thales   18
theological absolutism   186
theological anthropology   97
theology   5, 6, 41, 42, 72, 74–8, 92, 93, 100, 103, 105, 117, 175, 181, 190
  contemporary   117
  dogmatic   87
  German   91
  modern   40, 87
  natural   77
  speculative   80, 94
  traditional   124
Theoretische Biologie (Ehrenberg)   28
theosophy   42
Third Reich   98

thought and being   20, 42, 44
Torah   12, 13, 119–30, 132, 134, 135, 137, 139–43, 151–5, 157–60, 162, 163, 165, 167, 169, 171, 174, 177–81, 185, 194–6
totalitarianism   7, 126
totality   8, 9, 44, 46, 63, 74, 134, 140, 141
totemism   135, 139, 154–5, 157, 160, 165, 175
transcendence   24, 25, 43, 81, 96, 137, 138, 140, 160, 161, 169, 170, 179, 196, 197
transcendental imagination   172
transcendent organisms   134, 136
transhumanism   1
transnational community   9
Troeltsch, Ernst   16
truth   23–5, 27, 29, 31, 35, 38–40, 46, 77, 81, 93, 97
tumah   139, 158
Twentieth Century Mythos, The (Rosenberg)   126

überchristlich   16, 67
überjudisch   16, 67
Übermensch   22
Überwelt   22, 29, 52, 67
unanimity   6, 7, 17, 21, 68
Unger, Erich   6, 12, 120, 130, 137, 148–51, 154, 156, 157, 161, 174, 177, 178, 195
Unified States of Europe (*Vereinigte Staaten Europas*)   16, 17
United States. *See* America
unity of being   21
unity of world   26, 29, 30, 45, 50, 54, 64
unsere Empirie   134
Urjudentum   13, 124, 126, 128, 139, 164, 194
Urquelle   191

Verbindungsfäden   137
verbum externum   97, 103, 193
Verfall zur Normalität   139
verificationism   39, 40
Verkappte Religionen (Bry)   86

Verkündigung ('proclamation'/ 'preaching')   72
verschwinden   49
Vignoli, Tito   137–9
vitam aeternam   89
Vogt, Karl   6, 79
Voigts, Manfred   6, 7, 12, 235 n.209
Völkerwanderung   149
völkisch   32, 56
von dem gesunden Menschenverstand   33

Wagner, Andreas   236 n.226
Ward, Peter   188, 189, 196
Weikart, Richard   2
Weimar period   3, 7, 12, 39
Weimar Republic   3, 7, 157, 178
Weiterleben   60
Weltanschauung   33
Western Christianity   186
Western civilization   7, 40, 64, 123, 138, 191
Western messianism   237 n.10
Western philosophy   18, 56, 198
Widerspruch   172
will to power   107
Wirklichkeit   136
Wohlgemuth, Joseph   12
Wolfson, Elliot   37, 206 n.57
world history   51–3, 57–9, 61–4, 68, 86, 88
world of politics   29, 59
world of war   55
world politics   31
world-totality   19, 20, 33, 45, 49–50, 140

Yo Fukushima   9
Yoga   138
Yom Kippur   176

Zacharias, Edgar   12
Zeitanschauung   33
zero   175–7
Zionism   149
Zusatzbevölkerung   131, 150
Zwiespalt   119
Zweistromland   9

www.ingramcontent.com/pod-product-compliance
Lightning Source LLC
Chambersburg PA
CBHW062123300426
44115CB00012BA/1795